Jacques Le Moyne de Morgues, "A Young Daughter of the Picts" (front cover), ca. 1585. Watercolor and gouache on vellum. Painted or tattooed from neck to ankle with a variety of flowers, the young Pict is an instance not only of the *flors florum* (the "flower of flowers" that conventionally figures earthly and/or heavenly love) but also constitutes a meditation on the English word "pink"—a flower, an excellence, a tattoo. Le Moyne's fantasia on the classical theme of Pictish tattooing was subsequently engraved by the Flemish publisher Theodore de Bry as an ethnographic illustration of ancient British life. De Bry's engraving, "A Truue picture of a yonge dowgter of the Pictes" (back cover), is one of five illustrations of the ancient Britons that follow de Bry's engravings of the life and habits of the Carolina Algonquians in *America I* (1590). De Bry's stated purpose in appending these British figures to his account of life in America is to confront his readers with the barbarian status of their own ancestors; here the tattoo is the mark that links the Algonquians to the ancient Britons, while separating them from the early modern Europeans.

Before seeking religious refuge in England, Le Moyne has acted as artist recorder on the French expeditions to Florida in 1563 and 1565. His account of the enterprise, illustrated with engravings from his paintings of Florida, was published by de Bry as *America II* (1591). Le Moyne has been accused of "idealizing" his American subjects, but his work is characterized by a gentle mannerism that idealizes both the Europeans and the Timucua and produces ethnic difference by first proposing the similarity of the two peoples. In *Excubitorum socordia ut punitur*, or "The execution of negligent sentries" (inside front cover), and in *In cerui exuvio Soli consecrando solennes ritus*, or "The offering of a stag to the sun" (inside back cover), European and American figures are represented in very close juxtaposition or in poses that reflect each other. Their mutual embrace is emphasized by the fact that the slashed and pinked clothing of the French finds its reflection in the tattoos and body ornaments of the Timucua. Pace de Bry, Le Moyne's work suggests that the human body is always "pinked" (marked, altered, written upon).

Res 31   Spring 1997

Anthropology and aesthetics

Contents

Res 31 Spring 1997

Anthropology and aesthetics

EDITOR
Francesco Pellizzi

ASSOCIATE EDITORS
Remo Guidieri
Joseph Koerner
Joseph Rykwert

EXECUTIVE EDITORIAL COUNCIL
Francesco Pellizzi
Irven DeVore
William Fash

ASSISTANT EDITOR
Cynthia Elmas

EDITORIAL CONSULTANT
Ivan Gaskell (Harvard University Museums)

EDITORIAL ADVISORS

Alain Babadzan
Akeel Bilrami
Suzanne P. Blier
Sarah Brett-Smith
Edmund Carpenter
K. C. Chang
Clemency Coggins
Whitney Davis
Kurt Forster

David Freedberg
Oleg Grabar
John Hay
Jonathan Hay
Adrienne Kaeppler
C. C. Lamberg-Karlovsky
Michael W. Meister
Gulru Necipoglu
Douglas Newton

Thomas Reese
Marshall Sahlins
Carlo Severi
David Shapiro
S. J. Tambiah
Gianni Vattimo
Gordon R. Willey
Irene Winter
Nur Yalman

COPY EDITOR AND COORDINATOR (Peabody Museum) Amy K. Hirschfeld
DESIGNER Richard Bartlett
COVER DESIGN From a 1981 sketch by Dan Flavin
LAYOUT Glenna Collett

EDITORIAL OFFICE
12 East 74th Street, New York, NY 10021. Tel.: (212) 737 6109. Fax: (212) 861 7874.

PRODUCED AND PUBLISHED BY
The Peabody Museum of Archaeology and Ethnology, Harvard University
11 Divinity Avenue, Cambridge, MA 02138
Director of Publications: Margaret R. Courtney

DISTRIBUTED BY
The University of Pennsylvania Museum Publications, 33rd and Spruce Streets, Philadelphia, PA 19104

Manufactured in the United States of America
Printing by Henry N. Sawyer Company, Charlestown, Massachusetts
Binding by Acme Bookbinding, Charlestown, Massachusetts

ISSN 0277–1322   ISBN 0-87365-820-5

Editorial

The abject of art history

JOSEPH LEO KOERNER

Art historians today are rallying around a cry to "return to the object." Like the school reformer's slogan "back to basics," this call for a retreat passes judgment on a previous campaign. It deems the new art history to have been an indecisive expedition into the foreign territories of ideas and theories and away from the vulnerable disciplinary homeland of things and practices. To some who follow this call, returning to the object means restoring objectivity. It signals a realignment of the humanities with their original model, science, and a recuperation of the shared goal of positive knowledge. Purged once more of the fictions of a projective imagination, the art object can be studied like any other fact. Ritually submitted to what humanists alone take to be the most advanced techniques of visualization, it returns more thinglike than ever before. Scanned, sampled, tested, magnified, and digitalized, it becomes increasingly defaced or invisible, like the rubble of smashed idols that an earlier iconoclasm taunted with the appeal, "If you are God then defend yourself!"

To others, the return to the object represents art's total assimilation not to nature but to culture. In this reincarnation of the critique, the hegemony of theory is exposed and overturned by a democratizing attention to particulars, to the ordinary practices and sediments of everyday life. Redubbed "object" rather than "work," art thus takes its place beside all other human fabrications. Purged of the universalizing fiction of beauty or depth, it stands subsumed under the category of material culture, where it can be studied within the expanded field of anthropology. Whether in this spirit of revolution or as a mode of reaction, the return to the object represents but the latest episode in what Bruno Latour has termed the process of "purification" that constitutes our modernity.[1] Reified as matter or cultural materiality, the object is kept pure, either as nature or as culture, but never as a mixture of the two. Meanwhile, within the networks in which we actually operate, outside the Great Divide that we fancy separates us from premodern superstition, another hybrid has taken shape. Masked as something primitive, but reflecting our most contemporary concerns, it is coming to stand for all those mysteries once imputed to the idol "beauty."

Imagine, if you will, that the entire discipline of art history were suddenly to devote itself to ugliness. Imagine, in other words, that the *abject,* and not the *object,* was art history's accepted universal and that it adequately named what it is the discipline studies.[2] Much would remain the same, rather like a slide projected backwards and upside down. Questions about the canon would still be vigorously pursued, and with the familiar methods. Art works that had been dismissed as beautiful could be reclaimed as being, in their own historically specific ways, hideous enough for study. The nineteenth century could go on being blamed for all distortions in the canon. And *kitsch,* though now cautiously celebrated, would remain indefinable.

Indeed, like many controversies in contemporary art history, questions of the canon would actually be better answered through a focus on the abject. For unlike objects, which ask to be judged as what they in themselves are, abjection exists in its effects, as a response elicited in the subject. That is why, in fact, study of the abject has served the broader shift within our discipline away from traditional aesthetics and towards a new, affective approach to art. For feelings of nausea, unlike sentiments of beauty, cannot easily be projected or disgorged, no matter how hard we retch.

Academic protocol, of course, would be changed were the abject to be our object. During lectures, slides would be projected unfocused, or at a manic pace, or towards the audience, or in raging sunlight, or not at all. Talks would vary from *soto voce* filibusters to single, ear-

1. Bruno Latour, *We Have Never Been Modern,* trans. Catherine Porter (Cambridge: Harvard University Press, 1993).

2. My remarks were first formulated to introduce a session on "The Abject in Art History," which I organized for the 1996 College Art Association conference in Boston. The conference's general topic had been advertised as "The Object of Art History." Speakers at my session included Jeffrey Hamburger, Juliet Fleming, and Christine Ross. Their talks are published in this issue in altered form.

splitting screams. And conferences would be held, unscheduled, in elevators, to Muzak versions of Wagner's *Parzival*, or in hotel check-in lines when all the rooms in town are triple-booked, or in unattended shuttle buses filled with an overwhelming scent of artificial pine. Somewhere, though, a conference of *refusés* would convene to discuss the "object in art history." In talks of exactly twenty minutes, this furtive few would exemplify the subversive idea that persons, each in full possession of their thoughts, can reasonably study things—and not merely *things*, but crafted products that, by virtue of the work invested in them, have something of the character of minds. This exotic hybrid—the art "object"—would thus stand at the abject's horizon, as the border case where abjection's hybrid of the not-me and the me receives, exceptionally, a positive inflection. Canova and Chagall would again be hotspots; and even the scholars of abjection would relish the monstrous spectacle of objects being studied in order to preserve the soul.

I will admit that abjection does not yet embrace the historical practices of the academic study of art as amply as does the object. Yet as rubric of opposition, the abject, more so than the object, does encompass the practices of many contemporary artists, as well as the criticism that seeks to make sense of them. For in recent art, abjection denotes more than simply incorporating or indexing base and repellent things like garbage, shit, hair, and rotten meat into artworks. Abjection assaults the very notion of objects purified of affect. And the criticism developed to explicate this assault attempts, in turn, to undermine an art history that, undertaken as if by self-sovereign subjects, remains confident of its objectivity.

This criticism received its specific rubric from Julia Kristeva's 1980 text *Powers of Horror: An Essay in Abjection*.[3] It gained additional force from recent reassessments of the work of Georges Bataille (especially by Rosalind Krauss) and through the work of Judith Butler.[4] Its general outlook, however, has been shaped by the failure of two earlier critiques: on the one hand, semiotics, which valued meaning over meaning's

material supports, and on the other hand, Marxism, which regarded product and production as more real than the ideas they support. Attention to the abject reflected a broader reorientation within the humanities towards the "materiality of communication."[5] Against earlier materialisms, Marxist or otherwise, focus turned to the immateriality of information codes; against semioticism, these codes, to cite Jacques Lacan in a prophetic seminar of 1954, were interesting not for their meaning but for their "materiality."[6] The abject dramatized this reorientation by overinvesting base objects with subjective, carnal affect and by substituting for the old, static dyad of objects and meanings a new hybrid of things and bodies placed in contexts of performance. Several papers in the present issue of *RES* explore this domain. Juliet Fleming discerns in the tattoo an inscription of individual identity, but one located, scandalously, on a cadaverous exterior in indelible defacements of the skin. And Christine Ross considers how, in contemporary performance art, the female body is simultaneously absence and presence, chaos and order, being at once dematerialized through information technologies and rematerialized as mortal flesh. In these accounts, abjection revalues values. By disputing the fixity of objects, and of the human subjects rendered homologous to objects (in the symmetry of viewer to viewed), abject art exposes the mechanism whereby some subjects are expelled in order to objectify the sovereignty of others.

The contemporary abject demystifies. It is a new instrument of the critique, revealing the object's concealed truth. As Roland Barthes put it in an oft-cited essay of 1979, "The truth of things is best read in refuse."[7] Yet it would be wrong to presume that the titular "object in art history" is not already, and quite explicitly, abject. Today's return to the object is not simply a recuperated empiricism. Rather, it is a confession of the otherness of things, their hyper-

3. Trans. Leon S. Roudiez (New York: Columbia University Press, 1982).

4. Krauss, *The Optical Unconscious* (Cambridge: MIT Press, 1993); Judith Butler, *Gender Trouble* (New York: Routledge, 1990); id., "Beyond the Logic of Repudiation," in *Bodies that Matter* (New York: Routledge, 1993).

5. K. Ludwig Pfeiffer, "The Materiality of Communication," in *Materialities of Communication*, ed. Hans Ulrich Gumbrecht and K. Ludwig Pfeiffer, trans. William Whobrey (Stanford: Stanford University Press, 1994), pp. 1–14.

6. Seminar II, 1954–1955; cited in Pfeiffer (see note 5), p. 6.

7. "The Wisdom of Art," in *Cy Twombly: Paintings and Drawings 1954–1972* (New York: Whitney Museum of American Art, 1979), pp. 9-23; cited, for example, in Jack Ben-Levi et al., *Abject Art: Repulsion and Desire in American Art* (New York: Whitney Museum of American Art, 1993), p. 11.

incommensurability vis-à-vis the histories that would interpret them. If, in the past, art history modeled itself on the sciences, and therefore on practices aimed at purifying the distinction between persons and things, today's sciences have revealed such purity to be unattainable, and art history follows suit. Museums now exhibit objects in their most naked, unrestored, and contingent state, not to display them as they are, stripped of aura, but to render them potentially animate, like cadavers. Whether purified as natural fact or as social fiction, as the chemistry of paint, say, or as painted "discourse," today's return to the object is a return of the abject.

The abject is a novelty neither in the history of art nor in the attempts to write that history. For Baudelaire the ugly constituted the artist's ultima ratio and the mark of his modernity. And already in the eighteenth century, at the moment when, through Alexander Gottlieb Baumgarten, the new discipline of *Aesthetics* defined its goal as the attainment of beauty and the avoidance of ugliness, the appeal, in art, of the gruesome, repellent, and ridiculous became a central philosophical concern.[8] Paralleling debates about theodicy in ethics, discussion of how ugly art could be true and pleasing signaled the dissolution of the old, metaphysical equation of the good, the true, and the beautiful. In the *Laocoon*, Lessing asked how moral and physical abjection, exemplified in Homer's hideous villain Thersites, engendered good literature.[9]

But if, in the Enlightenment, the ugly was a border case for aesthetics, in Romanticism it became an artistic ideal. Celebrating Karl Rosenkranz's *Aesthetics of the Ugly* of 1853,[10] Gottfried Keller, writing to Hermann Hettner, exclaimed that "even the title is paradoxical and romantic."[11] And from the moment of its admission into the writing of art history, the ugly discovered its privileged historical instance in the art of the Middle

Ages.[12] According to Hegel, the novelty of Christian and Romantic art consisted in its taking the abject as its privileged object. Specifically, the tortured and crucified Christ, that ugliest of all creatures in whom divine beauty became, through human evil, basest abjection, functioned as the great exception to the self-evidence of beauty in classicism. In his essay "To Make Women Weep," Jeffrey Hamburger revisits this subject in late medieval images of the ruined Christ made by women for women. As intensely affective objects, such pictures raise the question whether today's abject, performative art represents a new gothicism. Even the histrionic format of the installation, meant to counter the iconoclastic purity of the modernist gallery, reimagines the ritual ostentation of holy relics. At the very least, such self-ironized superstition, restaging religion as ambivalence, should remind us of how powerful and enduring Gothicism has been during the modern period.

In the nineteenth century, the Gothic went hand in hand with an ideal of realism grounded in the abject particularities of the flesh. Medieval church art, rejected in the Reformation and Enlightenment as either idolatrous or quintessentially ugly, thus became an emblem of the historical contingency, and therefore transformability, of beauty, truth, and the good. And it served as a model for what critics like Victor Hugo celebrated as a new grotesque realism in modern literature and art. The "ugliness of reality"[13] revealed in the Gothic Christ was now the antidote to science's disenchantment of the real. Hard facts were still haunted and nowhere more than in the case of our material existence. The human body, that mere thing that we are, became the last remaining site of categorical impurity for a culture that believed it could keep separate subjects from objects.

In the contemporary discourse of the abject, the body evinces its hauntedness through the image of surface. Surface, existing neither inside nor outside, reveals that continuing impurity of facts and fictions, that inescapable permeability between nature and culture that keeps us from ever being modern.[14] Christine Ross's

8. Hans Rudolf Schweizer, *Ästhetik als Philosophie der sinnliche Erkenntnis* (Basel: Schwabe, 1973), p. 115.

9. Herbert Dieckmann, "Das Abscheuliche und Schreckliche in der Kunsttheorie des 18. Jahrhunderts," in *Die nicht mehr schöne Künste*, ed. Hans Robert Jauß, Poetik und Hermeneutik 3 (Munich: Fink, 1968), pp. 271–317.

10. *Ästhetik des Häßlichen* (1853; reprint, Leipzig: Reclam, 1996). I profited from Dieter Klicke's "Pathologie des Schönen—Die Ästhetik des Häßlichen von Karl Rosenkranz," in the 1996 reprint, pp. 401–427.

11. Letter of August 3, 1853, cited in Werner Jung, *Schöner Schein in der Häßlichkeit oder Häßlichkeit des schönen Scheins* (Frankfurt: Athenaum, 1987), p. 201.

12. Hans Robert Jauss, "Die klassische und die christliche Rechtfertigung des hässlichen in mittelalterlicher Literatur," in *Die nicht mehr schöne Künste*, ed. Hans Robert Jauss, Poetik und Hermeneutik 3 (Munich: Fink, 1968), pp. 143–168.

13. Georg Wilhelm Friedrich Hegel, *Vorlesungen über die Aesthetik*, Sämtliche Werke 14 (Stuttgart, 1954), p. 120; see the essay by Jeffrey Hamburger in this issue.

14. Latour (see note 1).

account of Mona Hatoum's 1994 video installation, *Corps étranger*, renders this condition palpable. The endoscope's eye seems to search the artist's own bowels for some inner resting place—her inner subjectivity, perhaps, which ought to be art's "content"—but all it sees is more impenetrable surface. Screened in a museum rather than a laboratory, however, that surface becomes haunted or uncanny. Translating the medical examination into a Romantic quest, Hatoum offers her "foreign" body as a house of the spirit. This haunting is felt in other papers presented here, as well: in the decorated skin discussed by Fleming; in the gore-covered surfaces of Hamburger's humble pietàs; and in the *Komo* masks discussed by Sarah Brett-Smith, where surface, formed of sacrificial blood mixed with porridge, indicates the fear and power of the female sex.

When Ross delivered her paper at the 1996 College Art Association, Hatoum's video played behind her continuously as she talked. From my position beside her as "moderator," I could observe the audience squirming uncomfortably, but also cheerfully, in their seats. In understanding the lure of abjection today, it will be crucial to judge precisely its affective tone, as something both comic and macabre. For especially in its popular forms the abject can never presuppose that condition of naive belief that it imputes to its "gothic" and "primitive" models. As a fiction it remains joyously pulp, like the graveyard novels of the past. Which brings me to my final reflection—today, as in the Middle Ages and Romantic period, the abject in art is a trope of power. Performing death in us, it is a gesture that seems unrepeatable. This singleness—each time—reconstitutes abjection's modernity, the sense it gives of having no past and of imagining no tomorrow. Yet despite its amnesia, the abject persists in art history. It comes to light in moments of pessimism, when the illusions of apocalypse and revolution are lost. But it also abides unseen within tradition as the power by which art, in its revulsion against itself and its past, constitutes itself *as* history.

"To make women weep"

Ugly art as "feminine" and the origins of modern aesthetics

JEFFREY F. HAMBURGER

According to Francisco de Hollanda, Michelangelo, when asked by Vittoria Colonna why Flemish painting "seems more devout than that in the Italian manner," replied, "Flemish painting . . . will generally please the devout better than any painting of Italy, which will never cause him to shed a tear, whereas that of Flanders will cause him to shed many; and that not through the vigor and goodness of the painting but owing to the goodness of the devout person. It will appeal to women, especially the very old and the very young, and also to monks and nuns and to certain noblemen who have no sense of true harmony."[1] The authenticity of the opinions Hollanda attributes to Michelangelo remains in dispute.[2] It has nevertheless taken modern scholarship much longer to come to a similar, if less contemptuous, conclusion: that women were among the primary and formative audiences for devotional imagery in northern Europe, and the meanings of these images were as much defined by affective response as by their aesthetic qualities.[3]

The opposition between affective response and *ingenium* or artistic talent was not new in Michelangelo's day. The *Libri Carolini*, an eighth-century treatise on the place of images in worship, also distinguishes between qualities intrinsic and extrinsic to the image. Why, its author, Theodulf of Orléans, asked, are some images considered beautiful ("*formosus*"), others ugly and detestable ("*foedus*"). Only, he replied, on account of their materials and the ingenuity with which they were wrought, not on account of the piety of the onlooker ("*fervor devotionis*").[4] For Theodulf, what

---

My thanks to Joseph Koerner for inviting me to present this paper in his College Art Association session on "The Abject in Art History." Some of the material in this essay borrows from my book, *Nuns as Artists: The Visual Culture of a Medieval Convent* (Berkeley and Los Angeles: University of California Press, 1997), although it is presented in a different context. I have also drawn, in part, on my review of *Sculpture of Compassion: The Pietà and the Beguines in the Southern Low Countries c. 1300–c. 1600*, by J. Ziegler, *Speculum* 69 (1994):992–994.

1. I employ the translation in R. Klein, *Italian Art, 1500–1600: Sources and Documents* (Englewood Cliffs, New Jersey: Prentice-Hall, 1966), p. 34. For Michelangelo and Vittoria Colonna, see, most recently, E. Campi, *Michelangelo e Vittoria Colonna: Un dialogo artistico-teologico ispirato da Bernadino Ochino e altri saggi di storia della Riforma* (Turin: Claudiana, 1994).

2. C. Gilbert, review of *Michelangelo's Theory of Art*, by R. J. Clements, *Art Bulletin* 44 (1962):347–353, argues that the Dialogues are fictitious. But see J. B. Bury, *Two Notes on Francisco Holanda*, Warburg Institute Surveys 7 (London: The Warburg Institute, University of London, 1981), pp. 1–27, and S. Deswarte-Rosa, "*Idea* et le Temple de la Peinture, I: Michelangelo Buonarroti et Francisco de Holanda," *Revue de l'Art* 92 (1991):20–41, the latter cited by P. Sohm, "Gendered Style in Italian Art Criticism from Michelangelo to Malvasia," *Renaissance Quarterly* 48 (1995):759–808, esp. 775, n. 42.

3. See J. F. Hamburger, "The Visual and the Visionary: The Changing Role of the Image in Late Medieval Monastic Devotions," *Viator* 20 (1989):161–182; E. Vavra, "Bildmotiv und Frauenmystik:

Funktion und Rezeption," in *Frauenmystik im Mittelalter*, ed. P. Dinzelbacher and D. R. Bauer (Ostfildern bei Stuttgart: Schwabenverlag, 1985), pp. 201–230; D. Rigaux, "Dire la foi avec des images, une affaire de femmes?" in *La religion de ma mère: Les femmes et la transmission de la foi*, ed. J. Delumeau (Paris: Editions du Cerf, 1992), pp. 71–90; J. Ziegler, *Sculpture of Compassion: The Pietà and the Beguines in the Southern Low Countries c. 1300–c. 1600*, Études d'Histoire de l'Art 6 (Brussels: Institute Historique Belge de Rome, 1992); P. Vandenbroeck, "Zwischen Selbsterniedrigung und Selbstvergottung: Bilderwelt und Selbstbild religiöser Frauen in den südlichen Niederlanden: Eine erste Erkundigung," *De zeventiende eeuw* 5 (1989):67–88; id., *Le Jardin clos de l'âme: L'Imaginaire des religieuses dans les Pays-Bas du Sud, depuis le 13e siècle* (Brussels: Martial et Snoeck, 1994).

4. For the moment, the only edition remains the unreliable text printed in *Patrologiae cursus completus: Series latina*, 221 vols. (Paris: J.-P. Migne, 1841–1864), vol. 98, col. 1147: "Nam cum imagines plerumque secundum ingenium artificium fiant, ut modo sint formosae, modo deformes, nonnumquam pulchrae, aliquando etiam foede, quaedam illis quorum sunt similimae, quaedam vero dissimiles, quaedam novitate fulgentes, quaedam etiam vetustate fatescentes, quaerendum est quae earum sunt honorabiliores, utrum eas que pretiosiores, an eae quae viliores esse noscuntur, quoniam si pretiosiores plus habent honoris, operis in eis causa, vel materiarum qualitas habet venerationem, non fervor devotionis." The passage is singled out for discussion by F. Bologna, "'Operis causa, non fervor devotionis': Spunti di critica d'arte medioevale," *Paragone* 12 (1961):3–18, esp. 11. For the *Libri Carolini*, see, most recently, A. Freeman, "Scripture and Images in the *Libri Carolini*," in *Testi e immagine nell'alto medioevo, 15–21 aprile 1993*, vol. 1, Settimane di Studio del Centro Italiano di Studi sull'Alto Medioevo 41 (Spoleto: Presso la sede del Centro, 1994), pp. 163–195; C. M. Chazelle, "Not in Painting, but in Writing: Augustine and the Supremacy of the Word in the *Libri Carolini*," in *Reading and Wisdom: The De doctrina christiana of Augustine in the Middle Ages*, ed. E. D. English, Notre Dame Conferences in Medieval Studies 6 (Notre Dame, Indiana: University of Notre Dame Press, 1995), pp. 1–22.

the observer brought to the image was more important than its aesthetic or material qualities. Modern critics, in passing judgment on medieval art or medieval mysticism, have been more inclined to side with Michelangelo, no matter how anachronistic his point of view; witness the dismissal of Margery Kempe, the early fifteenth-century English mystic, because "her tears would have flowed in the presence of any Pietà, no matter what its artistic values."[5] In contrast, Michelangelo, by inscribing his signature on the band between the Virgin's breasts, identified his Pietà as an expression of assertive artistry as well as devotion[6] (fig. 1).

It is not hard to see what Michelangelo meant by harmony if one contrasts his early Pietà—paradoxically the most famous incarnation of this typically transalpine subject—with a northern *Vesperbild*[7] (figs. 1–2). Compared with the technical virtuosity and classical grace of Michelangelo's sculpture, the fourteenth-

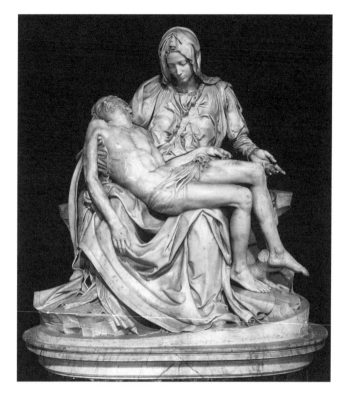

Figure 1. Michelangelo Buonarroti, *Pietà*, 1498–1499. Polished marble, H: 1.74 m, W (base): 1.95 m. Vatican, St. Peter's Basilica. Photo: Courtesy of Alinari/Art Resource.

century Röttgen Pietà is so forceful in its unidealized physicality that some might flinch before accepting it as "art."[8] In a word, it is ugly. In its explicit and exact delineation of Christ's excoriated flesh, it gives agonizing embodiment to Hegel's maxim: "Images had existed since time immemorial: piety needed them from its beginnings for its devotions, but it didn't need any beautiful images, indeed, these were disturbing to it."[9]

5. D. Gray, *Themes and Images in the Medieval English Religious Lyric* (London and Boston: Routledge and Kegan Paul, 1972), p. 28.

6. For the inscription, see K. Weil-Garris Brandt, "Michelangelo's Pietà for the *Capella del Re di Francia*," in *"Il se rendit en Italie": Etudes offertes à André Chastel* (Rome: Edizioni dell'Elefante and Paris: Flammarion, 1987), pp. 77–119, esp. pp. 92–93, who notes (p. 93) that, "He defined the *Pietà* beyond its function as a devotional image, specifically as a work of art." Not that medieval artists—especially in Italy—did not sign their works (see A. Dietl, *Italienische Bildhauerinschriften: Selbstdarstellungen und Schriftlichkeit mittelalterlicher Künstler* [Cologne-Opladen: Nordrhein-Westfälische Akademie der Wissenschaften, 1995]), but, as noted by L. Pon, "Michelangelo's First Signature," *Source: Notes in the History of Art* 15 (1996):16–21, esp. 16: "This first—and only—signature by Michelangelo on one of his sculptures is, like the Roman Pietà itself, both embedded in tradition and remarkably innovative." J. E. Ziegler, "Michelangelo and the Medieval Pietà: The Sculpture of Devotion or the Art of Sculpture?" *Gesta* 34 (1995):28–36, also compares Michelangelo's Pietà with medieval antecedents but overlooks Weil-Garris Brandt's lengthy account of the Pietà's own history of changing use and installation.

7. The literature on the Pietà in the Germanic-speaking world is vast. I cite only a few of the more significant recent studies: J. Michler, "Eine neuentdeckte frühe Bodensee-Pietà in Meersburg, I: Kunstgeschichtliche Einordnung und Bedeutung," *Zeitschrift für Kunsttechnologie und Konservierung* 6 (1992):315–323; M. Schawe, "*Fasciculus myrrhae*: Pietà und Hoheslied," *Jahrbuch des Zentralinstituts für Kunstgeschichte* 5–6 (1989–1990):161–212; G. Satzinger and H.-J. Ziegeler, "Marienklagen und Pietà," in *Die Passion Christi in Literatur und Kunst des Spätmittelalters*, ed. W. Haug and B. Wachinger, Fortuna Vitrea: Arbeiten zur literarischen Tradition zwischen dem 13. und 16. Jahrhundert, bd. 12 (Tübingen: M. Niemeyer, 1993), pp. 241–276. Michelangelo might have known images such as the Röttgen Pietà; see W. Körte, "Deutsche Vesperbilder in Italien," *Kunstgeschichtliches Jahrbuch der Bibliotheca Hertziana* 1 (1937):1–138.

8. See R. Haussherr, "Texte über die Pietà Röttgen," *Bonner Jahrbuch* 165 (1965):150–152.

9. My translation of the passage from the first edition of Hegel, *Vorlesungen über die Philosophie der Geschichte*, 1837, quoted without a precise indication of the source by H. R. Jauss, "Über religiöse und aesthetische Erfahrung: Zur Debatte um Hans Beltings *Bild und Kult* und Georg Steiners *Von realer Gegenwart*," *Merkur: Deutsche Zeitschrift für europäisches Denken* 45 (1991):934–946, esp. 934: "Bilder hatte man schon lange: die Frömmigkeit bedurfte ihrer schon früh für ihre Andacht, aber sie brauchte keine schönen Bilder, ja diese waren ihr sogar störend." For an equivalent passage in the only edition I was able to consult, see G. W. F. Hegel, *Sämtliche Werke*, 11 vols. (Stuttgart: Frommann, 1949), vol. 11, p. 516: ". . . wenn die

Figure 2. Röttgen Pietà, ca. 1350, Middle Rhine. Linden wood, polychromy partially restored, H: 89 cm with base. Rheinisches Landesmuseum, Bonn, Inv.-Nr. 24.189. Photo: Courtesy of Rheinisches Landesmuseum.

Yet even an image as abject as the Röttgen Pietà is not without calculated effects: for example, the huge, drooping heads or the stark contrast between the stiff, emaciated forms of Christ's broken body and the soft, mellifluous folds of Mary's mantle. Where blood once flowed down Christ's arms, it now flows up.[10] Gore also coagulates around the side wound, interpreted as the source of the Sacrament. Intensifying the imagery of Christ's sacrifice as a *Liebestod*, the gouts of blood congeal into red, roseate blooms.[11] Spiritual authors labeled Christ's life-giving blood *rosenfarbig,* or "rosecolored," an epithet given concrete form in the rosettes on the plinth.[12]

To sheer force of expression, the abject can add nuance and articulation. For example, in a Pietà from the Abbey of St. Walburg in Eichstätt, Bavaria (a community of Benedictine nuns), striking inconsistencies of scale reinforce the underlying message: the fortunate paradox of Christ's having been born to die on behalf of

Figure 3. Pietà, early fourteenth century. Wood, dimensions unknown. Eichstätt, Bavaria, Abbey of St. Walburg. Photo: © 1995 Belser Wissenschaftliche Dienst, Germany.

mankind (fig. 3). Christ's puny body and his mother's unflinching disposition recall images of the Virgin as the Throne of Wisdom[13] (fig. 6). Mary's pursed lips, drawn up to reveal the slightest smile, seem no less incongruous.[14] But the Virgin, who delights in the necessity of the Passion, embodies "sweet sorrow," a sentiment shared by the smiling Christ from the same convent[15] (fig. 4). In this context, the Pietà can be seen

---

Religion die Abhängigkeit seyn soll von einem wesentlich außerhalb Seyenden, von einem Ding, so findet diese Art Religion im Verhältnis zum Schönen nicht ihre Befriedigung, sondern für eine solche sind ganz schlechte, häßliche, platte Darstellungen das ebenso Zweckmäßige, oder das vielmehr Zweckmäßigere. Wie man denn auch sagt, daß die wahrhaften Kunstwerke, z. B. Raphael's Madonnenbilder, nicht die Verehrung genießen, nicht die Menge von Gaben empfangen, als vielmehr die schlechten Bilder vornehmlich aufgesucht werden und Gegenstand der größeren Andacht und Freigebigkeit sind."

10. A recent examination of the Röttgen Pietà indicates that the oldest, if not necessarily the original, layer of polychromy on the Pietà includes blood painted on the arms. My thanks to Dr. Ingeborg Krueger for sharing this information, not yet published. In the meantime, consult W. Krönig, "Die Vesperbilder in Münstereifel und Düsseldorf," *Jahrbuch der rheinischen Denkmalpflege* 27 (1967):19–26, esp. 25–26.

11. For the "Liebestod" in *Minnesang* as well as mystical thought, see A. M. Haas, "Mystik oder Erotik: Dialektik von Tod und Leben in Gottfried's *Tristan,*" and "Mors Mystica," both reprinted in A. M. Haas, *Todesbilder im Mittelalter: Fakten und Hinweise in der deutschen Literatur* (Darmstadt: Wissenschaftliche Buchgesellschaft, 1989), pp. 139–174, 222–232, with extensive bibliography.

12. Cf. the rose prominently displayed between the two kneeling donors immediately beneath the *sudarium* in the wall plaque from Bronnbach, second quarter of the fourteenth century, now in the Liebieghaus, Frankfurt, reproduced and discussed together with related representations by A. Legner, "Das Bronnbacher Wanddenkmal im Liebighaus," in *Kunstgeschichtliche Studien für Kurt Bauch zum 70. Geburtstag von seinen Schülern,* ed. M. Lisner and R. Becksmann (Berlin: Deutscher Kunstverlag, 1970), pp. 29–42, esp. pp. 33–35. For further discussion, see J. F. Hamburger, *Nuns as Artists: The Visual Culture of a Medieval Convent* (Berkeley and Los Angeles: University of California Press, 1997), pp. 63–100.

13. I. Forsyth, *The Throne of Wisdom: Wood Sculptures of the Madonna in Romanesque France* (Princeton, New Jersey: Princeton University Press, 1972).

14. See E. Reiners-Ernst, *Das freudvolle Vesperbild und die Anfänge der Pietà-Vorstellung* (Munich: Neuer Filser-Verlag, 1939). J. Svanberg, "The Gothic Smile," in *Künstlerischer Austausch—Artistic Exchange: Akten des XXVIII. Internationalen Kongresses für Kunstgeschichte Berlin, 15.–20. Juli 1992,* 3 vols., ed. T. W. Gaehtgens (Berlin: Akademie Verlag, 1993), vol. 2, pp. 357–370, makes no mention of the incongruous smile in some Pietàs.

15. To the best of my knowledge, the crucifix, which is kept in the nuns' choir, is unpublished; it is not listed in F. Mader, *Die Kunstdenkmäler von Mittelfranken I: Stadt Eichstätt* (Munich: Oldenburg, 1924). In all probability, portions have been restored. For the manuscript reproduced here, a Breviary from the Brigittine convent of Marienboom in the Netherlands, dated 1501 (Staatsbibliothek zu Berlin, Preußischer Kulturbesitz, Ms. theol. lat. qu. 19, 301v), see G.

as a combination of the two Christian cult images most familiar through much of the Middle Ages: the Virgin and Child and the crucified Christ.[16]

Art history has come to terms with images such as the Pietà under the anachronistic rubric, *Andachtsbilder,* or "devotional images."[17] To recount the career of this misleading moniker would be to trace the development of German art history in its formative years.[18] Harnessed to the twin engines of nationalism and romanticism, and later, expressionism, the Pietà provided the *"Urbild"* of an authentically German art and spirituality. In turn, it served as a point of departure for art historians such as Panofsky, who sought to internationalize the history of German art by placing it in an Italian perspective.[19] Both viewpoints have removed the Pietà and related imagery from the contexts in which they first emerged, of which (as recognized by Michelangelo as reported by Francisco de Hollanda) the most important was female monasticism.

Andachtsbilder have long since entered into the canon of art history, to the point that the term seems to have outlived its usefulness. One class of devotional imagery associated with women, however, has remained beneath contempt: the devotional drawings made by and for nuns known as *Nonnenarbeiten,* literally "nuns' work," or, as they are sometimes called, *Kleine Andachtsbilder,* or "small devotional images"[20] (fig. 5). Both terms define dumping grounds for objects with

Figure 4. Crucifix, early fourteenth century. Wood, dimensions unknown. Eichstätt, Bavaria, Abbey of St. Walburg. Photo: © 1995 Belser Wissenschaftliche Dienst, Germany.

which art history would rather not be bothered. In their modern variants, these small-scale devotional images come dangerously close to what commonly is called kitsch, in Germany linked with the "feminine" categories of *Heim und Herz,* or "domesticity and

Achten, *Das christliche Gebetbuch im Mittelalter: Andachts- und Stundenbücher in Handschrift und Frühdruck,* 2d rev. ed. (Berlin: Staatsbibliothek Preußischer Kulturbesitz, 1987), cat. no. 101, pp. 133–134.

16. On the theological implications of the image, see T. Dobrzeniecki, "Medieval Source of the Pietà," *Bulletin du Musée national de Varsovie* 7 (1967):15–24.

17. Schawe (see note 7), nn. 9–10, provides a convenient bibliography of the most important literature. For "Andacht" as defined in Middle High German texts, see K.-H. Göttert, "'Devotio-andâht': Frömmigkeitsbegriff und Darstellungsprinzip im legendarischen Erzählen des hohen Mittelalters," in *Zeiten und Formen in Sprache und Dichtung: Festschrift für Fritz Tschirch zum 70. Geburtstag,* ed. K.-H. Schirmer and B. Sowinski (Cologne: Bohlau, 1972).

18. See Ziegler (see note 3), pp. 25–51; K. Schade, *Andachtsbild: Die Geschichte eines kunsthistorischen Begriffs* (Berlin: Datenbank für Geisteswissenschaften, 1996), which appeared after this essay was completed.

19. E. Panofsky, *"Imago pietatis": Ein Beitrag zur Typengeschichte des Schmerzensmanns und der Maria Mediatrix,"* in *Festschrift für Max J. Friedländer zum 60. Geburtstage* (Leipzig: E. A. Seemann, 1927), pp. 261–308.

20. As noted by C. von Heusinger, "Studien zur oberrheinischen Buchmalerei und Graphik im Spätmittelalter" (Ph.D. diss., Albert-

Ludwigs-Universität, Freiburg, 1953), the terms *"Nonnenarbeit"* and *"Nonnenmalerei"* were coined by H. Wegener, *Beschreibendes Verzeichnis der deutschen Bilderhandschriften des späten Mittelalters in der Heidelberger Universitäts-Bibliothek* (Leipzig: J. J. Weber, 1927), and *Beschreibende Verzeichnisse der Miniaturen-Handschriften der preussischen Staatsbibliothek zu Berlin, V: Die deutschen Handschriften* (Leipzig: J. J. Weber, 1928). For a fuller discussion of these terms and the problems associated with them, see Hamburger (see note 12), esp. pp. 1–5, 177–212.

Figure 5. Pietà in prayer book from Marienboom, 1501. Colored inks and burnished gold on parchment, 168 x 116 mm. Staatsbibliothek zu Berlin—Preußischer Kulturbesitz—Handschriftenabteilung, Ms. theol. Lat. 4° 19, 301v.

The largest available corpus of small devotional images—Adolf Spamer's *Das Kleine Andachtsbild,* published in 1930—has been described as "a truly formidable collection of the mawkish and trashy in six centuries of popular Christian art."[23] Far from effusions of "popular piety," however, medieval *Nonnenarbeiten* can only be understood in relation to the monastic culture that produced them. A drawing of the crucified Christ, attributed to a draftswoman working in the Rhineland about 1350 offers a striking example (fig. 7). This startling image is best seen in color, as did the nuns for whom it was made.[24] Hardly an object intended for viewing at a disinterested distance, it asks to be handled and touched, as the body of Christ is itself caressed in

sentimentality."[21] Anachronistic considerations of quality need not, however, interfere with our appreciation of these objects, any more than they have with other genres that, while once disdained, have since found a fixed place in the art-historical firmament.[22]

21. See H. Kämpf-Jansen, "Kitsch—oder ist die Antithese der Kunst weiblich?" in *Frauen-Bilder-Männer-Mythen: Kunsthistorische Beiträge,* ed. I. Barta et al. (Berlin: D. Reimer, 1987), pp. 322–341; S. Schade and S. Wenk, "Inszenierung des Sehens: Kunst, Geschichte und Geschlechterdifferenz," in *Genus: Zur Geschlechterdifferenz in den Kulturwissenschaften,* ed. H. Bußmann and R. Hof (Stuttgart: Alfred Kroner Verlag, 1995), esp. pp. 357–358.

22. As noted by N. Ott, *Rechtspraxis und Heilsgeschichte: Zu Überlieferung, Ikonographie und Gebrauchssituation des deutschen*

'Belial', Münchener Texte und Untersuchungen zur deutschen Literatur des Mittelalters, bd. 80 (Munich: Artemis, 1983), pp. 195–202, 224–229 ("Qualität oder 'Anspruchsniveau'"); until recently, notions of quality prevented any serious consideration of most illustrated German vernacular manuscripts.

23. A. Spamer, *Das Kleine Andachtsbild vom XIV. bis zum XX. Jahrhundert* (Munich: F. Bruckmann, 1930). See E. Colledge and J. C. Marler, "'Mystical pictures' in the Suso *Exemplar,* Ms Strasbourg 2929," *Archivum Fratrum Praedicatorum* 54 (1984):293–354, esp. 319, n. 95. For early modern images classified as *Kleine Andachtsbilder,* see E. Launert, "The Small *Andachtsbild*: A Little-Known Aspect of European Religious Art," *Connoisseur* 166 (1967):164–169; G. Gugitz, *Das Kleine Andachtsbild in den Österreichischen Gnadenstätten in Darstellung, Verbreitung und Brauchtum nebst einer Ikonographie* (Vienna: Bruder Hollinek, 1950); M. Scharfe, *Evangelische Andachtsbilder: Studien zur Intention und Funktion des Bildes in der Frömmigkeitsgeschichte vornehmlich des schwäbischen Raumes,* Veröffentlichungen des Staatlichen Amtes für Denkmalpflege Stuttgart, Reihe C, Volkskunde, bd. 5 (Stuttgart: Muller u. Graff, 1968). The church historian and sometime art historian Stephan Beissel, "Religiöse Bilder für das katholische Volk," *Stimmen aus Maria Laach* 33 (1887):456–472 and 58 (1900):281–294, fulmigated against the *Kleine Andachtsbilder* of his own day yet blamed the most egregious excesses on French, not German, Catholics: "Die deutschen Verleger haben sich nicht so weit verirrt, wie die französischen; aber die Spielereien mit Blumensprache und leichtfertigem unkirchlichem Symbolismus sind auch bei uns zwar zu häufig." Beissel's condemnation formed part of a broader reaction against the proliferation of *Kleine Andachtsbilder,* discussed briefly by Scharfe (see this note), pp. 62–64. For a less biased account of French devotional imagery in the nineteenth century, see J. Pirotte, "L'Imagerie de dévotion aux XIXe et XXe siècles et la société ecclésiale," in *L'Image et la production du sacré,* ed. F. Dunand, J.-M. Spieser, and J. Wirth (Paris: Meridiens Klincksieck, 1991), pp. 233–249.

24. For a brief discussion of the drawing, see F. O. Büttner, *Imitatio pietatis: Motive der christlichen Ikonographie als Modelle der Verähnlichung* (Berlin: G. Mann, 1983), pp. 150, 215, fig. 162. It is also cited in passing in *Splendours of Flanders: Late Medieval Art in Cambridge Collections,* ed. A. Arnould et al. (Cambridge: Cambridge University Press, 1993), cat. no. 53, pp. 160–161, 185. The drawing appears as color plate 1 in Hamburger (see note 12).

the image. Like St. Bernard and the nun, we are compelled to identify with the body and blood of Christ through the sheer, livid profusion of red ink saturating the paper.[25] Almost entirely obscured by blood, Christ's body appears as one enormous wound. Even Christ's halo takes on the sanguine tincture. The pigment—thick and viscous—suggests a compact sealed in blood, like Christ's own assurance of salvation.[26] Although usually classified as a *Kleines Andachtsbild*, the drawing is anything but small. Its dimensions—25.5 x 18 cm, only slightly smaller than this journal—increase its impact.[27]

This Crucifixion rivets, even as it repels us. Yet where some might see only unbridled violence or unrestrained expression, the woman by and for whom it was made— represented by the nun at the foot of the cross—would have experienced more complex meanings and sensations. To see through her eyes and those of her contemporaries, we have to forget preconceived notions of "Art." Instead, we must try to inhabit her world, removed from the present by the passage of time and the seclusion of the cloister. Some insight comes from sermons: for example, the homily on the side wound by Konrad von Eßlingen, twice Dominican prior provincial

Figure 6. Imad Madonna, 1051–1058. Linden wood, H: 112 cm. Erzbischöfliches Diözesanmuseum und Domschatzkammer, Inv.-Nr. SK1 (62.1). Photo: Husgar Hoffmann.

of Teutonia (1277–1281; 1290–1293).[28] Delivered in 1318 to the female community at Adelhausen in Freiburg, his words survive as a *précis* recorded by the nuns, who heard him through a grille.[29]

Konrad's homily offers an analogy to the drawing without, however, accounting for its visceral power. In good scholastic fashion, the Dominican enumerates the qualities of Christ's blood: its heat, fluidity, and color. Likening the Eucharist to a pigment, Konrad argues that the red color of Christ's blood:

25. The image evokes the popular and oft-illustrated story of St. Bernard from Conrad of Eberbach's *Exordium magnum Cisterciense*, II, 7, which describes how a monk of Morimond witnessed Bernard embraced by an image of the crucified Christ. See B. P. McGuire, *The Difficult Saint: Bernard of Clairvaux and His Tradition* (Kalamazoo, Michigan: Cistercian Publications, 1991), esp. chap. 8, "Bernard and the Embrace of Christ: Renewal in Late Medieval Monastic Life and Devotion."

26. For the symbolism of the color red in Christian art and exegesis, see M. Pastoureau, "'Ceci est mon sang': Le Christianisme médiéval et la couleur rouge," in *Le Pressoir mystique: Actes du colloque de Recloses, 27 mai 1989*, ed. D. Alexandre-Bidon (Paris: Editions du Cerf, 1990), pp. 43–56; R. Suntrup, "Liturgische Farbendeutung im Mittelalter und in der frühen Neuzeit," in *Symbole des Alltags, Alltag der Symbole: Festschrift für Harry Kühnel zum 65. Geburtstag*, ed. G. Blaschitz, H. Hundsbichler, G. Jaritz, and E. Vavra (Graz: Akademische Druch- u. Verlagsanstalt, 1992), pp. 445–468, esp. pp. 459–461; C. Meier and R. Suntrup, "Zum Lexikon der Farbendeutung im Mittelalter: Einführung zu Gegenstand und Methoden sowie Probeartikel aus dem Farbbereich 'Rot,'" *Frühmittelalterliche Studien* 21 (1987):390–478. N. Bériou, "De la lecture aux épousailles: Les images dans la communication de la Parle de Dieu au XIIIe siècle," *Cristianesimo nella storia* 14 (1993):535–568, esp. 546, n. 25, cites a sermon that refers to a crucifix with its corpus completely covered in blood.

27. The measurements given in *Das Schnütgen-Museum: Eine Auswahl* (Cologne, 1968) are inaccurate; my thanks to the museum's director, Dr. H. Westermann-Angerhausen, for providing me with the correct dimensions.

28. For what little is known of Konrad, see D. Ladish-Grube, "Konrad von Eßlingen," in *Die deutsche Literatur des Mittelalters: Verfasser Lexikon*, 2d ed., ed. K. Ruh et al. (Berlin: De Gruyter, 1978–), vol. 5, p. 170.

29. For the convent and its history, see the exhibition catalogue, *750 Jahre Dominikanerinnenkloster Adelhausen* (Freiburg in Breisgau: Adelhausensenstiftung, 1985).

Figure 7. Crucifixion, mid-fourteenth century. Pen and colored inks on paper, 25.5 x 18 cm. Schnütgen-Museum, Cologne M 340. Photo: Rheinisches Bildarchiv Köln.

restores and renews the divine image imprinted in the soul; a person may never erase that image, whether he goes to heaven or to hell. With our sins, however, we often act like the man who took the emperor's shield and dunked it in a puddle, so that the image was besmirched and yet remained as it was. The red of the blood restores and revarnishes the divine image in the sinner.[30]

The shield to which Konrad alludes denotes not only the *imago Dei* imprinted on the soul, it also signifies a piece of armor that shields the soul from the ravages of sin.[31] In German, however, "*Schild*" refers specifically to a coat-of-arms, such as were often emblazoned on shields—in this instance, the *arma Christi*, the heraldic insignia of Christ's Passion[32] (fig. 8). Painting itself provides an emblem of the process of creation and redemption, with Christ's blood as the medium that binds image and artist, man to his maker. Konrad's metaphor represents a specialized application of the

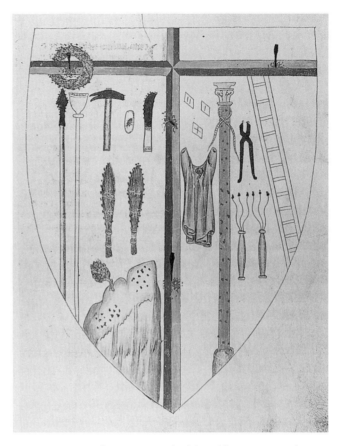

Figure 8. *Arma Christi*, Passional of the Abbess Kunigunde, ca. 1321. Parchment, 29.5 x 25 cm. Prague, National Library, XIV A 17, f. 3r.

comparison of God to an artist.[33] Whereas Christ works through the Sacraments to restore his image in the soul, men (or, in this case, the women who make up Konrad's listeners) commit through their sins an act of collective *lèse majesté*. According to the preacher, sinners besmirch the image of God stamped on their souls, which is then cleansed and restored by the blood of Christ.

In the drawing, the blood-drenched body of Christ also assumes sacramental significance. The vivifying fluid rains down and gathers in pools between Christ's

---

30. The precis of the sermon is appended to the chronicle of Anna von Münzingen, prioress of the Dominican convent of Adelhausen in Freiburg; see J. König, ed., "Die Chronik der Anna von Münzingen," *Freiburger Diözesan Archiv* 13 (1880):129–236, esp. 189–191: "Das dritte die röte: wan die farwe sines blůtes wider verwertet vnd wider nůweret das götliche bilde, das in die sele getruckt ist; das bilde mag der mensche nieme vertilgen, er kome in himelrich oder in helle. Wir tůnt aber dicke mit vnsern súndern als der des keysers schilt neme, vnd in truckte in die lachen, so wurde dz bilde vermasget vnd blibe doch an im selber, das wider verwet vnd wider firnisset die röti des blůtes." For the chronicle itself, see E. Krebs, "Die Mystik in Adelhausen: Eine vergleichende Studie über die 'Chronik' der Anna von Munzingen und die Thaumatographische Literatur des 13. und 14. Jahrhunderts als Beitrag zur Geschichte der Mystik im Predigerorden," in *Festgabe Heinrich Finke gewidmet* (Münster: Aschendorff, 1904), pp. 45–105; W. Blank, "Anna von Münzingen," in *Die deutsche Literatur des Mittelalters: Verfasser Lexikon*, 2d ed., ed. K. Ruh et al. (Berlin: De Gruyter, 1978–), vol. 1, cols. 365–366.

31. Cf. the characterization of the stigmata added at about 1480–1490 to the translation of Bonaventure's life of St. Francis (London, British Library Ms. Add. 15710), transcribed by Sibilla von Bondorf but attributed to Sibilla in *Bonaventuras Legenda Sancti Francisci in der Übersetzung der Sibilla von Bondorf*, ed. D. Brett-Evans, Texte des späten Mittelalters 12 (Munich: E. Schmidt, 1960), p. 192, ll. 60–64: "Uf daz zitt, do gott an sinen aller liepsten frúnd Sancto Francisco wolt legen daz wappenklaid der eren, daz er tragen, und bewaren sölt den kostparlichen schatz der fünf flús unser erlösung, durch die allain wir gerainget sind von unseren súnden. . . ."

32. For the *arma Christi*, see R. Suckale, "*Arma Christi*: Überlegungen zur Zeichenhaftigkeit mittelalterlicher Andachtsbilder," *Städel-Jahrbuch* 6 (1977):177–208; for the example reproduced here, from the *Passionale* of the Abbess Kunegonde, completed about 1321, see most recently A. Merhautová and K. Stejskal, *St.-Georgs-Stift auf der Prager Burg* (Prague: Art Folia, 1991), pp. 40–58, with additional bibliography.

33. For God as an artist, see A. Blunt, "Blake's *Ancient of Days*: The Symbolism of the Compasses," *Journal of the Warburg and Courtauld Institutes* 2 (1938–1939):53–63; E. R. Curtius, *European Literature and the Latin Middle Ages*, trans. W. R. Trask, Bollingen Series 36 (New York: Pantheon Books, 1953), pp. 544–546; F. Ohly, "*Deus geometra*: Skizzen zur Geschichte einer Vorstellung von Gott," in *Tradition als historische Kraft: Festschrift Karl Hauck*, ed. N. Kamp and J. Wollasch (Berlin: De Gruyter, 1982), pp. 1–42.

devotees. Both, however, maintain decorum and distance; for all their fervor, they remain untouched, as if to signify their purity having been restored by Christ's sacrifice. The saint grasps the beam of the cross, but the blood flows under, not over, his fingers. The nun is still further removed. Even as the image portrays such intimate and privileged proximity to the divine, it bars the participants from complete immersion in the Godhead.

In a time when professional artists increasingly mass-produced images—prints, paintings, and even altarpieces—for the market, this drawing and others like it stand apart by virtue of their singular, unprofessional character.[34] Like most *Nonnenarbeiten*, it was made by and for nuns lacking both systematic training in art and wide-ranging contact with images outside the convent. Art historians would never assign a *sacra conversatione* by Fra Angelico and a portrait by Fra Filippo Lippi to the same genre because both happen to have been painted by friars. Nor could one assume that in identifying both artists as mendicants one had identified all that was typical of their work. Far from providing an apt, let alone productive, characterization of the images it seeks to define, the term *Nonnenarbeit* stands by definition for deficiency: not only a lack of skill and sophistication, but also a lack of identity, an anonymity that represents the very opposite of the artistic self-assertion exemplified by Michelangelo's signature.

To an uncomeliness of subject, *Nonnenarbeiten* add what the modern critic might regard as an awkwardness of style. Some medieval observers, however, considered this particular form of ugliness a virtue. The Florentine, Giovanni Dominici (d. 1419) thought timeworn, smoke-stained images more likely to provoke piety than glossy, gilt novelties.[35] In the early thirteenth century, the

Cistercian Caesarius of Heisterbach reported a woman duly punished for having denigrated an old, unattractive image of the Virgin with the words, *Ut quid hic stat vetus haec rumbula*, or "Why's this old load of rubbish standing here?"[36] In pictures as in persons, age served as a sign of venerability that could, in turn, invite veneration. For example, the *Legatus divinae pietatis* attributes to Gertrude of Helfta (1256–1301/02) a vision in which the Cistercian nun is astonished at the lovely ("*amabilis*") appearance of John the Baptist, who reveals himself adorned in the resplendent flower of vernal youth ("*flore vernantissimae juventutis et gloriose praefulgens*")—altogether different from the haggard, despicable saint ("*senex et despicabilis*") she knows from pictures ("*valde dissimilis forma in pictura eum ostenderet*"). Gertrude is perplexed, so John explains that painters depicted him as old and infirm by way of indicating that he had spent his entire life in seeking after virtue, an allusion to Psalm 70:17–18: "Thou hast taught me, O God, from my youth: and till now I will declare thy wonderful works. And unto old age and grey hairs."[37] John's transformation and restoration identifies

---

34. For the mass production of imagery in Germanic-speaking regions, aside from prints, see W. Krönig, "Rheinische Vesperbilder aus Leder und ihr Umkreis," *Wallraf-Richartz-Jahrbuch* 24 (1962):98–101; *Meisterwerke massenhaft: Die Bildhauerwerkstatt des Niklaus Weckmann und die Malerei im Ulm um 1500* (Stuttgart: Württembergisches Landesmuseum, 1993); F. Arens, "Die ursprüngliche Verwendung gotischer Stein- und Tonmodel mit einem Verzeichnis der Model in mittelrheinische Museen," *Mainzer Zeitschrift: Mittelrheinisches Jahrbuch für Archäologie, Kunst und Geschichte* 66 (1971):106–131; L. Saurma-Jeltsch, "Auftragsfertigung und Vorratsarbeit: Kriterien zu ihrer Unterscheidung am Beispiel der Werkstatt Diebold Laubers," *Unsere Kunstdenkmäler* 36 (1985):302–309; id., "Buchmalerei in Serie: Zur Frühgeschichte der Vervielfältigungskunst," *Zeitschrift für Schweizerische Archeologie und Kunstgeschichte* 40 (1983):128–135.

35. Cited by K. Krüger, "Mimesis als Bildlichkeit des Scheins: Zur Fiktionalität religiöser Bildkunst im Trecento," in *Künstlerischer Austausch—Artistic Exchange: Akten des XXVIII. Internationalen*

Kongresses für Kunstgeschichte Berlin, 15.–20. Juli 1992, 3 vols., ed. T. W. Gaehtgens (Berlin: Akademie Verlag, 1993), vol. 2, pp. 423–436, esp. p. 426. C. Gilbert, *Italian Art 1400–1500: Sources and Documents* (Englewood Cliffs, New Jersey: Prentice-Hall, 1980), p. 146. Dominici's primary concern is idolatry: "avoid frames of gold and silver, lest they become more idolatrous than faithful, since, if they see more candles lit and more hats removed and more kneeling to figures that are gilded and adorned with precious stones than to old smokey ones, they will only learn to revere gold and jewels, and not the figures, or rather, the truths represented by the figures." See also, Blessed Giovanni Dominici, *Regola del governo di cura familiare (On the Education of Children),* trans. A. B. Coté (Washington, D.C.: The Catholic University of America, 1927).

36. Quoted and translated by D. Freedberg, *The Power of Images: Studies in the History and Theory of Response* (Chicago: University of Chicago Press, 1989), p. 312.

37. See J.-M. Clément, les Moniales de Wisques, and B. de Vregille, *Gertrude d'Helfta: Oeuvres spirituelles,* vol. 4 (Paris: Editions du Cerf, 1978), pp. 332–334 (Bk. 4, chap. 42): "Die sancti Johannis Baptistae, dum interesset Matutinis quanto devotius potuit, apparuit ei idem beatus Johannes, stans in conspectu throni gloriae Regis caelorum, miro modo amabilis, flore vernantissimae juventutis et gloriose praefulgens specialibus privilegiis specialis dignitatis: scilicet, quod dignus fuit esse baptista Christi et praecursor atque demonstrator, et caetera hujusmodi. Cumque ipsum considerando recoleret, quod valde dissimilis forma in pictura eum ostenderet, quia senex et despicabilis ubique depingeretur, beatus Joannes eam docuit quod hoc ipsum cumulum gloriae suae non desineret augmentare, quia ratione disponente ideo eum pictura provectae aetatis ostenderet, quia constantem animum habebat pro divino amore usque in senectam et senium ac consumptionem omnium virium

his ugliness—what Gertrude defines as his "dissimilitude"—not simply as a sign of sin, but of struggle and redemption.

The ugly could only function as a reminder of rectitude because it served simultaneously as a sign of corruption. In classic Augustinian terms, the ugly existed only as a deformation, a falling off from an ideal of beauty, just as Lucifer had fallen from his original perfection. Ugliness connoted debasement, not simply depravity. In art, as in life, the ugly was a moral as well as a descriptive category.[38] Evil figures—for example, demons and the tormentors of Christ—were depicted as repulsive, not simply because they were bad, but because they had fallen.[39] Jean Miélot's adaptation of Gautier de Coinci's *Miracles de Notre Dame* tells of a painter at work on a Last Judgment who "took great trouble" to make the devil "so hideous that no painting or sculpture was ever so ugly."[40] In an aesthetics based on Christian soteriology, however, the fallen can, through grace, rise again. As in Gertrude's vision, beauty itself is revealed as a sign of redemption.

The ugly also served as a signifier of social class.[41] Social and religious rank, however, did not necessarily coincide. Homely rustics—for example, the awkward shepherds who gawk at the Christ Child at the center of Hugo van der Goes's Portinari Altarpiece—denote more than the Savior's universal appeal (fig. 9). They represent humility—their own and that of the ideal onlooker, but also that of the *summum bonum*, Christ himself, the paradoxical figure of the defiled and degraded Godhead who, on behalf of mankind, underwent the ultimate humiliation, a literal coming down to earth.[42]

The depiction of the dead and suffering Christ raised delicate issues of decorum.[43] Christianity contrasted the transfigured Jesus of the Second Coming with the uncomely Christ of the Passion, employing the words of Isaiah 53:2–3: "there is no beauty in him, nor comeliness: and we have seen him, and there was no sightliness, that we should be desirous of him, despised, and the most abject of men, a man of sorrows" (fig. 10). In the Vulgate, the phrase, "despised and the most abject of men" reads *despectum et novissimum virorum*, or "despised and the newest of men," with "newest" also carrying the implication of "last" or "inferior." Beauty carries with it connotations of social status; in Isaiah's prophecy as in its Christian interpretation, the abject Messiah is a ruler stripped of honor, a degraded monarch.

The crucified Christ provided the paradigm of what Eric Auerbach called a specifically Christian aesthetic in which *sermo humilis*, a humble style, was applied, in a grave breach of classical decorum, to the most exalted of subjects.[44] As observed by Hans Robert Jauss, "the

sensuumque suorum fideliter in omnibus contra injustitiam decertare, et in omni vita sua ad summam perfectione intendere." Book 4 is no longer considered an authentic work by Gertrude, but that of an anonymous female follower, also a nun at Helfta, writing in the early fourteenth century; see K. Ruh, "Gertrud von Helfta: Ein neues Gertrud-Bild," *Zeitschrift für deutsches Altertum und deutsche Literatur* 121 (1992):1–20.

38. This is not to imply that ugliness in medieval art can only be interpreted within an overarching moral framework. For the functions and meanings of grotesque imagery in medieval art, see M. Camille, *Image on the Edge: The Margins of Medieval Art* (London: Reaktion, 1992), and my review in *Art Bulletin* 75 (1993):319–327.

39. For the ugly and grotesque as signs of social stigma, see E. Salter, "The Annunciation to the Shepherds in Later Medieval Art and Drama," in *English and International: Studies in the Literature, Art and Patronage of Medieval England*, ed. D. Pearsall and N. Zeeman (Cambridge: Cambridge University Press, 1988), pp. 272–292; T. A. Heslop, "Romanesque Painting and Social Distinction: The Magi and the Shepherds," in *England in the Twelfth Century: Proceedings of the 1988 Harlaxton Symposium*, ed. D. Williams (Woodbridge: Boydell Press, 1990), pp. 137–152; R. Mellinkoff, *Outcasts: Signs of Otherness in Northern European Art of the Late Middle Ages*, 2 vols. (Berkeley and Los Angeles: University of California Press, 1993); R. A. Wisbey, "Die Darstellung des Hässlichen im Hoch- und Spätmittelalter," in *Deutsche Literatur des Späten Mittelalters: Hamburger Kolloquium 1973*, ed. W. Harms and L. P. Johnson, Publications of the Institute of Germanic Studies, University of London, bd. 22 (Berlin: E. Schmidt, 1975), pp. 9–34.

40. Freedberg (see note 36), p. 307

41. See, for example, J. J. G. Alexander, "'Labeur' et 'paresse':

Ideological Representations of Medieval Peasant Labor," *Art Bulletin* 72 (1990):436–452.

42. For theological conceptions of ugliness or uncomeliness, see P. Michel, *Formosa deformitas: Bewältigungsformen des Häßlichen in mittelalterlichen Literatur*, Studien zur Germanistik, Anglistik und Komparatistik, bd. 57 (Bonn: Bouvier, 1976).

43. For issues of decorum in representations of the Passion, see F. O. Büttner, "Das Christusbild auf niedrigster Stilhöhe: Ansichtigkeit und Körpersichtigkeit in narrativen Passionsdarstellungen der Jahrzehnte um 1500," *Wiener Jahrbuch für Kunstgeschichte* 46–47 (1993–1994):99–130, 397–400; G. Wolf, "*Velaverunt faciem eius*: Überlegungen zum Christusbild der Quattrocento," *Kritische Berichte* 4 (1991):5–18.

44. E. Auerbach, "*Sermo humilis*," *Romanische Forschungen* 64 (1952):304–364. Auerbach touches briefly on the same theme in *Mimesis: The Representation of Reality in Western Literature*, trans. W. R. Trask (Princeton: Princeton University Press, 1953), p. 72. Auerbach was hardly the first to define an aesthetic of the ugly in anticlassical terms; see, for example, K. Rosenkranz, *Aesthetik des Häslichen* (Königsberg: Gebruder Borntrager, 1853), who, however, links the ugly with the demonic. J. Trilling, "Medieval Art without Style? Plato's Loophole and a Modern Detour," *Gesta* 34 (1995):56–62, traces the equation of abstraction and spirituality to

Figure 9. Hugo van der Goes, The Three Shepherds, detail from the *Adoration of the Shepherds*, known as the Portinari Altarpiece, ca. 1473–1478. Oil on panel, 249 x 300 cm. Uffizi, Florence, Italy. Photo: Courtesy of Alinari/Art Resource.

Christian concept of *humilitas passionis* shattered the canonical, classical pairing of the good and the beautiful and of the ugly with the depths of evil."[45] In the early-

fourteenth-century *crucifixus dolorus* from the Cistercian nunnery of Baindt, Christ appears gaunt, hollowed out, emaciated—almost a piece of antisculpture (fig. 12).[46]

Schopenhauer and Worringer. For a brief discussion of the context in which Auerbach's anti-idealism developed, see W. Kemp, *Christliche Kunst: Ihre Anfänge, Ihre Strukturen* (Munich: Schirmer-Mosel, 1994), pp. 15–16, who expresses reservations concerning Auerbach's thesis, especially as developed by H. R. Jauss, "Die klassische und die christliche Rechtfertigung des Häßlichen in mittelalterlichen Literatur," in *Die nicht mehr Schönen Künste: Grenzphänomene des Ästhetischen,* Poetik und Hermaneutik 3 (Munich: W. Fink, 1968), pp. 143–168, esp. pp. 156–158, reprinted in *Alterität und Modernität der mittelalterlichen Literatur: Gesammelte Aufsätze 1956–1976* (Munich: W. Fink, 1977), pp. 385–409.

45. See Jauss (see note 44) and in the same volume, J. Taubes,

"Die Rechtfertigung des Hässlichen in Urchristlicher Tradition," pp. 169–185, who also builds on Auerbach's argument. For continuities and contrasts between classical and Christian aesthetics, see W. Haug, "Die Voraussetzungen antiker Rhetorik und christlicher Ästhetik," in *Literaturtheorie im deutschen Mittelalter von den Anfängen bis zum Ende des 13. Jahrhunderts* (Darmstadt: Wissenschaftliche Buchgesellschaft, 1992), pp. 7–24.

46. See W. Urban, "Das Baindter Pestkreuz," in *Baindt, "hortus floridus": Geschichte und Kunstwerke der früheren Zisterzienserinnen-Reichsabtei. Festschrift zur 750-Jahrfeier der Klostergründung, 1240–1990,* ed. O. Beck, Grosse Kunstführer, bd. 173 (Munich: Schnell und Steiner, 1990).

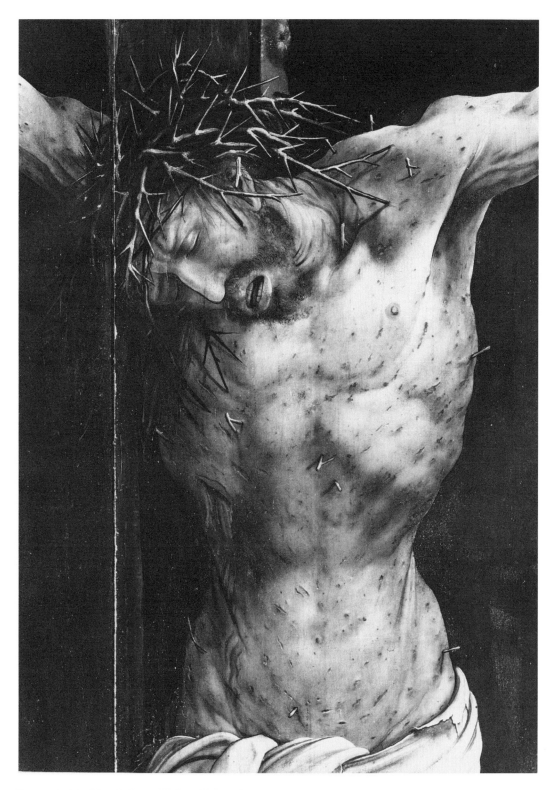

Figure 10. Matthias Grünewald, Crucifixion, detail from the Isenheim Altarpiece, ca. 1512/1513–1515. Oil on panel, 269 x 307 cm. Musée Unterlinden, Colmar, France. Photo: Courtesy of Giraudon/Art Resource.

Figure 11. Matthias Grünewald, Resurrection, detail from the Isenheim Altarpiece, ca. 1512/1513–1515. Oil on panel, 269 x 143 cm. Musée Unterlinden, Colmar, France. Photo: Giraudon/Art Resource.

St. Augustine's celebrated formulation states, *Pendebat enim in cruce deformis, sed deformitas illius pulchritudo nostra erat*, or "For he [Christ] hung ugly, disfigured [literally, deformed or misshapen] on the cross, but his ugliness was our beauty."[47] The clash between the ugly and the beautiful, between death and rebirth, received perhaps its most powerful (certainly its most celebrated) embodiment in Matthias Grünewald's Isenheim Altarpiece, whose gory, gruesome Crucifixion can only be understood in counterpoint to the mesmerizing,

incandescent figure of the resurrected Christ (figs. 10–11). Hegel did not know this altarpiece in Colmar, but one can imagine that for him, as for many in Germany immediately following the First World War, the Crucifixion would have exemplified what he characterized as the spiritual romanticism and "realism" of medieval painting. He considered one of the essential traits of medieval painting; not the abstraction with which today we often associate medieval art, but "the representation of suffering, the absolute ugliness of reality (*das Unschönen der Wirklichkeit*)."[48]

There is, ironically, more of a dialectic between the ideal and the "real," the beautiful and the ugly, both in Christianity and in Grünewald's altarpiece than Hegel's system allows for.[49] But in contrast to Michelangelo's classicizing aesthetic, a Christian artistic credo defined in paradoxical terms exalted the real over the ideal and expression over what Michelangelo called harmony. As in the German Pietàs, the ugly, the humble, and the degraded served as symbols, vehicles, and measures of ultimate transcendence. In mystical theology, especially

---

47. See Augustine, *Sermones de Vetere Testamento I–L*, Corpus Christianorum Series Latina 41 (Turnhout: Typographi Brepols, 1961), p. 365 (Sermon XXVII, 6, ll. 131–132). For this and related passages in Augustine's writings, see Jauss (see note 44), pp. 156–158.

48. Hegel (see note 9), vol. 14, esp. pp. 119–120: "Eine zweite Seite, welche Berücksichtigung verdient, ist der Uebergang . . . zur Darstellung von Martern, zum Unschönen der Wirklichkeit überhaupt." For a partial reception history of the altarpiece, in particular, the Crucifixion, see A. Stieglitz, "The Reproduction of Agony: Toward a Reception History of Grünewald's Isenheim Altar after the First World War," *Oxford Art Journal* 12 (1989):87–103, kindly brought to my attention by Neil Donahue; I. Schulze, *Die Erschütterung der Moderne: Grünewald im 20. Jahrhundert* (Leipzig: E. A. Seemann, 1991); A. Hayum, *The Isenheim Altarpiece: God's Medicine and the Painter's Vision* (Princeton, New Jersey: Princeton University Press, 1989), esp. chap. 4; C. Heck, "Entre le mythe et le modèle formel: Les Crucifixions de Grünewald et l'art de XXe siècle," in *Corps crucifiés, Catalog of an Exhibition Held at the Musée Picasso* (Paris: Reunion des Musées Nationaux, 1992–1993), pp. 84–107. D. B. Morris, *The Culture of Pain* (Berkeley: University of California Press, 1991), pp. 48–50, uses the image to exemplify a specifically Christian construction of pain according to which suffering "served as a sign and means of contact with the divine." The images of late medieval passion piety acquire new currency in a climate in which, as noted by H. Foster, *The Return of the Real: The Avant-Garde at the End of the Century* (Cambridge: MIT Press, 1996), p. 166, "truth resides in the traumatic or abject subject, in the diseased or damaged body."

49. Paradox is central to Christian doctrine; the virgin birth, the Incarnation, and the Trinity are all oxymorons. Paradox is also, not coincidentally, a central trope of Christian mysticism. See J. Keller, "The Function of Paradox in Mystical Discourse," *Studia Mystica* 6 (1983):3–19; R. Colie, *Paradoxia Epidemica: The Renaissance Tradition of Paradox* (Princeton, New Jersey: Princeton University Press, 1966), esp. pp. 22–28; A. M. Haas, "Überlegungen zum mystischen Paradox," in *Probleme philosophischer Mystik: Festschrift Karl Albert* (St. Augustin: Academia Verlag, 1991), pp. 109–124.

the tradition of apophatic or negative theology stemming from the pseudo-Dionysius, the paradox becomes more pointed still. Not only is God more beautiful than anything imaginable, he is beyond all predication to the point that all that can be said of Him is that He is. As God says of himself in Exodus 3:14: "I am who I am." Ugly, inapposite imagery, considered in relation to a Being so exalted and inaccessible, was deemed a more appropriate and less misleading way of approaching the Godhead than any analogy to beauty, goodness, or truth.[50]

Christianity, despite its insistence on the disparity between God and his creatures, presumed the ultimate coincidence of opposites. The Incarnation and, with it, the promise of the Resurrection, allowed the abject, if not beautiful in itself, to put on beauty, much as dry bones could once again put on beautiful, beatified flesh. In this sense, the ugly was also comic—comic in that, as in Dante's *Divine Comedy*, it entailed an ascent from the depths. Informed by this mode of vision, Bernard of Clairvaux could, along with the centurion Longinus, see beauty in the crucified Christ:[51]

The man who cried out: "Truly this man was the Son of God!" certainly perceived how great his beauty was. But where he perceived that beauty is for us to ascertain. For supposing he considered only what his eyes beheld, in what way was this man beautiful, how was he the Son of God? What did the eyes of the beholders see but a man deformed and black, his hands splayed out on the cross as he hung between two criminals, an object of laughter for the wicked.

As presented by Bernard, Longinus embodies the paradox of Christian vision: he sees, but only in his blindness, for which he is healed.[52]

The abject was linked not only to the new and inferior, but also to the feminine, witness the

feminization of the suffering Christ,[53] of whom it was said, in words spoken by the bride in the Song of Songs, *nigra sum, sed formosa*, or "I am black, but beautiful," a passage also glossed as a reference to the soul stained by sin.[54] In the words of Bernard of Clairvaux:[55]

The blackening of one makes many bright. . . . It is better that one be blackened for the sake of all "in the likeness of sinful flesh," than for the whole of mankind to be lost by the blackness of sin; that the splendor and image of the substance of God should be shrouded in the form of a slave, in order that a slave might live; that the brightness of eternal light should become dimmed in the flesh for the purging of the flesh; that he who surpasses all mankind in beauty should be eclipsed by the darkness of the Passion for the enlightening of mankind; that he himself should suffer the ignominy of the cross, grow pale in death, be totally deprived of beauty and comeliness that he might gain the Church as a beautiful and comely bride, without stain and fellows.

Even if, in Isaiah's formulation (53:2–3), there was in Christ "no sightliness that we should be desirous of him," Christ became in his unsightliness the object of the most ardent affection.

The ideas and emotions sketched so vividly by Bernard are enacted in the devotions of nuns. A vision ascribed to the nun, Elsbeth, in the early-fourteenth-century chronicle formerly associated with Kirchberg bei Sulz in Württemberg, frames Christ's crucifixion explicitly in terms of the contrast between the ugly and the beautiful.[56]

50. See Michel (see note 42); J. F. Hamburger, *The Rothschild Canticles: Art and Mysticism in Flanders and the Rhineland* (New Haven, Connecticut: Yale University Press, 1990), pp. 118–124; M. Büchsel, "Die von Abt Suger verfaßten Inschriften: Gibt es eine ästhetische Theorie der Skulptur im Mittelalter?" in *Studien zur Geschichte der Europäischen Skulptur im 12./13. Jahrhundert*, 2 vols., ed. H. Beck and K. Hengevoss-Dürkopp (Frankfurt: Henrich, 1994), vol. 1, pp. 57–73.

51. Bernard of Clairvaux, *On the Song of Songs*, Cistercian Fathers Series 7 (Kalamazoo, Michigan: Cistercian Publications, 1983), p. 91 (Sermon 28:4).

52. For Longinus as a figure of mystical vision, see Hamburger (see note 50), p. 75.

53. For the feminization of Christ in the later Middle Ages, see C. W. Bynum, *Jesus as Mother: Studies in the Spirituality of the High Middle Ages* (Berkeley: University of California Press, 1982), as well as many of the essays gathered in id., *Fragmentation and Redemption: Essays on Gender and the Human Body in Medieval Religion* (New York: Zone Books, 1991).

54. See K. Schreiner, *Maria: Jungfrau, Mutter, Herrscherin* (Munich and Vienna: C. Hanser, 1994), pp. 211–248. For the aesthetic implications of the phrase, especially in Cistercian thought and architecture, see Emma Simi Varanelli, "'Nigra sum sed formosa': La problematica della luce e della forma nell'estetica bernardina," *Rivista dell'Istituti Nazionale d'Archeologia e Storia dell'Arte*, 3d ser., 2 (1979):119–167.

55. Bernard of Clairvaux (see note 51), Sermons 25–28, pp. 50–101, esp. pp. 88–89 (Sermon 28:1–2).

56. F. W. E. Roth, "Aufzeichnungen über das mystische Leben der Nonne von Kirchberg bei Sulz Predigerordens während des 14. und 15. Jahrhunderts," *Alemannia* 21 (1893):103–148, esp. 144: "Zu einem mal da stund sie vor einem crucifix, das was gar peinlich und jemerlich gemalet, in gar grosser andacht. . . . Und ving an, und manet unsern herrn mit tieffem seüfczen aller seiner leidunge, und pat in, das er ir sünde vergebe. Als neiman mag an klein schulde gesein,

Figure 12. Crucifix, 1300–1325. Baindt, Cistercian nunnery (Kreis Ravensburg). Photo: Courtesy of Landesdenkmalamt Baden-Württemberg, Außenstell Tübingen, Dr. Hell/Reutlingen.

One time she [Elsbeth] was standing most piously in front of a crucifix that was painted in a particularly gruesome and sorrowful manner. . . . And, as she began, and our Lord demanded recompense with the deep sighs of all his suffering, she beseeched that he forgive her sins. For there is no one without a little sin—we are clothed and covered in dust and ashes. Our Lord then showed her spiritually his

noble, blissful humanity in a leprous image ["*in einem auss setzigen pild*"]. Then she said: Lord, I see with my eyes that you have been made a leper, and that on account of my sins. And she said all this with such crying, weeping, and heartfelt sorrow that he, in his divine mercy, did not leave her uncomforted. And afterwards our Lord once again was bright and desirable. She then said: 'Lord, you once again are beautiful and lovely ["*schön und mynicklich*"] and have forgiven my sins.' And with that she fell upon the ground again in a long prostration for our Lord as she thanked him for his mercy. Then she was entirely filled with joy, which she showed with affectionate, loving laughter and with sweet murmurings.

Elsbeth smiles in the face of suffering. Her vision instructs the reader that, properly understood, Christ's Passion is cause for blissful elation. From leprosy to laughter, Christ's transformation from glory to ugliness and back again defines the trajectory of the pious Christian made in God's image from the Fall to the Resurrection.

Elsbeth's exemplum teaches that, just as Christ suffered by way of expressing his love for mankind, so too the Christian who loves Jesus must study his wounds, a moral spelled out by the inscriptions on a single-leaf devotional drawing on parchment tipped into a paper manuscript compiled about 1440–1450 by a nun at the Dominican convent of St. Nicolaus in undis in Strasbourg.[57] The words at the top of the leaf read,

die weil wir mit staube und aschen gekleidet und überladen sein. Da zeiget ir unser herr gesichtiglich sein edel wunickliche menschiet in einem auss setzigen pild. Da sprach sie: 'Herr, ich sihe mit meinen augen, das du auss seczig pist worden, und das ist von meinen sünden,' und aus sprach da mit mit weinen und mit heülen und mit herczen leit in sein götlich erpermde, das er sie nit ungetröstet liesse, und dar nach ward unser herr wider klar und begirlich. Da sprach sie aber: 'Herre, du pist schön wider worden und mynicklich und hast mir mein sunde vergeben,' und da viel sie myder auff die erden an ir lange

venie für unsern herren, als sie im seiner erpermde danckte, und da was sie in ganzer voller freüde, als sie wol erzeiget mit zartem mynicklichem lachen und mit süssem weinungen." The vision comes from the second part of the chronicle, which, as noted by S. Ringler, *Viten- und Offenbarungsliteratur in Frauenklöstern des Mittelalters: Quellen und Studien*, Münchener Texte und Untersuchungen zur deutschen Literatur des Mittelalters, bd. 72 (Munich: Artemis Verlag, 1980), pp. 91–111, originated in another, as yet unidentified, community of Dominican nuns in Swabia.

57. See Achten (see note 15), cat. no. 89, p. 122–123; for a fuller description, see H. Degering, *Kurzes Verzeichnis der germanischen Handschriften der preussischen Staatsbibliothek*, vol. 2, *Die Handschriften in Oktovaformat* (1926; reprint, Graz: ADEVA, 1970), pp. 23–25. The image is followed (ff. 24r–33r) by prayers to Christ's wounds, of which the first is attributed to St. Bernard: "Dis ist sancte Bernhardus gebet von latin zü tützsche brocht vnd er machte do sich vnser herre zo ime neigete ab dem crúcze. Dis gehört zü den füssen unsers herren. . . ." T. Lentes, "Bild, Reform und Cura Monialium: Bildverständnis und Bildgebrauch im Buch der Reformatio Predigerordens des Johannes Meyer (+ 1485)," in *Dominicans et Dominicaines en Alsace, XIIIe–XXe siècle*: Actes du colloque de Guebwiller, 8–9 avril, 1994 (Strasbourg: Conseil Générale, 1996), pp. 177–195, esp. p. 188, discusses the same image in a similar light. Pending publication of Lentes's thesis on the prayer books from the

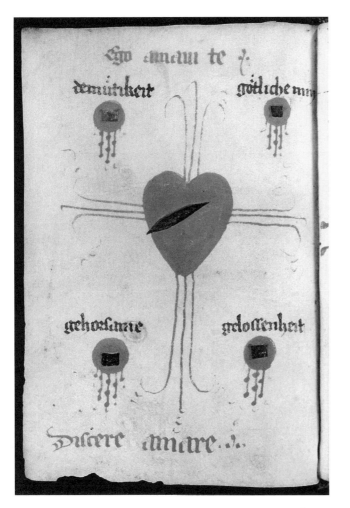

Figure 13. The Wounds of Christ, ca. 1440–1450, inserted into prayer book, Upper Rhine, Convent of St. Nicolaus in undis, Strasbourg. Red and brown ink on parchment leaf, 10 x 7 cm. Staatsbibliothek zu Berlin—Preußischer Kulturbesitz— Handschriftenabteilung, Ms. germ. oct. 53, f. 23v.

the wounds bespeaks physical suffering, but the red ink associates them with the crimson heart at the center and, hence, with Christ as the embodiment of charity. The image resembles so-called "*Speerbildchen*" from Nuremberg, small drawings or prints of Christ's heart that were impaled on the lance thought to have been used by Longinus to pierce the side of Christ and that hence assumed the status of contact relics.[58] But it also recalls allegorical illustrations of Christ crucified by the virtues, especially widespread in convents, in which Christ is presented as the embodiment of the virtues who nail him to the cross.[59] The labels attached to the four stigmata (*"demütikeit," "götliche min," "gehorsame,"* and *"gelossenhait"*) define a less corporeal form of discipline, the virtues highlighted in the Rule of St. Benedict: humility, divine love, obedience, and detachment. In spite of the drawing's apparent reference to extravagant asceticism of the kind celebrated in the literature of female spirituality, the image works to instill a less literal form of imitation, identifying the submission of the will embodied in a regular monastic routine as a sufficient ascetic regime.[60]

The drawing from the convent of St. Nicolaus in undis summarizes in emblematic fashion the conflation of love and suffering given archetypal expression by Christ's Passion, understood as both suffering and ardent desire.[61] The heart served as the locus of such affections: both the seat of compassion and the mystical bedchamber in which a nun consummated her marriage

Ego amavi te, or "I have loved you;" those at the bottom enjoin the viewer, *Discere amare,* or "Learn to love" (fig. 13). The declarations of amorous passion could be construed as spoken by either Christ or the onlooker, or as a dialogue between them. The blood dripping from

convent, see F. Rapp, "Zur Spiritualität in elsässischen Frauenklöstern am Ende des Mittelalters," in *Frauenmystik im Mittelalter,* ed. P. Dinzelbacher and D. R. Bauer (Ostfildern bei Stuttgart: Schwabenverlag, 1985), pp. 347–365.

58. Lentes (see note 57) makes the same comparison. For the *"Speerbildchen,"* see A. Bühler, "Die heilige Lanze: Ein ikonographischer Beitrag zur Geschichte der deutsche Reichskleinodien," *Das Münster* 16 (1963):85–116; T. Lentes, "Nur der geöffnete Körper schafft Heil: Das Bild als Verdoppelung des Körpers," in *Glaube, Hoffnung, Liebe, Tod,* ed. C. Geissmar-Brandi and E. Louis (Vienna: Albertina, 1995), pp. 152–155.

59. See H. Kraft, "Die Bildallegorie der Kreuzigung Christi durch die Tugenden" (Ph.D. diss., Frankfurt, 1976); H. M. Barth, "Liebe verwundet durch Liebe: Das Kreuzigungsbild des Regensburger Lektionars als Zeugnis mittelalterlicher Passionsfrömmigkeit," *Beiträge zur Geschichte des Bistums Regensburg* 17 (1983):229–268.

60. For this topic, see Hamburger (see note 12), pp. 94–100; id., "On the Little Bed of Jesus: Monastic Reform and the Rhetoric of Pictorial Piety," in *The Visual and the Visionary: Art and Female Spirituality in Medieval Germany* (New York: Zone Books, 1998, forthcoming).

61. The fundamental study remains E. Auerbach, "Gloria passionis," in *Literary Language and its Public in Late Latin Antiquity and in the Middle Ages,* trans. R. Manheim (Princeton, New Jersey: Princeton University Press, 1993), pp. 67–81.

Figure 14. The Heart on the Cross, ca. 1500. Inks on paper, dimensions unknown. Eichstätt, Bavaria, Abbey of St. Walburg. Photo: Jürgen Fuhrmann.

with the mystical bridegroom.[62] A *Nonnenarbeit* from St. Walburg—one of twelve drawings that can be attributed to the same nun—gives these mystical metaphors dramatic embodiment[63] (fig. 14). No matter how rough in execution, the drawing invites close inspection. We zoom in on the stunning, even shocking, image of the heart at the center, penetrating the gash to find

ourselves—in the person of the nun identified by her habit—nestled within the womblike space at the center, exchanging vows with Christ. The image defines the very act of viewing in scriptural terms. In irresistibly drawing our eye through the wound, it compels us, and, more specifically, the female viewer to whom it was originally addressed, to perform the act of penetration that in the Song of Songs 4:9 prompts the bridegroom to respond: "Thou hast wounded my heart, my sister, my spouse, thou hast wounded my heart with one of thy eyes." Simply in looking at the image, we fulfill the injunction and take on the role of the Virgin and bride. The gaze,

---

62. For representations of the heart in late medieval devotional art, see Hamburger (see note 12), pp. 101–175; Lentes (see note 57), pp. 136–155.

63. For this drawing, see Hamburger (see note 12), pp. 101–136.

defined as an act of penetrating vision, is here assigned to the Sponsa of the Song of Songs, and, more specifically, the female onlooker; a feminized Christ is its object.[64] Yet the central image evoked by the wound is less one of penetration than one of envelopment and enclosure—an appropriate displacement given the situation of the nuns for whom it was made. The small round object dangling from a cord attached to the lip of the wound sums up the sense of the image; it represents the seal of love invoked in Song of Songs 8:6: "Put me as a seal upon thy heart, as a seal upon thy arm, for love is strong as death."

As in a Coronation of the Virgin, the Infant Christ, at the right, places one hand behind the nun, as if to embrace her. With his other hand, Christ offers her a gift, not a ring, but a small golden pyx. The two inscriptions parallel to Christ's arms identify an offered embrace: the scroll to the left reads: *O herz zeuch mich [z]u dir In dich und nach dir*, or "O heart, draw me to you, into you and after you", an echo of Song of Songs 1:3, "Draw me: we will run after thee," a passage usually glossed as an expression of the soul's desire to imitate Christ.[65] In response to the bride's impassioned entreaty, the bridegroom replies in the words of the scroll that extends to the right: *Du bist gancz schon mein freundin*, or "You are completely beautiful, my beloved," a reminiscence of a refrain that recurs throughout the Song of Songs, for example, in 4:7, "Thou art all fair, O my love" (cf. 1:15, 4:1, and 7:6). The scroll that unfurls to the right in a descending diagonal corresponds to the ladder on the left; it reads, *Das ist mein ruestat; darinn ich will ruen ewigklich on end*, or "That is my resting place, within which I will rest eternally without end." The image exemplifies the reciprocity of imitation as defined by Catherine of Siena, who advised her own adviser, Raymund of Capua: "Let your heart and soul be grafted onto the tree of the most holy cross—with Christ crucified. Make his wounds your home."[66] The oversized heart, no longer Christ's alone,

also represents the interior of the nun's own being into which she welcomes Christ, just as he admits her to heaven through the portals of his wounds.

The crucifixion from St. Walburg epitomizes an entire system of devotion, one predicated on the devotee's ability to close the distance between herself and God through a step-by-step pursuit of the *imitatio Christi*. The ladder, its ten rungs labeled as virtues, represents the means of ascent towards union with the Godhead. Ladder imagery was a staple in mystical treatises and their illustrations.[67] But between the drawing from St. Walburg and this mass of material, there is a decisive difference; whereas in most images of ascent the worshiper appears at the bottom, looking up, in the drawing from St. Walburg, she already occupies the apogee, nestled in God's heart like the souls in the Bosom of Abraham. It was hardly accidental that Luther singled out the ladder as an emblem of all that he scorned in the piety of works: "A great deal has been written about how man shall be divinized; there they have made ladders with which one climbs up to heaven and many such things. It is, however, vain begging work [*eytel partecken werck*]."[68]

It is all too easy to dismiss the devotional drawings made by nuns as products of popular piety, quasi-magical objects with little, if any inherent aesthetic appeal. On closer examination, however, they address their onlookers in surprisingly complex and—more importantly—compelling ways. In addition to their idiosyncratic iconography, they possess a distinctive

---

64. For comparable instances in devotional poetry, see S. Stanbury, "The Virgin's Gaze: Spectacle and Transgression in Middle English Lyrics of the Passion," *Proceedings of the Modern Language Association* 106 (1991):1083–1093. See also Hamburger (see note 50), pp. 72–77.

65. See Hamburger (see note 50), pp. 48–49.

66. Cited by R. Kieckhefer, *Unquiet Souls: Fourteenth-Century Saints and their Religious Milieu* (Chicago: University of Chicago Press, 1984), p. 109. The imagery of mounting a ladder to enter into the wounds of Christ recurs in Jesuit devotional imagery of the

seventeenth century; see, for example, the images reproduced by E. M. Vetter, "'Dei famulam amplecti videbatur': zur Darstellung des Hl. Franziskus mit dem Gekreuzigten," *Das Münster* 25 (1972):341–348, esp. figs. 10–11.

67. See E. Bertaud and A. Rayez, "Échelle spirituelle," in *Dictionnaire de spiritualité*, ed. M. Viller (Paris: G. Beauchesne et ses fils, 1937–), vol. 4, cols. 62–86; J. O'Reilly, *Studies in the Iconography of the Virtues and Vices in the Middle Ages* (New York: Garland, 1988), pp. 349–359; R. Schleier, *Tabula Cebetis, oder "Spiegel des Menschlichen Lebens darin Tugent unt untugent abgemalet ist": Studien zur Rezeption einer antiken Bildbeschreibung im 16. und 17. Jahrhundert* (Berlin: Gebr. Mann, 1973); C. Heck, *L'Échelle céleste dans l'art du Moyen Âge* (Paris: Flammarion, 1997).

68. "Es ist viel davon gechrieben, wie der mensch soll vergottet werden, da haben sie leytern gemacht, daran man gen hymel steyge und viel solchs dings, Es ist aber eytel partecken werck," cited by G. Seebass, *Die Himmelsleiter des hl. Bonaventura von Lukas Cranach d.Ä.: Zur Reformation eines Holzschnitts*, Sitzungsberichte der Heidelberger Akademie der Wissenschaften, Philosophisch-Historische Klasse 1985, bericht 4 (Heidelberg: C. Winter, Universitatsverlag, 1985), p. 50.

visual rhetoric closely geared to the aspirations and training of their monastic audience. One could, of course, set aesthetics aside altogether and discuss *Nonnenarbeiten* solely in terms of their functions—by and large, the way most devotional imagery is approached today.[69] Monastic legislation encouraged nuns to think of their handiwork as a means of inculcating humility and obedience, nothing more, nothing less.[70] The Dominican constitutions for nuns defined their handiwork as an antidote to idleness, that "mother and nurturer of vices."[71] Never is there any mention of *otium*, the older monastic conception of contemplative leisure, let alone the notion that work itself might contribute a form of worship.[72] The virtuous nun was to emulate the Virgin at work in the Temple, a message instilled in part through images of the Virgin and her companions busy at their looms or engaged in other forms of artisanal activity.[73] Yet to emphasize

function over the distinctive visual rhetoric of nuns' work runs the risk of accepting the condemnation attributed to Michelangelo and its construction of gender. In fact, such constructions changed and continue to change; witness contemporary taste, which until recently tended less toward the grace and beauty of the early Michelangelo than the masculine "vigor" and "sublimity" of his mature works—all terms, it should be noted, used also by Michelangelo's contemporaries and successors.[74] By such standards, the ideal of "harmony" Francisco de Hollanda attributed to Michelangelo could itself be construed as having been feminized.

In theory, nuns' work left little room for religious, let alone artistic, expression. Yet nuns took pride in their craftsmanship. The thirteenth-century Cistercian mystic, Mechthild of Hackeborn reworked the familiar trope likening God to an artist, comparing artistic and, by implication, her own authorial premeditation with God's predestination of the Virgin. Mechthild defines Mary, and not only Christ, as the exemplar of all images and the Incarnation as the consummate act of divine artistry:[75]

> Just as the artist who determines to fashion a marvellous work thinks it over with great thought and premeditates it with pleasure in his heart, so too the venerable Trinity was pleased and delighted because it wished to make me [Mary] so remarkable an image in which the skill of all its wisdom and goodness would appear most elegantly.

69. See, for example, H. Belting, *Das Bild und sein Publikum: Form und Funktion früher Bildtafeln der Passion* (Berlin: Mann, 1981), who, however, also pays close attention to the visual rhetoric of the image. A still more strictly functional approach is taken by E. Lipsmeyer, "Devotion and Decorum: Intention and Quality in Medieval German Sculpture," *Gesta* 34 (1995):20–27.

70. See, for example, the regulations for the Poor Clares published by A. E. Schönbach, *Mitteilungen aus altdeutschen Handschriften*, pt. 10, *Die Regensburger Klarissenregel* (1909; reprint, Hildesheim: Olms, 1976), pp. 1–68, esp. p. 9, ll. 26–29: "Aber die swestern und die servicial die suln sich uben an nuzzer, und an erberre arbeit . . . under sogetaner fursichtekeit, daz sie die muzekeit vertrieben, die da ist ein vin der sele, und doch den geist heiliges gebetes und andacht."

71. *Analecta Sacri Ordinis Fratrum Praedicatorum seu Vetera Ordinis Monumenta*, vol. 3 (Rome, 1897), p. 346: "quia ociositas inimica est anime et mater et nutrix vitiorum, nullus sit ociosa." The passage continues: "Sed dilegenter observetur ut exceptis illis horis et temporibus quibus oracioni vel officio vel alii occupationi necessarie debent intendere: operibus manuum ad utilitatem communem omnes attente insistant."

72. See J. Leclercq, *Otia monastica: Études sur le vocabulaire de la contemplation au Moyen Age*, Studia Anselmiana 51 (Rome: Orbis Catholicus, Herder, 1963).

73. R. L. Wyss, "Die Handarbeiten der Maria: Eine ikonographische Studie unter Berücksichtigung der Techniken," in *Artes minores: Dank an Werner Abegg*, ed. M. Stettler and M. Lemberg (Bern: Stampfli, 1973), pp. 113–188, reproduces numerous examples. See also H. van Os, "Mary as Seamstress," in *Studies in Early Tuscan Painting* (London: Pindar, 1992), pp. 277–286; O. F. M. Meinardus, "Zur 'strickenden Madonna' oder 'Die Darbringung der Leidenswerkzeuge' des Meister Bertram," *Idea: Jahrbuch der Hamburger Kunsthalle* 7 (1988):15–22; C. Gerhardt, "Die Karitas webt die Einheit der Kirche: Der ungenähte Rock Christi in Otfrieds von Weißenburg *Evangelienbuch* (IV, 28–29)," in *Der Heilige Rock zu Trier: Studien zur Geschichte und Verehrung der Tunika Christi*, ed. E.

Aretz, M. Embach, M. Persch, and F. Ronig (Trier: Paulinus-Verlag, 1995), pp. 877–913; Z. Urbach, "'Ego sum deus et homo': Eine seltene Darstellung der *Infantia Christi* auf einem Triptychom des Christlichen Museums in Esztergom (Gran)," *Acta Historiae Artium* 36 (1993):57–76; F. M. Biscoglio, "'Unspun Heroes': Iconography of the Spinning Woman in the Middle Ages," *Journal of Medieval and Renaissance Studies* 25 (1995):163–176.

74. See Sohm (see note 2). I was unable to consult the recently completed dissertation by Rebekah Smick, "Images and the Rhetoric of Female Compassion: Art Critical and Poetic Reception of Michelangelo's Pietà in the 16th Century" (University of Toronto, 1996).

75. Mechthild of Hackeborn, *Revelationis Gertrudianae ac Mechthildianae*, 2 vols., ed. L. Paquelin (Poitiers-Paris, 1875–1877), vol. 1, p. 99 (Bk. 1, chap. 29): "Sicut enim artifex qui mirificum opus facere decrevit, magno studio praemeditatur, et in delectatione cordis sui praeimaginatur: sic veneranda Trinitas delectabatur, et gaudebat quia me talem imaginem facere volebat, in qua totius sapientiae et bonitatis suae artificium elegantissime appareret." For Mechthild, see M. Schmidt, "Mechthild von Hackeborn," in *Die deutsche Literatur des Mittelalters: Verfasser Lexikon*, 2d ed., ed. K. Ruh et al. (Berlin: De Gruyter, 1978), vol. 6, cols. 251–260.

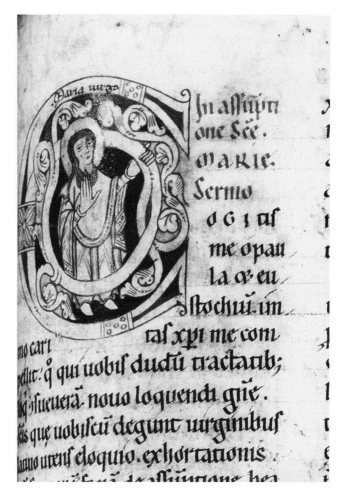

Figure 15. "Guda peccatrix," *Guda Homilary*, 1150–1200, Middle Rhine. Inks on parchment, 36.5 x 24 cm. Frankfurt, Stadt- und Universitätsbibliothek, Ms. Barth. 42, f. 110v. Photo: Courtesy of Stadt- und Universitätsbibliothek.

Figure 16. "Maria uirga," *Guda Homilary*, 1150–1200, Middle Rhine. Inks on parchment, 36.5 x 24 cm. Frankfurt, Stadt- und Universitätsbibliothek, Ms. Barth. 42, f. 196r. Photo: Courtesy of Stadt- und Universitätsbibliothek.

The *Guda Homilary*, a twelfth-century manuscript celebrated for its scribal self-portrait, implies a similar self-consciousness[76] (fig. 15). The initial with Guda has been reproduced countless times; with a touch of false modesty, the inscription intones: *GVDA peccatrix mulier scriptsit et pinxit hunc librum*, or "Guda, sinner and woman, wrote and painted this book." The manuscript's only other figural decoration, however, has never been reproduced (fig. 16). The initial, which introduces the homily for the feast of the Assumption of the Virgin, depicts Mary using a formula remarkably similar to that which Guda used for herself. Were it not for the halo and the inscription, "Maria uirgo," one might easily mistake the mother of God for Guda.

76. See G. Powitz and H. Buck, *Die Handschriften des Bartholomaeusstifts und des Karmeliterklosters in Frankfurt am Main,* Kataloge der Stadt- und Universitätsbibliotherk Frankfurt am Main, 3/II (Frankfurt: Klostermann, 1974), pp. 84–85, with additional bibliography. For other "self-portraits" by medieval artists, see M. Stevens,

"The Performing Self in Twelfth-Century Culture," *Viator* 9 (1978):193–212. See also B. Reudenbach, "Individuum ohne Bildnis? Zum Problem Künstlicher Ausdrucksformen von Individualität im Mittelalter," in *Individuum und Individualität im Mittelalter,* ed. J. A. Aertsen and A. Speer, Miscellanea Mediaevalia 24 (Berlin: De Gruyter, 1996), pp. 807–818.

Manuscripts signed by nuns are rare; signed *Nonnenarbeiten* are nonexistent.[77] As far as I know, only a single surviving *Nonnenarbeit* bears any indication of authorship. The drawing is glued into the cover of the pattern book for gold embroidery written in 1517 at St. Klara's in Nuremberg[78] (fig. 17). The inscription reads, *Dominus kindleín hat magdalenn lengen gemacht vnd gemalt*, or "Magdalena Lengen made and painted the little Christ Child." No less striking is the book's introduction, in which its author, Anna, notes: "I often couldn't sleep when I was thinking how I wanted to make a model," then adds, "it troubles me that I didn't compile this pattern book in my youth when I would have been more skillful. Although I am seventy years old, my dear sisters wouldn't leave me in peace."[79] Besides an unusual autobiographical touch, Anna's words suggest that in her old age she and her fellow nuns sought to codify a tradition that was in danger of dying out.

As recently as 1985, no less an authority than Margaret Miles asserted that medieval women had no

Figure 17. Anna Neuperin, Christ Child with the *arma Christi*, 1517, front paste down of Embroidery Pattern Book, St. Klara, Nuremberg. 18.5 x 11 cm. Wolfenbüttel, Herzog-August Bibliothek, Cod. Guelf. 57 Aug. 8°, 7 verso. Photo: Courtesy of Herzog-August Bibliothek.

autonomy or agency in either the making or reading of images. In her words, "As far as we can determine, not a single image of any woman—saint, Mary, scriptural or apocryphal figure—was designed or created by a woman. The images we must deal with are images provided for women by men."[80] The overlooked evidence of *Nonnenarbeiten*—let alone that of the textile arts—belies so bald and blind an assertion.[81] A considerable body of literature can be attributed to women; there is no reason to believe that they were not

77. For manuscripts signed by nuns, see, for example, A. W. Carr, "Women Artists in the Middle Ages," *Feminist Art Journal* 5 (1976):5–9; D. E. Miner, *Anastasie and Her Sisters: Women Artists of the Middle Ages* (Baltimore: Walters Art Gallery, 1974). The lack of signed material is surprising given that medieval art is not as anonymous as commonly thought; see the studies by P. C. Claussen, "Künstlerinschriften," in *Ornamenta Ecclesia,* 3 vols., ed. A. Legner (Cologne: Schnutgen-Museum der Stadt Koln, 1985), vol. 1, pp. 263–276; id., "Nachrichten von den Antipoden oder der mittelalterliche Künstler über sich selbst," in *Der Künster über sich in seinem Werk: Internationales Symposium der Bibliotheca Hertziana Rome 1989,* ed. M. Winner (Weinheim: VCH, Acta Humaniora, 1992), pp. 19–54; id., "Früher Künstlerstolz: Mittelalterliche Signaturen als Quelle der Kunstsoziologie," in *Bildwerk und Bauwerk im Mittelalter: Anschauliche Beiträge zu Kultur- und Sozialgeschichte,* ed. C. Clausberg et al. (Gießen: Anabas, 1981), pp. 7–34.

78. For a brief description, see O. von Heinemann, *Die Handschriften der Herzoglichen Bibliothek zu Wolfenbüttel: Zweite Abteilung. Die Augusteischen Handschriften,* bd. 5 (Wolfenbüttel: J. Zwissler, 1903), p. 88. It cannot be ruled out that, rather than a signature per se, the inscription is an addition intended to commemorate the artist. For the use of images in female communities as a means of commemoration, see H. Wunder, "'Gewirkte Geschichte': Gedenken und 'Handarbeit.' Überlegungen zum Tradieren von Geschichte im Mittelalter und zu seinem Wandel am Beginn der Neuzeit," in *Modernes Mittelalter: Neue Bilde einer populären Epoche,* ed. J. Heinzle (Frankfurt: Insel, 1994), pp. 324–354.

79. "ich hab meinen schlof oft dar durch geprochen wen ich gedocht wie ich je einem model wolt machen [f. 1v] . . . es mich rewt dz ich es nit in meinem jugent hab thu do ich geschiter wer geweßen. den noch lxx jaren so wolten mir mein lieb swest[ern] doch auch kein rw lasen."

80. M. R. Miles, *Image as Insight: Visual Understanding in Western Christianity and Secular Culture* (Boston: Beacon Press, 1985), p. 64. The recent issue of *Arte Cristiana* 82 (1994), devoted in its entirety to "Vocazione artistica dei religiosi," contained no article on nuns as artists.

81. Some of this material is discussed in J. F. Hamburger, "Art, Enclosure and the *Cura monialium*: Prolegomena in the Guise of a Postscript," *Gesta* 31 (1992):108–134.

Figure 18. The Consecration of Virgins, ca. 1500. Ink and pigments on parchment, dimensions unknown. Eichstätt, Bavaria, Abbey of St. Walburg. Photo: Jürgen Fuhrmann.

comparably active as artists.[82] The key question is not whether women made images of women for women; that much is certain. At issue is how women understood the images they made of and for themselves and how these images functioned in the contexts in which they circulated.

A second devotional drawing from St. Walburg illustrates the complex fashion in which *Nonnenarbeiten* were informed by the contexts in which they were created and informed them in turn (fig. 18). The drawing depicts in symbolic fashion the consecration of virgins, the defining moment in the life of any nun.[83] The Christ Child seated on the lap of the Virgin is outnumbered by his female companions eight to one. The nuns approach their heavenly bridegroom to receive a ring, just as in the actual ceremony they receive one from the officiating bishop. The scroll above the figures, spoken by the Virgin, opens with the injunction, *Accipe puerum Istum*, or "Take this boy," and closes with the promise, *ego dabo tibi mercedem tuam*, or "I will give you your reward." The words convey the essence of the rite, in which the nun accepts Christ in a vow of eternal marriage.[84] The Virgin's proclamation, however, is interrupted by an unexpected change of voice, in which the infant Christ issues an imperative of his own: *Nutri michi* [sic], or "Suckle me!"[85] Having first allowed the nun to identify herself with Mary in her role as Christ's bride, the drawing now encourages her to identify with

82. For some of the problems attendant on the interpretation of this body of literature, see P. Dinzelbacher, "Zur Interpretation erlebnismystischer Texte des Mittelalters," *Zeitschrift für deutsches Altertum und deutsche Literatur* 117 (1988):1–23, revised and reprinted in id., *Mittelalterliche Frauenmystik* (Paderborn: F. Schoningh, 1993), pp. 304–331; U. Peters, "Frauenliteratur im Mittelalter? Überlegungen zur Trobairitzpoesie, zur Frauenmystik und zur feministischen Literaturbetrachtung," *Germanisch-Romanische Monatsschrift,* n.f., 38 (1988):35–56; K. Greenspan, "Autohagiography and Medieval Women's Spiritual Autobiography," in *Gender and Text in the Later Middle Ages*, ed. J. Chance (Gainesville, Florida: University Press of Florida, 1996), pp. 216–236.

83. For a more detailed consideration of this drawing, see Hamburger (see note 12), pp. 56–61.

84. See R. Metz, *La Consécration des vierges dans l'église romaine: Étude d'histoire de la liturgie* (Paris: Presses Universitaires de France, 1954).

85. The imagery of suckling provided a common figure of spiritual inspiration and mystical union. Usually, however, it was the soul who played the role of nursling at the breast of Jesus; see C. W. Bynum, *Jesus as Mother: Studies in the Spirituality of the High Middle Ages* (Berkeley: University of California Press, 1982), pp. 110–169. For other examples and the origins of the motif, see N. Pike, *Mystic Union: An Essay in the Phenomenology of Mysticism* (Ithaca, New York: Cornell University Press, 1992), pp. 73–76; Hamburger (see note 50), pp. 78, 82; H. Rahner, "'De Dominici pectoris fonte potavit,'" *Zeitschrift für katholische Theologie* 55 (1931):103–108; id., "'Flumina de ventre Christi': Die patristische Auslegung von Joh. 7:37,38," *Biblia* 22 (1941):269–302, 367–401.

her ultimate exemplar, the Virgin, as Christ's mother.[86] Although hardly unique to images made for nuns, the infantilization of Christ was a strategy especially appropriate for an audience of cloistered women.[87] Christ appears not as a mature, marriageable male, but as a strapping, beefy boy, the object of exalted maternal instincts rather than sublimated sexual desire.

The images made by and for nuns raise fundamental questions about the changing relationship between art and devotion at the beginning of modernity. From the moment reformers sought to strip traditional cult objects of their aura comes compelling evidence of a fundamental shift in attitude toward devotional images such as *Nonnenarbeiten*. It takes the form of the forgotten correspondence between Willibald Pirckheimer, the dean of German humanists, and his sister Sabina (1482–1529), abbess of Bergen (Bavaria) from 1521 to 1529.[88] Sabina's letters refer often to painting; she and the convent's *Malerin* (or "painter," gendered feminine) relied on Willibald for supplies and prints, some of which they used as models. In one letter, Sabina describes vestments embroidered by her charges, adding "if we had our way, we'd like that you and Dürer should see them."[89] Most art historians still do not regard decorated textiles as "high" art—nor, perhaps, did Dürer or Pirckheimer—but in the early sixteenth century the modern distinction between the "fine" and the so-called "decorative" arts remained a novelty, at least in the North.[90]

In another letter, dated 1524, Sabina reveals her awareness of the extent to which her skills and those of her painter fall short compared with those of an artist like Dürer: "I have no recreation except painting; if I could only have Dürer for a fortnight so that he could instruct my painter."[91] Sabina's wish, no matter how charming, marks the passing of an era. A generation before nuns might never have doubted the efficacy and adequacy of their modest drawings. But by the eve of the Reformation their handiwork was suspect on both religious and aesthetic grounds. Religious imagery now had to be not only true but beautiful as well. In a word, it had to be "Art."[92]

None of Sabina's handiwork or that of her painter has survived. It was probably a far cry from the stylish sophistication of Dürer's prints. Not that men couldn't admire women's handiwork; in 1505 the humanist and prior of the Benedictine monastery of Maria Laach, Johann Butzbach, dedicated a short tract entitled *Libellus de preclaris picture professoribus* to Gertrude Buchel, abbess of Rolandswerth (later Nonnenwerth) from 1507 to her death in 1543.[93] In addition to

86. See R. Hale, "*Imitatio Mariae*: Motherhood Motifs in Devotional Memoirs," *Mystics Quarterly* 16 (1990):193–203. For the still poorly studied subject of the *imitatio Mariae* in female piety, see Hamburger (see note 50), pp. 88–104; M. Wehrli-Johns, "Haushälterin Gottes: Zur Mariennachfolge der Beginen," in *Maria, Abbild oder Vorbild? Zur Sozialgeschichte mittelalterlicher Marienverehrung* (Tübingen: Edition Diskord, 1990), pp. 146–167. The study by G. Lüers, *Marienverehrung mittelalterlicher Nonnen* (Munich: Rheinhardt, 1923), is disappointing.

87. See R. Berliner, "God is Love," *Gazette des Beaux-Arts* 43 (1953):9–26, esp. 23, who defines the feminization and the infantilization of Christ in late medieval devotional imagery as strategies for limiting the erotic suggestiveness of images depicting the love between Christ and the soul.

88. Lochner, ed., "Briefe der Aebtissin Sabina im Kloster zum heiligen Kreuz in Bergen an ihren Bruder Willibald Pirckheimer," *Zeitschrift für die historische Theologie* 36 (1866):518–566.

89. Ibid., pp. 530–531, letter 2: "wenn es mit wünschen zugieng, wollten wir gern, daß du und der Dürer si sollten sehen."

90. For a rare exception in modern times, see Gottfried Semper, "Style: The Textile Art," in *The Four Elements of Architecture and Other Writings*, trans. H. F. Mallgrave and W. Herrmann (Cambridge:

Cambridge University Press, 1989), p. 234, cited by M. Wigley, "Untitled: The Housing of Gender," in *Sexuality and Space*, ed. B. Colomina, Princeton Papers on Architecture 1 (New York: Princeton Architectural Press, 1992), pp. 327–389, esp. p. 372.

91. Lochner (see note 88), pp. 532–533, letter 3: "ich hab kein kurzweil denn malen, wenn ich nur den thürer ein xiiii tag het, daß er mir mein malerin unterwies."

92. For a similar distinction, see H. Belting, *Bild und Kult: eine Geschichte des Bildes vor dem Zeitalter der Kunst* (Munich: C. H. Beck, 1990).

93. For Butzbach and Maria Laach, see B. Resmini, *Die Benediktinerabtei Maria Laach*, Germania Sacra, n.f. 31, Erzbistum Trier 7 (Berlin: De Gruyter, 1993), pp. 71–74, 419–421; id., "Der Laacher Prior Johann Butzbach und der Humanismus rheinischer Benediktinerabteien," in *Ecclesiae Lacensis: Beiträge aus Anlaß der Wiederbesiedlung der Abtei Maria Laach durch Benediktiner aus Beuron vor 100 Jahren am 15. November 1892 und der Gründung des Klosters durch Pfalzgraf Heinrich II. von Laach vor 900 Jahren 1093*, ed. E. von Severus (Münster: Aschendorff, 1993), pp. 111–135. There remains no adequate edition of Butzbach's treatise, first published by A. Schultz, "Joannnes Butzbach's 'Libellus de preclaris picture professoribus' aus der Bonnenser Handschrift veröffentlicht," *Jahrbücher für Kunstwissenschaft* 2 (1869):60–72. O. Pelka, *Libellus de praeclaris picturae professoribus (mit der Urschrift in Nachbildung)* (Heidelberg: Weissbach, 1925), provides a facsimile and transcription of the sole surviving manuscript (Bonn, Universitätsbibliothek, Ms. S. 356, ff. 131r–138v) together with a German translation that, as noted by A. Beriger, *Johannes Butzbach Odeporicon (eine Autobiographie aus dem Jahre 1506): Zweisprachige Ausgabe* (Weinheim: VCH, Acta Humaniora, 1991), pp. 49, 57–58, is not free of errors. For further commentary, see W. Waetzoldt, *Deutsche Kunsthistoriker*, 2 vols.

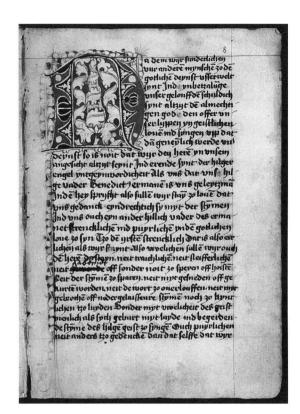

Figure 19. Gertrude Buchel, *Benedictine Rule*, 1497. Colored inks on paper, 192 x 132 mm. Staatsbibliothek zu Berlin—Preußischer Kulturbesitz—Handschriftenabteilung, Ms. Germ. 4° 555, f. 8r.

illuminating manuscripts, Gertrude produced *Nonnenarbeiten*, which she gave to Butzbach and his monks. Butzbach describes them as *corcula*, or "little hearts of our most blessed Savior and Redeemer."[94] Butzbach was no Vasari. His interest is neither aesthetics nor the history of art conceived as a history of style, but rather images as instruments of edification. His booklet nevertheless departs from medieval tradition. Butzbach dignifies the craft of painting by providing it with a historical lineage, classical as well as Christian. He also tailors his tract to his female audience by listing female artists of antiquity, all mentioned by Pliny, but probably

borrowed by Butzbach from Boccaccio.[95] Butzbach also likens Gertrude to, in his words, the "most subtle" of engravers, Israhel von Meckenem, a startling contrast to Sabina Pirckheimer's ready admission of Dürer's aesthetic superiority.[96]

The liturgical manuscripts linked with Gertrude can no longer be traced. She was, however, no figment of Butzbach's imagination. One manuscript signed by Gertrude survives, a translation of the Benedictine Rule dated 1497[97] (fig. 19). To judge from this book, Butzbach's praise outstripped Gertrude's talent. Like the letters of Sabina Pirckheimer, however, Butzbach's treatise testifies to a dramatic change in the standards by which images were evaluated. In setting Gertrude's painting in a historical continuum, he initiates the history of German art history by inserting the work of a woman into the discipline as it traditionally has been defined, an account of the making of art extending from the past to the present. How ironic, then, that our own histories have found next to no place for women like Gertrude and her anonymous contemporaries. After five hundred years, they and their work should compel us to reconsider the challenge posed by Michelangelo's contempt.

(Leipzig: E. A. Seemann, 1921, 1924), vol. 1, pp. 13–14; also J. L. Koerner, *The Moment of Self-Portraiture in German Renaissance Art* (Chicago: University of Chicago Press, 1993), pp. 123–126.

94. Pelka (see note 93), p. 27: "corcula scilicet benignissimi salvatoris et redemptoris nostri."

95. For early editions of Boccaccio, see F. S. Borroni, "L'incisione al servizio del Boccaccio nei secoli XV e XVI," *Annali della Scuola Normale di Pisa, Classe di Lettere e Filosofia* 7 (1977):595–734, cited by G. Schweikhart, "Boccaccios *De claris mulieribus* und die Selbstdarstellungen von Malerinnen im 16. Jahrhundert," in *Der Künstler über sich in seinem Werk: Internationales Symposium der Bibliotheca Hertziana Rome 1989,* ed. M. Winner (Weinheim: VCH, Acta Humaniora, 1992), pp. 113–136, esp. p. 114, n. 7, who, however, omits Butzbach from his account of Boccaccio's reception in the sixteenth century.

96. Pelka (see note 93), p. 37: "In arte sculpendi Israel, civis bucoliensis iam subtilissimus predicatur, ast te in arte pigendi ingeniosissimam cuncti mirantur."

97. For a description, see Degering (see note 57), vol. 2, p. 96. The Latin colophon is on f. 143v: "finitus et completus est iber iste per me sororem girdrudus buchel pro stellam monialem Insule rolandi anni domini Milesimo quadagintesimo nonagesimo septimo in vigilia mathie apostoli [=February 24, 1497]. Oretis dominum deum pro me." I am grateful to Dr. Peter Jörg Becker for supplying me with this information.

Figure 5. Jacques Le Moyne de Morgues, "A Young Daughter of the Picts," 1585–1588. Watercolor and gouache on vellum, 10 1/8 x 7 1/4 cm. Yale Center for British Art. Photo: Courtesy of the Yale Center for British Art, Paul Mellon Collection.

The Renaissance tattoo

JULIET FLEMING

I

It is the oddness of a structure that is at issue.

Lacan

For the past quarter-century, the West has been enjoying a "tattoo renaissance," according to Arnold Rubin, tattoo artist and theorist who popularized the term (1988:233–264; Sanders 1989a:232–241). It is a movement characterized both by refinements of conception (such as the influence of Abstract Expressionism and the introduction of the "photorealistic" tattoo, black graphic "tribal" styles, Japanese designs, and imagery adopted from the mass media) and by technical developments (single-needle techniques, an extended palette, and the refinement of procedure and equipment facilitated by the rise of mail-order suppliers, newsletters, and conventions; Tucker 1981). Unlike earlier or less elite tattooists, artists of the tattoo renaissance usually have professional art training and some association with the larger art world. They increasingly specialize in large-scale, custom designs and recognize and value each others' work (Rubin 1988:235). "Being a tattoo artist," they say, "is different from being a good tattooist" (Tucker 1981:44).

The tattoo renaissance comprises not the rebirth of a technique, but the social relocation of a practice; it is as tattooing becomes gentrified that it is elevated into a socially elaborated art form. As a consequence, western tattooing is now divided against itself in terms of class. On the one hand, it advances serious claims to be considered high art: an art whose products are commissioned, governed by canons of "taste" and knowledge, and shown in galleries and museums. On the other hand, tattooing remains, in theory and in fact, a demotic practice whose products include prison-made and homemade tattoos, as well as those done in commercial studios to more or less standard designs. The difference between "art" tattooing and the "rough neck, silly aspects" of the commercial trade is one on which tattoo artists insist (Rubin 1988:258), but they also acknowledge that the barrier separating the two modes is permeable. For tattoo art must not only redeploy the codified motifs of commercial practice (the "international style"); the perceived importance of tattoo as an artistic medium derives in part from its articulated deracination vis-a-vis middle-class values. Tattoo art understands itself to be, at some level, outré; like similar movements before it, its renaissance is predicated on a culture clash of which it is the reified effect.

The re-engrossing of the scandalous affect that the middle class projects onto its "outlaws" has been a standard high cultural practice and in the case of tattooing, its results are predictable. To its middle-class practitioners and clients, tattoo art now figures the domain of authenticity, the properly expressive, and (as the precipitate of "opposition") the individual. So Rubin considers tattoo the repository and expression of "unconventional, individualistic" values (1988:260); while for Michael Bakaty and others, it is "the only form of human expression we have left that has magic to it. Everything else is academic" (Tucker 1981:47). Tattoo artists sometimes dismiss commercial tattoos on the grounds that they are the derivative products of procedures inimical to the work of art—reproduction and commodification.[1] The desire to class tattooing among the arts drives some of its theorists to read ritual, supernatural, and therapeutic elements into their own practices with the same "striking lack of discretion" that Walter Benjamin attributed to the early theorists of film (1985:227). But lack of discretion is easy to identify within critical discourses surrounding new art forms. The therapeutic effect that often accompanies the acquisition of a tattoo within our culture is explained by tattoo artists and their clients according to the intellectual protocols of a magical thinking whose excesses have, in fact, been borrowed from more established accounts of the ethical and therapeutic functions of art.

Within tattoo's new representational economy, its traditionally marginal social status and its association

With thanks to Joseph Koerner for suggesting I write on abjection; Phillipa Berry, Joseph Boone, Dympna Callaghan, Stefan Collini, Katherine Craik, Ezra Getzler, Martin Hyland, Rayna Kalas, Steven Melville, Francesco Pellizzi, David Rollo, and Einar Steingrimsson for information and comments; and Charles MacQuarrie who generously shared his own work on tattooing with me.

1. For example, see Don Ed Hardy (1992:15): "Nonexclusionary and defiantly beyond the commodification inherent in all other mediums, tattooing is a universal body language bridging cultural differences with direct expression."

with ancient or primitive cultures only enhance its paradoxical value as a form of expression whose "low" or atavistic character allows it to function as a conduit for unconscious or instinctive forces. Here the archaic, preindividual drives of the Freudian unconscious are reinterpreted and given new valence as the creative "drives" of individuals alienated from contemporary "mass society." Witness Governor Jerry Brown, testifying at the opening of California's Tattoo Expo in 1982: "Once the power of the tattoo [was] intertwined with those who chose to live beyond the norms of society. . . . Today the realm of the outlaw has been redefined: the wild places which excite the most profound thinkers are conceptual" (Rubin 1981:255). Under the aegis of the California Expo, tattoo put its "wildness" (here troping a middle-class erotics) to work in support of the liberal-libertarian coalition represented by Governor Brown.

Even among tattoo artists and their customers, the tattoo retains its uncanny power to affront the liberal subject: a power of horror that is crucially coincident with the special effect identified by Julia Kristeva under the name of "abjection" (1982). To the person without tattoos, this horror articulates itself in the first instance around the question of permanency. The "problem" with tattoos, we say (as if we were all being forced to get one, this minute) is that they are indelible—"You can never get a tattoo off." The striking persistence of this complaint indicates its support within the social unconscious. The fantasy (since, even before ruby laser technology allowed their removal, it was always possible to write over, and so change, tattoos) is one that admits in the first instance to the negative possibility that the subject is named on the body. (The debate about tattooing is thus in part a debate about whether "individuality" can survive certain modes of representation.) The suggestion that identity is constituted not in the depths but at the outer surface of the subject is experienced by the Cartesian *cogito* as a type of claustrophobia: *nominor ergo sum.*[2] So the

thought of something sticking to the skin is ever a deep affront; even within a comic register it evokes Hercules trapped inside the poisoned shirt of Nessus. A protective covering that displaces and so destroys that which it should protect, the tattoo can be thought of as a poisoned (that is, poisoning) name. That this name is also a wound without depth—a wound from which, consequently, there can be no recovery—is a proposition with far-reaching implications.

Tattoo artists and practitioners, on the contrary, understand their art as being "antirepressive." Tattooing in prison is felt to be an affirmation that (at least) this body is yours; while artists such as Don Ed Hardy differentiate their practice from that of earlier American tattooists by invoking their own departure from the use of "flash" or pattern sheets. Where once customers chose tattoos from such sheets and so "had to fit their individual psyche into pre-congealed images that were often very out-of-date," today's tattoo artist functions as "a kind of therapist: a vehicle to help people channel their unconscious urges to the surface" (Juno and Vale 1991:52). British tattooist Chinchilla argues that she can see, as her clients cannot, what "crawls beneath their skin . . . everything I ink on people is already inside them, their history, sleeping creatures or saints, I only open up the skin and let it out, succubus, cherub, bike, snake, Betty Boop with a dildo" (*Tattoo International* 155, November 1994:11). It is at this moment in the tattoo renaissance—when tattooing comes to see itself, in Kristeva's terms, as a form of semiotic writing—that women enter the field, "probing tattooing's intuitive roots" as its practitioners and customers (Hardy 1992:13).[3] Arguing from an identity position predicated on the assumption that women have privileged access to the semiotic (that mode in which the drives of the pre-Oedipal phase manifest themselves through, but against the grain of, language), female tattoo artist Jamie Summers was able to pull rank on the pro-feminist Hardy in the 1980s by complaining that, in spite of his own claims, his "mastery of technique and tendency towards intellectualization" produced only "highly accomplished surface decoration, rather than the revelation of interior states," which had come to be her own sole objective (Rubin 1988:257–258).

In Chinchilla's formulation of the tattoo as an inner demon at once expelled and held at the border of the

---

2. Describing the Cartesian *cogito* as "the presence, inside man, of the celebrated little fellow who governs him, who is the driver," a notion "already denounced by pre-Socratic thought," Lacan offers instead his own formulation of the subject, a subject properly symbolized by the barred S ($\cancel{S}$) "in so far as it is constituted as secondary in relation to the signifier." The bar may be thought of as the stroke or notch of the signifier that, marking the subject off, situates him as such. The difference between Lacanian and Cartesian models of the self, the one "marked" and the other not, may be grasped by considering that the Lacanian subject is instantiated *as a tattoo*: "The subject himself is marked off by a single stroke, and first he marks himself as a tattoo, the first of the signifiers" (Lacan 1981:141).

3. One female customer described the acquisition of a tattoo as follows: "the unspeakable of the experience has been turned into an image on my arm" (*Tattoo International* 158, June 1995:12).

subject, lies not only an explanation for the overt content of many tattoos (devils, death's heads, monsters, birds of prey, statements such as "Born Criminal" or "*je finirai mal*"), but also a usefully precise figure for abjection. In Kristeva's work, the abject is a boundary phenomenon. Neither inside nor outside, at once "an excluded ground" and "a border that has encroached upon everything," the abject is "something rejected from which one does not part" (Kristeva 1982:3–4). A tattoo is caught in the same impossible situation, both conceptually and in fact. For in tattooing, as in fresco technique, molecules of dye or pigment form a surface beneath a surface. According to the deft formulation of Alfred Gell, "the defining feature of tattooing is that it is the making of indelible pigmented traces which are inside or underneath the skin . . . behind what seems like a transparent layer. . . . The basic schema of tattooing is thus definable as the exteriorization of the interior which is simultaneously the interiorization of the exterior" (1993:38–39). On the border between inside and outside, a tattoo is lodged in the no-place of abjection.

Abjection can also be thought of as a boundary effect within the functioning of the psychic apparatus itself, as something midway between the procedures of symptom-formation (understood as the somatic expression of something repressed) and sublimation (the deflection, without repression, of a drive) (Freud 1953:14:69; Kristeva 1982:4–11). The interim position between symptom production and sublimation is one that is often assumed for tattooing; understood as a self-inflicted wound, tattoo is seen as being both a mark that abjects the bearer and an assertion of control over abjection.[4]

As one of Chinchilla's tattooed clients reports, "I feel that what one does is ritualistically abrade the skin over the spot where a mark already existed. This, that rose through my muscle and psyche had always been there" (*Tattoo International* 153, June 1994:10–11). Here tattooing exemplifies Kristeva's definition of the artistic experience as something "rooted in the abject which it utters and by the same token purifies" (1982:17). At the frontier of what is "assimilable, thinkable," functioning to collapse the boundary between subject and object, tattooing is an act of catharsis par excellence.

However constructed, tattoo's claim to effectively represent the interior of the psyche is one of the things that permits its elevation to an art form in the West. Another is the irreducible authenticity—the aura—that a tattoo carries as a result of its "unique existence at the place where it happens to be," the simple fact that because its medium is the living body, a tattoo cannot be reproduced (Benjamin 1985:220). But the special consequence of tattooing as an art medium—perhaps the radical principle of its function as art—may finally depend on its evocation of the geometrical concern that structures Kristeva's formulation of abjection and may be said to comprise the simple proposition that it is a figure in two dimensions. This figure may be variously thought of as one that is all surface, or one whose inside is also its outside (an instance of "the intimate exteriority or 'extimacy' that is the Thing" in Lacan's important discussion of the wall paintings in the caves of Altamira [1992:139]). As a creature of the surface, a tattoo is an example of the first; as a disturbance to that surface, it is an instance of the second. Even where it is not deliberately recursive—a woman with a tattoo of a woman (with the tattoo of a woman) embracing death— the tattoo is an image of regression without recession, a geometrical paradox that marks the impossible profundity of the surface on which it is inscribed.[5]

4. Gell suggests a sociohistorical explanation for the radical bifurcation in the meaning of tattoos: "whereas in non-hierarchical societies body-markings reveal an immanent self which is inside the body, and can be made to appear on the skin, in hierarchical societies body markings are brands imposed from without, and signify the suppression of the devalued body" (1993:26). In today's western cultures, where a significant proportion of the population is tattooed, the case is less clear-cut, and the tattoo is understood as being *simultaneously* a symptom and the effect of sublimation. Italian criminologist Cesare Lombroso touched on the strange double nature of the tattoo in his analysis of the signs of criminality. Arguing that a disposition to criminality was inborn, the result of an ontogenetic deficit, Lombroso included among the signs of criminal tendencies large jaws, high cheek bones, handle-shaped ears, "insensibility to pain, extremely acute sight, tattooing, excessive idleness, love of orgies, and the irresistible craving for evil for its own sake" (Lombroso 1911:xv). In Lombroso's list, tattooing occupies the place of a hinge between physical symptoms and social characteristics; actively chosen by those who bear them, the tattoo is the product of an irresistible, biological disposition to become tattooed (Gell 1993:12). Lombroso's

conclusion, and the deductive method that produced and reproduced it, were taken to their logical conclusion by his contemporary, Adolf Loos: "If someone who is tattooed dies in freedom, then he does so a few years before he would have committed murder" (Loos 1966:226: cf. Gell 1993; Gould 1984).

5. Describing the "propensity for interpreters to regard tattooing as a kind of writing, legible if one just knew how to read it," Nicholas Thomas notes that apprehension of the curvilinear forms characteristic of Maori *moko* as "scrolls" constitutes "an effort to read the visual for what it [is] not. . . . Interpretative desire is defeated from the start if designs take the form of an archaic bearer of writing, a scroll which appears as such only in profile, its text surely there but unnecessarily seen. If only it could be looked at from a different angle, pleads the reader" (Thomas 1995:93–94). The skin is a two-dimensional surface that at once provokes and defeats a desire for depth.

In *The Skin Ego*, Didier Anzieu tests two dependent hypotheses: "what if thought were as much an affair of the skin as of the brain? And what if the Ego—now defined as a Skin Ego—had the structure of an envelope?" (1989:9). Anzieu begins his argument (one he sustains through the display of an astonishing and convincing array of cutaneous fantasies) with the observation that the organ of consciousness, the cortex (Latin: "bark," "shell," or "rind"), not only sits as "a sort of cap" on the white matter of the brain, but is embryonically a development of the surface of the early fetus, an introverted and reticulated "skin." "We are faced then, with a paradox: the centre is situated at the periphery" (ibid.). Anzieu notes this paradox is replicated in Freud's model of the psychic apparatus, according to which the ego "is not merely a surface entity, but is itself the projection of a surface" (Freud 1953:19:26; Anzieu 1989:85). To cite, as Anzieu does, Paul Valéry, "We burrow down in vain, doctor, we are . . . ectoderm!" (ibid., 60).

The figure whose depth is a feature of its surface, or the figure whose surface is, like that of a manifold, without edge, is a recurrent motif in contemporary French theory. It is encountered in the möbius strip that Lacan chose as an emblem for the journal *Scilicet*; in his figure of the mitre (a self-intersecting surface projected into three-dimensional space) in the seminar on *Identification*; and in the other "fundamental" topological objects (such as the Klein bottle and the Borromean rings) that organize his late work. Lacan cautions that, in everything concerning topology, "one must always be very careful to avoid attributing it with any kind of *Gestalt* function." But he goes on to demonstrate the pleasure to be gained from imagining biological life's "touching strivings after topological configurations" (especially when that life form is the erect, uncircumcised penis), and finally insists that only topological considerations can provide us with appropriate images to organize our thought "when it is a question of something inside that is also outside" (Lacan 1981:147).[6]

Valéry's proposition, "*C'est qu'il y a de plus profond dans l'homme, c'est la peau*" (Anzieu 1989:60), has important resonance within the work of reconception

that constitutes modernism and postmodernism. It is a proposition illustrated by the recurrence of the figures of fold, veil, and fan of Derrida's Mallarmé; in Derrida's own important concept of the hymen ("the fold in a lining by which it is, out of itself, in itself, at once its own outside and its own inside; between the outside and the inside, making the outside enter the inside and turning back the antre or the other upon its surface"); in the rhizome and fold of Deleuze and Guattari; and in Lyotard's work on discourse and figure (Derrida 1981:229; Deleuze 1993; Deleuze and Guattari 1987; Lyotard 1971).[7] But the uncanniness of the profound surface whose primary figure is the skin is not new in

experience as analysts, which may be taken in a metaphysical perspective" (1981:90). In Lacan's writing, the fact that the Ego "has" (or may be thought to have) the structure of the möbius strip goes some way towards accounting for its perversion and alienation. Anzieu's more complaisant conception of the Ego leads him to consider the möbius strip configuration as being specific only to borderline states (Anzieu 1989:124). But both theorists link psychic disturbance, pathological or not, to what they understand as geometrical disturbance, as does Kristeva when she describes *jouissance* as a "'structure' that is skewed, a topology of catastrophe" (1982:9). It is here that the question of the appropriateness of using topological figures to represent psychic phenomena may be raised—a question that, for the mathematician, marks a border dispute between the hard science of mathematics and a humanistic discourse that takes mathematical truths either for metaphors, or as models for psychic entities and effects. At issue is the fact that in mathematics, topological figures carry no affect: the Jordan curve theorem, for example, demonstrates the difficulty, but not the trauma, of proving that there are such concepts as inside and outside. Viewed from the perspective of mathematics, the purchase that topological paradoxes have on the humanities, their capacity to provoke and model intellectual anxieties, would dissolve as soon as those figures were properly, that is mathematically, understood. But such a view is motivated by suspicion of the productive conflation in Freudian and Lacanian psychoanalysis between bodily organ and image; between causal explanation and hermeneutics. It is consequently a suspicion that disables from the start any attempt to understand Lacan's account of the Cause at work in the midst of the field of hermeneutics (see Zizek 1994:29–54).

7. For Derrida, Mallarmé's fold marks the place at which conventional literary criticism fails and the work of deconstruction begins: "Now, if we can begin to see that the 'blank' and the 'fold' cannot in fact be mastered as themes or as meanings [in Mallarmé], if it is within the folds and blankness of a certain hymen that the very textuality of the text is re-marked, then we will precisely have determined the limits of thematic criticism itself" (Derrida 1981:245–246). Lacan's use of topological figures to describe the problematic relation of inside and outside is illuminated by Derrida's discussion of that relation as "the matrix of all possible opposition," and of writing as the term or practice that "opens up" the "very possibility" of these oppositions "without letting itself be comprehended by them." See Derrida 1981:103–104.

---

6. Pressed on his use of topological figures—"Is topology for you a method of discovery or of exposition?"—Lacan replied with enigmatic caution, "It is the mapping of the topology proper to our

modernism; indeed, one might consider it to be one result of the replacement of the "flat" plane of medieval representation with the perspectival space of the Renaissance. Within this new, Euclidean space, the skin functions as a Derridean supplement, the material remainder that haunts the objective spatial depth within which the Cartesian subject is driven to locate itself.

So Michelangelo's famous portrait of the artist as a flayed skin on the wall of the Sistine Chapel (1535) and Juan de Valverde's drawing of an anatomized figure carrying his own pelt (1560) seem freighted with surplus violence, one that resides in the revelation of two specific facts. The first, revealed by the successive removal of surfaces that comprises the art of anatomy, is that the body is nothing *but* surface.[8] The second is that while death happens in three dimensions, the skin, in two, can survive. The uncanny aspect of the undead skin may be confronted in the true story of Alfred Corder, sentenced to be hanged and dissected for his notorious murder of Maria Marten. After death, Corder's body was skinned, tanned, and used to bind a presentation copy of the printed account of his life and crime.[9] So treated, the skin becomes that impossible object, the material embodiment of abjection. When, in tattoo, the skin gives its own strange half-life over to a newly "living" image, it similarly asks and complicates the question of what becomes of our mortal envelope, either at the Resurrection or at the morgue.

But there is another dimension to the intellectual distress for which tattoo stands as a figure. For although we say, with horror, "a tattoo lasts forever"—as if, within our cultural or psychic economy, permanence were a recognized evil—most tattoos last only as long as the body endures, which is to say, not as long as ink on paper. Disapprobation of tattoo's permanence has a political, as well as a psychic, dimension. For where classical economic theory recognizes three types of property—the intellectual, the real or "immobile" (land), and the moveable (chattels)—tattoo announces itself as a fourth type: a property that is at once mobile *and*

inalienable. And here inalienability shows itself to be a disconcerting quality in property, as if not only the value but the *propriety* of property depended on its capacity to be exchanged. As is suggested by the popular narrative of the tattooed man who ends up on the wall of an unscrupulous art dealer, a tattoo is a property that, for a variety of ethical and practical reasons, cannot be sold.[10] Tattoo thus readily connotes a blockage in the free circulation of commodities that is understood to constitute economic health in the West; it is partly in this capacity that it has always been used to figure both the improvidence of the class that does not possess, and the culpable economic naiveté of native peoples.

II

Pain and history seem tied together.

Tattoo International

According to popular tradition, sanctioned by the Oxford English Dictionary, the word tattoo, adapted from the Tahitian "tatau," made its first English appearance in James Cook's account of his voyages to the Polynesian basin, published in London in 1769. Historians locate the origins of European tattooing in Cook's return from his South Sea Islands voyage of 1774 with the tattooed Tahitian known to the British as Omai: the "noble savage" whose appearance sparked a tattooing vogue among the English aristocracy.[11] It is one of the many weaknesses in the history of western tattooing as it stands that the definitive movement of tattoo from the center to the margins of British culture has been assumed (as a "trickle-down" effect) rather than documented or accounted for. Equally mysterious within this history is the alacrity with which certain groups of eighteenth-century Europeans, from ships' crews to the monarchy,

8. For a discussion of the difficult conditions under which Michelangelo worked on "The Last Judgment" and the real and fantasized cutaneous discomfort such conditions provoked, see Leibert 1983:331–360. For a discussion of anatomy as a method for revealing order that causes decay, see Hodges 1985.

9. *An Authentic and Faithful History of the Mysterious Murder of Maria Marten* (London: Thomas Kelly, 1828), is now in Moyses Hall Museum, Bury St. Edmunds, England.

10. In the course of his discussion of primitive accumulation, Marx offers a parodic, "nursery tale" account of the genesis of capitalism, one predicated on a division between the "frugal élite" and the "lazy rascals"—"Thus it came to pass, that the former sort accumulated wealth, and the latter finally had nothing to sell except their own skins" (Marx 1977:872). The bottom line that presents itself to Marx and, he imagines, to even the most irresponsible theorists of capitalism is the human skin—the commodity in which no one, even the person who owns it, has the right to trade. In actuality the tattooed skin can be bought and sold—but not without raising profound questions concerning human and property rights.

11. For description of the reception of Omai in Britain, see Guest 1992. For an extended discussion of the impact of European exploration on Polynesian tattooing, see Gell 1993.

adopted the practice. The seduction of Polynesian tattooing, both to those who saw it in situ, and to those who copied it from returning travelers, is rendered more surprising by the fact that the Europeans had already encountered and documented tattooing in the Americas, Asia, and Africa in the sixteenth and seventeenth centuries—in these earlier instances without being tempted to try it for themselves.[12]

The most useful recent account of the history of tattooing in Europe is Alfred Gell's brilliant analysis of tattooing as an encounter phenomenon (1993). Gell argues that western notions about tattooing derive from the overlay of perceptions of tattooing as a "stigma of the class Other" (the tattooed sailor or criminal) with "perceptions of the practice as characteristic of the ethnic Other—the tattooed native." But Gell is concerned with western tattooing only insofar as its practices and assumptions inform surviving European descriptions of tattooing in Polynesia; and he follows standard accounts of western tattooing when he begins his own with the heuristic assumption that "tattooing, as it is now practiced in western countries, originated as a consequence of European expansion into the Pacific" (Gell 1993:10). I propose to adopt a different assumption: that tattooing was occurring in Europe at the same time that European travelers documented its presence in the Americas, Asia, Africa, and later in the Pacific. The possibility that Polynesian tattooing reinflected, rather than began, an indigenous practice of European tattooing will not in itself explain the particular social patterns that it has subsequently assumed in the West. But it may enable us to see tattooing more clearly, both as the symptom of a colonial encounter and as an instance of a cultural practice that is typically overlooked by the societies in which it occurs.

In a recent interview, performance artist Genesis P-Orridge outlined a self-consciously "alternative" history for British tattooing: "The Romans found the Britons covered in . . . tattoos. The heritage of the pagan Britons was to be heavily tattooed, but of course we're not told of our tribal, integrated, celebratory culture in school. The history has been stolen and turned into a perversion called Christianity." Like Jamie Summers, P-Orridge

understands tattooing as an instance of the elevation of the semiotic into a principle of signification; the tattoo or cut is a "symbolic key" that "makes you open to your own unconscious." P-Orridge goes on to argue that societies that practice tattooing and scarification have been and will be characterized by a benign relational ethics and suggests that before the coming of the Romans, the Britons maintained a balanced relationship with the environment, understanding that "every being . . . should relate to [every] other as mortal and vulnerable" (Juno and Vale 1991:180). According to P-Orridge, for Britons both Ancient and New Age tattooing evidences man's proper and ethical acknowledgment of the semiotic processes of life and death.

This "alternative" history of British tattooing is not in serious conflict with the more standard accounts that locate its genesis in the eighteenth-century contact with Polynesia; in a history of Britain there is room for both. But it does bring into view an important set of meanings that structure demotic tattooing in Britain today, where "Celtic" designs may be used to articulate engagement with, for example, the concerns of Scottish nationalism or with the particular type of environmentalism associated with Wicca. Besides, as it happens, tattoo's alternative history is largely correct. In the years leading to the accession of James VI of Scotland to the English throne, the antiquary William Camden (newly interested in arguing for the tribal unity of the British people) marshaled evidence from classical and other sources (including Bede, Caesar, Herodian, Solinus, Tacitus, Tertullian, and Isidore of Seville) to prove that both the Picts and the insular Celts had been "painted peoples," set apart from later invaders by "their staining and colouring of their whole bodies" with woad and "their *cutting, pinking,* and *pouncing* of their flesh" (Camden 1610:115).[13]

"Listing," "rasing," "pricking," "pinking," and "pouncing" are the interlinked English terms for

---

12. In *Purchas His Pilgrimage,* Samuel Purchas reproduces many descriptions of tattooing from the accounts of earlier and contemporary European travelers (see, for example, Purchas 1617:487, 571, 743, 813, 853, 876, 955, 958).

---

13. In discussing the history of the Scots, Camden underlines his purpose in arguing for the racial unity of the ancient peoples of Britain and incidentally demonstrates the difficulty of producing a tactful account of Britain's barbarian past: "So far am I from working any discredit unto them, that I have rather respectively loved them alwaies, as of the same bloud and stoke, yes, and honoured them too, even when the kingdomes were divided: but now much more, since it hath pleased our almightie, and most mercifull God, that wee growe united in one Bodie, under one most Sacred head of the Empire, to the joy, happinesse, welfare, and safetie, of both Nations" (Camden 1610:119).

tattooing before the middle of the eighteenth century; Samuel Purchas says of the Algonquian Indians, "the women . . . with an Yron, pounce and raze their bodies, legs, thighes, and armes, in curious knots and portraytures of folwes, fishes, beasts, and rub a painting into the same, which will never out" (1617:955). The English term "pounce" was associated with writing as well as with face-painting; pounce is a powder used to dust cheeks, to prepare parchment to receive writing, or to transfer embroidery designs through a perforated pattern. "To pounce" is to tattoo, bruise, puncture, emboss, or engrave, to polish or erase, and to slash or jag the edges of a cloth for ornament, while "a pounce" may be a tattoo, an engraving instrument, or a "pink." Pinking (the cutting out of holes, figures, or letters to display skin, undergarment, or lining of a different colour) is a mode of ornament readily associated with excess; its depravity (which consists in the interesting proposition that it is a *superfluous taking away*) is regularly adduced in late-sixteenth-century attacks on fashion. Finally a "list" or "race" is a slit or scratch, a cut that marks. But to rase is also to remove by scraping or rasping, to erase. Remarkable in this early modern constellation of terms for tattoo is the fact that they each propose a logic of the mark whereby one can mark by detraction, detract by addition. In this they register one of the formal paradoxes that structures today's aversion to tattooing.

In his *Historie of Great Britaine*, a book whose frontispiece depicts a tattooed ancient Briton, John Speed echoed Camden's account of ancient British tattooing:

> Solinus likewise speaking of the *Britaines* saith, their Country is peopled by *Barbarians*, who by means of artificial incisions of sundry formes, have from their childhood divers shapes of beasts incorporate upon them; and having their markes deeply imprinted within their bodies, looke how their growth for stature, so doe those pictured characters likewise increase. . . . These skarres by Tertullian are tearmed *Britannorum stigmata*, *The Britaines markes* . . . and of this use of painting both the *Britaines* had their primitive derivation, and the *Picts* (a branch of British race) a long time after, for that their accustomed manner, were called *Picti* by the *Romanes*, that is, the *painted* people.
>
> Speed 1627:167; Camden 1610:31

Like Solinus and Camden before him, and many after him, Speed is arrested by the paradox of the tattoo as an

image fixed on a moving, in this case expanding, surface.[14] Later in his account he reproduces and glosses Claudian's description of Caesar's military triumph over the Picts—"*Perlegit exanimes Picto moriente figuras: On dying Picts he reads the breathless shapes*, as if the *Beasts* so lively portraited on them, seemed to lie dead together with the murdered bodies of the *Picts*" (Speed 1627:182; Camden 1610:115). Redolent of sympathy for the Picts, Claudian's proposition, underlined by Speed, is that as the tattooed image "lived" on the skin, so it should "die" in a gesture of respect for the body that supported it. The wit of the proposal depends on its acknowledged impossibility—an impossibility borrowed wholesale from the strange object (one that may be equally thought of as a dead image on a live skin, or as a live image on a dead skin) that is a tattoo. The larger question of a tattoo changing as the body changes, expanding or contracting in all its parts without entirely altering their relation to one another, is a formal proposition of some consequence. It is dealt with in the field of geometric topology under the rubrics of diffiomorphism and homeomorphism; and Lacan uses it in his discussion of anamorphosis to illustrate his formulation of the gaze as something excessive to perspectival optics.[15] In the work of Speed and his contemporaries, the formal proposition of an object that moves and grows, but can never change, takes on a primarily political dimension—one within which the

---

14. In Joyce's *Ulysses*, D. B. Murphy bears three tattoos, one "a young man's side face looking frowningly rather. . . . See here, he said, showing Antonio. There he is cursing the mate. And there he is now, he added, the same fellow, pulling the skin with his fingers, some special knack evidently, and he laughing at a yarn" (Joyce 1986:156; Levine 1994:277–300).

15. Lacan introduces a tattoo to illustrate "a dimension in the field of the gaze that has nothing to do with the vision as such," a dimension that may be apprehended operating within "all the paranoic ambiguities" to which distortion may lend itself. "How is it," he continues, "that nobody has ever thought of connecting this with . . . the effect of an erection? Imagine a tattoo traced on the sexual organ *ad hoc* in the state of repose and assuming its, if I may say so, developed form in another state" (Lacan 1981:88). Lacan's imaginary organ is, in his own argument, something of a chimera: one that is briefly standing in for the "gaze as such," that is, for the desire that articulates itself through optical distortion. But it is worth remaining with the tattooed penis long enough to note that in the stretching of the tattoo image we confront the propositions that semblance is subject to physical laws and that the image has an internal structure having nothing to do with appearance.

tattoo comes to stand as the sign of the irreducible difference between Europe and its others.

For the antiquaries and their sources, tattooing and body painting among the ancient Britons went hand in hand with the further distinguishing tribal practices of gynarchy and nakedness. The fact that the Picts were, as Tacitus puts it, "subject to the government of women" was fodder to the antiquarian argument that the Picts were descended from the ancient Britons: "neither [tribe] ma[king] any distinction of sex for government, or exclud[ing] women from bearing sceptre" (Camden 1610:30). Speed goes so far as to compare Queen Elizabeth to Bodicea, "another Great Lady of British race . . . whose juste, wise, and resolute kinde of Government hath justified that Custome of our old *Britaines* and *Picts* . . . that they made no difference for the Soveraigne command, yea, and used to warre under the conduct of women" (1627:183). Writing at the end of Elizabeth I's long reign, Camden and Speed felt there was nothing especially barbaric in the ancient British tolerance for female monarchy.[16] But when he addresses himself to the legendary nakedness of the Picts and Britons, Speed follows his sources in concluding that his barbarian ancestors went naked through their ignorance of cloth manufacture and other rudimentary arts of civilization. As Diodorus Siculus puts it in Camden's account, "The Britans live after the manner of the old world" (Camden 1610:29).

Even now, little is known about Pictish civilization and culture; a few inscrutable inscriptions aside, written sources are more or less limited to classical accounts of the Picts as primitive barbarians, and (for the period after the conversion) the sparse comments of Adoman and Bede.[17] Since these sources are almost unanimous

in their claims that both the Picts and other ancient British tribes tattooed, little more may be served in doubting the record than the satisfaction of a national pride that sets itself against the practice. The recent discovery by archaeologists of Scythian and Pazyrak bodies with extensive tattoo work may indicate that the element of fantasy in classical accounts of British tattooing resides less in the assertion that the barbarians tattooed, than in the implication that the Roman soldiers did not. The accuracy of the record aside, Speed's apparent purpose in invoking ancient British tattooing ("to propose unto the eyes of our now glorious and gorgeous *Britaines*, some generall draughts of our poor and rude progenitors") is to demonstrate the ancient (but new) identity of the British "race": a national group marked and set aside by its use of tattoo and body painting (Speed 1627:179). But the tattoo also marks a different, and conflicting, national concern. Housed in tents, dressed in skins, and eating sparely, ignorant of God, agriculture, and the value of gold, the Picts of the antiquarian account bear striking resemblance to the New World inhabitants whose existence was fast becoming a focus of British attention at the end of the sixteenth century. Under the pressure of this moment of encounter, the figure of the tattooed Briton finds itself pressed into the service of the newly emergent discourse of comparative ethnography.

The first volume of Theodore de Bry's famous work *America I* (1590a, 1590b, published simultaneously in Latin, English, French, and German) contains Thomas Harriot's account (1588) of the English expedition to Roanoke of 1585, together with thirteen engravings, "The True Pictures and Fashions of the People in that Part of America now called Virginia." Largely based on paintings of the Southeastern Algonquians made by John White, artist recorder to the first Roanoke expedition, the series also includes two engravings based on the work of Jacques Le Moyne de Morgues, artist to the earlier French expeditions to Florida of 1562–1565. A fuller set of Le Moyne's images of the Timucua people, with his written commentary on them, appeared in the second volume of *America* (de Bry 1591), together with Le Moyne's map of Florida and his own account of the attempted French colony.[18]

---

16. The association of tattooing with the rule of women reaches beyond its historical justification; where it emerges in the discourse of modern anthropology it is often used to mark the double abjection of native cultures. So Joseph Dowd suggested tattooing was a practice "which probably originated at a time when the matriarchate was universal and before children came to have individual names. Instead of giving a special name to each member of the family or tribe, all of the same blood on the mother's side were designated by a common tattoo mark" (Dowd 1907:42). In his 1898 essay "Matriarchy among the Picts" Heinrich Zimmer also linked the two practices when he insisted that tattooing, like matrilineal descent, was a savage custom not properly associated with the Aryan community (cited in MacQuarrie 1996:2).

17. The question of whether or not the Picts tattooed themselves has not been fully addressed; see MacQuarrie 1996:2–3. Part of the evidence for ancient British tattooing, as Claudian, Solinus, Camden,

---

Speed, and others point out, is comprised by the Roman name *Picti* (the painted men) and the ancient British name *Priteni* (people of the designs); see MacQuarrie 1996:7–10.

18. The first Roanoke expedition (June 1585–June 1586), for which John White acted as official recorder, was led by Sir Richard Greville

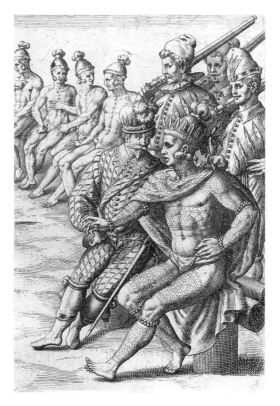

Figure 1. Theodore de Bry (after Jacques Le Moyne de Morgues), *In cerui exuvio Soli consecrando solennes ritus,* or "The offering of a stag to the sun" (detail). Engraving from *America II* (1591:pl. 35). Reproduced by permission of the Syndics of Cambridge University Library.

Figure 2. Theodore de Bry (after Jacques Le Moyne de Morgues), *Excubitorum socordia ut punitur,* or "The execution of negligent sentries" (detail). Engraving from *America II* (1591:pl. 32). Reproduced by permission of the Syndics of Cambridge University Library.

White and Le Moyne both recorded the practice of tattooing in their paintings of the native Americans. At least as engraved by de Bry, Le Moyne used tattooing in his paintings to posit an unexpected similarity between the body decoration of the Timucua and the slashed, pinked, and rased clothing of the French (fig. 1). Le

Moyne's account of Laudonniere's attempt to establish a Huguenot foothold in Florida is unusually sensitive to the impact made on Timucua by the arrival of the French. While he advises his reader to remember that "*istos Regulos, eorum´que uxores, corporiscutem puncturis quibusdam varia picturas imitantibus ornare*" (de Bry 1591:pl. 39) or "All these rulers and their wives

under the patronage of Raleigh. In July 1587, White returned to Roanoke as governor of "the city of Raleigh in Virginia." Shortly after his arrival there he was persuaded by the other settlers to seek further provisions and assistance back in England; returning to Roanoke in August 1590, he found the settlement (hereafter "The Lost Colony") deserted (see Hulton 1984).

Jacques Le Moyne accompanied Réné de Laudonniere on his expedition to Floria in 1563 and 1565. Laudonniere's expedition journal was published by Hakluyt in France in 1586, and in London in English in 1587 and 1589. Le Moyne's Latin account of the French expedition "Brevis narratio eorum quae in Florida etc," together with etchings of his paintings of Florida, was published by de Bry as

America II (1591). Le Moyne left France as a Huguenot refugee sometime after 1573; settled in Blackfriars as a painter and engraver under the patronage of Mary Sidney and Walter Raleigh; and died in 1588; see Hulton 1977. Theodore de Bry was a Flemish goldsmith, engraver, and publisher with strong Protestant sympathies. In 1587 he was commissioned to engrave Thomas Lant's drawings of Philip Sidney's funeral procession; on a return visit to London the following year he purchased Le Moyne's paintings from his widow. Two of Le Moyne's Florida paintings are used to illustrate *America I* (de Bry 1590), which is dedicated to Walter Raleigh; the rest appeared in *America II* (de Bry 1591); see Hulton 1984.

decorate the skin of their bodies with a kind of tattooing, in imitation of various painted designs" (Hulton 1977:151), Le Moyne also records that the Timucua were "somewhat astonished when they noticed the difference between the smoothness and softness of our bodies and theirs, and the unfamiliar clothing we wore" (Hulton 1977:120).

In Le Moyne's work, the difference between the Europeans and the Native Americans is produced through the proposition of an underlying similarity; European and American figures are often represented in very close juxtaposition or in poses that reflect each other (fig. 2). The paintings are vulnerable to the charge that they "idealized" (that is, "Europeanized") their American subjects; the majority of them were probably reconstructed from memory following Le Moyne's dramatic escape from the colony, and they are not held to be of the same ethnographical value as the work of his contemporary John White (Hulton 1977:70). But Le Moyne, whose characteristic style is that of a gentle but sustained mannerism, idealizes European as well as Native American figures and does so as part of a deliberative inquiry into the question of what it means to be civilized. So he advises readers that Christians have much to learn from the Timucua in terms of temperance and "deserve to be handed over to these base uncivilized people and brutish creatures to learn restraint" (Hulton 1977:148). The proposition that civilized peoples may learn civility from the uncivilized is a conventional piece of social criticism; it is nevertheless part of a serious attempt to theorize the ethical consequences of a colonial encounter.

John White did not include the arrival of the Europeans in his record of Roanoke; only two surviving paintings show scenes of the colonists, and those are of Puerto Rico (Hulton 1984:9). Thomas Harriot, with whom White worked closely to compile a full account of the area of the Roanoke landings, took a markedly functionalist view of Algonquian culture. The first version of his "Briefe and true report of the newfoundland of Virginia" was addressed to the "Adventurers, Favourers, and Welwillers of the action," and assures them that "in respect of troubling our inhabiting and planting, [the Algonquians] are not to be feared; but . . . shall have cause both to feare and love us, that shall inhabite with them" (Harriot 1588:E1v). Arguably, it was precisely Harriot's and White's refusal to concern themselves with their own relationship to the Algonquians that renders their account of Native

American culture more ethnographically accurate than that of Le Moyne.

White's illustrations corroborate Harriot's account of body painting and tattooing among the Carolina Algonquians: "the Princes of Virginia . . . ether pownes, or paynt their forehead, cheeks, chynne, bodye, armes, and legges." Secotoan women of rank are similarly "pownced," with the addition of a "chaine" around their necks, "either pricked or paynted" (de Bry 1590a:Sig A1v, Sig A2). Harriot's apparent uncertainty as to whether the body markings of the various Algonquian tribes were "pricked" and "pownced" or "painted" has led Paul Hulton to argue that "tattooing was probably confined to the women, while painting was used widely by both sexes" (1984:28). In fact, Harriot's hesitation concerns the distribution rather than the incidence of tattooing among the men and women of the different Algonquian groups; he argues further that the Algonquian warriors had "marks rased on their backs" for purposes of identification. An engraving of these marks, together with a key linking them to the names of different chiefs, is the final image in the series illustrating "the fashions of the people of America" (fig. 3; de Bry 1590a:Sig D4v). In order, as he says, "to shew that the Inhabitants of great Britain have bin in times past as savage as those of Virginia," de Bry then concludes *America I* with "Some Picture of the Pictes which in the olde tyme did habite one part of great Bretainne" (Sig E1).

In his introductory remarks to these engravings, which show three heavily tattooed Picts and two untattooed Ancient Britons "from neighbouring tribes," de Bry implies the images were copied by John White from "a oolld English cronicle" (Sig E1). The engravings are accompanied by a commentary, which details the weapons, ornaments, hairstyles, and body decorations of the Picts, and explains, in accordance with the engravings, that the Picts "did paint all their bodye"; the men affecting suns, monsters, and snakes (Sig E1v), while the women wore moon and stars, figures of animals, and abstract designs (Sig E2v). But the image that was to prove the most memorable to his contemporaries was de Bry's "Truue picture of a yonge dowgter of the Pictes," an engraving that shows a female nude wearing a sword, holding a spear, and "painted over all the body . . . of sondrye kinds of flours, and of the fairest that they cowld feynde" (fig. 4).[19] Pace de Bry,

---

19. White is known to have made direct copies of Le Moyne's work, and it is possible that de Bry was working from such a copy when he engraved "The Truue picture of a yonge dowgter of the

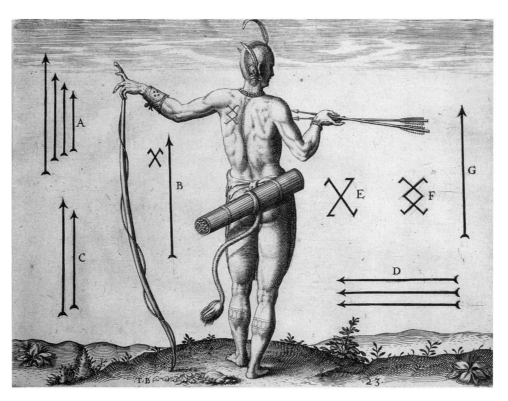

Figure 3. Theodore de Bry (after John White), *Aliquot Heroum Virginiae Notae* or "The Marks of sundrye of the Cheif mene of Virginia." Engraving from *America I* (1590:pl. 23). Reproduced by permission of the Syndics of Cambridge University Library.

this image at least is based on the work not of John White, but of Jacques Le Moyne, whose painting, "A Young Daughter of the Picts" (fig. 5) is now in the Yale Center for British Art (Hulton 1984:18). Le Moyne's Pict stands to the front of a landscape, in the mid-distance of which can be seen the people and buildings of a small but prosperous town. She stands in a relaxed but artificial pose, her face turned half right, her body half left; her right hand on her hip, she carries a slim spear in the left. Her carefully tended hair falls in virgin profusion down her back; except for an elegant iron necklet and a girdle, from which a curving sword depends from the impossible support of a golden chain, she is naked.

Most striking, of course, is that the young Pict's body is painted or tattooed from neck to ankle with a variety

of flowers, among which Paul Hulton has identified the single and double peony, delphinium, hollyhock, heartsease, double columbine, orange lily, tazetta narcissus, cornflower, rose campion, yellow-horned poppy, mourning iris, tulip, and marvel-of-Peru (1977:2:164). Hulton points out that the last three varieties had only recently been introduced to western Europe from America and the Balkan peninsula and concludes "it was anachronistic indeed of Le Moyne to adorn a Pictish maiden with such newly arrived flowers" (Hulton 1977:1:57). But Le Moyne, author of a volume of woodcuts of beasts, birds, and plants intended for decorative patterns and responsible for a large group of exquisite watercolor drawings of plants (now in the Victoria and Albert Museum), would certainly have known what he was doing in decorating the body of an Ancient Briton with the marvel-of-Peru. The deliberate anachronism is the first in a series of gestures designed to mark the wit of this thoroughly mannerist painting.

Pictes." For an account of the complicated relationship between the work of Le Moynes, White, and de Bry, see Hulton (1984:17–18).

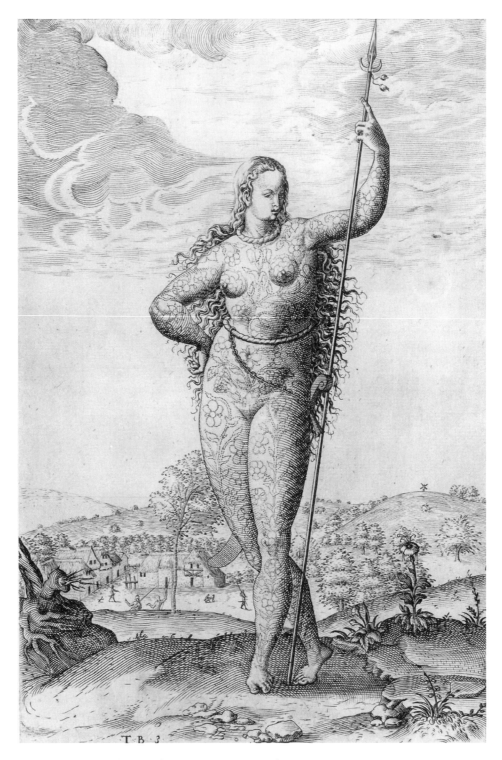

Figure 4. Theodore de Bry (after Jacques Le Moyne de Morgues), *Virginis Pictae icon III* or "Truue picture of a yonge dowgter of the Pictes." Engraving from *America I* (1590). Reproduced by permission of the Syndics of Cambridge University Library.

In its entirety, Le Moyne's painting constitutes a series of visual and verbal puns, ranging from a joke concerning the impropriety of "painting" a nude to a meditation on the sixteenth-century English word "pink," which signifies not only a tattoo, beauty, or excellence, but also a flower. (The sixteenth-century French word *fleurdeliser* carries some of the same determinants; it is defined in Randall Cotgrave's *Dictionarie of the French and English Tongues* [1611] as "to set a flowerdeluce between the shoulders with a hot yron [the mark of a rogue]; also, to flourish, beautify, sticke, set thicke, with Flowerdeluces.") As a "pink," the young Pict is herself an instance of the *flors florum*, the "flower of flowers," which is the conventional floral trope for heavenly and/or earthly love (Peterson 1994:24). In its insistent proposition that woman is like a flower—a proposition that involves both a reversal between form and content and a self-conscious refusal to distinguish between the real and the figural—Le Moyne's painting reveals itself as the painting not of a woman, but of metaphor itself. Its purpose, in brief, is to evoke admiration for the impossible achievements of art.

"A Young Daughter of the Picts" was probably painted in London about 1585–1588, while Le Moyne was living in Blackfriars as a Huguenot refugee. Although he seems, like de Bry, to have enjoyed the patronage of Raleigh and the Sidney Family, Le Moyne was still in possession of the painting at his death. He had, on an earlier occasion, refused to sell his work to de Bry, and it is tempting to conclude that "A Young Daughter" was painted for no occasion other than the exercise of his own virtuosity. While the painting may, as Paul Hulton suggests, owe something in style to the miniatures of Hilliard and Oliver, in conception there is nothing like it among contemporary English paintings (Hulton 1977:78). Certainly Le Moyne's wit was lost on his peers or at least hidden from them by de Bry, who bought the painting from Le Moyne's widow and engraved it as an illustration of the historical appearance and manners of the Picts. De Bry's elliptical comment on the engraving may indicate his own reservations about this use of Le Moyne's image. According to him, the daughters of the Pict were "painted over all the body, so much that noe men could not faynde any different, yf they had not use of another fashion of paintinge, for they did paint themselves of sondrye kinds of flours, and of the fairest that they could fende" (de Bry 1590a:Pictae Icon III). Like Harriot and like Le Moyne, who had suggested that Timucuan tattooing was done "in imitation of various

painted designs," de Bry is uncertain how to distinguish between tattooing and the use of body paint. But the problem he is facing here is that, according to his own evidence, girls are tattooed with flowers, women with animals and planets.

The paradox was given sharper formulation by Speed, who, in reproducing four of de Bry's engravings, two of the Picts and two of neighbouring British tribes, added tattoo work to the female ancient Briton:

> By these varieties of picturing (if some have not misinformed us out of their alleged ancient *Authors*) those people so distinguished themselves, that their *married women* were knowne by having pictured on their shoulders, *elbowes*, and *knees*, the heads of some four beasts, as Lions, Gryphons, etc. On their belly, the Sunne spreading his beames: on their *Pappes*, Moones and Starres etc. On their *Armes*, *thighes*, and *legges*, some other fancies of their owne Choice. But for their *Virgines*, their whole body was garnished over with the shapes of all the fairest kinds of flowers and herbes; which (to speak indifferently) could but yield, though a strange, yet no unpleasing aspect . . . yet, this scruple will not easily be removed (if it be true, *that from their childhood their prints increased with their bodies*) how those, who being *Virgins*, had no prints but of hearbes and flowers, becoming *Wives*, were so easily transformed into Beasts or heavenly creatures.
> *Speed 1627:180–182*

A marginal note identifies the source of possible "misinformation" as "the Appendix to Harriot's Virginia"; all the same, Speed is happy enough to reproduce and further disseminate the error, which now takes the form of a conundrum. A tattoo is forever, a virgin is not; a tattooed flower may grow with the body, but it cannot grow into an animal or star. Standing in the place that Derrida calls the hymen ("Neither future nor present, but between the two"—that is, as the figure of surface in the dimension of historical time) within Speed's account the daughter of the Pict suggests not so much the developmental trajectory of ancient or primitive peoples, but their irrevocably barbarian status. Looking back over Britain's hybrid past, Camden had been moved to take stock of his present moment: "Since that for so many ages successively ensuing, we are all now by a certain ingraffing or commixtion become one nation, molified and civilised with Religion, and good Arts, let us mediate and consider, both what they were, and also what we should be" (1610:110). But in his comments on the figure of the young female Pict, Speed introduces a wrinkle into Camden's account of the progress of British civilization, using the isotopic property of the tattoo (which may grow, but cannot change) to illustrate the impossibility of getting from past to present, or from America to Europe, while remaining the same. In so doing, he raises the specter of an incommensurability that is no longer confined, as Le Moyne confined it, to the structure of the signifier, but has become instead a question of cultural codes.

Within the terms of the uneven cultural grammar that is the ground on which the early modern antiquarians began to work out a discourse of British national sentiment, the tattooed ancestor stands for a barbarian past that is at once acknowledged and disavowed. That tattooing, the *Britannorum stigmata* as Camden calls it, is the fetish permitting this avowal-that-is-not-one explains, I think, the curious combination of levity and anxiety with which tattoos are treated in the antiquarian account and as they have been treated ever since. But the fact that the early modern English described tattooing in other times and places as a foreign practice, one whose technologies and functions were unknown within their own culture, should not be taken as evidence that they did not tattoo themselves. For pace Camden and others after him, tattooing is not incompatible with Christianity in any simple sense and survived the coming both of Christianity and the Romans to Britain.

Famously, tattooing is prohibited in Leviticus 19:28 ("You shall not make any cuttings in your flesh for the dead, nor print any marks upon you"). But in his letter to the Galatians 6:17, St. Paul seems to suggest that tattooing is an acceptable sign of Christian commitment, one that may, indeed, be preferable to circumcision: "For in Christ Jesus neither circumcision availeth any thing, nor uncircumcision. . . . From henceforth let no man trouble me, for I bear in my body the marks of the Lord Jesus." The practice of branding or tattooing for Jesus was recorded by the fifth-century Greek historian Procopius of Gaza, by the seventeenth-century traveler Fynes Moryson, and by Emile Durkheim and others as being a practice still extant within the Eastern Church in the twentieth century (Durkheim 1976 [1915]:232; Moryson 1617:1:233–234; see also Carswell 1956; Keimer 1948). Reviewing the evidence for tattooing in medieval Irish and Hiberno-Latin literature, Charles MacQuarrie concludes that tattooing in medieval Europe had a bifurcated set of associations. On the one hand, it was associated with the wounds of Christ (with what, after St. Francis, came to be known as the stigmata) and

with the writing that appears on Christ's thigh in Revelations 19:16; on the other hand, it was associated with paganism and outlawry (MacQuarrie 1996:28–29).

In 786 c.e., Hadrian's Papal Legates reported tattooing among members of the church in Northumbria; an "injury of staining" (*tincturae injuriam*) they condemned if done for purposes of pagan superstition but were prepared to allow if undergone for the sake of Christ (MacQuarrie 1996:12–13; Sinclair 1908:369). William of Malmesbury stressed the second meaning of tattoo when he described the English at the time of the Norman conquest "laden with golden bracelets, their skin tattooed with colored designs" (*armillis aureis brachia onerati, picturatis stigmatibus cutem insigniti*); he went on to suggest that they imparted the barbaric practice to the invaders (Stubbs 1887:2:305). But throughout the medieval period it was common practice for pilgrims to have themselves tattooed in Jerusalem, returning home bearing indelible marks as evidence both of their journey and of their commitment to the service of God. The Jerusalem tattoo was a common sight in fifteenth-, sixteenth-, and even seventeenth-century Europe. As the English traveler George Sandys recorded in his eyewitness account, "They use to mark the Arms of Pilgrims, with the names of Jesus, Maria, Ierusalem, Bethlehem, the Ierusalem Crosse, and sundry other characters" (Sandys 1615:56).[20]

Although the Reformation technically put an end to pilgrimages from Protestant countries, travelers continued to make the difficult journey to Jerusalem from Scotland and England. Protestants though they were, the majority went on to receive tattoos, either at the site of the Holy Sepulchre in Jerusalem or in Bethlehem, which seems to have been something of a

---

20. See also Henry Maundrell's (1707) laconic but detailed account: "*March 27* [1697]—The next morning nothing extraordinary passed, which gave many of the pilgrims leisure to have their arms marked with the usual ensigns of Jerusalem. The artists who undertake the operation do it in this manner. They have stamps in wood of any figure you desire, which they first print off upon your arm with powder of charcoal; then, taking two very fine needles tied close together, and dipping them often, like a pen, in certain ink, compounded, as I was informed, of gunpowder and ox-gall, they make with them small punctures all along the lines of the figure which they have printed, and then, washing the part in wine, conclude the work. These punctures they make with great quickness and dexterity, and with scarce any smart, seldom piercing so deep as to draw blood" (Maundrell 1707:445–446). For a set of traditional tattoo patterns, and a careful description of the history of the practice in Jerusalem, see Carswell 1956.

tattoo center.[21] Thomas Coryat had a Jerusalem cross put on his left wrist and a cross, three nails, and the inscription *Via, Veritas, Vita* on the right while in Jerusalem, according to Edward Terry, who was with him when he died in India. Coryat evidently wore his tattoos with pride, understanding them as a type of stigmata, as Terry recounts:

> All these impressions were made by sharp *Needles* bound together, that pierced only the skin, and then a black Powder put into the places so pierced, which became presently indelible *Characters*, to continue with him so long as his flesh should be covered with *skin*: And they were done upon his Arms so artificially, as if they had been drawn by some accurate Pencil upon Parchment. This poor man would pride himself very much in beholding of those characters, and seeing them would often speak those words of St. Paul, written to the Galatians, Gal 6. 17 (though far besides the Apostles meaning) *I bear in my body the marks of Lord Jesus.*
> Terry 1655:sig E8v–r

Fynes Moryson and his brother, who visited Bethlehem in the company of some French pilgrims, took pains to avoid getting tattooed, since it was a procedure they associated with the Roman church: "And when our *consorts* at Bethlehem printed the signe of the Crosse with inke and a pen-knife upon their armes, so as the print was never to bee taken out, wee would not folow them in this small matter, but excused our selves, that being to passe home through many kngdomes, we durst not beare any such marke upon our bodie, whereby wee might bee knowne" (Moryson 1617:1:237). But another Scotsman, William Lithgow, one of James I's courtiers, had no such qualms, receiving extensive tattoo-work in Jerusalem. There he elaborated a standard pattern (a Jerusalem cross) with some devices of his own:

> In the last night of my staying at Jerusalem, which was at the holy grave, I remembring that bounden duty, and loving zeale, which I own unto my native Prince; whom I in all humility (next and immediate to Christ Jesus) acknowledge, to be the supreme head, and Governour of the true

Christian and Catholicke Church; by the remembrance of this obligation, I say, I caused one *Elias Bethleete*, a Christian inhabitour of *Bethleem*, to ingrave on the flesh of my right arme, *The never-conquered Crowne of Scotland,* and *the nowe inconquerable Crowne of England,* joyned also to it; with this inscription, painefully carved in letters, within the circle of the Crowne, *Vivat Iacobus Rex.*
> Lithgow 1614:R3–R3v

In the 1640 edition of his text, which he dedicated to Charles I, Lithgow included a woodcut illustration of his tattooed cross and crown (fig. 6) and described a third tattoo, which he now claimed to have had added beneath them: "Returning to the fellow two piasters for his reward, I fixed these lines for King James. "Long may he live, and long may God above / Confirm, reward, increase his Christian love / That he (bless'd king of men) may never cease / To keep this badge, the sacred prince of peace/ And there's the motto of his maiden crown / *Haec nobis invicta miserunt,* ne'er won" (Lithgow 1640:269). Lithgow's tattoo is particularly interesting in that it is partially detached from its religious context as it matches the Cross with the Crown, and the name of Christ with that of James I ("Prince of Peace"). By Lithgow's own account, the Jerusalem official who saw the tattoo was "greatly offended with me, that I should have polluted that holy place with the name of such an arch-enemy to the Roman church" (ibid., 269).

In the figure of William Lithgow, returning tattooed to the English court, we can no longer refuse to recognize the Renaissance tattoo. Our certainty that the British did not tattoo themselves during the early modern period marks us as the descendants of Camden and Speed, British men and women for whom tattoo is visible as the mark of an ethnic status that we have long claimed, as a nation, to have outgrown. But if tattoo has a generalizable function across different cultures, it is precisely to stand as the mark of "foreignness." So Gell notes that at the moment of encounter, the Polynesians, like the British today, thought of tattooing as a foreign practice—as one adopted, for example, from a different island in the archipelago, or from the European sailors who, increasingly tattooed, moved among them (Gell 1993:10). To the early modern Europeans, tattooing may have appeared as a sign of ethnic difference simply because it was available to perform the work of such a sign. In this case, it would have been the attempt to assert their own difference from other native peoples that drove the Europeans to identify tattooing as a cultural practice that they were prepared, newly, to disavow.

---

21. In his seventeenth-century account, Thevenot suggests that tattooing is the characteristic practice of both pilgrims and a Christian sect living in Bethlehem: "Nous emploiâmes tout le Mardi 29 Avril à nous faire marquer les bras, comme sont ordinairerment tous les Pélerins, ce sont des Chrêtiens de Bethlehem suivant le rit Latin qui font cela. . . . Ils ont une petite canne où sont deux aiguilles, qu'ils trempent de tems en tems dans l'ancre mêlée avec du fiel de boeuf, et vous en piquent suivant les lignes marquées par le moule de bois . . . les marques restent bleuës, et ne s'effacent jamais, parce que le sang se mêlant avec cette teinture d'ancre et de fiel de boeuf, se marquer encor dedans sous la peau" (Thevenot 1689:638–639).

Figure 6. William Lithgow's tattoos: a Jerusalem cross and the united crowns of Scotland and England (detail). From William Lithgow, *The Totall discourse* (1640), p. 285. Reproduced by permission of the Syndics of Cambridge University Library.

Caused by the introduction of a foreign body under the skin, under certain circumstances (such as those under which we encounter it today), the tattoo marks the self as foreign. It consequently stands as a ready figure for the border skirmishing that defines conceptual relations not only between the inside and the outside of the body, but also between the inside and the outside of social groups. Harriot and Speed themselves understood tribal tattooing as a system of identification; Speed describes Pictish tattoos as "badges of their Noblenes, thus endamasked," while Harriot argued the Algonquian warriors wore tattoos "whereby it may be knowen what Princes subjects they bee" (Speed 1611:182; de Bry 1590a:pl. 23). Like all naming practices, tattooing accords an individual an identity predicated on the partial dispossession of the self. It is as such, I propose, that it attracts the fetishized recognition of both the native and the colonial gaze.

BIBLIOGRAPHY

Anzieu, D.
  1989   *The Skin Ego*, trans. Chris Turner. Yale University Press, New Haven.

Benjamin, W.
  1985   *Illuminations*, ed. Hannah Arendt, trans. Harry Zohn. Schoken Books, New York.

de Bry, T.
  1590a   *America I: Admiranda narratio fida tamen, de commodis et incolarum ritibus Virginiae.* De Bry, Frankfürt.
  1590b   *America I: A briefe and true report of the new found land of Virginia.* De Bry, Frankfürt. (English edition.) See Harriot 1588.
  1591   *America II; Brevis narratio eorum quae in Florida etc.* De Bry, Frankfürt. See Le Moyne 1591.

Camden, W.
  1610   *Britannia* (1586), trans. P. Holland. G. Bishop, London.

Carswell, J.
  1956   *Coptic Tattoo Designs.* Karam Press, Jerusalem.

Cotgrave, R.
  1611   *Dictionarie of the French and English Tongues.* Adam Islip, London.

Curtis, J.
  1828   *An Authentic and Faithful History of the Mysterious Murder of Maria Marten.* Thomas Kelly, London.

Deleuze, G.
  1993   *The Fold: Leibnitz and the Baroque*, trans. Tom Conley. Athlone, London.

Deleuze, G., and F. Guattari
  1987   *A Thousand Plateaus: Capitalism and Schizophrenia*, trans. Brian Massumi. University of Minneapolis Press, Minneapolis.

Derrida, J.
  1981   *Dissemination*, trans. Barbara Johnson. University of Chicago Press, Chicago.
  1982   *Margins of Philosophy*, trans. Alan Bass. University of Chicago Press, Chicago.

Dowd, J.
  1907   *The Negro Races: A Sociological Study.* Macmillan, London.

Durkheim, E.
  1976 *Elementary Forms of Religious Life* (1912), trans. J. W. Swain. George Allen and Unwin, London.

Freud, S.
  1953–1974 *The Standard Edition of the Complete Psychological Works of Sigmund Freud*, trans. James Strachey. Hogarth Press, London.

Gell, A.
  1993 *Wrapping in Images: Tattooing in Polynesia.* Claredon Press, Oxford.

Gould, S.
  1984 *The Mismeasure of Man* (1981). Penguin, Harmondsworth.

Guest, H.
  1992 "Curiously Marked: Tattooing, Masculinity and Nationality in Eighteenth-Century British Perceptions of the South Pacific," in *Painting and the Politics of Culture: New Essays on British Art, 1700–1850*, ed. John Barrell, pp. 101–134. Oxford University Press, Oxford.

Hardy, D. E.
  1992 *Forever Yes: Art of the New Tattoo.* Hardy Marks Publications, Honolulu.

Harriot, T.
  1588 *A briefe and true report of the new found land of Virginia.* R. Robinson, London.

Henderson, I.
  1967 *The Picts.* Thames and Hudson, London.

Hodges, D.
  1985 *Renaissance Fictions of Anatomy.* University of Massachusetts Press, Amherst.

Hulton, P.
  1984 *America 1585: The Complete Drawings of John White.* University of North Carolina Press, Chapel Hill.

Hulton, P., ed.
  1977 *The Work of Jacques Le Moyne de Morgues, a Huguenot Artist in France, Florida, and England.* British Museum Publications Ltd., London.

Joyce, J.
  1986 *Ulysses* (1922). Bodley Head, London.

Juno, A., and V. Vale
  1991 "Interview with G. and P. P-Orridge." *Research* 12:164–181.

Keimer, L.
  1948 *Remarques sur le Tatouage dans l'Eqypte Ancienne.* Mémoires Présentés a l'Institute D'Égypte, Cairo.

Kristeva, J.
  1982 *Powers of Horror: An Essay on Subjection*, trans. Leon S. Roudiez. Columbia University Press, New York.

Lacan, J.
  1981 *Four Fundamental Concepts of Psycho-Analysis* (1973), trans. Alan Sheridan. Norton, New York.
  1992 *The Ethics of Psychoanalysis 1959–60* (1986). Routledge, London.

Leibert, R.
  1983 *Michaelangelo: A Psychoanalytic Study of his Life and Images.* Yale University Press, New Haven.

Le Moyne, J.
  1590 *Brevis narratio eorumquae in Florida Americae provincia Gallis acciderunt.* De Bry, Frankfürt.

Levine, J.
  1994 "James Joyce, Tattoo Artist: Tracing the Outlines of Homosocial Desire." *James Joyce Quarterly* 31(3):277–300.

Lithgow, W.
  1614 *A most delectable, and true discourse, of an admired and painfull peregrination in Europe, Asia, and Africke.* N. Oakes, London.
  1640 *The Total Discourse of the Rare Adventures etc.* J. Oakes, London. (Later edition of Lithgow 1614.)

Lombroso, C.
  1911 *Criminal Man*, comp. G. Lombroso-Ferriero. Putnam's Press, New York.

Loos, A.
  1966 "Ornament and Crime (1908)," in *Adolf Loos: Pioneer of Modern Architecture*, L. Münz and G. Künstler, trans. Harold Meek, pp. 226–231. Thames and Hudson, London.

Lyotard, J.-F.
  1971 *Discours, figure.* Klincksieck, Paris.

MacQuarrie, C.
1996 "Insular Celtic Tattooing: History, Myth, and Metaphor." Unpublished manuscript.

Marx, K.
1977 *Capital* (1867), vol. 1, trans. Ben Fowkes. Random House, New York.

Maundrell, H.
1707 *A Journey from Aleppo to Jerusalem at Easter 1697.* Jonah Bowyer, Oxford.

Moryson, F.
1617 *An Intinerary.* John Beale, London.

Peterson, J.
1994 "Writing Flowers: Figuration and the Feminine in Carmina Burana 177." *Exemplaria* 6(1):1–34.

Purchas, S.
1617 *Purchas his Pilgrimage.* W. Stansby, London.

Rubin, A.
1988 "The Tattoo Renaissance," in *Marks of Civilization: Artistic Transformations of the Human Body*, ed. A. Rubin, pp. 233–262. Museum of Cultural History, University of California, Los Angeles.

Sanders, C.
1989a "Organizational Constraints on Tattoo Images: A Sociological Analysis of Artistic Style," in *The Meanings of Things: Material Culture and Symbolic Expression*, ed. I. Hodder, pp. 232–241. Unwin Hyman, New York.
1989b *Customizing the Body: the Art and Culture of Tattoo.* Temple University Press, Philadelphia.

Sandys, G.
1615 *A Relation of a Journey begun An.Dom. 1610.* W. Barrett, London.

Sinclair, A.
1908 "Tattooing—Oriental and Gypsy." *American Anthropologist* n.s. 10(3):361–388.

Speed, J.
1627 *The Historie of Great Britaine (1611).* G. Humble, London.

Stubbs, W.
1887, 1889 *De gestis regum Anglorum.* Her Majesty's Stationery Office, London.

Terry, E.
1655 *A Voyage to East India.* J. Martin, London.

Thevenot, J. de
1689 *Voyages de Mr de Thevenot.* Charles Angot, Paris.

Thomas, N.
1995 "Kiss the Baby Goodbye: *Kowhaiwhai* and Aesthetics in Aotearoa New Zealand." *Critical Inquiry* 22(1):90–121.

Tucker, M.
1981 "Tattoo: The State of the Art." *Artforum* May:42–47.

Zizek, S.
1994 *The Mestastases of Enjoyment: Six Essays on Woman and Causality.* Verso, London.

Blood in flux, sanctity at issue

JOAN R. BRANHAM

The Sages spoke in a parable about woman: There is in her a chamber, an ante-chamber, and an upper-room. Blood in the chamber is unclean; if it is found in the ante-chamber, its condition of doubt is deemed unclean, since it is presumed to be from the fountain.

Niddah, 2.5, The Mishnah

"Words are not the only bearers of meaning. Matter, too, is a matrix of meanings, and as such it invites interpretation," begins Heinrich von Staden's article "Women and Dirt."[1] Von Staden's conjecture, that corporeal *things* solicit interpretation—a relevant citation it seems to bring to a journal dubbed *RES*—points to the sine qua non of the art historian's work. In this case, however, it prompts my investigation into the meaning and figuration of blood. Ancient Jewish, Greek, and Roman societies read blood as a purifying *and* defiling substance. Sacrificial blood, for example, cleanses and sanctifies spaces, people, and objects. Menstrual blood, conversely, profanes and contaminates the very same. How is it that the substance of blood carries such apparently irreconcilable connotations? And are these connotations as contradictory and absolute as they seem?

The familiar *topoi* that menses and sacrificial blood have occupied in anthropological studies over the last century have led historians to interpret them as binary opposites, positing sacrificial blood in the sacred slot and menses in the profane one. A closer examination reveals, however, a much murkier picture. Blood seems to be laden with overdetermined significance, especially in ancient temple traditions. Literary evidence from late antiquity even discloses startling references to the sacred powers of menses as well as to the figurative parallels between menstrual blood and sacrificial blood. Such approximations between the two substances have been, for the most part, overlooked by scholars. Could it be that female reproductive blood—almost universally excluded from sacred spaces—is forbidden not because it is considered an "inferior blood," in some way, to sacrificial blood? Rather, might menses represent a forceful agent, *competitive and threatening* to the powers of sacrificial blood?[2] The similarities that exist between sacrificial blood and women's reproductive blood may, in fact, stem from a similar source—their association with life-forces. Their kindred link with generative powers seems to create a certain tension in dominionship and therefore restricts the simultaneous presence of sacrificial blood and menses in the same charged religious setting.[3]

As the rabbinic parable at the lead of this essay indicates, I have chosen to examine the relationships among blood, space, and the body in more than contextual terms alone. Like blood, space also carries meanings multivalent and in flux, rarely monolithic or stationary.[4] This understanding of space has led many cultures to differentiate among varying types of space, as they do bloods, by physically marking off their limits. Disparate methods of establishing spatial inequities and hierarchies determine an extended network of

1. Heinrich von Staden, "Women and Dirt," *Helios* 19, nos. 1–2 (1992):7.

I thank the American Association of University Women, the Getty Research Institute for the History of Art and the Humanities, and the École Pratique des Hautes Études in Paris for their generous support and resources during my research. This essay makes up a larger discussion on sacred and profane space in my forthcoming book, *Sacred Space in Ancient and Early Medieval Architecture* (New York: Cambridge University Press). I thank Francesco Pellizzi for the many editorial improvements he suggested here. I would also like to thank Richard Brilliant, John Scheid, Carol Krinsky, Paul Flesher, and Joseph Rykwert for their criticisms, as well as Francis Schmidt and Veronique Gillet-Didier for their invaluable assistance in Paris.

2. Here, the exemplary work and methodology of Page duBois guide my argument. DuBois disputes psychoanalytical propositions that render the female body as an historically perceived castrated or inferior male body and offers alternative metaphors that conceptualize the female anatomy as fruitful earth ready for sowing. *Sowing the Body* (Chicago: University of Chicago Press, 1988), p. 3.

3. Scholars have argued that sacrifice and other blood-spilling rituals find their very origins in a mimetic desire to emulate female menstruation. For example, Chris Knight has recently made this point regarding Wogeo Islanders—males who cut themselves to imitate female menstruation in order to gain power during the hunt. Knight states that "menstruation had been culturally constructed as a source (perhaps even *the* symbolic source) of ritual power—power which these 'menstruating men' were now motivated to usurp and appropriate for themselves." *Blood Relations: Menstruation and the Origins of Culture* (New Haven: Yale University Press, 1991), p. 37.

4. This precept has traditionally formed the core of theories on sacred space. See Mircea Eliade, *The Sacred and the Profane* (San Diego: Harcourt Brace Jovanovich, 1959), p. 20. Also see W. Robertson Smith's chapter on human perceptions of holy places in *Religion of the Semites* (Edinburgh: Adam and Charles Black, 1889), pp. 132–149.

relationships—between space and participant, space and matter, space and gender.[5] Once again, like purifying and defiling bloods, "sacred space" and "profane space"—theoretical rubrics commonly afoot in anthropological discourse—can be somewhat misleading if taken to refer to fixed descriptive categories. Characteristics that render a space or blood sacred in one specific time and place may, in fact, make it profane in another context. This capacity of elements to shift dramatically between sacred and profane categories frames the following discussion of sacrificial blood, female reproductive blood, and ritual space as reciprocally governing agents that negotiate, configure, and define each other.

Body and space: demarcating the sacred

The boundaries of geographical space and the boundaries of bodily space both exhibit limits of safety and danger. Whereas structured cities commonly employ grids, walls, and gates to flag the intersection between exterior threat and interior protection, the body carries its own natural border of skin. Substances either leaving or entering the body's epidermal envelope represent potential sources of pollution once they are displaced and in a new environment.[6] For example, a certain skin ointment may be vital to the health and survival of the body's outer surface area, but can prove fatal if passed into its inner regions. Anthropological studies have shown that some cultures have even modeled the safety and unity of their villages on the coherence of the human anatomy; the Gourmantche in Africa, for example, call their bounded settlements

"skinned lands."[7] This notion—that space and body are parallel, demarcated zones—determines the spatial system of the primary model of sacred space under consideration here, the ancient Jewish Temple in Jerusalem. The organizational scheme embodied in this liturgical complex sets the stage for the problematic proximity of sacrificial blood and menstrual blood.

The Hebrew root for "sacred" or "holy"—qdsh (קדש)—means "to be separated" or "to be cut off."[8] This linguistic base makes up the rabbinic term most often used in reference to the Jerusalem Temple—bet hamiqdash (בית המיקדש)—that is to say, "the house that is separated" or "cut off" from the more profane surrounding area.[9] Indeed, holiness and separation are concepts intimately linked in biblical and rabbinic literature.[10] Several Talmudic passages discuss the

5. Roberta Gilchrist defines *gender* as an aspect of society that "is socially created and historically specific, in contrast with categories of male and female sex which are fixed and biologically determined." *Gender and Material Culture* (New York: Routledge, 1994), p. 1. Part of the feminist endeavor has been, in fact, to determine the process that takes place in the establishment of gender categories; that is to say, when does being male or female start to mean identifying with socially constructed gender roles? I will attempt to address this question in relation to the *actual places* in which gender ideologies and religious conventions are played out. Specifically, I want to examine the notion of "sacred space" as "gendered space," casting liturgical space not only as the palpable forum in which the interaction of ritual and gender materializes, but also as the place in which gender roles and religious hierarchies mutually define each other.

6. We will return to this notion below in light of Mary Douglas's work in *Purity and Danger* (1966; reprint, London: ARK Paperbacks, 1984).

7. Michel Cartry noted that for the Gourmantche in Africa, problems presented by the limits of the body were the same as those of the village. Gourmantche language reflects this perception in its appellation of the village as *tin'gban'yendo*, or in Cartry's words, "peau terre." "Du village à la brousse ou le retour de la question," in *La fonction symbolique*, ed. Michel Izard and Pierre Smith (Paris: Gallimard, 1979), p. 279. Also see the theoretical discussions of Charles Malamoud on the symbiotic relationship of the enclosed village and its periphery in "Village et forêt dans l'idéologie de l'Inde brahmanique," reprinted in *Cuire du monde, rite et pensée dans l'inde ancienne* (Paris: La Découverte, 1989), pp. 93–114, as well as Victor Turner's explanation of ritual enclosures in Ndembu society in *The Ritual Process: Structure and Anti-Structure* (Chicago: Aldine Publishing Company, 1969), p. 24. For a more general discussion of the human body as a model for sociopolitical communities, see Mary Douglas's chapter "The Two Bodies," in *Natural Symbols* (1970; reprint, Harmondsworth: Penguin Books, Ltd., 1973), pp. 93–112.

8. Marcus Jastrow, *A Dictionary of the Targumim, the Talmud Babli and Yerushalmi, and the Midrashic Literature* (New York: The Judaica Press, 1982), pp. 1319–1321; Francis Brown, S. R. Driver, and Charles A. Briggs, *A Hebrew and English Lexicon of the Old Testament* (Oxford: Clarendon Press, 1951), pp. 871–874. See also a good overview of the meaning of קדש in Jacob Milgrom's entry, "Sanctification," in *Interpreter's Dictionary of the Bible Supplement*, ed. Keith Crim (Nashville: Abingdon, 1976), pp. 782–784.

9. Curiously, *bet hamiqdash* (בית המיקדש) is used only once in the Hebrew Bible (2 Chronicles 36:17); other terms like *habeit* (הבית), simply "the house," or *bet Yahweh* (בית יהוה), "house of the Lord," are employed more often. But in postbiblical, rabbinic literature, *bet hamiqdash* is the term used most frequently in relation to the Temple. See Menahem Haran, *Temples and Temple Service in Ancient Israel* (Oxford: Clarendon, 1978), p. 5; id., "Temple and Community in Ancient Israel," in *Temple in Society*, ed. Michael V. Fox (Winona Lake: Eisenbrauns, 1988), p. 17.

10. To orient the reader, I will be dealing with the following rabbinic texts: the Mishnah, written after the destruction of the Temple and compiled around 200 C.E.; the Tosefta (a supplement to the Mishnah), edited some time during the third century C.E.; and the

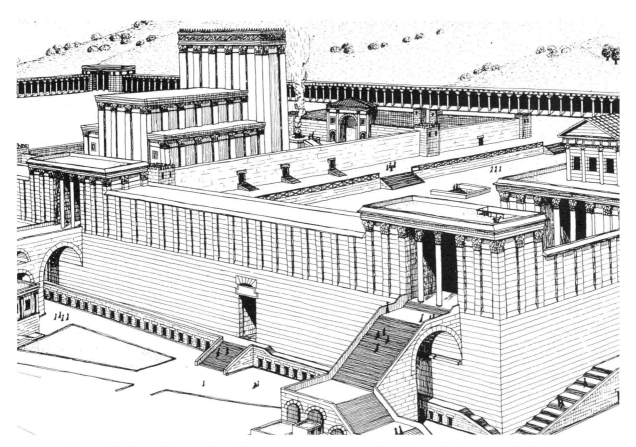

Figure 1. The Temple of Herod in Jerusalem, first century B.C.E.–70 C.E. A low balustrade, the *soreg*, divides the inner sacred precincts from the Court of the Gentiles. Reconstruction: Leen Ritmeyer.

enabling and disabling features that control inclusion in and exclusion from the successive temples that stood on Jerusalem's Temple Mount, particularly the Second Temple built by Herod in the first century B.C.E. and destroyed by the Romans in 70 C.E. (see figs. 1–2). Kelim, 1.8–9 in the Mishnah, for example, maps out geographical limits of holiness by matching those divisions to disparate human conditions. Each area accounted for—from the greater Temple Mount to the exclusive Holy of Holies (God's private chamber)— measures incrementally more sacred than the previous one in terms of the individuals restricted from the spaces in question. To every physical area corresponds an equal or opposite type of individual, included in or excluded from it. Moreover, the status of the participant often

depends on the intactness of his or her own bodily envelope. In one passage, the Mishnaic text explains that the Temple Mount is more holy than the city around it "for no man or woman that has a flux, no menstruant, and no woman after childbirth may enter therein."[11] Here, the permeable nature of the body's casing plays a significant role in dictating the penetrability of the Temple's very courtyards. Corporeal edges and spatial limits go hand in hand in an inverse system: closed temple to open body, open temple to closed body. In the Jerusalem Temple then, the definition of architectural space, a person's place in society, and the repair of bodily borders mutually fashion and construe one another.[12]

Babylonian Talmud (an extensive legal and ethical commentary consisting of the Hebrew Mishnah and Aramaic Gemara), written between 200 and 500 C.E.

11. Kelim, 1.8–9, in *The Mishnah*, trans. Herbert Danby (Oxford: Oxford University Press, 1933), pp. 605–606. Below I will return more specifically to the status of the menstruant.

12. I thank Donald W. Parry for giving me a copy of his paper "Stratification of Sacred Space and Gradations of Humanity: The

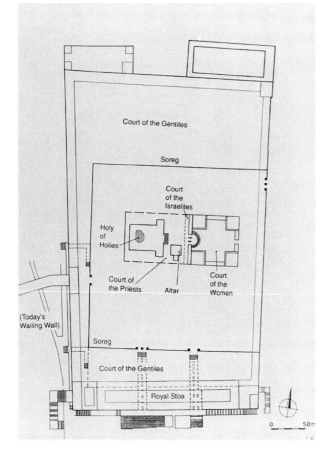

Figure 2. Plan of the Jerusalem Temple courtyard surrounded by the *soreg*. Reconstruction: Leen Ritmeyer.

Coexistent with these echelons of space, social positions, and anatomical boundaries are stone barriers that actually "cut off" designated areas in the Jerusalem Temple. While various stairs, portals, and low walls marked the different degrees of sacrality within the interior courts of the Temple, providing entry only to authorized worshipers,[13] one crucial barrier separated Jews from non-Jews (read, Jews from external threats).[14]

A stone balustrade running around the perimeter of the inner courtyards warned Gentiles of the death penalty should they pass the highly charged border (see fence structure in fig. 1).[15] The Hebrew term for this spatial barrier, the *soreg*, comes from the verb *srg* (סרג), meaning "to gird." In this sense, the *soreg* acted as a type of architectonic skin, girding and embracing the Temple's sacred grounds. Furthermore, a secondary definition of *srg* (סרג) is "to knit," suggesting the permeable, latticelike nature of the wall itself—a structural form common to ancient temple borders.[16] One might say that the interlacing, woven composition of the device symbolizes the point at which sacred and profane are severed *and* woven together. The multidimensional import of such devices—impregnable, yet penetrable—parallels the shielding, yet porous nature of bodily skin. Gates and points of passage within architectural space approximate breaks and orifices in bodily space.

Preserved Greek inscriptions from the Jerusalem Temple *soreg*, no doubt positioned near its points of passage, state, "No alien may enter within the balustrade around the sanctuary and the enclosure. Whoever is caught, on himself shall he put blame for the death which will ensue."[17] The New Testament

Temple of Herod Model," presented at the Symposium on Sacred Space in Oxford, Ohio, March 6, 1993. See also Francis Schmidt's discussion of the Temple and its divisions in *La pensée du temple: De Jérusalem à Qoumrân* (Paris: Seuil, 1994), pp. 94–105.

13. See F. J. Hollis, *The Archaeology of Herod's Temple* (London: J. M. Dent and Sons Limited, 1934), p. 153; Meir Ben-Dov, *The Dig at the Temple Mount* (Jerusalem: Keter, 1982), p. 102 (in Hebrew).

14. For a recent, concise overview of biblical and rabbinic attitudes toward Gentiles as either impure or profane presences, see

Jonathan Klawans, "Notions of Gentile Impurity in Ancient Judaism," *Association for Jewish Studies Review* 20, no. 2 (1995):285–312.

15. Josephus, *Jewish War* 5.5,2 nos. 193–194, trans. H. St. J. Thackeray (London: William Heinemann Ltd., 1928), pp. 256–259; see other references to this boundary marker in ibid., 4.3,10 nos. 182–183, pp. 56–59 (τῶν βεβήλων); ibid., 6.2,4 nos. 124–128, pp. 412–413; *Jewish Antiquities* 15.11,5 no. 417, trans. Ralph Marcus (1963; reprint, Cambridge: Harvard University Press, 1980), pp. 202–205; ibid., 12.3,4 no. 145, pp. 74–75; *Against Apion* 2.8 no. 103, trans. H. St. J. Thackeray (1926; reprint, London: William Heinemann Ltd., 1966), pp. 332–333. See Philo, *The Embassy to Gaius* 31 no. 212, trans. F. H. Colson (Cambridge: Harvard University Press, 1962), pp. 110–111. Also see E. Schürer, G. Vermes, F. Millar, and M. Black, *The History of the Jewish People in the Age of Jesus Christ*, vol. 2 (Edinburgh, Scotland: T. & T. Clark, Ltd., 1979), pp. 284–286.

16. M. Middoth, 2.3 in the Mishnah calls this marker a *soreg* (סורג). See a further discussion of the term *soreg* and its hypothetical, reconstructed form in my essay "Vicarious Sacrality: Temple Space in Ancient Synagogues," in *Ancient Synagogues: Historical Analysis and Archaeological Discovery*, vol. 2, ed. Dan Urman and Paul Flesher (Leiden: E. J. Brill, 1995), pp. 319–345. For a study of balustrades around pagan temples and the *soreg*'s legacy in the form of synagogue and church chancel screens, see my article "Sacred Space Under Erasure in Ancient Synagogues and Early Churches," *The Art Bulletin* 74, no. 3 (1992):375–394.

17. Translation by Elias Bickerman in, "The Warning Inscriptions of Herod's Temple," *Studies in Jewish and Christian*

confirms this exclusionary system against foreign pollution in its account of Paul when he presumably brought Gentiles past the *soreg* and into the inner precincts. Acts 21:28 describes a chaotic scene: Jews inside the Temple seize Paul, drag him outside the gates, and start to beat him, exclaiming, "Men of Israel, help! This is the man who is teaching men everywhere against the people and the Law and this place; moreover he also brought Greeks into the Temple, and he has defiled this holy place (ἅγιον τόπον)."[18] Punctuating, classifying, and sheathing space in this way carries serious implications for certain members of the population and, as we shall see further below, particularly for women in antiquity.

Like the Hebrew word used for the Jerusalem Temple—*bet hamiqdash* (בית המיקדש), or "the house that is separated"—*temenos*, or "precincts" of a Greek temple, has at its root the verb *temno* (τέμνω), signifying "to cut." The construction of a *temenos* implies, then, the actual cutting out of a space. Homeric usage originally speaks of a *temenos* simply as a land segmented off for a king's benefit.[19] Eventually, however,

temenos singularly denoted "a piece of land marked off from common uses and dedicated to a god, a precinct."[20] Similarly, the Latin noun *temlum* or *templum*,[21] related to the Greek *temenos*, historically signifies in the Roman world, according to George R. H. Wright:

> a place marked off on the ground by the (Etruscan) augurs for observations (of the flight of birds) to take auguries. By extension it is a place set apart or consecrated by the augurs for public functions and hence metaphorically it is the "region" of anything, and in particular of a god.[22]

A *temenos* or *templum* implies, therefore, a place that is "cut off" from all other areas and that maintains divine associations.[23] Sometimes unwrought stones, perceived as holy, natural formations, are set up to mark the site.[24] These stones, or *horoi*, are often engraved with warnings to prohibit unknowing parties from wandering into a potentially charged space. In one Greek temple site, for instance, six inscriptions repeating the formula ΤΕΜΕΝΟΣ ΔΙΟΣ were found carved on rocks surrounding the *temenos* of Zeus at Neandria.[25] By the first century C.E., human-built walls or fences that "cut off" spatial entities associated with the sacred replaced

History, vol. 2 (Leiden: E. J. Brill, 1980), pp. 210–211. Also see Peretz Segal, "The Penalty of the Warning Inscription from the Temple of Jerusalem," *Israel Exploration Journal* 39, nos. 1–2 (1989):79–84. Two of these plaques exist today, a complete one in the Istanbul Museum and another fragment in Jerusalem at the Rockefeller Museum. See Moshe Schwabe, "Greek Inscriptions from Jerusalem," in *Sepher Yerushalayim*, ed. Michael Avi-Yonah (Jerusalem: The Bialik Institute and Dvir Publishing House, 1956), pp. 359–368 (in Hebrew); J. H. Iliffe, "The ΘΑΝΑΤΟΣ Inscription from Herod's Temple," *Quarterly of the Department of Antiquities in Palestine* 6, no. 1 (1936):1–3.

18. For a discussion of purity in relation to Gentiles, see E. P. Sanders, *Judaism: Practice and Belief, 63 B.C.E.–66 C.E.* (Philadelphia: Trinity Press International, 1992), pp. 72–76.

19. See Robert Parker's etymological discussion of *temenos*, from its mundane beginnings indicating land "cut off" for royalty to the post-Homerian meaning as land "cut off" for divinity. *Miasma: Pollution and Purification in Greek Religion* (New York: Oxford University Press, 1983), pp. 160–163. Sacrality is of course invested in the person of the king and so also in his separated land. See John Pairman Brown's comparison of *temenos* and תמנה in "The *Templum* and the *Saeculum*: Sacred Space and Time in Israel and Etruria," *Zeitschrift für die alttestamentliche Wissenschaft* 98 (1986):427. Vincent Scully examines *temenos* planning in Greek temples in *The Earth, the Temple, and the Gods: Greek Sacred Architecture* (New Haven: Yale University Press, 1962), pp. 54–55. Also see Walter Burkert, *Greek Religion*, trans. John Raffan (Cambridge: Harvard University Press, 1985), p. 86. A temple, *naos*, draws its meaning from *naiein*, or "to dwell." See Burkert's article, "The Meaning and Function of the Temple in Classical Greece," in *Temple in Society*, ed. Michael V. Fox (Winona Lake: Eisenbrauns, 1988), p. 27.

20. Henry George Liddell, Robert Scott, and Sr. Henry Stuart Jones, *A Greek-English Lexicon* (Oxford: Clarendon Press, 1968), p. 1774. See Plato's use: "They sanctified oracles and statues and altars and temples, and marked off (τεμένη) for each of them sacred globes." *Laws*, vol. 1, book 5, trans. R. G. Bury (Cambridge: Harvard University Press, 1967), pp. 358–359.

21. An insertion of a *p* as an explosion of the *m* before an *l* brings us the word "templum," according to Ernout and A. Meillet, *Dictionnaire Étymologique de la Langue Latine* (Paris: Librairie C. Klincksieck, 1959), pp. 680–681.

22. George R. H. Wright, *Ancient Building in South Syria and Palestine* (Leiden: E. J. Brill, 1985), p. 225.

23. While *naos* in Greek and *aedes* in Latin have parallel meanings of "temple" and "house" (*bet* in Hebrew), I am more interested in the descriptive resonance among these traditions that linguistically qualifies sacred structures as entities "cut off" or "separated" from surrounding sites. Also see an examination of "the sacred woods" as another separated region in Roman and Greek cultures in John Scheid, *Les bois sacrés*, Actes du colloque international organisé par le Centre Jean Bérard et l'École Pratique des Hautes Études (Naples: Centre Jean Bérard, 1993), pp. 13–20.

24. Burkert, *Greek Religion* (see note 19), pp. 84–85; id., "Meaning and Function" (see note 19), p. 35.

25. Phyllis Williams Lehmann and Denys Spittle, *Samothrace: The Temenos*, vol. 5 (Princeton: Princeton University Press, 1982), p. 81. See also Walter Burkert, *Homo Necans: The Anthropology of Ancient Greek Sacrificial Ritual and Myth*, trans. Peter Bing (Berkeley: University of California Press, 1983), p. 39.

natural markers.[26] In their capacity to cut off restricted regions, then, barriers surrounding Greek and Roman temples and the *soreg* in the Jerusalem Temple helped to conjure and define sacred sites by wrapping them with symbolically protective but permeable enclosures.

Shifting boundaries

The ability of stone barriers to redefine spatial zones points to the transformative, fluctuating nature of space, bodies, and borders. Concrete markers, signaling the shifts between sacred and profane space are, however, not the only devices that evoke alternate meanings. Intangible entities, like actions or spoken words, also work both to designate and transform certain elements.[27] The Jewish marriage ceremony, for example, represents one such ritual that implies "separation." The rite pivots

around the recitation of a traditional formula containing the root for sacred, *qdsh*. After placing the ring on the bride's finger, the groom recites: הרי את מקודשת לי בטבעת זו, כדת משה וישראל, or "Behold you are consecrated to me with this ring according to the law of Moses and Israel."[28] The adjective "consecrated"—*mequdeshet* (מקודשת)—contains *qdsh* (קדש), meaning "sacred" or "to be separated." A woman who is "consecrated" is, thereby, set apart for the groom alone at the pronunciation of this expression.[29] On one level, the utterance renders a woman "sacred" to a man; she is singled out as "different" and "authorized" in relation to other female partners. On another level, the age-old recitation proscriptively "cuts off" a woman's sexuality, situating it in a qualified, marital institution. Like demarcated liturgical spaces, her status changes; she is "set apart" as inaccessible to others.

In the Talmud, B. Berakot 28b describes the shifting nature of spaces and persons in its narrative of Rabban Johanan ben Zakkai lying ill on his deathbed. His students come into his room to visit him and "at the moment of his departure he said unto them: Remove the vessels so that they shall not become unclean." Whatever these "vessels" may have been (Torah scroll, kiddush cup, prayer shawl?), he believed that the nature of the space surrounding his body would undergo a metaphysical transformation at the instant of his death. This view indicates that a spatial context not only governs the meaning of an object, but that an event— death, in this case—has the power to change the character of a *topos*. Death, in fact, represents a transitive occurrence, a passage or threshold between two states of being. The corpse is no longer a person, nor is it a nonperson; it is a presence out of its natural place. Here then the moment of death, the subsequent corpse, and the indeterminate, ambiguous associations that they embody profane both the room and the physical entities in it.

Corpse contamination figures prominently in biblical literature as a catalyst for change between sacred and profane definitions. The puzzling case of the red heifer,

---

26. According to Jeanne Robert and Louis Robert, the Greek word for such barriers *kagkellos* (κάγκελλος) is a transcription of the Latin *cancellus* and appears in a number of inscriptions in Asia Minor during the Imperial period. For κάγκελλος, see Jeanne Robert and Louis Robert, "Inscriptions et reliefs d'Asie Mineure," *Hellenica* 9 (1950):47–48; Liddell, Scott, and Jones (see note 20), p. 848. Martin Price and Bluma Trell have published many numismatic representations of temples with barriers surrounding them in *Coins and their Cities* (London: Friary Press Ltd., 1977), pp. 9, 18–19, 144–146, 264–265. For a description of the fences and their functional uses, see E. Will, "L'espace sacrificiel dans les provinces romaines de syrie et d'arabie," in *L'espace sacrificiel dans les civilizations méditerranéennes de l'antiquité*, ed. Roland Étienne and Marie-Thérèse Le Dinahet (Lyon: Bibliothèque Salmon-Reinach, 1991), p. 259. Grillwork screens were used, in fact, as common architectural motifs in sacred and secular Greek and Roman enclosures. See Peter E. Corbett's discussion of Temple "F" at Selinunte and the "screen-walls" that existed in front of the cella in "Greek Temples and Greek Worshippers: The Literary and Archaeological Evidence," *Bulletin of the Institute of Classical Studies* 27 (1970):153, n. 29. And see Scully's (see note 19), p. 207, fig. 405, reference to a "high wall" delineating the *temenos* of Asklepieion at Corinth. Such grillwork formed perforated barriers in upstairs balustrades, windows, and doors precisely because it allowed one to see what lay on the other side of the barrier. The reconstruction of the Temple of Hera at Olympia reveals latticework doors barring access to the sanctuary. See E. Curtis and F. Adler, eds., *Olympia: Die Ergebnisse der von dem Deutschen Reich veranstalteten Ausgrabung* (Berlin, 1890–1897), Tafelband II, Tafel LXXXIV. Rex D. Martienssen discusses varied degrees of visual restrictions and vertical screenings in *The Idea of Space in Greek Architecture* (Johannesburg: Witwatersrand University Press, 1956), pp. 6–7.

27. Not unlike Josephus's description of the *soreg* in the Jerusalem Temple, the Babylonian Talmud elucidates the function of boundary markers in domestic surroundings and their role in disclosing sacred objects and spaces. See my discussion (see note 16), p. 322.

28. The Talmud states only הרי את מקדשת לי, Qiddushin 5b; Yad, Ishuth 3:1. Aryeh Kaplan states that the additional wording זו בטבעת כדת משה וישראל is first found associated with the ketubah in Tosefta, Ketubot 4:9. See his book, *Made in Heaven: A Jewish Wedding Guide* (New York: Maznaim Publishing Corporation, 1983), p. 180.

29. On such "performative language," see J. L. Austin, *How to Do Things with Words* (Cambridge: Harvard University Press, 1962), pp. 4ff.

as told in Numbers 19:2, presents an enigmatic scenario where priests are commanded to slaughter and burn a red, female cow outside the camp in order to remove impurity contracted by someone who has encountered a corpse. The ashes produced by this ritual have the mysterious power of purifying the contaminated person and at the same time defiling the priests officiating. Ritually pure priests who handle these ashes during the procedure "become unclean," must bathe, and wait until sundown in order to enter the Temple again.[30] The simultaneous and inverse power of the ashes—to sanctify that which is unclean and to defile that which is pure—gives testament not only to the fine line that divides the sacred and profane, but also to their interchangeable and transmutable natures. In an instant, the sacred becomes profane and the profane sacred, throwing these polar opposites into dramatic proximity.

Such resonance and slippage between sacred and profane states has occupied much of the theoretical work of Jonathan Z. Smith. Revising elementary distinctions between antithetical constructs, Smith affirms that neither space nor action is inherently sacred or profane, but that both depend upon "emplacement."[31] While working on a dairy farm, for example, Smith observed the head farmer rise every morning, wash his hands thoroughly, and then step outside only to pick up a fistful of soil and rub it over his clean hands. When asked about this, the farmer replied, "Inside the house it's dirt; outside it's earth." On another occasion he remarked, "There's really no such plant as a weed. A rose bush, growing in my cornfield, is a weed."[32] The farmer's outlook confirmed Smith's

view that nothing in itself is intrinsically clean or unclean, pure or impure, sacred or profane. Diverse rules govern incongruous spaces and the boundaries that map out those limits arbitrarily maintain the integrity of "place."[33] Only when something is set within a system of classification does it gain definition; it assumes the "character of its place." Meanings behind the words "dirt," "weed," and even "ashes" can be shuffled to fit different definitions. The tangible and disparate contexts of physical substances "place" them conceptually and ontologically.[34]

Reproductive blood versus sacrificial blood

Perhaps the most striking example of a material substance with oscillating, multifarious meanings in antiquity is blood. Genesis 31:19ff attests to the incompatibility of sacred objects and menstrual blood, for example, in its description of Jacob and Rachel's flight from Laban. In their escape, Rachel steals Laban's religious idols, hides the shanghaied booty in her camel's sack, and sits upon the idols (not exactly a neutral gesture). When her father comes to search for the idols, she apologizes that she cannot rise up before him, saying that the "way of women"—*derek nashim* (דרך נשים)—is upon her. Josephus retells this passage, adding his Second Temple-period interpretation that "Laban then desisted from further search, never supposing that his daughter in that condition would approach the images."[35] Here, menstrual blood and

---

30. Jacob Milgrom explains that the power of the red heifer's ashes depends on the blood contained in the ashes. Moreover, the red of the cow symbolizes the blood needed for purgation in a purification offering. "The Paradox of the Red Cow," *Vetus Testamentum* 31, no. 1 (1981):67. Albert Baumgarten presents another interesting angle on the power of the ashes, speculating that being "too close" to the sacred is dangerous and therefore can bring on a state of impurity. The priests, who are already sacred, come into contact with even more sacredness—the ashes—thereby placing them in greater proximity to the sacred. They must bathe to neutralize this sanctity. Similarly, the High Priest bathes after coming out of the Holy of Holies (Lev. 16) on the Day of Atonement in order to return "to the level of normalcy after his encounter with the sacred." "The Paradox of the Red Heifer," *Vetus Testamentum* 43, no. 4 (1993):446.

31. Jonathan Z. Smith, *To Take Place: Toward Theory in Ritual* (Chicago: University of Chicago Press, 1987), p. 104.

32. Id., *Map is Not Territory* (Chicago: University of Chicago Press, 1978), p. 292.

33. For an examination of shifting spatial meanings in museum-constructed space, see my piece, "Sacrality and Aura in the Museum: Mute Objects and Articulate Space," *The Journal of the Walters Art Gallery* 52/53 (1994/1995):33–47.

34. Another example of objects with changing meanings depending on their contexts can be found in Homer's *Odyssey* where Odysseus takes an oar from his ship and carries it inland until it is mistaken for a winnowing fan used to separate grain. In its migration from the coast, the oar not only loses its naval connotations as it is introduced into a culture unfamiliar with seafaring instruments but gains agricultural associations within the farming community. *The Odyssey* 11.121–137, 23.265–284, trans. Albert Cook (New York: W. W. Norton and Company, 1974), pp. 148, 318. I thank Lewis Hyde for sharing this passage with me.

35. Josephus, *Jewish Antiquities* 1.10 nos. 322–323, trans. H. St. J. Thackeray (Cambridge: Harvard University Press, 1978), pp. 154–155. For one of the best surveys to date on menstruants and their relationship to holiness, see Shaye J. D. Cohen, "Menstruants and the Sacred in Judaism and Christianity," in *Women's History and Ancient History*, ed. Sarah B. Pomeroy (Chapel Hill: University of North Carolina Press, 1991), pp. 271–299.

sacred objects—pagan ones in this case—are figured as mutually exclusive entities.

Within the context of other states of human impurity, Leviticus 12 describes the status of a woman who is associated with lochia (blood from childbirth) or menses; these conditions render her ritually impure and prohibit her from entering a sacred sphere.[36] Leviticus 15:31 explains, "You shall put the Israelites on guard against their uncleanness, unless they die through their uncleanness by defiling My Tabernacle which is among them." Individual uncleanness, therefore, has the power to profane a whole architectural complex. Kelim, 1.3 in the Mishnah further underscores the communicable properties of menses: "blood of a menstruant . . . convey(s) uncleanness both by contact and by carrying."[37]

Mary Douglas has interpreted blood from the female reproductive system, along with other profaning substances emitted by the body, as "marginal stuff" without coherent, definable categories.[38] By being out of its place, menstrual blood—having crossed its natural bodily border—enters the realm of dangerous, threatening substances. Although marginality may explain the exclusion of menses from liturgical spaces, it does not fully account for the spilling of animal blood in sacred, sacrificial rituals. In fact, it is only through the deliberate severing of animal skin and issuing forth of blood from its natural, bounded place and into the sacred altar area that purification and ritual cleansing take place. After a lengthy passage specifying the ritual impurity of female reproductive blood, Leviticus commands the deliberate spreading of sacrificial blood around the altar area and in the Holy of Holies on the Ark of the Covenant. Leviticus 16:14–19 states that Aaron, the High Priest,

> shall take some of the blood of the bull and sprinkle it with his finger over the cover [of the Ark]. . . . When he has made expiation for himself and his household, and for the whole congregation of Israel, he shall go out to the altar that is before the Lord and purge it: he shall take some of the blood of the bull and of the goat and apply it to each of the horns of the altar; and the rest of the blood he shall sprinkle on it with his finger seven times. Thus he shall cleanse it [*tohoro* (טהרו)] of the uncleanness of the Israelites and consecrate it [*qodsho* (קדשו)].

In this ritual context, blood actually "cleanses" and "consecrates" unclean objects and people.[39] Within the realm of sacred space, therefore, different types of blood oscillate between categories of sacred and profane in conjunction with certain rituals, personages, and places.[40] While female reproductive blood is singled out as *the* pollutant demanding the longest period of purification, sacrificial blood is likewise singled out as *the* mandatory substance for successful, sacred ritual.[41]

---

36. For an excellent study examining the meanings of menstrual taboos in various cultures, see Thomas Buckley and Alma Gottlieb, eds., *Blood Magic: The Anthropology of Menstruation* (Berkeley: University of California Press, 1988), especially the Introduction, pp. 3–50. For a less theoretical work, see Arthur Frederick Ide, *Women in Ancient Israel and Under the Torah and Talmud* (Mesquite, Texas: Ide House, 1982), pp. 3–4.

37. David P. Wright discusses the communicability of impurities in his fascinating book, *The Disposal of Impurity* (Atlanta: Scholars Press, 1987), pp. 163ff., 189ff. Menstruation and the process of generation was one female activity that eluded men's control. See Helen King's treatment of the negative and positive perceptions of menstruation in antiquity in her essay, "Bound to Bleed: Artemis and Greek Women," in *Images of Women in Antiquity*, ed. Averil Cameron and Amélie Kuhrt (London: Croom Helm, 1983), p. 111. The Hebrew word *niddah* (נדה) means "isolation," or "condition of uncleanness." As Jacob Milgrom has pointed out, by extension the term was used for a menstruant as well, that is, that which is isolated. *Leviticus 1–16: The Anchor Bible* (New York: Doubleday, 1991), p. 745; Jastrow (see note 8), p. 878.

38. Mary Douglas (see note 6), p. 121, explains: "All margins are dangerous. . . . Any structure of ideas is vulnerable at its margins. We should expect the orifices of the body to symbolise its specially vulnerable points. Matter issuing from them is marginal stuff of the most obvious kind. Spittle, blood, milk, urine, faeces or tears by simply issuing forth have traversed the boundary of the body." Also see the discussion of "released" female blood among the Bamana and the inherent powers possessed by the blood after its departure from the body in Sarah C. Brett-Smith's essay, "Symbolic Blood: Cloths for Excised Women," *RES: Anthropology and Aesthetics* 3 (1982):16.

39. For a discussion of blood as well as other defiling substances and activities that exclude admittance in ancient temple *temene*, see Parker (see note 19), pp. 37, 50, 64–66, 352–356.

40. B. Berakot 32b in the Talmud describes another association with blood, specifically in murder, that changes the status of a sacred personage. "R. Johanan said, A priest who has committed manslaughter should not lift his hands [to say the priestly benediction] since it says [in this context], 'Your hands are full of blood.'" Here and in the case of a menstruant, certain categories of blood defile both a personage and space. See also Parker's chapter on murder and sacrifice (see note 19), pp. 104–143. M. Qiddushin 1:8 states that men, not women, must sprinkle the blood of women's sacrificial offerings. Also see Léonie J. Archer, "The Role of Jewish Women in Religion, Ritual and Cult of Graeco-Roman Palestine," in *Images of Women in Antiquity*, ed. Averil Cameron and Amélie Kuhrt (London: Croom Helm, 1983), p. 279.

41. As I shall discuss further in this article, impure conditions, such as corpse contamination, scale disease, and emission of semen, require a one- to eight-day period of purification, while parturients require forty to eighty days of purification after the birth of a child. See

Robert Parker comments that the power of sacrifice in ancient societies is linked precisely to "the contact with blood, a repugnant, polluting substance, in a controlled ritual context that renders the threat tolerable."[42] Animal blood—out of its normal, bodily borders—figuratively changes by reason of its new context and association with ritual. Bounded temple space becomes, in essence, its new skin. In the words of Mircea Eliade, "any object becomes *something else*, yet it continues to remain *itself*" when placed in relation to the sacred.[43]

The chameleon-like nature of blood is even more evident in the sacrificial ritual. At a critical moment within the Temple service, leftover blood from the sacrificial victim must be discarded carefully. As a highly charged substance within the Temple's precincts, this superfluous element risks contaminating the entire area. In the Jerusalem Temple, small holes in the southwest corner of the altar's base lead to a water channel that carries unused sacrificial blood out of consecrated space and into the Kidron Valley where it is sold to farmers for fertilizer.[44] Here, sacrificial blood navigates its way geographically and symbolically through a complicated system of identifiable states: from its mundane existence within the victim's body, to a consecrated status in relation to sacred ritual and space, and finally to its metamorphosis into purchasable commodity. Sacred and profane, clean and unclean are defined by closely knit, permeable membranes that allow blood to circulate among them.

Unlike sacrificial blood, however, menstrual blood remains disconnected from any regulated system of ritual practices inside temple precincts and prevails as a threatening impurity.[45] Howard Eilberg-Schwartz has suggested that "controllability"—a crucial factor that distinguishes sacrificial blood from menstrual blood—may determine the meaning of other bodily fluids as well. Sacrificial blood, like the blood of male

circumcision, is *shed with intent* and ritual design. The shedding of circumcised blood requires no purification period for those who come into contact with it while a woman's defilement does. Eilberg-Schwartz states:

> The distinction between control and lack of control is . . . implied in the contrast between circumcision (male blood) and sacrifice, on the one hand, and blood of birth on the other. In circumcision and sacrifice, blood is intentionally spilled, whereas a woman's blood flows uncontrollably during and after the birthing process.[46]

In accordance with this theory, the emission of semen—a substance associated with reproductive powers, like menses or lochia—renders a Jewish male unclean depending on the controllability of the emission. Leviticus 15 confirms this by describing two categories of male impurity linked to semen. If a man has an uncontrollable issue of semen, he is unclean for seven days and must present a sin offering and burnt offering at the Temple for purification.[47] If, however, a man has an issue of semen during intercourse with a woman—that is, an emission with intent—he and his partner will be unclean only until the same evening. While the ability to govern bodily emissions reveals one differentiating characteristic between sacrificial and menstrual blood, it does not fully account for all types of blood spilling (such as murder—an act carried out with decisive intent). The following ancient source further complicates the problem.

Josephus, the first-century Jewish historian who officiated in the Jerusalem Temple, delineates its spatial limitations by stating:

> The outer court was open to all, foreigners included; *women during their impurity were alone refused admission.* To the second court all Jews were permitted and, when uncontaminated by any defilement, their wives; to the third, male Jews, if clean and purified; to the fourth, the priests.[48]

We learn from this passage that "the outer court was open to all," including potentially impure foreigners and Jewish males (see figs. 1–2). Only menstruants were

---

Jacob Milgrom's "Table of Purification Procedures and Effects" (see note 37), pp. 986–987, which clearly lists a variety of impurities and their purification regulations.

42. Parker (see note 19), p. 373.

43. Eliade (see note 4), p. 12. See Smith (see note 31), p. 110.

44. See David Wright's (see note 37), pp. 155–156, examination of the Temple's "sewer for sacrificial refuse."

45. Paradoxically, however, the very word "rite" seems to come from the Sanskrit "ritu," which means "any settled point of time, fixed time, time appointed for any action" *and* "the menstrual discharge." See Rosemary J. Dudley, "She Who Bleeds, Yet Does Not Die," *Heresies* 5 (1978):112.

---

46. Howard Eilberg-Schwartz, *The Savage in Judaism* (Bloomington: Indiana University Press, 1990), pp. 180–182.

47. See this interpretation of the text in Cohen (see note 35), p. 274.

48. Emphasis added. Josephus, *Against Apion* 2.8 nos. 102–105 (see note 15), pp. 332–335; *Jewish Wars* 5.5.2 nos. 193–194 (see note 15), pp. 256–259. Note the discrepancy with M. Kelim, 1.6–9. For a discussion of the inclusion and exclusion of Jewish women from liturgy, see Archer (see note 40), pp. 278ff; Cohen (see note 35), p. 282.

excluded. According to Josephus, it seems that a foreigner or Jewish male with a bodily issue—a bloody cut?—could enter where a menstruating woman could not. Even in the exterior court, outside the bounds of the symbolically charged *soreg*, menstrual blood alone is deemed taboo. As we begin to see, bodily issues—controllable or uncontrollable—are not homogeneously perceived or defined. In the case of menses and circumcision blood, Eilberg-Schwartz further explains their discrepancy in terms of the "gender of blood."[49] Here we begin to scratch the surface of the incredibly complex associations of blood. The *telos* or destination of women's reproductive blood implies life-giving functions. And the basic importance of blood as the agency of life in ancient Hebrew traditions cannot be over emphasized. The Hebrew God explicitly forbids the consumption of blood, saying "the flesh with its life, which is its blood, you shall not eat" (Genesis 9:3) and:

> I will set my face against that person that eats blood, and will cut him off from among his people. For the life of the flesh is in the blood, and I have given it to you upon the altar to make atonement for your souls, for it is the blood that makes an atonement for the soul.
>
> *Leviticus 17:10ff*

Blood unquestionably means life in the Hebrew tradition. As Jacob Milgrom has interpreted it, "Life is inviolable; it may not be treated lightly. Mankind has a right to nourishment, not to life. Hence the blood, the symbol of life, must be drained, returned to the universe, to God."[50] Sacrificial blood and female reproductive blood are both associated with the forces of life. Moreover, the discrepancy even between monthly menses and the blood of childbirth points to the extra attention given to the life-engendering powers of lochia. After completing menstruation, a woman must wait seven days before gaining access into sacrosanct grounds. After childbirth, that is to say after generating life, she must wait forty days if it is a boy child and

eighty days if it is a girl child. A girl child represents yet another potentially life-bearing power. The danger presented to sacred space by a woman who has just created a female infant is unrivaled.

Creation, of course, belongs to the divine realm. In the beginning, Genesis tells us that God creates. The text also belies, however, that woman creates as well. After the first human birth, Eve says a curious thing: קניתי איש את-יהוה (Genesis 4:1). Scholars have anguished over the translation of this enigmatic phrase. It is the only biblical passage that allows a mortal "to create" with the same verb with which God creates—*qnh* (קנה). Umberto Cassuto's classic translation, "I have created a man equally with God," places the female act of giving birth on par with powers in the sacred sphere.[51] Umberto Cassuto even interprets Eve's maternal proclamation as "arrogance," commenting, "the first woman, in her joy at giving birth to her first son, boasts of her generative power, which approximates in her estimation to the Divine creative power."[52] In any event, the explicit biblical linking of God's creative potency to giving birth has far reaching implications for the traditional conception of women's procreative potentials. While it is God's breath that endows human beings with life and soul, it is Eve's blood that acts as the generative agent, further establishing the soul-blood connection associated with sacrificial blood. Do human creation and the life-embodying (female) blood that accompanies it represent comparable, yet antagonistic forces to those embodied by sacrificial blood within Temple territory?

Biblical texts figure both blood on the altar and female reproductive blood linguistically as "purifying bloods." Leviticus 12:4 states that a woman, after giving birth to a child, "shall then continue in *the blood of her purifying* (תשב בדמי טהרה) . . . she shall touch no

49. "The relationship of circumcision (male blood) to blood of birth corresponds to the oppositions between men and women as well as to the opposition between control and lack of control. Through a kind of ritual transitivity, the contrast in bloods generates an association between gender and control." Eilberg-Schwartz (see note 46), p. 188.

50. Milgrom (see note 37), p. 713. Such prohibitions against consuming blood have given rise to Jewish Orthodox customs of preparing or "koshering" meat by soaking or salting the blood out of it. See these methods in Hayim Halevy Donin, *To Be a Jew* (New York: Basic Books, 1972), pp. 107–111.

51. The verb קנה has elicited considerable conjecture because it mostly means "to buy, possess, acquire" when a human being is its subject. In this sense, Eve acquires a man-child. But קנה also carries the meaning "to form, produce, create," in a variety of passages (Gen. 14:19, 22; Exod. 15:16; Deut. 32:6; Ps. 74:2; 78:54; 139:13; Prov. 8:22). In all of these, however, God is the subject of the verb. Such divine powers are further indicated in the last part of the phrase את-יהוה. This construction has been hotly debated. It has been translated as, "with the help of the Lord," "from Yahweh," or even "equally with the Lord." See Claus Westermann, *Genesis 1–11: A Commentary* (Minneapolis: Augsburg Publishing House, 1974), pp. 281–292, for a listing of the most prominent interpretations. I thank Rabbi Paul Laderman for pointing this passage out to me.

52. Umberto Cassuto, *A Commentary on the Book of Genesis*, trans. Israel Abrahams (Jerusalem: Magnes Press, 1961), p. 201.

hallowed thing, nor come into the sanctuary until the days of her purifying are fulfilled."[53] Analogously, sacrificial blood represents a purifying mechanism in its own setting.[54] Both bloods, from radically disparate sources with seemingly opposite relationships to the sacred, are joined in function by the same term, *thr* (טהר), meaning "to purify." Could the evidence pointing to parallels between female reproductive blood—a profane substance with generative, purifying powers— and sacrificial blood—a sacred, purifying substance containing the essence of life—position the two bloods too close for comfort? And might this proximity present an "adversarial" relationship? The answer lies in Leviticus itself. After a parturient completes her blood of purifying, the text states:

> And when the days of her purifying are fulfilled, for a son or for a daughter, she shall bring a lamb . . . and a young pigeon, or a turtledove, for a sin offering, to . . . the priest who shall offer it before the Lord, and make atonement for her; and she shall be cleansed [*tohorah* (טהרה)] from the source of her blood. [55]

Leviticus 12:6–7

Sacrificial blood on the altar cancels out reproductive blood from a woman's procreative source. The operative principle at work here is blood against blood. And if sacrificial blood negates the hazardous powers of reproductive blood in a sacred space, might lochia present the same danger to sacrificial ritual? To help illuminate this question, we must determine the shifting significance of blood in the broader context of antiquity and bring into the discussion relevant Greek and Roman sources.[56]

Blood: anointing pollutant

According to Greek religious customs, birth, defecation, sexual intercourse, and death were generally banned from sacred *topoi*.[57] The expressions reserved for women and foreigners under such religious restrictions were *ou themis*, or "it is not sanctioned by custom," and *ouch hosia/ouch hosion*, or "it is not sanctioned by divine law."[58] Analogous to Israelite taboos, certain restrictions kept menstruants out of sacred places in the ancient pagan world as well. Prohibitive inscriptions concerning menstruants have been found from the second century B.C.E. on and in wide-ranging locations, such as Arcadia, Delos, Ptolemaïs, Attica, and Lindos.[59]

"Whatever complexities, layers, and changes in cultural tradition underlie the individual peculiarities, it is astounding, details aside, to observe the similarity of action and experience from Athens to Jerusalem and on to Babylon." The history of the Jewish tradition and its sacrificial system developed in relation to various Near Eastern cultures long before its practice in the Roman-period edifice in Jerusalem. My aim, then, is not to examine the mutual influence among Greek, Roman, and Jewish sacrificial systems, as others before me have done (see Royden Keith Yerkes, *Sacrifice in Greek and Roman Religions and Early Judaism* [London: Adams and Charles Black, 1952]; W. Robertson Smith [see note 4], and his discussion of blood, pp. 239–270); nor is it to provide a comprehensive survey of the perception of blood and sacrifice in these societies. Rather, I set out to underscore some points of resonance and dissonance in these traditions' respective treatments of menstruants and their relationship to sacred, sacrificial spaces.

57. Susan Guettel Cole, "*Gynaiki Ou Themis*: Gender Difference in the Greek *Leges Sacrae*," *Helios* 19, nos. 1–2 (1992):107. See Burkert (see note 19), p. 35. Also see his discussion of laws against sexual intercourse within temple precincts in relation to mythological exceptions and the sacrificial associations of deflowering in the cult of Aphrodite. Burkert (see note 25), p. 60, n. 11, pp. 62–63.

58. Cole (see note 57), p. 106. Like the Jerusalem Temple, each Greek and Roman temple carried its own specific legal system of admittance. In Greece, for example, foreigners were universally excluded without the official intervention of a Greek citizen. See Marcel Detienne, "Violents *eugénies*: En pleines Thesmophories des femmes couvertes de sang," in *La cuisine du sacrifice en pays grec*, ed. M. Detienne and J. P. Vernant (Paris: Gallimard, 1979), p. 186.

59. Because many of these sacred laws are associated with immigrant cults (Isis and Sarapis, the Syrian gods, a Hellenistic cult in Egypt, and Men Tyrannos) and because no epigraphical evidence about menstruation exists from sacred *topoi* before the second century B.C.E., Cole and von Staden suggest that laws stipulating purity from menstrual pollution may express an Eastern influence on Greek and Roman practices. See Cole (see note 57), p. 111; von Staden (see note 1), p. 14. Robert Parker (see note 19), p. 102, postulates, however, that there are limited explicit references to menses as pollution at temple entrances because female menstruation "was so secret and shaming that it could not be alluded to at all, even to the extent of requiring purity from it in sacred law." Also see Sarah B. Pomeroy, *Women in*

53. Emphasis added. Lev. 12:5 repeats the same phrase with a prepositional change: תשב על-דמי טהרה. Jacob Milgrom (see note 37), p. 749, translates דמי טהרה (*deme tohorah*) as "blood purity" and speculates that it is "a frozen idiom that refers exclusively to the parturient's state."

54. Sacrificial blood is used with the verb טהר, "to purify," in Lev. 16:19 and Ezekiel 43:26.

55. For commentary on the "sin" aspect of this offering, see Milgrom (see note 37), p. 760. For rabbinic interpretation, see Jacob Neusner, *The Idea of Purity in Ancient Judaism* (Leiden: E. J. Brill, 1973), pp. 84–85.

56. In this transition I take note of Bruno Dombrowski's warning (meant as a critical review of Walter Burkert's work) against equating sacrificial systems "across the board." "Killing in Sacrifice: The Most Profound Experience of God?" *Numen* 23 (1976):138. Burkert (see note 25), pp. 9–10, affirms that "ritual details varied greatly among the Greeks themselves," and points out parallel methods of sacrifice between Old Testament rites and Greek practices, stating that,

Sacred rules designate specific periods of time before ritually impure women were allowed to enter a sacred precinct: a day or less after intercourse, six to nine days after menstruation, a minimum of nine and up to twenty-one days after giving birth, and forty days after miscarriage.[60] Menstruation, childbirth, and miscarriage require the longest periods of purification and all of these biological activities involve a flow of blood from the reproductive system. Furthermore, the event of miscarriage comprises three polluting taboos—menstruation, childbirth, and death—and hence calls for a lengthier purification period.

A woman's state of ritual impurity bears heavily not only on her own status for cult participation, but on those who come into contact with her. The earliest text to mention women contaminated by childbirth derives from a Cyrene purification law:

> the woman in childbed shall pollute the roof . . . she shall not pollute (anyone) outside the roof unless he comes in. The man who is inside, he himself shall be polluted for three days, but he shall not pollute anyone else, not wherever this man goes.[61]

This passage emphasizes the spatial limits of defilement connected to a woman, the source and carrier of impurity, and the nature of her architectural surroundings—any area under the same structural roof. The law is not, however, concerned with the cultic status of the laboring mother as much as it is with how she affects others. The Jewish tradition similarly places a great emphasis on female purity precisely because it determines the cultic purity of men with whom they have relations. In the Mishnah, for example, the discussion of female menstruation does not even appear under the Division on Women, Nashim, which is devoted to women's matters. Rather, menstruation appears in the Division on Purity, Tohoroth, because a menstruant affects the cultic purity of others.[62] Both

Greek and Hebrew examples underscore, then, the communicability of menstrual impurity.

Nevertheless, not all ancient sources figure menstrual blood as an unequivocal pollutant; several in fact frame menses as a conveyor of sacral powers, perceived as both positive and negative.[63] Greek and Roman writers—from Aristotle, pseudo-Democritus, and Aelian to Plutarch and Pliny the Elder—attribute miraculous forces, agricultural and medicinal, to menstrual blood. While menses, on the one hand, can separate asphalt, dim mirrors, spoil wine, blight trees and crops, blunt knives, kill bees, corrode metal, and madden dogs,[64] menstrual blood also has the ability to kill locusts, cure fevers, act as a fertility drug, relieve tumors, and avert hail or whirlwinds from vineyards.[65] Pollutants are, therefore, simultaneously contaminating and powerfully effective against pollution itself.[66]

This idea of using pollutants to cancel out other pollutants lies at the heart of the sacrificial ritual within the bounds of temple *temene*. Blood, a substance loaded with dangerous, forbidden properties connected to life itself, is shed to erase other dangerous forces. We have already seen this in the ritual cleansing of Jewish parturients through the shedding of sacrificial blood. The

Hellenistic Egypt from Alexander to Cleopatra (New York: Schocken, 1984), pp. 136–137.

60. See Cole (see note 57), p. 110; von Staden (see note 1), p. 14.

61. *Lois Sacrées des Cités grecques*, supplement, ed. F. Sokolowski (Paris, 1969), 115A.16–20; Cole (see note 57), p. 109; Parker (see note 19), p. 336.

62. Judith Romney Wegner, *Chattel or Person? The Status of Women in the Mishnah* (New York: Oxford University Press, 1988), p. 163. For a sociological study of menstruating women as defilement to the purity of men, see the chapter "Menstrual Restrictions and Sex Segregation Practices" in *The Politics of Reproductive Ritual*, Karen

Ericksen Paige and Jeffrey M. Paige (Berkeley: University of California Press, 1981), pp. 209–254.

63. Compare with the work Mary Douglas has done on Australian aborigines, the Murngin and Arunta, where female menstruation is seen as a show of creative force; therefore, the genitals of boys are incised during initiation rites to draw blood in imitation of the menstrual flow of women. *Implicit Meanings* (London: Routledge & Kegan Paul, 1975), p. 65.

64. Pliny, *Natural History* 7.15.64–65, trans. H. Rackham (Cambridge: Harvard University Press, 1942), pp. 548–549.

65. Ibid., 17, 47, pp. 266–267. Pliny states, "There is no limit to woman's power. First of all, they say that hailstorms and whirlwinds are driven away if menstrual fluid is exposed to the very flashes of lightening . . . wild indeed are the stories told of the mysterious and awful power of the menstrous discharge itself. . . . Of these tales I may without shame mention the following: if this female power should issue when the moon or sun is in eclipse, it will cause irremediable harm. . . . So much greater then is the power of a menstrous woman. . . . I have said much about this virulent discharge . . . not even fire, the all-conquering, overcomes it. . . ." Ibid., 27, 23, pp. 77–87. See also von Staden (see note 1), pp. 14–16, nn. 53, 67; Parker (see note 19), pp. 102–103, nn. 116–117. For a less academic discussion of the powers of menstruation, see Judy Grahn, "From Sacred Blood to the Curse and Beyond," in *The Politics of Women's Spirituality*, ed. Charlene Spretnak (Garden City, New York: Anchor Books, 1982), pp. 267ff.

66. Several authors have said this before. In this context, for example, see von Staden (see note 1), p. 16.

ceremonial effectiveness of blood lies, then, in its own "defiling power." Blood stands as a metonymic referent for the pollution destined to be effaced.[67] The most famous of such nullifications in the Greek world were absolutions from murder through the killing of the sacrificial victim. Hence Heraclitus criticizes the practice stating, "Vainly they cleanse themselves with blood when they are polluted by blood, as if a man who had stepped into mud were to wash himself in mud."[68] Likewise, the use of menstrual blood, an impure and taboo substance, to work beneficial magic against other impurities, indicates the sacral power attributed to menses, especially concerning matters of fertility, life, and death.[69]

In addition to Pliny's list of the polluting effects of menses, he also acknowledges that this "pernicious mischief" that occurs in a woman every month "is the material for human generation." It represents the very stuff that "inspires life" and "endows body" to the human form.[70] In its generative abilities then, reproductive blood achieves something akin to the divine. In this sense, Parker maintains that "in some contexts, pollution acquires positive powers; the impure, normally shunned, becomes 'sacred' in the sense that it is marked out as powerful in contrast to the nonpolluted objects of familiar use."[71] This multivalent nature of pollution lies at the very heart of the word "taboo." The etymology of taboo, from the Polynesian word *tapu*, renders *ta* as a verb meaning "to mark," and *pu* as an adverb signifying "intensely." Something *tapu*, or "taboo," is "marked thoroughly"; it is neither positive nor negative, simply highly marked. The opposite of taboo, therefore, is something "unmarked" or "common," that is to say without holy or forbidden distinctions.[72] The question arises again: in its highly marked status as a taboo substance, could menstrual blood risk canceling out the potency of sacrificial blood if present within the same sphere?

Figure 3. Greek red-figure lecythus showing a woman approaching the altar and bearing a basket—a *canoun*—used to hold the sacrificial knife and other ritual objects, second quarter of the fifth century B.C.E. H: 12.9 cm. FR,CA 2567. Photo: Courtesy of Musée du Louvre, Département des Antiquités grecques, étrusques et romaines, Laurence Fossé.

The answer may reside in the religious roles allowed and denied women in sacred spaces. Biblical and Talmudic passages consistently describe the exclusion of Jewish women from priestly, sacrificial duties and from sacred areas immediately surrounding sacrificial places. In Greek and Roman religions, on the other hand, ancient sources inform us that women participated in liturgical practices and performed most cultic activities—that is, except for the actual shedding of blood in sacrifice. The Canephorae, for example, were young women who carried the sacrificial knife in their baskets of barley but were not allowed to use it. The Greek lecythus in figure 3 (ca. 480 B.C.E.) depicts such a basket bearer approaching the altar within a temple setting, synecdochally indicated by the single, standing column behind her. She holds a three-pronged wicker

67. Parker (see note 19), p. 233. See also Brett-Smith (see note 38), pp. 23–24.

68. Quoted by Parker (see note 19), pp. 371–372, n. 10.

69. See von Staden's (see note 1), pp. 9–14, discussion of animal excrement, a pollutant, used in order to render women "pure."

70. Pliny, *Natural History* 7.15.64–65 (see note 64), pp. 548–549.

71. Parker (see note 19), p. 233.

72. I draw here from Franz Steiner's *Taboo* (London: Cohen and West, Ltd., 1956), pp. 32, 82. Also see Buckley and Gottlieb (see note 36), p. 8.

basket, a *canoun*, that traditionally housed the sacrificial knife, seeds to be thrown on the fire and altar, as well as bandalets to be attached to the sacrificial victim.[73] Likewise, female water carriers provided the liquid used for honing the sacrificial knives and axes in the Bouphonia festival in Athens, but they did not employ the instruments of sacrifice.[74] A fifth-century, white-figure dish used for ritual libations shows a *chorus* of women—including a female musician playing a reed flute (*aulos*)—actually dancing around a sacrifice burning on the altar (fig. 4).[75] If we take these representations as any indication of actual practices, women's proximity to the altar and sacrifice is striking, yet no indication exists of their actually executing the sacrificial act itself. Similarly, the Vestal virgins, as public priestesses in Rome, were also central to sacrificial ritual but were only allowed to enact the final phase of animal sacrifice by burning the part of the victim passed to them after its death.[76] The Thesmophoria, a festival connected to Demeter and Kore, is one of the most telling Greek ceremonies in this respect, because it was solely administered by women. On the third day there was a blood sacrifice that the women oversaw but did not themselves execute. The final, fatal blow represented the single ritual act that stood beyond their functions. Instead, inscriptions attest to a *mageiros*, a male butcher or cook, who entered the *temenos*, delivered the sacrificial stroke, and immediately fled the temple

grounds.[77] The *Dyskolos* of Menander mentions the same practice of *mageiroi* carrying out sacrifices that were offered by women to Pan.[78] And as Marcel Detienne points out, the very term for slaughterer in sacrificial systems, *mageiros*, does not even exist in the feminine form in ancient Greek.[79]

These sources indicate that Greek and Roman women had access to sacred spaces and could participate in cultic activities except for the actual blood-shedding of the sacrificial animal. And yet in spite of women refraining from ritual sacrifice, it seems that they were still banned from sacrificial areas when associated with the blood of childbirth, miscarriage, or menstruation. These biological states are closely linked, of course, to sexuality and reproduction. Such human, generative associations may be incongruous with spaces designated for the gods. Astonishingly, *temno*—the verb root for *temenos*, or "sacred precinct"—additionally carries the meaning "to castrate." In Lucian's work, *De Dea Syria*, for example, Rhea ritually castrates Attis (ἔτεμεν) to prepare him for religious service for her.[80] Could a *temenos* also be considered a "castrated space?" For ritual precincts to be effective, must mortal powers of sexuality and reproduction be severed from them? Such neuterment manifests itself in the universal prohibitions against birth, death, sexual intercourse, and menses within temple *temene*, as well as in the important role that virgins and eunuchs play in certain temple traditions. Moreover, certain pagan practices of castrating sacrificial victims represent actions that would both underscore the animal's virility and simultaneously cancel it out.[81]

---

73. See François Lissarrague, "Figures of Women," in *A History of Women in the West*, ed. Pauline Schmitt Pantel (Cambridge: The Belknap Press of Harvard University Press, 1992), p. 186.

74. See Louise Bruit Zaidman, "Pandora's Daughters and Rituals in Grecian Cities," in *A History of Women in the West*, ed. Pauline Schmitt Pantel (Cambridge: The Belknap Press of Harvard University Press, 1992), pp. 344–345.

75. Lissarrague (see note 73), p. 184.

76. See Ovid, *Fasti* 4, 637–640; Tertullian, *Spectacles* 5; Prudentius, *Contra Synmachus* 2.1107; all quoted in John Scheid's excellent article discussing women's sacrificial rites, "The Religious Role of Roman Women," in *A History of Women in the West*, ed. Pauline Schmitt Pantel (Cambridge: The Belknap Press of Harvard University Press, 1992), p. 383, nn. 22–23, 25. We learn of only two festivals where women might have actually carried out the sacrifice themselves. At Fortuna Muliebris, during a celebration of a war against Coriolanus where women, not men, saved the republic, the story indicates a symbolic change of gender: "On this occasion matrons acted like men at war, and so too they acted like men in the commemorative cult." Ibid., p. 389. Similarly, women might have administered sacrifices in the cult of Bona Dea, which represented "an upside-down world in which women assume masculine roles." Ibid., p. 393.

77. See Isaeus 8.19–20, quoted in Zaidman (see note 74), p. 351. See another discussion of the Thesmophoria festival and women's control of agricultural fertility *through their menstrual blood* in a book by Penelope Shuttle and Peter Redgrove, *The Wise Wound: Eve's Curse and Everywoman* (New York: Richard Marek Publishers, 1978), pp. 182–183. For Roman traditions, Scheid (see note 76), pp. 379, 388, states that "women of all ranks bore responsibility for a public festival, but . . . one that concerned them directly and involved no blood sacrifice." *Lanii*, always male butchers, often carried out the sacrifice itself for both men and women.

78. Detienne (see note 58), p. 109, n. 3.

79. Ibid., p. 207.

80. Lucian, *The Syrian Goddess* 15, trans. Herbert A. Strong (London: Constable & Company, Ltd., 1913), p. 56; Liddell, Scott, and Jones (see note 20), p. 1775.

81. For castration and abstinence in preparation for sacrifice in relation to early hunting rituals, see Burkert (see note 25), pp. 59–69.

Figure 4. Interior of Attic white-ground dish used for libations with depiction of female chorus dancing around burning sacrifice on the altar, ca. 440 B.C.E. Diam: 22.5 cm. Inv. 65.908. Edwin E. Jack Fund. Photo: Courtesy of Museum of Fine Arts, Boston.

If temple *temene* can be thought of as places purified of human sexuality, the analogy between the life-forces of sacrificial blood and women's reproductive blood would tend to establish a tension between the religious realms of these two bloods. Helen King has shown, in fact, that ancient Greek perceptions of menses are strongly connected with sacrificial imagery.[82] Aristotle, for example, explicitly compares the *gyne* (a woman after puberty) to a sacrificial animal, saying menstrual blood is "like that of a freshly slaughtered beast" (*hoion neosphakteon*).[83] The Hippocratic texts further state that in a healthy woman during both childbirth and menstruation, "the blood flows like that of a sacrificed victim" (*choreei de haima hoion apo hiereiou*).[84] And Empedocles calls the fetal sac an *amnion*, the same term Homer employs, exceptionally enough, for the bowl that collects blood in sacrifice.[85] Crucial to these comparisons of women's blood to sacrificial blood is the striking absence of similar analogies with any other kind of bleeding. Such approximations between human blood and sacrificial blood are exclusive to gynecological tractates.[86]

Literary and iconographical traditions further associate women's blood with sacrifice. A Greek amphora by the Timiandes Painter shows Polyxena held over a burning altar as her throat is cut in sacrificial ritual (fig. 5).[87] Another image, taken from an Etruscan sarcophagus in Volterra, shows the sacrifice of Iphigeneia from Aeschylus's *Agamemnon* (fig. 6). The text tells us that Agamemnon commands his henchmen to "hoist her over the altar like a yearling, give it all your strength!" [88] The slayer holds the *amnion* symbolically over her head, visually connecting the blood-collecting vessel with Iphigeneia's female reproductive potential. Additional linguistic evidence accentuates the affinity between women's blood and sacrificial blood. The Hippocratic writings refer to menstruation with precisely the same terms—*katharsis, kathairô*—employed to describe ritual sanctification from defilement.[89] This parallels Hebrew notions of "purification" in conjunction to sacrificial and reproductive bloods. In antiquity, the power of women's blood seems to be inextricably linked—linguistically, conceptually, and materially—to the force and function of sacrificial blood in its relationship to life, death, and purification.[90]

Blood represents a complex fabric of sacred and profane associations decipherable at several levels. Menses is an ungovernable, nonritualized, female-gendered matter, as opposed to the blood of sacrifice, a substance easily controlled and manipulated almost entirely by men. Women's reproductive blood is endowed with procreative forces similar in importance to the life-force of sacrificial blood. Consequently, it is

82. See Helen King's valuable study, "Sacrificial Blood: The Role of the *Amnion* in Ancient Gynecology," *Helios* 13, no. 2 (1987):117–126. Also see Ann Ellis Hanson's treatment of sacrifice and defloration in "The Medical Writers' Woman," in *Before Sexuality: The Construction of Erotic Experience in the Ancient Greek World*, ed. David M. Halperin, John J. Winkler, and Froma I. Zeitlin (Princeton: Princeton University Press, 1990), pp. 326–327; and Anne Carson's discussion of Greek women as "leaky" and "boundless" in "Putting Her in Her Place: Woman, Dirt, and Desire," in *Before Sexuality: The Construction of Erotic Experience in the Ancient Greek World*, ed. David M. Halperin, John J. Winkler, and Froma I. Zeitlin (Princeton: Princeton University Press, 1990), pp. 153–164.

83. Aristotle, *Historia Animalium* 581b 1–2; see King's discussion of this passage (see note 37), pp. 120–122, (see note 82), p. 117.

84. *De morbis mulierum* 1.6, 1.72, and 2.113; also *De natura pueris* 18; also cited in King (see note 82), p. 117.

85. *Odyssey* 3.444. See King's (see note 82), p. 121, etymological treatment of this term and comparison with *sphageion*, the classical word for the bowl that collected sacrificial blood.

86. King (see note 82), p. 119. Her interpretation of these comparisons is very different from mine, although no doubt correct at a social-critical level. She sees the semblance of women's blood with sacrificial blood as a Greek inclination to place women on an animal, subhuman level and as part "of a wider system of classification of male and female, in which women are excluded from culturally significant acts which involve shedding the blood of others (war, sacrifice, butchery), and that can be extended to the way in which female anatomy and physiology are imagined to work. Men shed the blood of others: women naturally bleed from their own bodies." Ibid., p. 120.

87. I was first introduced to this imagery in Joan B. Connelly's "Parthenon and *Parthenoi*: A Mythological Interpretation of the Parthenon Frieze," *American Journal of Archaeology* 100, no. 1 (1996):62–63. See also A. J. N. W. Prag, *The Oresteia: Iconographic and Narrative Tradition* (Chicago: Bolchazy Carducci, 1985), pp. 61–67; Gabriella Barbieri and Jean-Louis Durand, "Con il bue a spalla," *Bolletino d'arte del Ministero della Pubblica Istruzione* 29 (1985):1–16.

88. Aeschylus, *The Orestia*, trans. Robert Fagles (New York: The Viking Press, 1975), p. 100, ll. 229-232.

89. Von Staden (see note 1), p. 15, n. 59.

90. This rapport with sacrality might be described as both holy and profane at the same time. In fact, the Greek term for sacred—*hagios* (ἅγιος)—contains meanings that are, likewise, potentially contradictory. While the primary definition of something *hagios* is "revered and pure," the secondary sense situates it as something "accursed, taboo, and dangerous." Liddell, Scott, and Jones (see note 20), p. 9. The fine line between the bivalency of this single term corresponds to the fine line between the symbolic powers of sacred purity and profane impurity. Burkert (see note 19), p. 270; Parker (see note 19), p. 328.

Figure 5. Timiandes Painter, Tyrrhenian black-figure amphora illustrating the *Sacrifice of Polyxena*. H: 15 in. No. 1897.7-27.2. Photo: Courtesy of Trustees of the British Museum, London.

prohibited from places that are designated for divine commission because of its human generative powers. Moreover, within the sacred, sacrificial precincts of ancient traditions, the hierarchy of mortal performers did not permit females to carry out the actual sacrificial act. Women would have wielded an immense religious power had they been able both to spill the blood of animals in rituals of fertility, propitiation, and purification *and* to control the natural processes of procreation. Extraordinary Greek and Latin sources figure menstrual blood—an impure and taboo substance in most contexts—as an element that actually cancels out other impurities. While these literary sources expound on the symbolic powers of menses, explicitly comparing female reproductive blood to the blood of sacrificed animals, biblical texts point to the immense forces contained in blood in general and to the cleansing and expunging powers of female reproductive blood in particular. The tension fostered by the synchronous presence of sacrificial blood and reproductive blood in the same bounded, sacred spaces may have given rise to prohibitions impeding the

convergence of these opposing and dangerous forces. If sacrifice can cancel out the impurity of childbirth, then lochia might extinguish blood on the altar as well. Reproductive blood is, in this context, taboo in the truest sense of the word—it is a substance *both endowed with divine powers and forbidden at the same time*. Sacrificial blood and menses could be figured, then, as similarly charged elements comparable to the positive ends of two mutually repelling magnetic poles.

After the destruction of the Jerusalem Temple, the study of Torah and prayer in the synagogue supplanted the defunct sacrificial ceremony. Purity laws necessarily underwent revision in relation to the Torah scroll—the new focus of sacrality. One intriguing rabbinic text informs us, "*zavim, zavot* (those with oozing discharges), menstruants, and parturients are permitted to read the Torah, and to study Mishnah, Midrash, laws, and homilies" (Tosefta Berakot 2:12).[91] This early, post-

91. See Shaye Cohen's (see note 35), p. 283, explanation of the alteration of this law, the sexual politics among the rabbis, and their desire to limit sexual activity among their students, the Talmudim.

Figure 6. Etruscan relief on sarcophagus from Volterra representing the *Sacrifice of Iphigeneia*, ca. second–first century B.C.E. L: 70 cm. Inv.-Nr.Bc 2. Sarcophagus destroyed in World War II. Photo: Courtesy of Archäologische Sammlungen im Reiss-Museum der Stadt Mannheim.

Temple purity revision may indicate that the absence of sacrificial blood in the synagogue attenuated any competitive dynamic that might have existed between menses and sacrificial blood in earlier Temple practices.[92] In its highly marked status, then, menstrual blood fluctuates once again between sacred and profane identities.

---

92. By contrast, see my treatment of the early church and its appropriation of ancient sacrificial traditions in chapter three of my forthcoming book (see note 1).

The mouth of the *Komo*

SARAH BRETT-SMITH

The elders say that seeing a naked woman is seeing the
Komo.

Nyamaton Diarra, Interview of April 18, 1984[1]

My purpose is to reexamine the significance of the
Bamana and Malinke *Komo* mask in the light of new
data collected in the Kita and Beledugu regions of Mali,
West Africa (fig. 1).[2] This information suggests that the
headdress incorporates several levels of meaning and

that an intense concern with the control of masculine
sexuality and the mastery of human reproduction
informs one of the less easily accessible, but crucially
important, metaphors that lie concealed within the
mask. The data also suggests that a deep-seated fear of
the female sex is an important motivation for the
creation of secret male associations and the artworks
used in them.

Let us begin by seeing how the *Komo* functions in
daily life. The *Komo* is still the most widespread of the
six 'secret' associations (*jow*) that formerly structured the

---

1. The Bamana text is as follows:

Cèkòròbaw ko, muso lankolon ye, Kòmò ye don.

Second interview with Nyamaton Diarra, 4/18/84,
Book 19, pp. 19–20 of transcribed tapes

Unfortunately, there is no single standard written form for Bamana
and Malinke. The interviews used as data for this article were
transcribed by M. Seku Ba Camara using the orthography preferred by
the Direction Nationale de l'Alphabétisation Fonctionelle et de la
Linguistique Appliqué (DNAFLA), Mali. However, there may be times
when the Bamana or Malinke text presented here differs from what
might be an official DNAFLA transcription. I have judged it wiser to
publish M. Camara's transcriptions word for word, since the spoken
Malinke or Bamana of many of my interviews departs considerably
from urban Bamana speech. It is hoped that the meticulous
transcription of the oral text will give the Bamana- or Malinke-
speaking reader the flavor of the original text.

The reader should also be aware that Bamana texts published in
Mali do not use either capital letters or punctuation. I have inserted
both in order to make the Bamana transcriptions and their translations
more accessible. The plural form of nouns is indicated by adding a *w*
to the end of the word.

When translating and interpreting Bamana or Malinke terms, I
have used double quotation marks (") to indicate when I am
employing a word that is a direct translation of the original Malinke
or Bamana and single quotation marks (') to denote a word that forms
part of my own interpretation.

My use of single quotation marks is also designed to highlight
terms that have been subject to question and controversy, such as
'caste,' and terms that are derived from Western art history and
whose use may be somewhat inappropriate in the Bamana context,
such as 'realistic.' In these cases the single quotation marks should
alert the reader to the fact that I am somewhat skeptical of the term
used, but that it seemed the best choice from among a group of
unsatisfactory alternatives.

2. The research and writing of this article were supported by a
number of grants and fellowships. I would like to thank the John
Simon Guggenheim Memorial Foundation and the Fulbright-Hays
program for funding field research in 1984–1985 and 1984 respectively.

When I returned to the United States, the translation and cross-
referencing of the data used in this article were funded by a series of
grants from Rutgers University: in 1988–1989 and in 1989–1990, two

---

Rutgers University Research Council Fellowships; in 1989–1990, the
Henry Rutgers Research Fellowship; and in 1989–1990, a Rutgers
Council on International Programs Fellowship.

I would also like to express my gratitude to David Robinson, who
negotiated my award of an NEH grant for the translation, "Bamana
Origins and the History of the Komo Society," through the
"Translations of African Historical Sources" project administered via
Michigan State University. This funding was instrumental in allowing
me to translate the interviews with Nyamaton Diarra that make a
critical contribution to "The Theft of the Komo."

I would like to thank the National Endowment for the Humanities
for the award of a Fellowship for University Teachers (1990–1991) and
the School of Historical Studies at the Institute for Advanced Study in
Princeton for a Herodotus Fellowship (1990–1991). These fellowships
allowed me to begin this article.

Finally, I am grateful to the Sainsbury Research Unit for the Arts
of Africa, Oceania, and the Americas at the Sainsbury Centre for
Visual Arts, University of East Anglia, for the award of a Visiting
Research Fellowship (autumn 1995), a grant that enabled me to
complete this paper.

It may seem improbable for a woman to discuss the *Komo*, but the
reader should remember that a foreign female researcher is often
regarded as having a male persona and is therefore permitted access to
information that might not be available to Bamana women. This switch
in gender identification occurred in my own case and is described in
Brett-Smith (1994:4–5).

Another factor was the collaborative research method that evolved
from long-term fieldwork with my colleague, Mr. Adama Mara. For a
description of this method, see the introduction to Brett-Smith (1994),
especially pp. 1–2.

According to McNaughton, the Malinke and the Wasulu Bamana
call the *Komo*, *Koma* (1979:17). I have used the term *Komo* simply
because that was the name used the most consistently by my
informants, whether Malinke or Bamana. It may be that *Koma* is the
earlier term and that it has given way to *Komo* because radio
broadcasts are almost invariably in Bamana not Malinke.

McNaughton's 1979 account is the best monograph in English on
the *Komo* and its art. In French, the most detailed account is that of
Dieterlen and Cissé (1972).

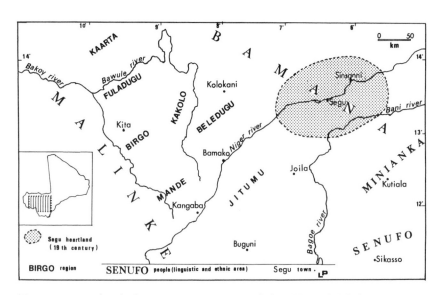

Figure 1. Map of Mali showing Bamana area and also Kita and Beledugu areas.

lives of Bamana and Malinke men.[3] In most farming villages, it continues to enroll young men in its ranks, its dignitaries and elders are still consulted about difficult family problems, and it remains the most feared of all the male associations. The fear surrounding the *Komo*

stems, at least in part, from the society's precolonial role as the highest known judicial authority within a village or an association of villages (*kafo*). Traditionally, the *Komo* wielded powers of life or death over anyone within its territory; this included its own members,

3. McNaughton (1979:2–9) provides a comprehensive overview of the secret associations and succinctly summarizes how different scholars have classified them over time. Most researchers have noted the existence of at least six male associations (*N'tomo, Tyi Warra, Komo, Nama, Konon,* and *Kore*) and two female ones (the *Guan* and the *Nyakuruni*), but the number varies from region to region. The *Kore* seems to be limited to the eastern Bamana and Minianka area; my Beledugu informants knew nothing about it. In the central Bamana area, most villages possess only one of the adult male power associations, the *Komo, Nama,* or *Konon,* although individuals may travel to another village in order to enroll in a second or third *jo.* Finally, in the Ganadugu region around Buguni, there seems to be only one male association, the *Jo* (this is distinct from the term *jo,* which means any secret society).

In addition to the problems posed by geographic complexity, researchers disagree about the exact status of the *N'tomo, Tyi Warra, Kore,* and *Nya* (a male association more commonly found among the Minianka than the Bamana, although some scholars occasionally add it to the list of Bamana associations). My own impression is that the *Tyi Warra* is an "eating society," or *ton* (see next part of this note), not a *jo,* and that the *Kore* and *Nya* are Minianka, rather than Bamana, associations. The *N'tomo* appears to be a *jo,* but a less secret one than the others, since it is made up of uncircumcised boys, and women view its performances.

McNaughton (1979:9–17) categorizes four of the adult male *jow* as "power associations" (*Komo, Konon, Nama, Nya*), grouping these societies together because they seem to wield political and mystical

power at a higher level than the other associations. In the past, all these *jow* had a significant ability to enforce their rules through the use of violence, and all possessed a similar ability to harness or unleash intensely destructive spiritual powers.

For the special status of the *Komo* within the group of "power associations," see Brett-Smith (1994:262, n. 6).

There is considerable debate as to whether the male associations can be labeled 'secret.' Z. S. Strother (Nooter 1993:161, 178, n. 5) prefers the term 'fraternity' suggested by Kassim Kone. However, my informants made a clear distinction between the *tonw,* or fraternal societies, and the *jow,* or 'secret' associations (Brett-Smith 1994:285, n. 21). Whereas *tonw* were based on villagewide work groups formed for farming and carrying out other tasks of community importance, such as road maintenance (Hopkins 1971:104–106), *jow* were associations specifically concerned with the teaching and use of 'secrets.' A *ton,* such as the *Tyi Warra,* could include both male and female branches, but *jow* were either male or female exclusively. *Tonw* entrance was usually automatic (Hopkins 1971:105), whereas admission to any *jow* demanded a sacrifice, a formal initiation, and the swearing of a loyalty oath to the society in question. These oaths always involved the commitment not to divulge the society's 'secrets.'

However, the word *ton* has also acquired the more general sense of "association," and informants sometimes spoke of the *Komo ton* or "*Komo* association" as a shorthand way of referring to the *Komo jo.* However, they were always careful to give the specific name of the society in question—the *Nama ton,* the *Komo ton,* etc.—in order to

women, and uninitiated men. With the introduction of a Western-based legal system, its overt power has diminished, and the elderly *Komo* leaders who discussed the society with me complained bitterly about

make clear that they were actually talking about a 'secret' association, not an eating society. When asked specifically about the meanings of the two words, my informants backtracked and cited the differences outlined in the preceding paragraph.

This paper is based on the premise that the Bamana consciously define *jow* in terms of 'secret' knowledge, and that they distinguish between 'secret' and non-'secret' associations. It also adopts the view that the information encapsulated in 'secrets' is both more important to society and more emotionally charged than that which remains open to all. In this sense, both my data and my point of view as author follow a more standard analytical paradigm than that proposed by Poppi (Nooter 1993:197–203). Poppi suggests that the content of an association's 'secrets' may be less important than the fact that it possesses and manipulates information that is ostensibly off limits to those outside the association's boundaries. For him, the significance of the 'secret' is its framing, not its actual 'meaning.' In fact, he suggests that the actual content of an association's 'secrets' is often banal and already familiar to the initiates. For Poppi, interpretations and objects are 'secret' not because they or their 'meanings' are either esoteric or unknown, but because a specific group within society (e.g., elderly men, women) declares them to be outside normal discourse.

My own point of view is closer to that of D'Azevedo (in Blakely, Van Beek, and Thomson 1994:342–362) who, although he notes that the Western idea of a 'secret' society is at least in part a colonial creation, describes one specific 'secret' manipulated by the Gola women's association, Sande, and attempts to identify its possible meanings. While issuing caveats about the use of the term 'secret society,' D'Azevedo actually proceeds on the basis that the Gola themselves recognize some knowledge as 'secret' and that these 'secrets' have important meanings.

Both its content and the reluctance with which my informants divulged the data presented here indicate that the Bamana and Malinke consider this information 'secret.' I would also suggest that the relative value of a 'secret' depends on the cultural frame of the viewer. To dismiss the content of non-Western 'secrets' as trivial because it often involves the revelation of basic information about the female reproductive system, is to impose a Western point of view on the Bamana or Gola definition of 'secrets.' Modern Western society is unusual in its demystification of sexual behavior and biological processes, and this demystification clearly depends on our access to and belief in scientific explanations. In fact, although we no longer consider human reproduction sacred, sexual behavior and even information are still emotionally charged subjects in our own society. We need to remember that sex remains a sacred 'secret' for those living in traditional societies and that, even among the educated elite, there may be very little access to information about female bodily processes. As D'Azevedo points out (1994:353–354), even Western-educated Gola men have surprisingly little access to information about the female body or how it functions reproductively; his statement that most Gola men have never seen even their wives' vaginas (1994:354) might also be made for the Bamana. As will be discussed later in this article, the sexual symbolism and the beliefs

their loss of authority.[4] Nevertheless, younger men and women remain convinced of the association's uncanny reach, and trade tales of local *Komow* who are reputed to enforce their decrees covertly through the judicious use of poison and, on occasion, outright violence.[5] Thus when an active *Komo* society leader says that the business of the *Komo* is killing people, he is simply stating what continues to be an obvious truth for most Bamana and Malinke.[6] The *Komo* may have acquired a shadowy status, but no one, not even the most powerful modern bureaucrat, will knowingly take the risk of acting against a famous *Komo* leader or, if he does, he has already settled his affairs.

Both foreign scholars and the Bamana and Malinke themselves link the *Komo*'s exceptional stature to its power to kill and, in particular, to its categorical ban on women and its right to execute any woman who views the society's mask. According to *Komo* leaders, the power of the association and its objects rests on the absolute avoidance of women and their contaminating fluids, and the only substance that can denude the

about female sexuality encapsulated in the *Komo* mask are far from trivial to those who use it.

4. Each local association has its own *Komotigi*, or "owner of the *Komo*," who is the executive decision-maker for the society. He is usually, but not always, a member of the blacksmith 'caste' (*numu*). He must be an expert in ritual practice, divination, and poisons and their antidotes. He may or may not wear the society's mask during the *Komo*'s celebrations; often the performer is a much younger man who has the endurance to sustain the prolonged dancing and acrobatic feats expected of the masquerader.

The data presented in this paper is largely that collected from two such *Komotigiw*, Kojugu Cissoko and Nyamaton Diarra. It is unusual for *Komotigiw* to agree to talk frankly about the association.

5. The most feared *Komow* are usually those in either remote and/or fervently traditional villages.

For an eyewitness account of secret association violence, see Brett-Smith (1994:319, n. 15). In this case, the informant was Minianka, and his mother was killed by a man who came up behind her and cracked her skull in two with a club. It is unclear whether his mother was deliberately forced to view a *Komo* mask or whether the object shown to her belonged to another secret association, but was also off limits to women. The Minianka possess the *Komo*, but it is a relatively recent introduction and is often imported from Bamana villages.

6. Interview with Kojugu Cissoko, 6/14/84, Cissoko6-14, Book 7, p. 74 of transcribed tapes.

Kojugu was also a gifted sculptor, who had carved seven *Komo* masks, and an inspired diviner. For a description of Kojugu's personality and the circumstances that allowed the author to work with him, see Brett-Smith (1994:3–4). This book presents the greater part of the data collected from Kojugu.

Komo mask of its power is menstrual blood.[7] On the surface, at least, the *Komo* is the most explicitly masculine of all the Bamana and Malinke 'secret' associations, and in the past young men could not marry or have intercourse until they had first been circumcised and then inducted into the society.[8] In fact, one could

---

7. Dieterlen (1951:150). Dieterlen notes that in order to prevent any mishap, society members whose wives are menstruating are forbidden to attend *Komo* festivities.

While both male and female informants agreed that menstrual blood could remove the power of any male ritual object, including the *Komo*, Kojugu Cissoko made specific observations about the rules that protect a sculptor from this substance.

Kojugu said that the sculptor must protect the *jagi*, a curved chisel for scraping out mortars, from contact with women. The reason for this precaution is that if a woman has just had sex and has not washed or if she is menstruating, she will contaminate the instrument, causing it to wound the artist the next time he uses it. Furthermore, this wound will be resistant to healing. (See Brett-Smith 1994:151, 306, n. 143; Interview with Kojugu Cissoko, Outils-1, Book 12, p. 64 of transcribed tapes.)

He also observed that sculptors never cross the boundaries of the kitchen for fear of stepping in the footsteps of a woman who may be menstruating (a menstruating woman may sit in the kitchen area to cook her own meal, or simply to talk with the other women; see Brett-Smith 1994:158, 307–308, nn. 10–11; Interview with Kojugu Cissoko, 8/9/84, Questions-1, Book 13, pp. 74–75 of transcribed tapes). If he were to have such contact, whatever object the artist carved would not only be devoid of spiritual power, but it would also lack any ability to act in the world.

Finally, Kojugu reports that artists try to avoid carving figures of women when their wives are menstruating. If an artist were to carve such an image at this time, his wife's menstrual blood would act at a distance to render the figure useless, even if the sculptor himself avoided any direct contact with her (Interview with Kojugu Cissoko, 8/9/84, Questions-3, Book 15, p. 91 of transcribed tapes). However, in theory at least, the sculptor can make other ritual objects, such as masks, at this time, provided he avoids his wife.

In a continuation of the passage just cited, Kojugu gives an additional explanation of the reasons why it is not good to carve any human figure, male or female, while one's wife is menstruating. He says that sculptors avoid carving human figures at this time, because if they were to break the interdictions that forbid sex with a menstruating woman, either the child produced by this union would die (allowing the wooden figure to function), or the figure would be useless (allowing the child to live). Kojugu's discussion of this entire issue is far from clear, but what he does communicate is that both sexual relations and contact with a woman's menstrual flow are inimical to the creation of ritual objects that will function correctly. For the passage in question and a more detailed analysis of its meaning, see Brett-Smith (1994:232, 330, n. 113; Interview with Kojugu Cissoko, 8/9/84, Questions-3, Book 15, pp. 92–93 of transcribed tapes).

8. McNaughton (1988:130). Zahan (1963:123) reports that men are initiated into the *Komo* association on the sixth day after circumcision.

Both Bamana and Malinke male and female informants asserted that indiscriminate sexual activity and the breaking of the ritual interdictions (*tanaw*) that traditionally controlled sexual behavior were

say that among the Bamana, to be a man was to be a member of the local *Komo*.

The *Komo*'s ubiquitous, if unseen and often subtle, presence continues to dominate village life and structure the passage of time for both men and women.[9] The

---

unknown at the village level prior to Malian independence in 1960 (for date, see Murray 1981:152). Up to this time, grandparents arranged the marriages of their grandchildren, and no one, male or female, 'experimented' with sex before marriage.

Along with some readers of this paper, I have been skeptical that such strict abstinence requirements could have been observed in reality. However, at the 1996 African Studies Association meetings in San Francisco, Kassim Kone and another Malian scholar stood up after a presentation on contemporary premarital pregnancy in Bamako to say that during their childhoods, sexual rules were strictly enforced and premarital pregnancies were almost unheard of. Both men are probably in their late thirties or early forties, which would place their childhoods in the late 1950s. One tends to dismiss elderly informants' tales of abstinence as fabrications, but every Western-educated Malian I have consulted who was alive at this period has agreed that today's sexual behavior was unknown in the 1950s. They have also agreed that the changes I describe here did, in fact, happen.

From the precolonial through the early postcolonial period, women had to be excised before they could marry or bear children, and men had to be circumcised. Since girls underwent clitoridectomy at about age 16 or 17, and men were circumcised at about age 25, this rule imposed a considerable period of sexual abstinence on both men and women.

According to my informants, sexual rules were not only rigid but were rigidly enforced; a girl was required to be a virgin at marriage, and a child born to either an unexcised girl or an uncircumcised boy was exposed to die in the bush (Interview with a group of women elders at a Beledugu village, 5/21/78, p. 2). Because excision was the gateway to sexual experience and adult, married status, many young women actually looked forward to the successful completion of their surgery and its accompanying rituals. This attitude was still evident in the pride with which both Nansun Suko and Araba Diarra spoke of their recent excisions in 1978 (Brett-Smith 1982b). While I do not possess equally detailed data on circumcision, all the male elders I interviewed agreed that it would have been just as unthinkable for an uncircumcised young man to break the sexual code as for an unexcised girl. Thus the data suggests that recently circumcised men (who had also just been initiated into the *Komo*) were virgins when they married their first wives.

Both circumcisions and excisions are normally performed at the height of the dry season in February or March, and both men and women would have consummated their arranged marriages during the rainy season. Since the *Komo* initiations take place at the society's yearly sacrifices (in early June just prior to the first rains) men would have received their assigned brides after both circumcision and initiation into the *Komo*. Zahan (1963:123) notes a variant of this timetable in which men are inducted into the *Komo* on the sixth day after circumcision, which would then occur in late May.

See note 66 for a discussion of changes in the ages at which circumcision and excision are performed.

9. Its celebrations take priority over all other events (especially those planned by women's associations) with the possible exception of

Figure 2. *Komo* mask, late nineteenth or early twentieth century. Wood, horn, porcupine quill, hair, metal, pigment, encrustations, H: 59.06 cm, D: 83.19 cm. The Seattle Art Museum, Gift of Katherine White and the Boeing Company. Photo: Paul Macapia.

Komo's ritual calendar is complex, and the information collected by different researchers at different time periods suggests considerable variation from village to village and region to region. However, all the reports agree that every functioning *Komo* society holds annual celebrations in late May or early June just before the beginning of the rainy season, and that these festivities involve the appearance of the society's medium wearing the famous mask (figs. 2–6, 8).[10] Dieterlen (1951:159–160) says that the *Komo* also celebrates the year's harvest and that it appears during the dry season when a circumcision is held.[11] Travélé (1929:137)

mentions a number of other *Komo* festivities, including a ritual clearing of the bush and a communal fishing effort. Both Travélé (1929:137) and Pâques (1954:85) describe yearly ceremonies where, in order to reinvigorate them, *Komo* objects are first immersed in the society's sacred pool and then removed from it.[12] On a more practical level, McNaughton (1979:20–21)

modern, government-sponsored festivities, such as independence day (Sept. 22).

10. The *Komo*'s annual sacrifice marks the inauguration of the planting season after the first rains and the beginning of a new year.

All the scholars who have worked on the *Komo* agree that its celebrations cannot occur during the rainy season (my informants also reported this). The sole exception to this rule might occur in case of the death of a *Komo* society head.

11. The harvest celebration occurs at the end of the rainy season, probably in October or November.

Circumcisions usually occur during the hot season, which begins at the end of January and lasts until the first rains in early June.

12. If the identifications provided by Travélé are correct, these objects are the association's wooden trumpets (1929:pl. 1). However, Dieterlen and Cissé's description of a similar ceremony (1972:252–254) involves the immersion of *boliw*, or portable altars.

On the basis of the following data collected among the Minianka, Dieterlen and Cissé's description seems more probable to me. On 5/16/79, Bakari Traore, the head of his local *Komo* association, reported that among the Minianka, men did not save their children when a village was attacked; rather, they ran to get their *boliw* so as to hide them from the enemy by throwing them into a nearby river (Interview with Bakari Traore, region of Koutiala, 5/16/79, p. 173; Brett-Smith 1983:60).

Pâques (1954:85) and Dieterlen and Cissé (1972:287–295) also discuss the rituals that are performed on the death of a society leader.

Figure 3. *Komo* mask, late nineteenth or early twentieth century. Wood, feathers, horns, and other organic substances, L: 65 cm. Lowie Museum of Anthropology, University of California, Berkeley, 5-12980.

reports that throughout the dry season, fully functioning associations hold weekly performances at night, where the masked medium becomes possessed and provides inspired answers to the dilemmas that have been set before the association's leader during the preceding seven days. Whether exceptional or expected, all these events interrupt daily life and reinforce the fear that surrounds the association and its mask, for they require

Figure 4. *Komo* mask, late nineteenth or early twentieth century. The Brooklyn Museum, Brooklyn, 69.39.3.

the uninitiated—women, children, and strangers—to lock themselves inside their houses on pain of death until the festivities have ended.

In actuality, *Komo* celebrations usually occur without interruption, since the society's medium usually wears the mask at night, and women receive numerous warnings letting them know when they must remain hidden. Nevertheless, both men and women refer to the *Komo* headdress as an object of terror. That women should be frightened of the mask is understandable, but why men? When the *Komo* medium performs, he not only has license to kill any woman he may encounter but also to eliminate any initiated man who is judged to have broken the rules of the association. Dieterlen (1951:163) reports that the masquerader wounds the culprit with a metal hook impregnated with poison and that the erring society member dies within the next few

days.[13] Kojugu corroborated this, and he also emphasized the rigid hierarchy that holds sway within the *Komo*, commenting that older members use force to make the younger initiates obey orders:

___

13. Dieterlen (1951:151, 163) notes that the masquerader carries a hook (*koli*) in each hand. Both hooks are soaked in poison, which is renewed annually. Dieterlen reports that the right-hand hook is used to kill erring *Komo* members, while she says that the left-hand hook is waved in front of faithful society members to defend them against the poisons that emanate from the masquerader's right hand.

Kojugu says that it is the left hand, not the right-hand hook, that kills, and it is the right hand, not the left, that has a protective role. Clearly, Kojugu's opinion on this matter contradicts Dieterlen's.

Interestingly, this contradiction echoes another concerning the identification of the left and right hands as male and female respectively (see Brett-Smith 1994:127, 296–297, n. 53). Dieterlen (1951:69) and Kojugu (Interview of 6/14/84, Book 7, pp. 88–89 of transcribed tapes) both identify the right hand as male and the left as

The whip, it is the whip which demonstrates it to you clearly, and you will do that thing.[14]

In fact, Kojugu viewed both the whips and the Komo mask as essential tools with which the leader of the association and his elderly advisers control the young. The sculptor, who had himself carved seven Komo headdresses, indicated that the mask is deliberately designed to terrify young initiates.[15] He observed that older initiates are less impressed by the mask, since they know that the association's stock of poison is kept inside one of its ritual iron flutes (Komo saman), not on the imposing carving.[16] Nevertheless, Kojugu indicated that

when carving a Komo mask, the sculptor's task was to create a headdress that would terrify.

What are the forms through which sculptors convey the unique sense of fear which surrounds the Komo and intimidates the young initiate? In fact, Komo masks have a relatively standard form, and no sculptor can deviate too far from this norm without incurring severe criticism (figs. 2–6). On most headdresses, a small, rounded dome covers the masquerader's head like a cap. Large, curving horns sprout from the back of this dome, while in front the wooden cap develops into an elongated jaw bearing numerous teeth. The mouth usually opens to reveal a gash of gaping space between the upper and lower jaws, a gap that accentuates the ferocity of the teeth. The dome-shaped head and the top of the upper jaw are frequently decorated with smaller animal horns, porcupine quills, and iron spikes that protrude menacingly up and outwards. Much of the mask's visual effect depends on the contrast between the thrusting forms of these "ornaments," and the hollow, 'empty' space outlined by the mouth. In fact, the width of the mouth and its yawning quality, the sense that it is about to consume something or someone, is one of the most prominent identifying characteristics of Komo masks; other headdresses, such as those used by the Konon and Nama associations, have elongated muzzles, but these

---

female, but Nyamaton (First interview, 4/15/84, Book 17, pp. 70–71 of transcribed tapes) identifies the left hand as the "man's" and the right hand as the "woman's." I have been unable to unravel this confusion, except to note that all the sources (Dieterlen, Kojugu, and Nyamaton) agree that ritual and sexual acts are performed with the left hand and that the right hand is used for ordinary actions.

In the case of the Komo masquerader striking a victim with intention to kill, it would seem to make more sense for this to be carried out with the left hand, since this is reserved for ritual "work" (killing an offender would fall within this category of actions).

Kojugu says that there is no remedy for being struck with the left hand; inevitably the victim dies within the next few days.

But, if you put on the entire costume of the Komo [the masquerader], at that moment you become the Komo. Indeed, you are feared on your left and on your right. At that time, hitting someone with your right hand is better than hitting them with your left. If you hit someone with your left hand, in any case, that is, that person is a dead man. There is no remedy for that. There is nothing against that. There is no sacrifice for that. There is nothing against that. That is why we fear the left side. May this be pleasing to Allah and to you.

Interview with Kojugu Cissoko, 8/14/84, Boliw-2, Book 16, p. 64 of transcribed tapes

The Bamana text reads:

Nka n'i donna a nyèngènmafèn kònò, awa o tuma na i kèra Koma ye. I tè kè mògò ye tugun dè, i bè kè Koma de ye. Wa i kini n'i numan, siran bè kè olu nyè. I ka mògò bon i kini na o waati la, o ka fisa i ka mògò bon i numan na. N'i ye mògò bon i numan na, o koni ye, o kèra, o kèra su ye ka ban mènè; lankari t'o la, foyi t'o la. Saraka t'o la, foyi t'o la. O kosòn, siran bè kè numan lanfanfèla nin nyè. Allah sako i sako.

Also see Brett-Smith (1994:140, 303, n. 101).

14. Bisan, bisan de b'o yira kènèkisè jè kan, aw b'a kè.
Interview with Kojugu Cissoko, 6/14/84, Book 8, pp. 14–15 of transcribed interviews

15. See also Dieterlen (1951:149) for corroboration of this point.

16. Nyamaton Diarra (Interview of 4/15/84, Book 17, pp. 31–33 of transcribed tapes) identified the pair of flutes as the Komo saman and the association's mask as the Komo suruku (see note 22), and this is the identification used here.

Kojugu Cissoko provided ambiguous and confusing information when asked to identify the Komo saman and the Komo suruku. In an early interview (6/14/84, Cissoko 14, Book 8, pp. 11–12), Kojugu identified the Komo suruku as a small metal flute and the Komo saman as a larger metal flute or horn. However, in the later interview, Modèles-2, he was less precise, identifying both terms simply as names for the musical instruments that are part of the paraphernalia of all Komo associations (Interview of 6/22/84, Modèles-2, Book 12, pp. 94–96). Finally, in the interview Outils-2 (6/24/84, Book 13, p. 46), Kojugu identifies the Komo saman as one of a pair of iron flutes of which the other is the Komo suruku.

Mr. Adama Mara confirmed the identification of the pair of flutes as the Komo saman on the basis of his own further research in Guinea. He also confirmed what both Kojugu and Nyamaton indicated, that the flutes are far more important and powerful than the mask and that one cannot commission or use the mask without previously obtaining the flutes (pers. comm. 7/27/93).

Few historical sources distinguish between the Komo suruku and the Komo saman, and Moussa Travélé's article (1929) is exceptional in this respect. He identifies the Komo saman as carved from wood or forged from iron (Travélé 1929:134, pl. 1). He adds that each Komo association possesses at least one Komo saman and may possess several different-sized trumpets.

For a more detailed discussion of the Komo saman and the Komo suruku, see Brett-Smith (1994:286, n. 27).

Figure 5. *Komo* mask, late nineteenth or early twentieth century. Wood, antelope horns, porcupine quills, cotton, and plant material, H: 50 cm, L: 70 cm. Collection Musée de l'Homme, Paris, M.H. 63.81.1.

masks lack both the gaping space between the jaws and the sense of aggression typical of *Komo* headdresses.

Most *Komo* masks display a rough, indeterminate surface created by layer upon layer of sacrificial blood mixed with millet porridge (*dègè*).[17] This encrustation envelops both the wooden headdress and its attached decorations, obscuring the sharp outlines of the original forms so that it becomes difficult to determine the features of the mask with any precision (figs. 2, 4).[18] One has the impression of gazing at the materialization of a shadow, rather than an actual object.[19] The Bamana and Malinke enhance this effect of imprecision and fluidity by performing with the mask at night under the diffuse light of the moon or in an open space lit by the flickering flames of a bonfire. Furthermore, as with the society's portable altars, or *boliw*, the original lines of most *Komo* masks are highly abstract (figs. 2–7). Although, as in the mask reproduced in figure 2, these abstract forms often convey extraordinary animation and the sense of a distinct personality, no visual clues inform the viewer as to exactly what animal is being represented. While carved and adorned to give an impression of lifelike vitality and threatening aggression, the mask never reveals its features or its identity with any exactitude. Perhaps it is this imprecision that adds an uncanny dimension to the headdress, since the fluid forms allow the terrified initiate to interpret the mask according to his own fears. In the end, the "head of the *Komo*" seems to defeat precise identification, presenting any interpreter with a set of complex and apparently irresolvable iconographical problems.

Numerous scholars have worked on the *Komo*, and the death-dealing mask has often been interpreted as some type of animal head. Dieterlen (1951:149) identifies the mask generically, as simply human or animal, while specifying that individual *Komo* masks represent panthers, swans, eagles, elephants, and vultures. She also reports that many masks are composites created from parts of animals, such as buffalos and crocodiles, but she never discusses whether the generic *Komo* headdress possesses any fundamental meaning.[20] McNaughton (1988:129) offers a more subtle interpretation when he relates a cautionary comment made by one of his informants, Sedu Traore, in September of 1973:

> The *kòmò* mask is made to look like an animal. But it is not an animal; it is a secret.

He suggests that *Komo* masks may be enigmas, complex power objects that incorporate the violence and energy

---

17. For a comprehensive discussion of the sinister meanings attached to *dègè*, see Brett-Smith (1994:300–301, n. 79).

18. See McNaughton (1979:44; 1988:138) for a discussion of the spiritual message conveyed by the encrustation that covers most *Komo* masks.

19. I am indebted to William Tronzo for this observation.

20. Dieterlen (1951:149); Dieterlen and Cissé (1972:48–51). McNaughton (1979:32) notes that antelope horns and wild pig tusks can sometimes be attached to the top of *Komo* masks.

Figure 6. *Komo* mask, late nineteenth or early twentieth century. Wood, iron, animal horns, blood, H: 90 cm. Collection Musée de l'Homme, Paris, M.H. C61.706.493.

of the animals they evoke. He stresses that the headdresses do not actually "represent" any particular animal, interpreting the mask's forms as a series of visual metaphors that express in a general way the *Komo*'s aggressive power and uncanny abilities.[21] I shall argue that we have enough data to discern at least one basic metaphor that unites McNaughton's interpretation of the mask as a mysterious "secret" with Dieterlen's disparate menagerie of birds and animals.

Among all the scholars who have studied the *Komo*, perhaps only Zahan (1960b:80–81) begins to unify all the possible 'meanings' attributed to the mask when he reports that the Bamana associate the headdress's gaping mouth with the hyena's voracity.[22] The hyena's capacity

to devour anything it encounters presumably represents the *Komo*'s power to "devour" those who break its rules.[23] Yet it still remains unclear why other devouring animals are mixed with the hyena image and whether any more fundamental metaphor lies hidden behind the mask's aggressively yawning mouth.

I believe that we must stop trying to understand *Komo* masks literally and begin to read them as complex symbolic constructions built out of layer upon layer of associations. The interpretations discussed so far—from Dieterlen's swan to Zahan's hyena—assume that the animals, birds, or "secrets" represented by the mask express the essence of Mande masculinity.[24] On a surface level, this is obviously true; in the Malinke and

21. McNaughton (1988:138). McNaughton comments that when blacksmiths say that *Komo* masks look like horses' heads, they do not really mean that *Komo* masks "represent" horses, but that they "resemble" these animals. This perceptive interpretation agrees with my data and my own discussion of the issue of representation and resemblance (Brett-Smith 1994:171–172).

For McNaughton's discussion of the aggressive power of the animal tusks, quills, horns, and teeth attached to *Komo* masks, see McNaughton (1979:32–36; 1988:136–138).

22. Zahan interprets this association as representing the voracious desire for ritual knowledge. However, my informants never offered this philosophical explanation, and it seems uncharacteristically abstract for the Bamana and Malinke.

One reason (among others) that Zahan's suggestion of a generic link between *Komo* masks and hyenas is plausible is that the masked medium is called the *Komo suruku* or "hyena of the *Komo*." The same term is also used for the musical instrument made from a stick of bamboo that the mask wearer and medium uses to distort his voice (this is a different instrument than either the wooden or metal flutes or the trumpets discussed in note 16).

For the companion term to *Komo suruku*, *Komo saman*, see note 16 of this paper. For further discussion of the phrase, *Komo*

suruku, and the sources that mention it, see Brett-Smith (1994:286, n. 27).

23. This is my interpretation based on my own field data. See note 22 for Zahan's interpretation.

24. I use the word Mande as an adjective to denote the cultural values common to those ethnic groups that speak a core Mande language. The Mande language family includes Bamana, Malinke, Jula, Manya, Khasonke, Wangara, Marka-Dafin, Kuranko, Vai, Susu, Mende, Kpelle, Loma, Mano, Dan, and a number of other relatively local languages (Brett-Smith 1996:19, n. 5).

The term Manden designates the geographic heartland of the thirteenth- to late-sixteenth-century empire of Mali. The Manden is centered on the upper valley of the river Niger and includes Malinke-speaking areas in both the Republic of Mali and the Republic of Guinea-Conakry.

When one talks of 'Mande values' or a 'Mande ethos,' one is usually referring to the cultural beliefs shared by the Mande-speaking ethnic groups (the Bamana, Malinke, Marka) who live within the core area of the Manden. Much of this cultural ethos is shard by other Mande-speaking groups outside the Manden geographic region. For the precise borders of the Manden, see Brett-Smith (1996:19, n. 5).

Zahan (1960b:33) says the following of the *Komo* society: "Son domaine est marqué par la monovalence sexuelle du mâle. . . ."

Bamana world hunters adorn their jackets with horns and quills, and spikes and teeth are clear indicators of the animal aggression associated with powerful men. McNaughton correctly tells us that a famous *Komo* mask, like a renowned *Komo* leader, can be referred to by a phrase usually employed to designate an old and powerful male elephant or bush buffalo.[25]

However, the *Komo* headdress is multivalent, and there may be something even more terrifying for Bamana men than the accumulated powers of a male elder, particularly if we remember that the primary audience that views the mask and for which it is designed, consists of young, newly initiated men, who, in the traditional context, would still be virgins.[26] Perhaps it is revealing that informants refer to the mask as a *warra*, or "clawed animal," without being able to provide a more precise identification.[27] In Mande legend, the most terrifying clawed animal is not the lion, the anteater, or the roan antelope, but the sorceress who disguises herself in animal form to entrap the unwary hunter. In tale after tale, a woman assumes the shape of a mysteriously attractive clawed animal in order to defeat a hero who is the embodiment of male power. If one takes the hint offered by these tales and looks beyond the obvious 'masculinity' of the *Komo* mask, perhaps one will find that its features express male fears, not male prowess. Perhaps the bestiality of the mask conveys a more subtle meaning than at first appears, for the worst "clawed animal" of all may be woman herself.[28]

Figure 7. *Boli* or portable altar, late nineteenth or early twentieth century, region of San. Earth, wax, wood, blood. Collection Musée de l'Homme, Paris, M.H. 31.74.1091.

25. The phrase is *dan kelen*, which means, "isolated one." See McNaughton (1979:30) for this information.

26. Women almost never view the mask, and if they do, they do not live to talk about it.

27. McNaughton (1979:30, n. 34). The source is the famous hunter's bard Seydou Camara. Also see ibid., p. 35.

The Bamana and Malinke term *warra* denotes an animal category that does not exist in Western classification systems. *Warra* is a general reference word for any wild animal with claws that can scratch and wound (see Zahan [1980:35] for a slightly different definition of the term). This category includes animals as diverse as the lion (the *warra* par excellence), the pangolin (*n'koson, Manis tricuspis*), the anteater (*timba, Orycteropus afer*), and the roan antelope (*dage, Hippotragus equinus*).

For additional information on the nature of *warraw* and their relationship to the *Tyi Warra* association and masks, see Zahan (1980).

28. In this context, it is interesting to note that the modern Malinke singer, Salif Keita, praises the African woman and girlfriend as a true *warra* in his song *Waraya*, or "Wildness" (on the tape, *Amen*, Island Records, 1991). Here, Salif is using the term *warra* in order to celebrate the ferocity and physical strength valued in a traditional woman. He implicitly contrasts the strength of the African woman with the faults of Western women, who are generally viewed as too frail to withstand either a tropical climate or 'real' lovemaking. Traditionalists

Let us begin our investigation of the *Komo*'s 'animality' with some new and unexpected data. In the spring of 1984, Mr. Mara and I presented Nyamaton Diarra, the former head of a Beledugu *Komo* society, with an open-ended question about the meaning of the *Komo* mask. We expected that Nyamaton might refuse to answer or, if he did, that he would simply identify the association's mask as one of the many creatures already recorded by other scholars. Instead, the *Komo* leader bluntly stated the following, as if it were a well-known fact:

Old men say that to see a woman naked is to see the *Komo*.[29]

Nyamaton then elaborated on his statement as follows:

Seeing the *Komo* is the same kind of thing. Because, what is seeing the *Komo*? If you have seen a woman, if you have

consider many aspects of what we would call romantic lovemaking (for instance, kissing) to be corruptions of the truer and stronger methods of traditional intimacy.

29. *Cèkòròbaw ko, muso lankolon ye, Kòmò ye don.*
Interview with Nyamaton Diarra, 4/18/84,
Book 19, pp. 19–20 of transcribed tapes

seen her naked, and if it has excited you, if she doesn't keep her feet together [that is, prevent you], you will sleep with her. This is as though you have seen the *Komo*. For instance, your female relative, if you see her naked sex and if you say, 'I want you, I am going to have sex with you,' then you will obtain her and have sex with her. And if you have sought after your female relative, then you have seen the *Komo*.[30]

How can we make sense of these statements? Before we begin our exploration of their enigmatic content, it is necessary to have some idea of how the Bamana and Malinke view human sexuality. Specifically, we need to know what they think about the female genitals, since this is the key body part to which Nyamaton refers.

For traditional Malinke and Bamana, sex is an important and indeed almost sacred activity, since children are essential for individual security in old age and the survival of the group. Like a religious mystery, the sexual act is viewed as profoundly incomprehensible; no one really understands what determines either sterility or successful conception and childbirth. What is known is that the female sex is essential for these processes and that its pleasures exert a compelling power over men. Apart from that, the reproductive process remains an unknown quantity: something that women apparently control, at least in regard to menstruation, conception, and childbirth, for these are events from which Bamana and Malinke men feel they are completely excluded.[31]

---

30. *Kòmò ye don o cogo rò. Parce que kòmò ye ye mun ye? N'i ye a ye, n'i y'a lankolon ye, n'i jarabir'a la, n'a m'a senw kè nyògòn kan, i bè si a fè. O bè kòmi i ye kòmò ye. I balemamuso, n'i y'a ju lankolon ye, n'i y'a fò ko 'n' b'i nyini n' bè si i fè,' i bè se k'a sòrò, k'a k'a la. N'i ye i balemamuso nyini, i ye kòmò ye.*
Interview with Nyamaton Diarra, 4/18/84,
Book 19, p. 20 of transcribed tapes

31. Biology excludes men from menstruation and childbirth in a direct physical sense. However, they are also socially excluded from these events, since they are forbidden any direct contact either with a menstruating woman and menstrual cloths or with a woman in childbirth and childbirth cloths. Men also believe that they are excluded from control of conception, since sexual activity is viewed as a basis for conception, but not necessarily the cause of conception. Everyone knows that a woman has to be having sexual relations to conceive, but just because she has these relations does not necessarily mean that she conceives. Actual conception or sterility is thought to be dependent on other factors, such as the woman's communication with the spirit world, her breaking or not breaking ritual interdictions (*tanaw*), and her human relationships (for instance, the goodwill of her mother's cowives). For an extended discussion of this issue and male fears concerning their exclusion from the reproductive process, see Brett-Smith (1994:222–223).

Despite the availability of modern health clinics in large towns and cities, a generic sense of exclusion and an attitude of ritual awe still pervade male attitudes towards sexuality. A small boy who accidentally finds his mother's first menstrual cloth as he plays in her bed will never forget her expression. However, her calm explanation that it is the preservation of this cloth that guarantees her continued ability to have more children inspires her son with a profound respect, fear, and awe for the creative powers materialized in the blood-soaked rag. Such a rag is not a source of shame, guilt, or evil; rather, it is one of life's most powerful objects, and no one, least of all a man or boy, takes such an object lightly.[32]

This sense of ritualized respect, of almost incredulous disbelief at a woman's power to create new life, affects Bamana and Malinke sexual behavior in concrete ways. Sex is too important and too sacred to be left to the individual; in the past, grandfathers not only arranged the marriages of their grandsons but taught the basic rules of sexual conduct, many of which are still followed to this day. Almost every detail of sexual behavior was regulated by some rule, and young men learned most of these during the retreat period following their circumcision (Dieterlen and Cissé 1972:58–59).

This sexual code is pertinent to our understanding of Nyamaton's enigmatic statements regarding the *Komo* and the female sex. First of all, the female sex, the only observable part of the female body that is clearly necessary for conception and childbirth, is surrounded with an atmosphere of fearful reverence. Men not only think of the female genitals as erotically exciting, but as sacred and terrifying. The female sex itself is a ritual tool, and every woman carries within her own body a weapon capable of destroying the most powerful man. When a woman is angered or shamed beyond the point of no return, she has only to detach her skirt in public, place her hand on her naked genitals, and curse the offending male, for her oppressor to face universal ostracism and social ruin. No one will speak to, feed, or have any dealings whatsoever with a man so cursed. The fact that few women ever resort to this extreme gesture adds to its power; the gesture continues to exist as a measure of last resort, and men continue to fear it. Furthermore, the female sex has other capacities that inspire caution; in an instant, a woman's menstrual

---

32. See Brett-Smith (1994:206) for a more extended discussion of this example.

Figure 8. *Komo* costume. Mask: wood, animal horns, porcupine quills, and other unidentified materials. Costume: Western and traditional cotton cloth and vulture and cock feathers. Collection Musée de l'Homme, Paris, M.H. 31.74.1066.

blood can empty a man's carefully husbanded store of ritual objects of all their power, and women are not always careful to say when they are bleeding. The list of dangers inherent in male contact with the female sex is endless, but our immediate concern is with the practical rules generated by this overriding sense of danger.

Because of its uncanny power, young men are taught that they must never approach the female sex casually. The Bamana and Malinke consider that the female genitals are too dangerous to be seen directly or clearly. A man is free to initiate sex with his wife, but he must avoid gazing directly at her genitals. If a man breaks this rule and looks at the naked female sex and breathes its vapors, he will either go blind or become sick and die of incurable tuberculosis (Brett-Smith 1994:208–209, 319, n. 16). Elders also caution young men to use only their left hands to handle their penises during sexual encounters and to begin and end sexual relations abruptly;[33] kissing, lengthy embracing, or touching the woman's sex is considered almost as dangerous as the sight of female genitalia (Brett-Smith 1994:210). Furthermore, many men take the precaution of washing with special medicinal leaves after sexual relations in order to remove the *nyama*, or unreleased energy, that attaches itself to them from the experience.[34]

33. The information concerning the use of the left hand was first told to us by Nyamaton. See Brett-Smith (1994:210, n. 21) for Nyamaton's exact words.

34. *Nyama* is a concept that is almost indefinable, so pervasive is the idea within Bamana society. Bird describes it as the "energy of action," or the energy released by any act, whether positive or negative (1974:vii–ix; Bird & Kendall 1980:16–17, nn. 4–6). This ever-lurking but invisible force, which flows through both animate and inanimate things, inevitably seems to have more negative than positive consequences. Few will attribute success in difficult, and seemingly hopeless, marriage negotiations to *nyama*, but everyone can explain a woman's recurrent miscarriages as the result of unleashed *nyama*. Perhaps the woman touched her husband's hunting shirt, inadvertently letting loose the *nyama* of the animals he had killed on their unborn child, perhaps she unknowingly ate a sauce containing a *nyama*-filled medicinal plant, or perhaps the long-term *nyama* from her constant attempts to injure her cowife's many sons rebounded on her own pregnancies.

As this example suggests, reproductive failure provides fertile territory for the action of *nyama*. Nevertheless, the female sex itself is invested with a sacredness that cannot be defined simply by saying that it has *nyama* or is *nyama*-filled, since the female genitals have important powers of creation as well as destruction. *Nyama* flows through a woman's sex, but the sex itself is conceived of as separate from and different than this abstract energy.

The rules of sexual behavior described in this paper are essential defensive tools that allow a man to have creative contact with the

As these examples suggest, the Bamana and Malinke surround sexual activity with a series of ritualized rules that channel and control men's behavior. These rules, and the atmosphere they engender, are strikingly similar to those that surround ritual objects, whether they are blood-soaked menstrual rags or *Komo* masks.[35] In the light of these associations, Nyamaton's comparison does not seem eccentric, but rather logical and rational. Let us then return to his statements and see whether we can get a better grasp of their meaning.

When one rereads Nyamaton's declarations, it appears as though the *Komo* leader is saying several things at once. He begins by asserting that seeing any female sex is the equivalent of seeing the *Komo*. He then gives a reason for this equation: such a sight might lead a man into initiating incestuous sexual relations, and such relations are just as forbidden as seeing the *Komo*. However, Nyamaton's enigmatic way of speaking leaves us unclear as to whether seeing a female sex is similar to seeing the *Komo* simply because both involve the breaking of ritual rules (*tanaw*) and the committing of forbidden acts, or whether the female sex in and of itself is an object equivalent to a *Komo* mask.

I suggest that Nyamaton intends to convey both meanings and that each is relevant for an analysis of the *Komo* mask. Just as a woman who views the *Komo* mask is immediately executed, so too the incautious man who sees a female sex will die from tuberculosis as a result. The female sex and the *Komo* mask are "the same," because both are sacred objects whose sight results in the viewer's death. Secondly, the sight of a female sex may lead a man to incest, and the traditional punishment for incest was and continues to be suicide by both participants. Thus the viewing of a woman's sex may lead to an even more dangerous situation—incest—

female sex without bringing its inherent *nyama* down upon him. This defense system is more subtle than it may seem at first; both Nyamaton and Kojugu are well aware that a man will not recoil and curl up to die immediately if he does see his wife's genitals, but they are not worrying about short-term consequences. Rather, their perspective on sex is colored by long-term fears, since *nyama* inherent in the female genitals usually manifests itself in the unexpected aftereffects of sexual activity, not in the sexual encounter per se.

For a more thorough definition of *nyama*, see Brett-Smith (1994:38). For the *nyama* attached to the female genitals, see Brett-Smith (1994:209, 215, 319–320, n. 17).

For the most succinct current summary of this concept, see McNaughton (1988:15–16).

35. For a lengthy discussion of these similarities, see Brett-Smith (1994:chap. 6).

and this, in turn, leads to an immediate and violent, if self-inflicted, death. Whatever way one turns, the result of viewing both a woman's sex and the *Komo* is death.

However coherent Nyamaton's statements may become, once one understands the Mande view of human sexuality and what the Bamana and Malinke believe are the consequences of seeing the female genitals, these passages still reflect the views of a single informant. In June of 1984, Kojugu Cissoko, a sculptor who had carved seven *Komo* masks and who was currently the head of his village's *Komo* in the Kita area, independently confirmed Nyamaton's statements. After listening to the tape recording of the earlier interview with Nyamaton, Kojugu commented:

> If you have heard that you don't leave the place of sacrifice to the *Komo* to have sex with a woman, the meaning of that, the thing which the old man said about the *Komo*, where he explained to you, saying that it was the same thing as the sex of a woman, that is the truth. But whoever shall say that this is not the truth, may I become a child once again and put us together sitting side by side, and I will interrogate him severely and pursue him so that at that moment he will realize that he doesn't even know about the fact that the *Komo* can kill people. The person who said that, that it isn't true, he doesn't know anything at all. In fact, it is made with the sex of a woman. . . . [36]

Initially, Kojugu refused to explain in detail what he meant by his tantalizing statement, "it is made with the sex of a woman. . . . ," but later in the same interview he did repeat his assertion that seeing a woman nude was "the same" as seeing the *Komo*:

> To say that to see a woman nude, that this is to see the *Komo*, it is to see the *Komo*, it is to see the *Komo*, the old man [that is, Nyamaton] didn't lie about that.[37]

In assessing Kojugu's statements, it is important to know that the sculptor did not personally know Nyamaton,

nor was he even aware of Nyamaton's name or village, since we concealed this information from him. It is also significant that Kojugu's desire to convince us that he was more knowledgeable than any other informant actually gave him a strong inducement to contradict the tape recording in order to enhance his status in our eyes. Yet, despite his competitiveness, Kojugu unhesitatingly confirmed Nyamaton's assertion.

Furthermore, two of Kojugu's own statements reinforce the idea, already raised by Nyamaton, of an explicitly physical correspondence between a woman's sexual parts and the *Komo* mask. When Kojugu says, "in fact, it is made with the sex of a woman. . . ." (*A dilala de k'a ni muso nyèkun. . . .*), he uses a verb, *ka dlan*, that means, "to make" or "to fabricate," in the sense of "physically construct."[38] Sculptors commonly use this verb to describe the actual carving of an object, while they employ an entirely different verb, *ka dan*, or "to create," to express the idea of conceptual thinking and creative invention.[39] *Muso nyèkun* simply means "a woman's front parts." Kojugu's Malinke is unequivocal; the mask is made with the sex of a woman.

When pressed to explain this abrupt and disturbing statement, Kojugu implied that constructing a *Komo* mask with the sex of a woman probably belongs to the domain of history. In the following passage he grudgingly reveals that the female sex used to make the first *Komo* headdress was taken from a child of the griot 'caste.' According to Kojugu, this is the reason why these bards and oral historians are the one social group completely excluded from the *Komo*:[40]

> *Question:* You spoke about the manner of making the *Komo*?
> *Kojugu:* It is a child. Nhun. It's not made with an old woman.
> *Question:* Of approximately what age?
> *Kojugu:* At the time when it was [first] made, aaa, my grandfather didn't tell me the number of her years. If I

---

36. *N'i y'a mèn, i tè bò Komosòn yòrò ka taa muso ko kè, a kòrò ye, cèkòròba dò in ye, min f'i ye ko, Komo, a ye yòrò min yir'i la kafò ani muso nyèfèla ye kelen ye, o ye tinyè de ye. Min ko, ko, tinyè tè, ne ka kè denmisènnin ye, n'i y'an sigi nyògòn kan, n' b'a fèsèfèsè k'a gèn k'a lò a rò, kafò a tè hali Kòmò mògòfaga yòrò lòn. Min ye nin fò dè, ko tinyè tè dè, a t'a lòn. A dilala de k'a ni muso nyèkun. . . .*
> *Interview with Kojugu Cissoko, 6/14/84, Cissoko6-14, Book 7, pp. 75–76 of transcribed tapes*

37. *A fò, ko, muso lankolon yeli, k'o ye Kòmò ye de ye, Kòmò ye don. Cèkòròba ma nkalon tigè o la.*
> *Interview with Kojugu Cissoko, 6/14/84, Cissoko6-14, Book 7, p. 91 of transcribed tapes*

---

38. Interview with Kojugu Cissoko, 6/14/84, Cissoko6-14, Book 7, pp. 75–76 of transcribed tapes.

39. For an extended discussion of both *ka dilan* (*ka dlan*, "to fabricate") and *ka dan* ("to create"), see Brett-Smith (1994:169).
   Bazin (1906:103) translates *ka dlan* as "to arrange, repair." Dumestre (1983, no. 2:290–291) translates it as "to make, fabricate, arrange, repair, prepare."

40. Of course women of all 'castes' are automatically excluded, as has already been stated.
   Interview with Kojugu Cissoko, 6/14/84, Cissoko6-14, Book 7, pp. 76–77 of transcribed tapes.

should say something and speak about it, I will lie and that isn't good.

Question: But was this a blacksmith child, or a child of some other caste?

Kojugu: It was a griotte.

Question: Hun?

Kojugu: It was a griotte.

Question: Aa?

Kojugu: Haven't you heard that griots don't enter the assembly of the *Komo*? The reason for this comes from this [the fact that a griotte child was used to construct the first *Komo*].[41]

Both the use of the past tense and the reference to Kojugu's grandfather as the source of the information

41. *Question: I ko, ko Kòmò dila cogo?*
Kojugu: Denmisènnin don. Nhun. A tè dila muso kòròba la dè.
Question: A bè san jòli bò hakè?
Kojugu: A bè dila tuma min, aa Adama n' mòkè ma o san hakè fò n' nyèna dè. Ni n' ko ten, ko n' b'o fò, n' bè nkalon tigè. O dun ma nyi.
Question: Mais, est-ce que o ye numu den de ye wa, wala siya wèrè?
Kojugu: O ye jeli de ye.
Question: A?
Kojugu: Jeli don. I m'a mèn, ko jeli tè ta Kòmò jè la? A baju de bòra yen.

Interview with Kojugu Cissoko, 6/14/84, Cissoko6-14,
Book 7, pp. 76–77 of transcribed tapes

Several readers, including Francesco Pellizzi, have suggested that the use of a child rather than an adult woman as a sacrifice for the *Komo* may be a clue as to the meaning of this offering. One reader doubted that the sex of a child would have the same level of power as that of an adult woman.

Pellizzi suggested that the use of an unexcised and therefore unsocialized female sex in the creation of the *Komo* headdress would transfer original generative powers to the mask, thereby endowing it with wild and antisocial force. The mask might then represent the unbridled seeking of pleasure, while the initiation itself would parallel women's excision in placing limits on the exploration of sexual enjoyment.

I find the suggestion of diminished power unconvincing, partly because of data that suggests that an uncircumcised male sex has more power than a circumcised one. This is why it is recommended that an uncircumcised boy carve the "[objects] that you make to kill people" (Interview with Kojugu Cissoko, 8/9/84, Questions-1, Book 13, p. 56 of transcribed tapes). For an extended discussion of the superior powers of an uncircumcised boy, see Brett-Smith (1994:235–236). The data on excision support a parallel attribution of superior power to an unexcised female sex.

Pellizzi's suggestion is more convincing and might be explored further if additional data could be collected from Kojugu or other ritual experts. Unfortunately, Kojugu made it clear that he was only speaking of the griotte sacrifice in very vague terms and that it would be useless to ask him what his own interpretation of the offering was. Given

suggest that we are dealing with a longstanding oral tradition, not with an account of something the sculptor had experienced in his lifetime. Furthermore, the interdiction that forbids male griots to participate in the *Komo* is so old that no one knows when it began, thus Kojugu's reference to it places the use of the child's sex in early, if not mythic, times. Nevertheless, the statement and its explanation remain somewhat unclear, except that the sculptor's words imply a physical use of the female sex in the construction of at least one *Komo* mask.

Kojugu's statements tell us that a *Komo* mask and a woman's sex possess some kind of physical correspondence that goes far beyond the fact that the sight of each object may cause the viewer's death. Furthermore, in a postscript to his confirmation of Nyamaton's statements, Kojugu implies that a *Komo* mask and a woman's sexual parts are visually similar:

The *Komo* is made to become like the sex of a girl. If you have learned that women don't see the *Komo* and that women never eat meat from its sacrifices—indeed, this has many meanings.[42]

Kojugu makes this identification even more explicit when he says of the *Komo*'s mouth:

It resembles a woman. It really resembles the sex of a woman.[43]

Here, it is worthwhile to examine the words that Kojugu uses. He says:

A bòlen muso la. A bòlen muso lasiri yèrè yèrè la.

Kojugu's refusal to explain his statements, one can only speculate about the significance of the sacrifice at this point.

Kojugu seemed to indicate that the offering had a very important meaning that might be quite different than anyone could reasonably expect and that he was not going to reveal it. My own guess is that his reluctance to explain the griotte offering had to do with the balance of power and the inter-'caste' relationship between griots and blacksmiths. It is possible that any mention of this sacrifice still carries political overtones having to do with the origin of the griot and blacksmith 'castes' and that the 'meaning' of the offering is to be found more in the domain of politics than of ritual.

42. *Komo de dilala k'a kè o* [this particle refers back to the subject of the preceding sentence, *denmisènnin musoman,* or "a young girl"] *nyèfèla cogo ye. N'i y'a ye, u ko, muso tè a ye, muso tè a sòn sogo dumu, a kòrò ka ca dè.*
Interview with Kojugu Cissoko, 6/14/84, Cissoko6-14,
Book 7, p. 76 of transcribed tapes

43. *A bòlen muso la. A bòlen muso lasiri yèrè yèrè la.*
Interview with Kojugu Cissoko, 8/11/84, Djinns/Ciw,
Book 14, p. 93 of transcribed tapes

The expression *A bòlen . . . la* or *A bòlen bè . . . fe* is commonly employed when discussing a physical likeness between two things or people, as in the phrase, "He resembles Mamadou." By using this construction, Kojugu is stating that there is a visual similarity between the appearance of a *Komo* mask and a woman's sex. Furthermore, Kojugu does not use one of the more euphemistic expressions, such as *ju* ("base") or *nyèfela* ("front"), that men usually employ when they refer to the female genitals.[44] Rather, he makes a deliberate choice to use the word, *lasiri*. *Lasiri* is far more specific than either *ju* or *muso nyèfela* ("a woman's front parts"), since it is a technical medical term that midwives use when they refer either to the uterus or to the actual entry into the vagina.[45] Kojugu's choice of *lasiri* suggests that he is making a specific visual comparison between the gaping jaw of the typical *Komo* mask and the entrance to a woman's vagina.

Given the appearance of *Komo* masks, the reader may well view the sculptor's assertion with skepticism (figs. 2–6, 8). However, I would suggest that when Kojugu says, "The *Komo* is made to become like a woman's sex," and, "It really resembles the sex of a woman," he is not stating that *Komo* masks are realistic depictions of the female genitals as we, in the West, understand them. Rather, he is viewing the mask as a graphic exaggeration of all those visual characteristics that make the female sex so terrifying to Bamana and Malinke men. Kojugu's *Komo* does not correspond to an illustration in a Western biology book, but to a nightmare image, rapacious and devouring.

In fact, this graphic image of an intensely destructive female sex occurs in the description of one of the most important women in Mande oral literature, Sogolen Wulen Condé. Many versions of the Sunjata epic describe the marriage of the great king's father, Fara Magan Cenyi, to his short, hunchbacked, limping, bald mother, Sogolen Wulen Condé.[46] Although Sunjata's father has been told that he will obtain a famous son by marrying Sogolen, he is not anxious to consummate the marriage when she arrives in his courtyard. Sogolen is brought to Sunjata's father by two hunters who have won her by killing the mysterious and destructive buffalo of Do (an aged sorceress with powers of animal transformation). Not only is Sogolen the epitome of ugliness, but she is also a sorceress with the power to defend herself against the loss of her virginity. Sogolen has already successfully resisted the advances of the two hunters, and when she is finally married to Fara Magan Cenyi and enters the marriage chamber, she brings forth an entire armory of defenses. From her eye she shoots an iron needle at her husband, trying to pierce his eyes. She also attempts to spear him with an iron-tipped staff and bombards him with other, similar rods.[47] In some versions, Sogolen's pubic hair is transformed into porcupine quills to prevent both the hunters and her royal husband from touching her sex (Laye 1978:65–66; de Zeltner 1913:6). Such defenses—iron spikes, rods, needles, and porcupine quills—are exactly what one finds on *Komo* masks (see figs. 3–6).[48] The description of

---

44. Bazin (1906:175–176) defines *ju* as "base, foundation, lower part, behind." He also gives a second definition as "beginning, end." He does not give the sexual meaning.

Bailleul (1981:89–90) defines *ju* as "the buttocks" in an anatomical sense, and when used in an insult, as "the sexual parts." When used in a figurative sense, he translates it as "base, beginning, origin, motive, and cause."

Today, the most common use of the word *ju* occurs in sexual insults. Neither Bazin (1906), Dumestre (1981–1989), or Bailleul (1981) define *nyèfela*.

45. Bazin (1906:364) defines *lasiri* as "to be full, pregnant."

Dumestre (1989, no. 7:1085) defines *lasiri* as "to be pregnant, to be full, to make pregnant, pregnancy; sex, anus, base, cause, reason, the bottom of a basin."

Bailleul (1981:129) simply translates *lasiri* as "to make pregnant."

My own experience is that *lasiri* tends to carry an objective, anatomical connotation and that it denotes either the uterus itself or the entry into the vagina. Whereas a young man or woman might use *lasiri* as a general term for the female sex, an experienced midwife or a knowledgeable male elder, like Kojugu, would employ it in a specific sense.

46. Sunjata is the famous thirteenth-century king who first defeated the great blacksmith sorcerer and tyrant, Soumaoro, then united the entire Mande area into the kingdom of Mali, and finally set forth the code of traditional law, which was observed in principle up until colonization.

There are multiple published versions of the Sunjata epic. I have consulted Johnson (1986), Laye (1978), Niane (1960), and de Zeltner (1913) and have also made extensive use of Conrad's forthcoming article on the image of Mande women (1997). I am indebted to Stephen Belcher for drawing my attention to some of the texts cited above.

Sunjata's father has a variety of names. Here, I am using the one suggested by Stephen Belcher (pers. comm., 9/17/95). Conrad prefers Farako Manko Farako Ken (pers. comm., 9/2/95). Niane (1960) uses Maghan Kon Fatta.

47. My description of this event is drawn from Conrad (1997:10–13).

48. The reader may question how the feathers attached to the *Komo* masquerader's tunic and the resulting image of a predatory bird (Dieterlen's vultures, swans, and eagles) relate to the interpretation

Sogolen's mystical equipment fits well with Nyamaton's and Kojugu's statements, and we must conclude that the appearance of the *Komo* mask expresses a similar belief in the possible danger of the female sex. The mask gives a concrete shape to the ideas (such as quills replacing pubic hair) that we might view as exclusively metaphorical when we find them in Mande oral literature.

Given that the nightmare image of the female sex has an important role in epic poetry, we might expect to find some mention of the female genitals in the oral literature associated with the *Komo* mask and *Komo* ceremonies. Unfortunately, Kojugu was only willing to divulge one of the songs and speeches used in *Komo* society celebrations. We had asked the sculptor whether any songs existed that related the *Komo* to the female sex. He replied that certain *Komo* songs focused on this theme, and he reluctantly agreed to recite two stanzas from one such song:

> Byè ka dun de
> Byè ka jan de
> Byè sima da dumani
> Byè bo diyaro.

> Byè ka bon de
> Byè ka jan de
> Byè si ma
> Nanyumani byè bo
> Diya ro.

> The vagina is deep
> The vagina is large
> The hairy vagina has a small, sweet mouth
> to reach the sweetness of the vagina.

> The vagina is broad
> The vagina is large

but no vagina has ever achieved the sweetness of the thing of Nanyumani.[49]

As one might suspect, the song is ritual speech, not normal Malinke discourse, and the sculptor's voice became almost unbearably tense when he recited the verses. Kojugu then added that the song is learned mandatorily by all *Komo* initiates and that the day one sings it is "a red thing," that is, a time of many sacrifices. Beyond this, he would not elaborate.[50]

To understand the significance of the song and what it evokes for the Bamana or Malinke listener, one must comprehend the meaning of the word *byè*. This word does not simply refer to the female sex. Both men and women will use the words *ju*, or "root, base," and *musoya*, or "womanness," as somewhat impolite but vague terms appropriate in personal discussions of infertility and sexuality.[51] However, *byè* is practically unpronounceable. Everyone knows the word, everyone knows that some people use it, but no well brought up person of either sex will ever employ it voluntarily, unless they are a midwife engaged in a serious medical consultation.[52] *Byè* is a ritualized term that denotes the

---

suggested here. First, the comparison of women to birds of prey is fairly common in Africa; the *Gelede* masquerade among the Yoruba is one tradition that uses such imagery. Second, a look at the Bamana terms for feathers, *siw* and *jolow*, reveals several interesting usages. *Jolo* refers only to quills and bird feathers or plumage (Bailleul 1981:87); it cannot be used in reference to human hair. Significantly, my informants never used *jolow* to refer to *Komo* mask decorations, but always employed the word *si*. *Si* can refer to birds' feathers or porcupine quills, but it can also mean hair, even pubic hair. In the light of the descriptions of Sogolon's magical armory cited here, it is tempting to regard the birds' feathers and the porcupine quills on *Komo* masks as references to female pubic hair.

Bazin (1906:172) defines *jolo* as "animal quill," and *si* (1906:530) as "hair, wool, horse hair, beard, feather, etc."

49. Interview with Kojugu Cissoko, 8/11/84, Djinns/Ciw-2, Book 14, pp. 94–95 of transcribed tapes.

50. At least not in terms Mr. Mara and I could understand. Kojugu continues by saying that on this day, water is turned into wine and into milk and that several other miraculous transformations occur, but he does not explain what he means by these comments or how they relate to the song. Interview with Kojugu Cissoko, 8/11/84, Djinns/Ciw-2, Book 14, p. 95 of transcribed tapes.

Francesco Pellizzi commented that if the mask is the female sex, then the sacrifices made to or on it may correspond to menstrual blood. He suggests that the sacrificial blood, produced artificially through acts of violence by men, may function as a compensation for the disappearance of menstrual blood during pregnancy. He proposes that because women withhold their blood in order to create, men compensate for this loss by spilling blood during sacrifices to the ritual objects that represent an abstract sex. I suspect that this challenging idea may well prove correct, but my current data is too limited for me to use this hypothesis in an analysis of the *Komo* material presented here. I hope that future field work will shed additional light on this suggestion.

51. For the meanings of *ju* see note 44.

Bazin (1906:414–415) gives *musoya* the meaning, "quality of being a woman, effeminacy."

Bailleul (1981:145) translates *musoya* as "state or condition of being a woman," and as a "polite term for the sexual parts of a woman."

52. Bazin (1906:93) translates *byè* as "a woman's sexual parts."

Bailleul (1981:24) lists *byè* as an impolite term for the sexual parts of a woman.

Dumestre (1981, no.1:195) translates *byè* as "vulva, a woman's sex."

vagina itself and, like the body part, the word is regarded as sacred, never to be uttered even in the privacy of one's own bedroom. One can use *ju* or *musoya* in insults or lovemaking and be forgiven, but the use of *byè* will never be forgotten. Whereas *ju* and *musoya* have an abstract quality that blunts their meaning, and *lasiri*, although specific, has largely anatomical overtones, *byè* conjures up an obscene and grossly realistic physical image of the female genitals. In singing "*byè* is broad, *byè* is large," the *Komo* initiates are evoking a visual confrontation with the vagina itself, a confrontation that is metaphorically acted out when the young men face the *Komo* mask for the first time during their initiation.

Let us look at this moment when mask and initiate come face to face. According to Dieterlen (1951:155), the young man does not simply view the *Komo* mask, but he is forced to lick both the headdress and the metal hooks carried by the masked medium three times, while swearing that he will place the *Komo* ahead of everything else in his life, even his father and mother. In the concrete action of licking, the initiate comes face to face, and one could even say mouth to mouth, with the mask. The action of licking is so physically explicit, one can even suggest that prior to 1960, it was this confrontation with a metaphorical vagina that was a young man's initiation into sex, not the loss of his virginity with a real woman.[53] Significantly, this confrontation involves the performance of the most forbidden and dangerous sexual act—licking—within the boundaries of a ritual context. By committing this metaphorical transgression and by subsequently swearing allegiance to the *Komo*, the young man acknowledges that unbridled, 'wild' sexuality belongs within the domain of the *Komo*, and that he accepts the association's charge not to let his own sexuality break the established boundaries of daily life.[54]

Although the postindependence dissolution of traditional sexual mores has obscured the connection between *Komo* initiation and sexuality, a *Komo* leader such as Kojugu still views the young man's traumatic entry into the society as fundamentally similar to sexual experience. When he discusses *Komo* initiation, Kojugu compares this ritual to the experience of having sex for the first time:

> The first day that you enter into the *Komo,* the thing that you have never seen, you will see that thing, the thing that you have never done, you will do that thing. That is like the fact that you have never had sexual intercourse and then you touch a woman [that is, her sex]. Yes, your hand touches first of all, your hand is placed on her breasts, good, and then when you mount her, too, it will be another experience that you aren't accustomed to. That is the same thing as entering the *Komo.*[55]

Both Kojugu's song and his description of the initiation into the *Komo* evoke images of the society's mask as a vagina in disguise, but the song also makes a somewhat confusing declaration. After praising the depth and sweetness of the female body part, it concludes by asserting that the vagina cannot provide a man with the ultimate in human satisfaction:

> no vagina has ever achieved the sweetness of the thing of Nanyumani.

What is the "thing of Nanyumani," and how can it be sweeter than the real vaginas that await the young men after they are initiated? Kojugu never explained his phrase, "the thing of Nanyumani," directly, but data collected from Nyamaton Diarra suggests a plausible interpretation.

Nanyumani is similar to many Bamana and Malinke names for women, and the sentence construction itself ("the thing of Nanyumani") suggests that we are dealing with the name of a person. Among knowledgeable

---

53. Francesco Pellizzi suggests that if the initiate licks the "top" of the mask, the section that Kojugu insists is the most dangerous, he may be licking the area that represents the 'clitoris' of the unexcised griotte who was sacrificed to make the first *Komo*. It would be very interesting to find out if the top of the *Komo* mask is in any way associated with the clitoris and if this is one of the reasons it is so dangerous, but so far my field data is silent on this point. Furthermore, Dieterlen's description does not really clarify where the initiate licks or even if there is a chosen spot. What my interviews with Kojugu do suggest is that the initiate is licking the two objects most likely to be covered with poison—the mask and the metal hooks carried by the masquerader.

See note 13 for citations concerning the poison carried by the masquerader's iron hooks. Also see my discussion of the *Nyè Tenen* horn further along in this article. The *Nyè Tenen* horn contains poison and is inserted into the top of some but not all *Komo* headdresses.

54. I am indebted to Francesco Pellizzi for this analysis of the licking procedure.

55. *I don don fòlò Kòmò la, i ma deli ka fèn min ye ban, i b'o ye. I ma deli ka ko min kè, i b'o kè. O ye komi i ma deli ka muso ko kè ban, e sera muso ma. Awa, i bolo fòlò ser'a ma, i bolo dara si kan, bon, n'i dun nana yèlèn fana, aa, i bè kè cogoya dò la min ma deli ka k'i la. O ni Kòmòrò donni cogo bèe ka kan.*
Interview with Kojugu Cissoko, 8/11/84, Djinns/Ciw, Book 14, pp. 96–97 of transcribed tapes

elders, it is fairly common to use a code word, such as a woman's name, to refer to a secret association and its objects. We also know that at least one woman's name does function as such a code word and that it explicitly refers to the *Komo* mask. When questioned about the meaning of the common female name Tenen and its associated but less common variant, NyèTenen, Nyamaton Diarra revealed that Tenen is a name that can be given to a baby girl by the owner of the *Nyè Tenen* ritual object. Nyamaton then explained that the *Nyè Tenen* is actually a horn (presumably filled with ritual substances) that is placed in the center of the forehead of a *Komo* mask to endow it with power. The *Nyè Tenen* horn functions as a type of lie detector, since it enables the *Komo* that possesses it to detect uninitiated men within the crowd at a *Komo* celebration.[56] In daily life, it is quite common for women to be called Tenen, and this name does not necessarily have the direct relationship to the *Nyè Tenen* horn mentioned by Nyamaton. However, Nyamaton's comments tell us that when the name Tenen or the phrase *Nyè Tenen* is used by elders in the context of a discussion about *Komo* matters, the name has a specific meaning that is disguised by its everyday usage. Furthermore, as we shall see later in this paper, both male and female elders preserve traditions that attribute the origin of the *Komo* to women, so that it would make sense for elders to refer to pieces of *Komo* equipment, or even the society itself, as "the thing of X," where X is a woman's name with specific associations to the *Komo*.

So far, I have not collected data that directly associates the name Nanyumani with the *Komo*. However, the NyèTenen example suggests that one can interpret the name Nanyumani in a similar fashion. Thus it is plausible to hypothesize that when Kojugu says, "no vagina has ever achieved the sweetness of the thing of Nanyumani," he means that no vagina has ever equaled the sweetness of the *Komo*. This interpretation would also make sense when one considers the literal meaning of the name, Nanyumani. *Na* is an alternative form of the honorific prefix, *Ma*, or "mother," which is often attached to female names. Among the Malinke (and Kojugu essentially speaks Malinke rather than Bamana) especially, one tends to say Ma Tenen or "mother Tenen," instead of the simpler "Tenen," in order to show respect for a woman. Thus, Nanyumani can be broken

down into Na Nyumani, where Na means "mother," and Nyumani means "sweet thing," or "good thing." A literal interpretation of the name Nanyumani would then be, "mother sweet thing," or perhaps even "mother of sweet things," an honorific title that would be entirely appropriate for the *Komo* society.

If we accept this interpretation as a plausible working hypothesis, the last line of Kojugu's song can be recast as:

> but no vagina has ever achieved the sweetness of the *Komo* society.

In teaching the young men this song, a song whose meaning seems completely at odds with the reality of sexual experience, the *Komo* elders were asserting their categorical power over the initiates.[57] For unless the new society member could accept and memorize the declaration that no sexual experience with a living woman would ever compare in sweetness to membership in the *Komo*, he was not allowed to pass out of the initiation and marry. Only after swearing primary loyalty to the *Komo* mask, the metaphorical vagina owned by the group of men, could the young initiates gain access to real vaginas.

The elders who teach the young men Kojugu's song are trying to convince them that the mask, the objectified wooden vagina, has something special to offer, a power that real women lack. Yet their insistence on the mask's "sweetness," a sweetness that will shortly be disproven by the physical experience of the initiates' marriages, suggests a profound sense of lack, a fear of that very "sweetness" represented by the mask. For, in fact, it is women, not men, who possess vaginas. Despite the generalized belief that the *Komo* mask and its accompanying *boli* can inflict sterility or impregnate women, it is still women, not men, who conceive and bear children. In a society where one can still reasonably expect only half of one's children to survive,

---

56. See Brett-Smith (1996:107–108). Fifth interview with Nyamaton Diarra, 4/20/84, pp. 45–47 of transcribed tapes.

57. Many scholars have already noted that the *Komo* dignitaries use the association's mask to control both younger men and women socially and politically.

See McNaughton (1979:17–23) for a thorough and cogent overview of different scholars' opinions of the *Komo*'s origins and function.

Dieterlen and Cissé (1972) identify the *Komo* as the most important initiation association among the Bamana (p. 17). Their description of the *Komo*'s functions underlines the society's ability to organize and train young men in arcane knowledge (pp. 17–19) and its absolute closure to women (p. 35).

Dieterlen (1951:164–165) stresses the extent to which the *Komo* infiltrates every aspect of Bamana life.

children are essential, and men cannot make them. In an environment where only reproduction guarantees survival, men are profoundly aware of their deep dependence on women, for they and they alone can produce children.

Nyamaton's and Kojugu's statements and Kojugu's song tell us that *Komo* members perceive their mask as the metaphysical transformation of an ideal vagina. Clearly, understanding the mental equation, mask equals vagina, is a critical first step in understanding the mask. However, this identification does not tell the full story, for the owners of the mask are men, not women. Why do men own a power object that functions as a symbolic vagina? Does our analysis of the *Komo* mask reveal anything more general about gender relations and the power to reproduce in Bamana and Malinke society?

Several elderly men and one female elder agreed that a myth about the *Komo's* origin explains male ownership of the association and its mask. The myth explores the imbalance of power between men and women, and it also leads to a more subtle interpretation of the mask-equals-vagina equation. The story suggests that the *Komo* headdress represents generative power and not merely a feared and desired body part. While M'Fa Sory Traore and Kojugu Cissoko recounted truncated versions of the myth and other male elders agreed on the story's general outlines, the only informant able (or perhaps willing) to recite the full version was a woman, Salimata Kone.[58] She told us that:

> I learned something from my grandfather. He was talking in front of us when we were children. The thing which caused the *Komo* to belong to men—we women were having a celebration and the *Komo* [the mask] jumped [out of our grasp]. Some were in front, and some were behind. The

Nyamaton's and Kojugu's statements and Kojugu's

58. M'Fa Sory Traore at Kurusa provided us with a truncated version of the myth while we were sitting with him and several other elders under an outside shelter on a hot afternoon. The shelter happened to be just outside Salimata Kone's room; at first she was silent while the men were talking, but then she interrupted M'Fa Sory to give us a fuller version of the myth. This is the version translated here.

Later, when we interviewed Kojugu Cissoko in Bamako, he told us another version of the myth:

Kojugu: They said it [that is, they recounted the myth]. The beginning of the *Komo* is with women. People say it. The *Komo* fell in the space of knowledge for women.

Interviewer: What is the meaning of the space of knowledge for women?

Kojugu: The meaning of their space of knowledge, no one has told me that. We simply hear the word *lònkènè* [see explanation

Komo slipped and fell into a well. It fell into a well, and they said that the women should get it out, not the men. We all came, we came with our waistbands and we tied them end to end, transforming them into one, and then we tied them around the middle of the *Komo*. When the rope had been tied around the middle of the *Komo*, it broke. We took the rope away. We went to get our old skirts. We tied all our old skirts together. When we put this rope around the middle of the *Komo*, it broke. Then we said that we could not get this thing out of the well. Then we went to see the head of the village—we asked him to bring men to get it out. We went to see the head of the village; the head of the village asked us how the men could get the *Komo* out of the well? Because a person who has his eyes blindfolded cannot get the *Komo* out of the well, and at that time the men did not view it [the *Komo* mask]. We said

below]. The *lònkènè* is a thing, but is it that it is the place of knowledge, or is it that it is the place of sorcery, or is it that it is the place of the *nyaguan* [a redoubtable all-female association of "sorcerers," which no informant, either male or female, was able or willing to define further], in any case, people say *lònkènè*. The men and the women met each other in this place. The *Komo* [that is, the mask] fell in the well [this implies that the *lònkènè* is a flat open space, since such spaces are usually created around wells]. The women were unable to get it out until the men brought it out. That is the meaning of this (that the *Komo* began with women).

> *Interview with Kojugu Cissoko, 8/9/84, Questions-1, Book 13, pp. 83–84 of transcribed tapes*

The Malinke text is as follows:

Kojugu: U b'a fò. Kòmò jujòn ye musow ye. A bè fò. Kòmò de tun binna musow la lònkènè kan.
Interviewer: Lònkènè, o ye mun ye?
Kojugu: U ka lònkènè, a kòrò ye min ye, o ma fò n' ye. An b'a mèn, ko, lònkènè. Dònkènè ye fèn min ye, dònni kènè do wa, suya kènè do wa, nyaguan kènè do wa, a koni bè fò, ko lònkènè. Cè ni muso ye nyògòn sòrò yen. Kòmò de binna kòlòn nò, musow ma se k'a labò, fo cèw y'a labò. A kòrò filè nin ye.

Kojugu uses the term *lònkènè*, which I translate as "space of knowledge for women." This is a location chosen as a meeting place by senior women who meet there to exchange secret knowledge and to display the depths of their expertise to each other. It is unclear whether the *lònkènè* is a secret clearing in the depths of the bush (like the men's *tu* or sacred wood), whether it is a village square, or simply some other meeting place agreed upon by all women. Because women's secrets are both more dangerous than men's and also subversive of the overt political structure, the *lònkènè* is very carefully hidden. While men acknowledge that it exists and that they are afraid of what happens there, they never know its location and are reluctant even to discuss it.

For the reasons why Salimata had access to this information from her grandfather, and for a discussion of her personality and our work with her, see Brett-Smith (1994:5–6).

that if they succeeded in getting it out, we would give it to them. They agreed. They asked us if their eyes were going to be blindfolded. We said that they would not be blindfolded. The first thing that they had to do however, they all had to go and get a chicken and bring it to us. They went and got the chickens and came with them. These chickens for releasing the blindfolds, we killed them; once they had been killed, the men went and took the cords for their trousers, and then they tied them together one by one, and took the *Komo* out of the well. When the *Komo* got near the top of the well, it cried out. When the *Komo* came out of the well, it said that whatever women had stayed there, if they didn't offer the chicken for entering [the *Komo*], they would die; they would vomit and die. And if there were a child born after this time, if the child were a girl, if it were not given to it [the *Komo*], and if the child saw it [the *Komo*], she would also vomit and die.[59] And, if it [the *Komo*] saw an uncircumcised boy, if it were a young man, if he were circumcised and did not enter its place [that is, the *Komo* association], the chickens that were taken from the men [as the sacrifice necessary to take the blindfolds off], if that chicken were not to be offered, and if his eyes were not to be blindfolded [presumably a part of the young man's initiation into the *Komo*], then he too would die vomiting—he would die. My grandfather recited this account to me. Then, all the women fled, running into their houses. And the young boys, those who were about the age of this one here [pointing one out], those who could not yet reflect on things seriously, they also ran away and they entered the houses with the women. Then, they shut the doors. My grandfather told this story to me—this is the story he told me. It was in this way that the *Komo* came to belong to men. Originally, however, the *Komo* belonged to us. However, we couldn't get it out of the well—that was the reason that we lost it. My grandfather recounted this story to me—this is the one he told me. However, it did not occur in my lifetime.[60]

59. Here it is unclear whether "it" refers to the sacrificial chicken or to the baby girl. When a child is born, it is often "given" or dedicated to a particular cult.

60. As discussed above, Salimata recited this myth in a spontaneous response to a statement by M'Fa Sory Traore that:

The *Komo*—long, long ago the *Komo* belonged to women. (Interruption while the tape is changed from side A to side B.) Women—long ago, the *Komo* belonged to women. Men took it from them [the verb M'Fa Sory uses, *ka boshi*, implies the forcible alienation of something from someone].

The Bamana text is as follows:

Komo, fòlò, fòlò, Komo tun ye musow de ta ye. (Interruption for change of tape from side A to side B.) *Musow, fòlò, Kòmò tun ye musow ta ye. Cèw y'a bòshi u la.*
    Interview with M'Fa Sory Traore and Salimata Kone,
    3/30/84, Book 3, p. 90 of transcribed tapes

If we use Nyamaton's and Kojugu's declarations that the *Komo* mask is a female sex as keys for decoding the myth, we arrive at some revealing equations. Women once possessed the group's vagina, but they were unable to control it, and it leapt out of their hands and into a well from which only men could retrieve it. The women then lost the communally owned mask/vagina to the men, who thereby acquired political and ritual dominance.

If we interpret the equation, mask equals vagina, broadly as a visual condensation of men's belief in women's absolute capacity to control conception and birth, Salimata's story makes sense. The myth suggests that among the Bamana and Malinke, each sex believes that the other controls fertility. Ritual, social, and marital life might well be described as a continual squabble over the reproductive process. Do women, with their exclusive control of childbirth, mastermind human reproduction or do men, with their secret objects,

Salimata's version is found in the same interview on pp. 90–92 of the transcribed tapes.

Nka, n' ye ko dòn n' mòkè nyèna, o tun bè baro bò an denmisènlama nyè na. Min ye Kòmò kè cèw ta ye, musow, an bè nyanajè la. Awa, Kòmò gininna. Dòw bè nyè, dòw bè kò. Kòmò nana jigin kòlòn nò. A jiginna kòlòn nò, u ko, ko musow k'a bò, ko, cè tè a bò. An nana, ka na an cèsiri jalaw, ka na olu tugun nyògòn na, ka kelen don, ka n'o siri Kòmò cè rò. A ser'a tilancè rò, o tigèra. An y'o bò yen. An taara taafe kolonw ta, ka na olu siri, siri, siri nyògòn na. A ser'a tilancè rò, a tigèra. An ko, an tè se ka fèn bò. An ka taa se dugutigi ma, o n'a ka cèw n'a bò. An taara se dugutigi ma. Dugutigi ko olu bè se ka Kòmò bò cogo di? Barisa, maa nyè sirilen tè se ka Kòmò bò, olu de t'a ye. An ko, n'u sera k'a bò, tinyè na, an b'a d'u ma. U ko, basi tè. O tuma, u nyè bè siri wa? An ko, u nyè tè siri. U don fòlò, fòlò, fòlò a rò, k'u bèe ka taa shè minè ka na. U taara shèw minè ka na. Anw ye u nyèminèshèw in, an ye olu faga. U fagalen, cèw taara u ka kulusi jala, u taara olu tugun, tugun, tugun nyògòn na, ka Kòmò bò. Kòmò surunyana da la, Kòmò pèrènna. A mana bò ka muso o muso to yen, n'o fana ma a don shè bò, n'o satò sera, o ka funu, o ka sa. Ni den min mana kè o kò rò, ni o den ye muso ye, n'o ma di ale ma, n'o nyè y'a ye, a fana ka funu, o ka sa. N'a ye bilakoronin ye, a kòròta ye bilakoronin ye, n'a cè la ma don, n'a bolokora, n'a ma don ale de rò, n' ye ka shè min minè cèw de la, o shè de ma bò, k'a fana nyè siri, o fana satò o ka funu, o ka sa. Ne mòkè tun bi o sala n' ye. Muso bèe bolila, ka don so kònòn. Cèmisènnin minnu bè ni waati bòlen bè olu kun, ni min hakili sigilen tè, olu bolitò, olu donna musow fè so kònòn. Olu datugura. Ne mòkè tun ye min masala bò n' nyè na, o de ye ninnu. O de ye Kòmò kè cèw ta ye. O kò Kòmò tun ye an musow ta ye fòlò. Nka an ma se k'a bò. N' y'i bilasira ni nin yòrònin ye. N' mòkè ye ni masala nin bò n' nyèna, o ye nin. N'o tè a ma kè n' nyè na. Kòmò kè sin ka kè cèw ta ye, o koni ye nin.

manipulate fertility? In the myth, women are seen as the original owners of generative power. After all, the mask belonged to them first. However, the women lose their control of reproductive power, just as the mask evades their grasp and falls into the well. By rescuing the mask the men are able to appropriate it, transforming it into a 'man's vagina.' Salimata's story informs us that men took creative power from women.

While the myth clearly reflects the ongoing struggle between men and women over reproductive control, it can also be interpreted more specifically in the light of what we know about *Komo* initiation. During the first stage of their initiation into the *Komo*, society members tell the new initiates that, "You will die; you will rot, we have summoned no one. Welcome!"[61] After these warnings, the terrorized young men crouch down against the earth in a ritualized but explicit enactment of death. They must remain in this position until they are sprinkled with water drawn from the village's sacred pond.[62] The crouching gesture and the initiate's resuscitation when touched with sacred water find echoes in Salimata's myth. The men's dangerous climb down into the well and their successful reappearance bearing the *Komo* mask can be interpreted as a representation of the *Komo* initiate's death and rebirth. Specific details of the myth suggest even more precise interpretation; the "cords of their pants" may stand for the invisible ties that link *Komo* members through their initiation and oath swearing, while the water in the well may correspond to the sacred water with which the new *Komo* members are sprinkled. The newly circumcised young man descends into the well (the *Komo* society), dies there, and then reemerges as an adult who has mastered the coveted secret knowledge that allows him to have sex (the *Komo* mask) safely.[63]

The connection between *Komo* initiation and Salimata's story becomes stronger when we explore a third and even more specific interpretation of the descent into the well. We should remember that in a traditional setting, young men married and had sex for the first time shortly after *Komo* initiation. Thus the fall into the well can also be read as a metaphor for the pleasures and dangers of the sexual experience that awaits the new initiates. The young man, who in real life must avoid gazing at the female sex, in the myth removes both his blindfold and the belt of his pants to clamber down into the well naked. Furthermore, the male complaints that they cannot perform this feat blindfolded suggest that the descent into the well is dark and terrifying as well as thrilling. Who knows whether one will not remain in the shadowy depths of the well with the mask? The men's fear suggests that the well represents the unknown territory of sexual pleasure, a territory where a man can easily lose himself. The metaphor is based on experience, for the gases that often build up in the lower reaches of a deep well can cause the man digging or cleaning it to lose consciousness, and deaths from well digging, although unusual, are not unknown among the Bamana and Malinke.[64]

This feared loss of consciousness represents something more sinister than the total relaxation of sexual release. If one wishes to use Freudian language, the treacherous climb down into the well expresses both castration anxiety and an identifiably Mande fear of losing vital energy during intercourse.[65] We have already noted that, prior to Westernization, initiation into the *Komo* and a man's first head-on sight of the *Komo* mask occurred on the sixth day after circumcision (Zahan 1963:123), an operation that was bound to arouse castration anxiety when performed without anesthetic on a fully adult young man.[66] In fact, it was not unusual

---

61. Quoted in Bamana and translated into French in Dieterlen and Cissé (1972:255).

62. This is usually a pool of water located in the middle of the *Komo tu*, the circular area of uncut primary forest just outside the village dedicated to *Komo* rituals. For the Bamana and Malinke, the village *tu* serves a purpose similar to our churches, mosques, or synagogues. One might perhaps consider the *tu* as a kind of environmental architecture since, apart from the circular area on the inside where rituals occur, it is deliberately kept as virgin forest.

63. I have also considered a parallel interpretation where the descent into the well and the reemergence of the men carrying the mask is viewed as a metaphor for childbirth. Francesco Pellizzi suggested an interesting elaboration of this idea, proposing that the

"cords of their pants" can be viewed specifically as an umbilical cord, the mask itself as a child, and the hidden water of the well as amniotic fluid. In this reading, the *Komo* members become the 'mothers' of generative power, giving satisfactory birth to the reproductive secrets that elude women.

64. It is interesting to note that the men known as specialists in well digging and cleaning are *numuw*, or "blacksmith/sculptors." *Komo* leaders are also usually *numuw*, and it is quite possible for the local *Komo* leader and the best-known well digger in the community to be one and the same person.

65. Of course, similar fears are found in many other societies, but both the Bamana and Malinke identify this fear in proverbs and in the advice given to young men. Within the broad spectrum of traditional thought, the idea that men will lose vital energy during intercourse appears as a consciously acknowledged, known fact of life.

66. Also see note 8. It is important to realize that the analysis presented in this paper is based on the assumption of adult

for young men to be told that circumcision was only the beginning and that their entire sex would be cut off when they emerged from the circumcision retreat and were inducted into the *Komo*. During the *Komo* initiation, elders would counsel the initiates to steer a middle course between complete abstinence and sexual indulgence. The young men would be warned that women will delight in sucking them dry like oranges, and it would be suggested that they aim to take a second wife, so as to diminish the power of the first. In the myth, the descent into the depths of the well expresses deep-seated male fears about the irresistible pull of the female sex. For what both the circumcision ritual and the *Komo* initiation teach is that it is women who are the wild beasts; it is women and their sexuality that cause men to act out of character, to abandon themselves, to lose consciousness, and to vanish in a bottomless well of sexual pleasure.

Now, perhaps, we can begin to understand why informants have identified the fundamentally abstract mask with such a diverse array of animals and birds. If, at a fundamental level, the mask represents a nightmare vision of the vaginal mouth, it is hardly surprising that it should be difficult, if not impossible, to pin down a specific animal reference. In fact, the only thing that Dieterlen's panthers, swans, eagles, elephants, vultures, buffalos, and crocodiles and Zahan's hyena seem to

---

circumcision (ages 20–25) and excision (ages 16–18). In country towns and remote villages, young women may still be excised in their late teens, but most boys are now circumcised at age six or seven, or even at birth; adult male circumcision has become a thing of the past.

In 1971, Hopkins (1971:105) also reported a progressive lowering of the age for circumcision. He states that, at the time of his research, boys living in urban areas were circumcised between the ages of eight and ten, while the age for boys in villages was 10–14 years. A generation earlier the age for the operation had been 18.

The shift to a younger age for circumcision resulted, at least in part, from the colonial need for teenage, male labor and the ensuing impracticality of sequestering young adult men for the long period of recuperation and initiation that followed the surgery. The Bamana also say that the telescoping of the adult ritual ensures that their children will be, at least nominally, 'adult' and will therefore be protected against the danger of breaking traditional sexual rules while uncircumcised or unexcised, once they are placed within the ruleless, 'anything goes' environment of a Western primary school. For many elders, the fact that Western-style primary school classes include both boys and girls is absolute proof of the corruption inherent in this method of education. Traditional learning was always acquired within a same-sex context; young boys learned their skills from men, and young girls learned from women. Men were supposed to remain ignorant of women's knowledge, and vice versa.

have in common is their aggressive veneer and their rapacious or destructive powers. Similarly, what is constant in *Komo* masks is not their particular features or their relationship to a particular animal, but the sense of devouring aggression projected by the headdress's 'abstract' forms. This animalistic voracity, which is such a fundamental characteristic of *Komo* masks, expresses the male conviction that women—wild beasts far worse than any in Dieterlen's list—will devour their partners as inevitably as a hyena devours carrion. My data suggests that, at a conscious but deliberately hidden level, the *Komo*'s gaping mouth expresses men's pervasive fears of women's sexuality. The mask is much more than an instrument of male power; it is also a warning, an icon to the fears that haunt Bamana men.

SELECTED BIBLIOGRAPHY

Bailleul, Charles
    1981 *Petit Dictionnaire Bambara-Français Français-Bambara*. Avebury Publishing Company, England.

Barth, Fredrik
    1975 *Ritual and Knowledge among the Baktaman of New Guinea*. Yale University Press, New Haven and Oslo.

Bazin, Jean
    1975 "Guerre et servitude à Ségou," in *L'esclavage en Afrique précoloniale*, ed. Claude Meillassoux, pp. 135–181. François Maspero, Paris.

Bazin, Monsignor Hippolyte
    1965 *Dictionnaire Bambara-Français (1906)*. Gregg, Ridgewood, New Jersey.

van Beek, Walter E. A.
    1994 "The Innocent Sorceror: Coping with Evil in Two African Societies (Kapsiki & Dogon)," in *Religion in Africa: Experience and Expression*, ed. Thomas D. Blakely, Walter E. A. van Beek, and Dennis L. Thomson, pp. 196–228. David M. Kennedy Center for International Studies at Brigham Young University Monograph Series, vol. 4. Heinnemann, Portsmouth, New Hampshire.

Bellman, Beryl L.
    1984 *The Language of Secrecy: Symbols & Metaphors in Poro Ritual*. Rutgers University Press, New Brunswick.

Bird, Charles S., trans.
   1974   *The Songs of Seydou Camara*. Vol. 1, *Kambili*. African
          Studies Center, Bloomington, Indiana.

Bird, Charles S., and Martha B. Kendall
   1980   "The Mande Hero," in *Explorations in African
          Systems of Thought*, ed. Ivan Karp and Charles S.
          Bird, pp. 13–26. Indiana University Press,
          Bloomington, Indiana.

Blakely, Thomas D., Walter E. A. van Beek, and Dennis L.
Thomson, eds.
   1994   *Religion in Africa: Experience and Expression*. David
          M. Kennedy Center for International Studies at
          Brigham Young University Monograph Series, vol. 4.
          Heinnemann, Portsmouth, New Hampshire.

Boyer, Pascal
   1980   "Les Figures du Savoir Initiatique." *Journal de la
          Société des Africanistes* 50(2):31–57.

Brett-Smith, Sarah
   1982a "Iron Skin: The Symbolism of Bamana Mud Cloth."
          Ph.D. diss., Yale University.
   1982b "Symbolic Blood: Cloths for Excised Women." *RES:
          Anthropology and Aesthetics* 3:15–31.
   1983   "The Poisonous Child." *RES: Anthropology and
          Aesthetics* 6:47–64.
   1984   "Speech Made Visible: The Irregular as a System of
          Meaning." *Empirical Studies of the Arts* 2(2):127–147.
   1987   "Bamanakan ka Gelen." *Art Tribal* 2:3–15.
   1994   *The Making of Bamana Sculpture: Creativity and
          Gender*. Cambridge University Press, New York.
   1996   *M'Fa Jigi: The First Mande Artist*. University of
          Wisconsin Press, Madison.

Cashion, Gerald A.
   1982   "Hunters of the Mande: A Behavioral Code and
          Worldview Derived from the Study of Their Folklore."
          Ph.D. diss., Indiana University.

Cissé, Youssouf Tata
   1985   "Les nains et l'origine des boli de chasse chez les
          Malinke," in *Fétiches: Objets enchantés mots réalisés*,
          pp. 13–24. Systèmes de pensée en Afrique noire, vol.
          8. Ecôle pratique des hautes etudes, Paris.

Colleyn, Jean-Paul
   1975   "Sur le chemin du village: l'initiation au *Koro*
          Minyanka." *Journal de la Société des Africanistes*
          45(1–2):115–126.
   1982   "'Le chiot court mais ne connaît pas les odeurs':
          Notes sur la société et les systèmes de pensée des
          Minyanka du Mali." *Africa* 52(1):3–14.

   1985   "Objets forts et rapports sociaux: Les *Yapèrè*
          Minyanka," in *Fétiches: Objets enchantés mots
          réalisés*, pp. 221–261. Systèmes de pensée en Afrique
          noire, vol. 8. Ecôle pratique des hautes etudes, Paris.

Conrad, David C.
   1990   *A State of Intrigue: The Epic of Bamana Segu
          According to Tayiru Banbera*. Oxford University
          Press, Oxford.
   1997   "Mooning Armies and Mothering Women," in *In
          Search of Sunjata: The Mande Epic as History*, ed.
          Ralph Austen. Indiana University Press, Bloomington,
          Indiana. Forthcoming.

D'Azevedo, Warren L.
   1973   "Mask Makers and Myth in Western Liberia," in
          Primitive Art and Society, ed. Anthony Forge, pp.
          126–150. Oxford University Press, Oxford.
   1994   "Gola Womanhood & the Limits of Masculine
          Omnipotence," in *Religion in Africa: Experience and
          Expression*, ed. Thomas D. Blakely, Walter E. A. van
          Beek, and Dennis L. Thomson, pp. 342–362. David
          M. Kennedy Center for International Studies at
          Brigham Young University Monograph Series, vol. 4.
          Heinnemann, Portsmouth, New Hampshire.

Dieterlen, Germaine
   1951   *Essai sur la religion Bambara*. Presses Universitaires
          de France, Paris.

Dieterlen, Germaine, and Youssouf Tata Cissé
   1972   *Les fondements de la société d'initiation du Komo*.
          Mouton & Co., Paris.

Douglas, Mary
   1966   *Purity and Danger: An Analysis of the Concepts of
          Pollution and Taboo*. Routledge & Kegan Paul, London.

Dumestre, Gérard
   1981–1989 *Dictionnaire Bambara—Français*, nos. 1–7.
          INALCO, Paris.

Garnier, Pierre
   1976   "Noms des plants en langue mandingue: Bamana
          (Bambara), Dioula, Maninka (Malinké), Mandingo.
          Langue Baoulé. Essai de classification logique des
          noms populaires de plantes." Ph.D. diss., Université
          d'Aix-Marseille.

Goldwater, Robert J.
   1960   *Bambara Sculpture from the Western Sudan*. Museum
          of Primitive Art, New York.

Goody, Jack
  1972 *The Myth of the Bagre.* Oxford University Press,
        Oxford.

Griaule, Marcel
  1952 "Le savoir des Dogon." *Journal de la Société des
        Africanistes* 22:27–42.

Henry, Abbé Joseph
  1910 *L'ame d'un peuple africain: Les Bambaras leur vie
        psychique, éthique, sociale, religieuse.*
        Aschendorffschen Buchhandlung, Munster.

Hopkins, Nicholas S.
  1971 "Mandinka Social Organization," in *Papers on the
        Manding,* ed. Carleton T. Hodge, pp. 99–128. Indiana
        University Press, Bloomington, Indiana.

Jamin, Jean
  1977 *Les lois du silence: Essai sur la fonction sociale du
        secret.* François Maspero, Paris.

Johnson, John William
  1986 *The Epic of Son-Jara: A West African Tradition.*
        Indiana University Press, Bloomington, Indiana.

Jonckers, Danielle
  1979 "Notes sur le forgeron, la forge et les métaux en pays
        minyanka." *Journal de la Société des Africanistes*
        49(1):103–124.

Knight, Chris
  1991 *Blood Relations: Menstruation and the Origins of
        Culture.* Yale University Press, New Haven,
        Connecticut.

Laye, Camara
  1978 *Le Mantre de la Parole: Kouma Lafolo Kouma.*
        Plon, Paris.

McNaughton, Patrick
  1979 *Secret Sculptures of Komo: Art and Power in Bamana
        (Bambara) Initiation Associations.* Working Papers in
        the Traditional Arts, vol. 4. ISHI, Philadelphia.
  1982 "Language, Art, Secrecy and Power: The Semantics of
        Dalilu." *Anthropological Linguistics* 24(4):487–505.
  1988 *The Mande Blacksmiths: Knowledge, Power and Art
        in West Africa.* Indiana University Press,
        Bloomington, Indiana.

Meillassoux, Claude
  1968 *Urbanization of an African Community: Voluntary
        Associations in Bamako.* University of Washington
        Press, Seattle.

Murray, Jocelyn, ed.
  1981 *Cultural Atlas of Africa.* Phaidon, Oxford.

Niane, D. T.
  1960 *Soundjata ou l'épopée mandingue.* Présence
        Africaine, Paris.

Nooter, Mary, ed.
  1993 *Secrecy: African Art that Conceals and Reveals.* The
        Museum for African Art, New York.

Pâques, Viviana
  1954 *Les Bambara.* Presses Universitaires de France, Paris.

Poppi, Cesare
  1993 "Sigma! The Pilgrim's Progress and the Logic of
        Secrecy," in *Secrecy: African Art that Conceals and
        Reveals,* ed. Mary Nooter, pp. 197–203. The Museum
        for African Art, New York.

Strother, Z. S.
  1993 "Eastern Pende Constructions of Secrecy," in *Secrecy:
        African Art that Conceals and Reveals,* ed. Mary
        Nooter, pp. 157–178. The Museum for African Art,
        New York.

Thoyer-Rozat, Annik
  1981 *Plantes medicinales du Mali.* OCGE, Bordeaux.

Travélé, Moussa
  1929 "Le Komo ou Koma." *Outre-Mer* 1:127–150.

Zahan, Dominique
  1960a "L'ataraxie et silence chez les Bambara." *Zaire* 14:
        491–504.
  1960b *Sociétés d'initiation Bambara: Le N'Domo, le Korè.*
        Mouton, Paris.
  1963 *La dialectique du verb chez les Bambara.*
        Mouton, Paris.
  1974 *The Bambara.* E. J. Brill, Leiden.
  1980 *Antilopes du soleil: Arts et rites agraires d'Afrique
        noire.* Schendl, Vienna.

de Zeltner, Frantz
  1913 *Contes de Senegal et de Niger.* Leroux, Paris.

Death of the deodand

Accursed objects and the money value of human life

WILLIAM PIETZ

"Whereas the Law respecting the Forfeiture of Chattels which have moved or caused the Death of Man, and respecting Deodands, is unreasonable and inconvenient": Be it enacted by the Queen's most Excellent Majesty, by and with the Advice and Consent of the Lords Spiritual and Temporal, and Commons, in this present Parliament assembled, and by the Authority of the same, That from and after the First Day of *September* One thousand eight hundred and forty-six there shall be no Forfeiture of any Chattel for or in respect of the same having moved to or caused the Death of Man; and no Coroner's Jury sworn to inquire, upon the Sight of any dead Body, how the Deceased came by his Death, shall find any Forfeiture of any Chattel which may have moved to or caused the Death of the Deceased, or any Deodand whatsoever; and it shall not be necessary in any Indictment or Inquisition for Homicide to allege the Value of the Instrument which caused the Death of the Deceased, or to allege that the same has no Value.[1]

With these words the British Parliament, in the summer of 1846, passed "An Act to Abolish Deodands," thereby undoing a law that had been in effect in England for over six centuries. A deodand was "an accursed thing."[2] The term itself comes from the Latin phrase *deo dandum*, which means "that which must be given to God." It is an example of the idea that evil objects are sacred, that they are charged with divine power, and that they therefore belong to God. In English law prior to 1846, any moveable material object—more specifically, any piece of personal chattel property—that

directly caused the death of an adult human being became deodand and, as an accursed thing, was held to be forfeit to God (whose earthly representative in such cases was the royal sovereign).

The abolition of the law of deodand was a relatively minor, but essential, part of a much more sweeping transformation in British social institutions of the 1840s that established legal structures better suited to capitalist enterprise and liberal society. But the issue it addressed was far from minor. Fatal accidents are a form of historical trauma common to any culture. For those who love and materially depend on the deceased, their disruptive force becomes a negatively lived object, an impassioned fixation, which represents a crisis not only in the violated hearts of certain individuals, but in the general structure of material social relations. Any culture must establish some procedure of compensation, expiation, or punishment to settle the debt created by unintended human deaths whose direct cause is not a morally accountable person, but a nonhuman material object. This was the issue thematized in public discourse by the debate on the law of deodand. Moreover, with its abolition, British legal institutions articulated the solution of liberal capitalist society to the general problem of the relation of the value of money to the value of human life.

Since the proximate cause of the death of the deodand as a social reality was itself an inanimate material object, the locomotive, I want to begin with an event that took place sixteen years prior to the statute of abolition. From consideration of this concrete event, I am going to indulge in some inexcusably far-ranging historical reflections on accursed objects and monetary debt as material embodiments of national sovereignty. I will, however, conclude with a somewhat more scholarly account of the abolition of deodand in 1846.

The unfortunate death of the Honourable William Huskisson

In September of 1830, the world's first public railroad, the Liverpool and Manchester line, made its inaugural run. The day had been carefully orchestrated

Thanks to Michael Taussig for inviting me to give the talk from which this essay is drawn as part of the Columbia University Department of Anthropology's "Angel of History" lecture series. Cordial apologies to Shael Herman, who so generously sent me the manuscript of a work of scrupulous scholarship that I have used so cavalierly. Thanks also to Tomoko Masuzawa for her interest in this essay and for inviting me to give the talk at the University of North Carolina "Fetishism" conference that began my interest in developing a materialist critique of the work of Georges Bataille, which has been continued in this essay.
1. *The Statutes of the United Kingdom of Great Britain and Ireland*, vol. 18, Acts 9 & 10 Victoria (1846) c. 62 (London: Eyre and Spottiswoode, 1847), p. 233.
2. Oliver Wendell Holmes, Jr., *The Common Law* (Boston: Little, Brown, 1881), p. 35.

not only as a business promotion, but as a national celebration. Liverpool and Manchester, the two great cities of the English cotton industry, had arranged for brass bands, speeches by local dignitaries, and a number of allegorical pageants celebrating English nationalism and industrial progress. Banners, grandstands, and archways of flowers were placed at gathering points along the route. The steam-powered cavalcade that set out from Liverpool at a stately 12 miles per hour consisted of eight locomotives, each flying a different colored flag and given striking names such as the Phoenix and the Rocket. These pulled a train of curiously upright carriages—their design was basically that of a stage coach on railroad wheels—that were occupied by notable men of British industry and politics. There were eleven Lords, four Viscounts, and one Marquis, the ambassadors from Austria and Russia, as well as the owners of the railroad. Among the politicians were Sir Robert Peel, the cotton magnate who, as Home Secretary, had just established the world's first modern police force and William Huskisson, a popular liberal Tory from Liverpool who, inspired as a young man by the American and French Revolutions, had been present at the storming of the Bastille but had since become a progressive conservative and tireless advocate of free enterprise.

Great crowds, estimated at half-a-million people, had turned out that day not to see any of these men, nor even the new technological wonder, but rather to catch a glimpse of the Duke of Wellington, hero of Waterloo and more recently England's Prime Minister. The crowd was mostly festive, though a few red republicans showed up waving tricolored flags and carrying signs demanding the extension of voting rights to a larger segment of the population. Unfortunately, the celebration was disrupted by what the *London Times* called a "dreadful accident" that occurred when the procession made a stop to add water to the locomotives' boilers. Among the passengers who got off to stretch their legs was William Huskisson. Huskisson had walked over to the Duke of Wellington's car—with the intention (so the newspapers said) of shaking hands with the great man in order to make up "an old quarrel"—and was standing on the tracks chatting with a group of politicians and railroad promoters. Let me quote the account of a *Times* correspondent for what happened next:

> Whilst he was standing with them, the Rocket engine, which, like the Phoenix, had to pass the Duke's car, to take up its station at the watering place, came slowly up, and as the engineer had been for some time checking his velocity, so silently that it was almost upon the group before they observed it. In the hurry of the moment all attempted to get out of the way. . . . [But Huskisson] hesitated, staggered a little as if not knowing what to do, then attempted to run forward, found it impossible to get off the road, on account of an excavation of some 14 or 15 feet in depth being on that side of it, on which he was, attempted again to get into the car, was hit by a motion of the door as he was mounting a step, and was thrown directly in the path of the Rocket, as that engine came opposite the Duke's car. He contrived to move himself a little out of its path before it came in contact with him, otherwise it must have gone directly over his head and breast. As it was, the wheel went over his left thigh, squeezing it almost to a jelly, broke the leg, it is said, in two places, laid the muscles bare from the ankle, nearly to the hip, and tore out a large piece of flesh, as it left him. Mrs. Huskisson, who, along with several other ladies, witnessed the accident, uttered a shriek of agony, which none who heard it will ever forget.[3]

Huskisson was dragged into the Duke of Wellington's car and a tourniquet applied to his leg, but it was clear the accident was fatal. The Duke and Sir Robert Peel insisted that the celebration be canceled and the train return to Liverpool. While the newspapers reported this merely as the expression of an admirably humane emotion, there was far more going on.[4] Wellington, Peel, and Huskisson led the three factions of a Tory Party that had been the ruling party in England for nearly half a century but that was now facing complete collapse. Wellington, the national hero, led the conservative Tories who wished to maintain the old political order that relied on a divinely ordained monarch, an established Anglican church, the army, and unreformed judicial and financial institutions. Peel, the innovative and authoritarian Home Secretary, led those Tories who recognized the need for strong new institutions to maintain social order and fiscal efficiency. Huskisson, who had pushed through major reforms as president of the Board of Trade and then as Colonial Secretary, represented those Tories most deeply involved in the global economy and who believed in the principles of free trade and "liberalism" before all else. When

---

3. London *Times*, September 17, 1830.

4. My characterization of this political moment relies on Jonathan Parry, *The Rise and Fall of Liberal Government in Victorian Britain* (New Haven: Yale University Press, 1993).

Wellington had been called upon to form a new government in 1828, Huskisson and other critics of the Duke's "illiberal" policies (they became known as Huskissonites) had bolted. The Tory coalition had been further weakened in 1829 as ultraconservatives became infuriated when Wellington had reluctantly pushed through a heavily hedged bill of Catholic emancipation. Worse yet, the winter of 1829–1830 saw a terrible economic depression set in. Many hard-pressed workers joined activist Political Unions. Local violence by the poor and unemployed surged. This, along with their own straightened circumstances, sent the middle classes into an apocalyptic fear of social chaos that expressed itself in a general demand for a more activist government and in a politicization of revived religious values whose focus became the demand for an immediate abolition of slavery in Britain's West Indian colonies. In June, the king had died, and a new king meant new elections in a year of crisis. The dire possibilities of such an election had been played out the following month in France, when a new election solidified an opposition backed by liberal business groups that, by the end of the month, had forced the king to abdicate. By September 15, the day of Huskisson's death, the Tory party was facing complete disaster in next month's election. The only hope of avoiding a transfer of governmental power to an opposition Whig party subject to unprecedented new social forces was to get the Huskissonites back on board. Astute politicians, Wellington and Peel saw in this bloody corpse not only a personal tragedy, but a new political fact whose ramifications had to be divined at once. However widely disliked Huskisson may have been in political circles for his vacillating unreliability, any treatment of the liberal Huskissonites fallen leader that might be perceived as disrespectful had to be avoided. (What happened, of course, is that the Whigs swept the election of November, 1830, and the way was opened for the Reform Act of 1832 that transformed the political constitution of England, which the Tories had so long defended.)

However, the railroad promoters of Liverpool and Manchester were part of the very social force that Huskisson represented, and they objected to turning a great ritual of commercial celebration into a procession of political mourning. They insisted that Wellington and Peel had a public duty to continue, that "the success of the project, on which they had expended so much capital, might depend on their [the procession] being regularly finished." They warned that if the expectations of the crowd of spectators in Manchester were not fulfilled, a riot might ensue:

> The public expected that they would have the satisfaction of seeing the road opened that day, and the directors were bound to fulfill their expectations to the best of their ability. It was quite certain that the news of the melancholy accident which had befallen Mr. Huskisson would reach Manchester, and that consideration rendered it still more imperative that the whole procession should move on, to correct any exaggerated reports of mischief which might get abroad, and to show the public *that the accident which happened was a mere accident, and had not happened through any fault of the machinery.*[5]

Wellington reluctantly agreed, and the procession continued, thereby averting a disastrous impression regarding the newborn railroad industry from being made upon that newly powerful political entity, public opinion.

But there was one more hurdle that had to be cleared. Would a coroner's jury declare that the locomotive involved deodand? Huskisson's body was taken back to Liverpool where it was laid on display in the city's principal public building. In any such case of suspicious death, the country coroner was required to impanel a jury of local citizens. The jury was first required to view the body and form a personal impression of the death. They then heard testimony from eye witnesses and other concerned parties, whereupon they decided whether a criminal homicide had taken place or merely an accidental death. If the latter, their last act was to decide whether or not an object was at fault and, if so, to declare the object deodand and estimate its money value, which became an amount of debt owed to the crown. In this case, as the always pro-railroad *Times* duly reported, the jury "returned a verdict of 'Accidental Death,' but affixed no deodand on the engine, from which it may be fairly inferred that they acquitted the engineers *and the machinery* of all blame."[6]

Oliver Wendell Holmes on the problem of the deodand

There are few ideas less rational to a modern mind than the idea of holding an inanimate object to be morally guilty for some effect it has caused. In his book

---

5. London *Times*, September 17, 1830. Emphasis added.
6. London *Times*, September 18, 1830. Emphasis added.

of 1881, *The Common Law*, Oliver Wendell Holmes traced the basic concept of deodand back to ancient German, Roman, and Biblical laws that required the physical surrender and sacrificial destruction of any lethally noxious thing, whether it was a knife purposefully directed by the hand of a murderer or some legally inanimate object that killed a person apart from the intention of its owner. The ox that gored a neighbor to death, the wagon that ran over a stranger in the marketplace, or the slave who killed a citizen must be surrendered, although experts disagreed whether this functioned primarily as a mode of expiation for the sin-tainted owner or as a way to satisfy the demand for revenge on the part of the victim's family and thereby avoid a blood feud. Holmes agreed with the latter view, since early law pursued the guilty thing itself even when its ownership had passed from the hands of its owner at the time of the death. As Holmes put it, "the liability seems to have been regarded as attached to the body doing the damage, in an almost physical sense."[7] This was in accord with Holmes's general view that "all law is directed to conditions of things manifest to the senses."[8] Hence his famous statement on the opening page of *The Common Law*: "The life of the law has not been logic; it has been experience."[9] Holmes explained his understanding of deodand, as well as his larger claim that the impulse for revenge was the origin of law, by locating its origin in an immediately lived response, specifically "the desire of retaliation against the offending thing itself," as exemplified in the angry desire one has to kick a door that has pinched one's finger.[10]

The reason why the apparently antiquarian problem of "the liability of inanimate things" was a central problem for Holmes in his effort to rethink modern liability law is illustrated by the confrontation between nineteenth-century industrial capitalism and the English law of deodand that is the subject of this essay. Earlier in the nineteenth century, jurists had tried to frame a legal theory adequate to the new industrial world by generalizing the principles of contract law. Such a framework worked well enough for controversies that could be understood in terms of intentional agreements between voluntary parties. But the new technologies

also multiplied the sorts of events in which injury occurred as an unintended consequence of mechanical operations, and the law of torts, that is, the body of laws compensating accidental wrongs occurring outside any preexisting contractual relation, had grown from a minor supplement to contract law to a separate field of equal importance. But the principles of tort law were far from certain. In *The Common Law*, Holmes attempted to establish these principles through what could be termed a historical phenomenology of material sensibilities (in opposition to the excessive formalism and Hegelianism that dominated the legal theory of his day). The task of the modern jurist was thus to discover the "anthropology contained in the history of law."[11] Influenced especially by the work of E. B. Tylor, Holmes sought to ground liability law in culturally specific standards of reasonable behavior, which in turn rested on what he called the "felt necessities" of a particular historical moment.

However, Holmes ultimately rejected this as a satisfactory solution to the nineteenth-century crisis in the understanding of civil and criminal liability.[12] The drawback of a method of cultural phenomenology as legal anthropology is its failure to take into account the conceptual effects of the multiple and often competing political institutions whose power shapes the legal discourse of a society. This is well illustrated by the concept of deodand itself. A law dictionary of 1579 inadequately defines the term thus:

> Deodande is when any man by misfortune is slaine by an horse or by a cart, or by anie other thinge that moveth, then this thing that is cause of his death, and which at the time of the misfortune mooved, shall be forfayte to the Queene, and that is called deodande, and that perteyneth to the Queenes Almener for to dyspose in almes and in deedes of charities.[13]

Although the paradigmatic event for deodand was indeed that of a material object that killed a person by its physical motion, this definition overlooks the fact that in concrete decisions about deodands, the operative

---

7. Holmes (see note 2), p. 11.
8. Ibid., p. 49.
9. Ibid., p. 1.
10. Ibid., pp. 34, 11.

11. Ibid., p. 37.
12. The reasons why Holmes abandoned custom as the standard for reasonableness in liability law are discussed by Morton J. Horwitz, "The Place of Justice Holmes in American Legal Thought," in *The Legacy of Oliver Wendell Holmes, Jr.*, ed. Robert W. Gordon (Stanford: Stanford University Press, 1992), pp. 31–71.
13. John Rastell, *An Exposition of Certaine Difficult and Obscure Words and Termes of the Lawes of this Realme* (Amsterdam: Da Capo Press, 1969), p. 62.

distinction was the feudal, institutional one between real and personal property. Real property formed a landed estate; the division or transfer of such property fell under the normal jurisdiction of the king's courts. Moveable objects that were personal chattel property, however, were transferred either through sales falling under the law merchant or through inheritance after a natural death, which was handled by ecclesiastical courts. The violence that made a chattel deodand was thus an exception to the normal division of property laws, since it placed a case involving personal property under the jurisdiction of the sovereign. It is the distinction between real and personal property that explains the oddity that a bell that fell and killed someone was not ruled deodand, despite the fact that its motion was the cause of death (because it was classified as real property, part of an estate). On the other hand, the lethal fall of a man off a stationary wagon could make the wagon deodand, despite its lack of motion (because a wagon was chattel property). Deodand is thus more accurately defined as "whatever personal chattel is the immediate occasion of the death of any reasonable creature."[14] (The latter qualification indicates that the death of an infant, who lacked reason and free will and hence the capacity for expiable sin, could not be the occasion for a judgment of deodand.)

While a historical materialist phenomenology of the sort Holmes attempted in *The Common Law* is necessary to grasp the idea of the deodand, it seems that it must be combined with a historical analysis of the theoretical discourse forged by a society's political institutions. In the case of the English law of deodand, this means examining the political theory established to legitimate a Christian state.

The pious use value of accursed objects and the fiscal body of the Christian sovereign

The English law of deodand differed from earlier Germanic and Mediterranean laws pertaining to guilty objects since it was shaped by Christian and feudal political institutions. The deodand that was forfeit to God was not destroyed in a public sacrifice but was rather surrendered for what the Church called "pious use." That is, its material use value was transferred from the private economy of material life to what we might call the Christian economy of charity and salvation. The accursed thing or, more often, an amount of money equal to the monetary value of that thing, was surrendered by the owner to the state for use in relief of the poor and other charitable activities. Things that had caused a human death became the rightful property of the sovereign and were given over to the king's high almoner.

The deodands responsible for sudden death were classified under a legal category of sovereign property that included any catastrophic source of royal revenue. Other examples were cargo washed ashore from shipwrecks, prizes seized in war, and chance discoveries of hidden treasure or gold mines. Various events of sudden violence and fortuitous encounter (what miners used to call a "lucky strike") produced a type of wealth that was held to belong to the sovereign if these occurred within the sovereign's territorial jurisdiction; they fell outside the normal privileges and protections inhering in real and personal property against the power of the state. The owner of such wealth was not the king in his status as a mortal person, but rather the monarch in his or her identity as the immortal body of the nation's sovereignty. As Kantorowicz mentions in his book on medieval political theology, *The King's Two Bodies*, this was conceived not through the modern distinction between the private sphere and the public sphere, but rather through the peculiar medieval distinction between the king feudal and the king fiscal. The king feudal was a particular mortal individual placed at the top of the hierarchy of voluntarily contracted feudal relationships. The king fiscal was the immortal king as the sovereign "crown." The latter, in Latin, was also called the *res fisci* (literally, "the fiscal thing"). The fiscal sovereign consisted of those materialities sacralized in the world of secular time by mundane historical events, as opposed to those objects sanctified through the divine salvational power that had entered the world through Christ. The wealth that became part of the king's fisc was conceived as a permanent, inalienable component of the sovereign, unlike the property that belonged to the king in his capacity as a mortal feudal lord, which could be sold off at need. As the fourteenth-century legal theorist, Bracton, wrote:

A thing quasi-sacred is a thing fiscal, which cannot be given away or be sold or transferred upon another person by the Prince or ruling king; and those things make the

---

14. *Jacob's Law Dictionary*, vol. 2 (New York: Riley, 1811), p. 245.

crown what it is, and they regard to common utility [what moderns would call "the public good"] such as peace and justice.[15]

This Christian feudal ideology produced what Kantorowicz calls "that seemingly weird antithesis or parallelism of *Christus* and *fiscus.*"[16] The *Christus*, the ecclesiastical body of Christ in this world, that is, the church with its eucharistically present Christ, its divinely empowered priests, and its sacramental objects, was concerned with the salvation of people's immortal souls. The *fiscus*, the fiscal body of the crown, that is, the king in his divine right as monarch, his officers, and the quasi-sacred objects that were the sovereign's wealth, was—in theory, at least—concerned with enacting God's law of Christian charity in the historical world of mortally embodied life. (I might note that while the use of wealth and money for the purpose of salvation in heaven corrupted and delegitimated the church, most spectacularly in the practice of selling indulgences, the use of wealth and money for the purpose of charity on earth successfully helped legitimize both the modern state and the charitable institutions, such as hospitals, to which the state granted special privileges.)

In the late twelfth century, the responsibility for deodands became part of the new office of the coroner. As is implied by the name itself, which is derived from corona, the Latin word for crown, the coroner was the direct agent and chief accountant of the sovereign in local affairs. The coroner's duty was to safeguard the rights of the crown by impaneling juries and holding courts of inquest into such things as shipwrecks, treasure-trove, and any unexplained death that might bring revenue to the crown.[17] As I have already mentioned, in late medieval times revenue derived from deodand judgments usually took the form of the money value of the accursed object rather than the thing itself. In the terminology of English common law, this meant that the thing had become liable for an action of debt, since the term "debt" referred to a specifically monetary obligation. This also meant that if the deodand object

was destroyed, the debt was canceled, since it was the thing itself, not its owner, that was the debtor. If the owner wished the continued use of the guilty object, then the money owed for its killing of a person was determined by the value of that particular object, be it a sword, an ox, a slave, or even, once such things came into existence, a locomotive.

The incorporation of capitalist debt into the sovereign body

Before turning to the abolition of deodand, I need to mention two important changes affecting the relation between deodand judgments and monetary debt that occurred prior to the nineteenth century. One need only be noted: the institution of the coroner had undergone a democratic transformation that altered it from being a direct agent of the crown in local affairs to being a representative of the local interests that was able to use the powers of the crown. This occurred not only because local citizens made up coroner's juries, but also because the coroner himself became a locally elected official. The other, however, requires a longer discussion; the fiscal body of the state underwent a fundamental transformation by its incorporation of a capitalist system of debt.

Since the time of the emergence of Christianity as the state religion of Rome in the fourth century, the law of Christian states had been characterized by an absolute ideological opposition to commercial debt, that is, to trade credit in the form of interest-bearing loans. The lending of money for profit, no matter how small, was condemned as usury, as a violation of the fundamental Christian principle of *caritas* (charity). As Shael Herman notes in his book, *Medieval Usury and the Commercialization of Feudal Bonds*, the main scriptural authority for this injunction was Luke 6:35, "Lend: expect nothing in return."[18] This position had only been reinforced with the development of European canon law in the twelfth century:

> Assuming money had immutable and absolute value, the Church apparently considered the idea of the time value of money as heretical as the teachings of Galileo and Copernicus. The autonomous system of canon law established by Gratian about 1142 had as one of its

15. Henry of Bracton, *De legibus et consuetudinibus Angliae,* 4 vols., ed. G. E. Woodbine (New Haven: Yale University Press, 1915–1942), fol. 14, translated by Ernst H. Kantorowicz in *The King's Two Bodies: A Study in Medieval Political Theology* (Princeton: Princeton University Press, 1957), p. 173.

16. Kantorowicz (see note 15), p. 173.

17. William S. Holdsworth, *A History of English Law*, vol. 1 (London: Methuen, 1903), pp. 82–85.

18. Shael Herman, *Medieval Usury and the Commercialization of Feudal Bonds* (Berlin: Dunker and Humblot, 1993), p. 14.

foundation stones an absolute ban on usury. In 1139, the Second Lateran Council deprived the unrepentant usurer of church sacraments and barred his burial in sacred ground.[19]

Lending money at interest was sacrilege because it exercised a power akin to unholy magic. Money was the tool of the great magician himself, the figure of the Antichrist, Simon Magus, when he tried to buy the miraculous power of the Holy Spirit from Saint Peter (in Acts 8:9–22). It was the need to preserve the holy power actualized in the sacrament of the Eucharist from corruption by the unholy power of money that made simony (a term derived from Simon Magus) the central issue in the Gregorian reformation of the Catholic Church.[20] Outside the church, whose priests held a monopoly on the power of the Holy Spirit, piety in the secular world was expressed in the act of charitable giving. Charity was the most godly of acts because it came closest to God's mode of action, the gift of the natural world that God created. The realm of secular temporality was itself a gift. As Karl Pribram has written, "Time was regarded as a common property given to all men as a free gift."[21] The gift of time, with its natural fruitfulness, came under man's stewardship in the form of real property (farmland and durable goods able to produce new things because they embodied the power of nature). But consumer goods and other movable personal property lacked such productive capacity; their "intrinsic goodness" could only be consumed by the owner or given away for another to consume. Since Aristotle, money had been classed among the consumer goods. Money could only be spent or lent, and lending was properly giving since money was naturally barren. The usurer who lent money at interest was corrupting the holy gift of time in the same way that Simon Magus tried to use money to acquire the power of the Holy Spirit from Saint Peter. Charging interest was thus not merely an unnatural use of money; it was a quasi-magical act entailing spiritual pollution.

Given the inevitable need for legitimate institutional structures to accommodate the monetary credit-debt relations crucial to the development of any widespread commerce, medieval states developed a number of creative evasions of the ban on usury. One, of course,

was the use of non-Christians as agents for loans. This received institutional form in England in the curious office called the Exchequer of the Jews. Another evasion, one available to land-rich monasteries and Christian lords, was the ruse of subinfeudation; agricultural land was nominally transferred as a nontenurial lease to a lender, in his guise as vassal to the borrower, so that a loan given to a feudal debtor could masquerade as rent and the interest on the loan paid to the creditor could masquerade as direct income earned by a feudal vassal from agricultural production.[22]

By the fifteenth century, laws against interest-bearing loans had been sufficiently undermined and European commerce had reached a sufficiently critical mass so that the greatest among the financiers providing intermediation services to commercial enterprises were able to draw enough currency from the web of monetarized debt values realized in bills of exchange and other financial credit instruments to begin making very large loans to the sovereigns of Europe. Monarchs of the sixteenth century like Charles V fought their wars on credit supplied by bourgeois bankers like the Fuggers and the Medici. Moreover, they increasingly fought these wars with weapons bought on credit from commercial industrial enterprises located in free cities. The expansion or contraction of the monetary value realized by private merchants in the form of capitalized debt and trade credit became precariously dependent on the fortunes of war and the victory or defeat of the particular sovereign a money lender or materials supplier had decided to back. That is, prior to the great overseas expansion that opened a vast field for speculative investment in colonial adventures and slave plantations, great merchant capitalists wagered their surplus money on great sovereigns who waged war.

In sixteenth-century Europe, the institutional linkage between the monetary values produced by commercial credit and those arising from public debt was still rather inchoate. My favorite example of this concerns a shipload of bullion belonging to Genoese merchant-bankers that was intended as a loan to the Spanish forces in the Netherlands who were fighting against the revolt of the Protestant Dutch. The dangers of the high

---

19. Ibid., p. 24.

20. Colin Morris, *The Papal Monarchy: The Western Church from 1050 to 1250* (Oxford: Clarendon Press, 1989), p. 101.

21. Karl Pribram, *A History of Economic Reasoning* (Baltimore: Johns Hopkins University Press, 1983), p. 18.

22. Elaborate notions of leasing have seen a great revival since 1995, when Citibank and other Western banks, in conjunction with financial institutions in Malaysia and the Gulf states, began to invent the accounting methods of "Islamic banking." Like medieval Christian law, Islamic Shari'a law bans the charging of interest.

seas forced the ship to take refuge in an English port, and Queen Elizabeth seized the treasure, which she desperately needed for her efforts to support the Dutch against the Spanish. Her seizure was legitimate according to the medieval law of sovereignty that I have already discussed, but Elizabeth, for practical political reasons, chose to treat this money as a loan, that is, as a debt owed to the bankers of Genoa who would have to be repaid. The Italian financiers accepted this shift of sides in their funding of the continental war. They couldn't do anything about it anyway and, after all, the money was not lost, only lent to an unexpected borrower.[23]

The crucial transformation in the fiscal body of the English sovereign occurred at the end of the following century, long after European monarchs had become thoroughly dependent on commercial credit. The great event was the founding of the Bank of England in 1694 and the creation of the first modern national debt. Unlike previous state debts, the British national debt that secured the Glorious Revolution was intended as a permanent entity that was never to be paid off. Individuals could invest in this debt by buying what we would call government bonds, from which they derived specified interest payments at specified times and which they could cash in at any time, making it a floating debt that came to be funded by all of the monied classes in the English nation. It thus became a political vehicle for building a national alliance between previously hostile agricultural and commercial economic interests, as well as an economic vehicle that provided the public money with which the new British state could build a navy whose primary political purpose was the protection and expansion of an overseas commercial empire.[24] Since the Bank of England was also the dominant source of private business loans in the nation, this institution for the first time enabled a functional unification of the body of monetary values existing in the form of private trade credit within a national economy and the body of monetary values created through public borrowing and the other fiscal activities of a sovereign state. This

innovation not only transformed the nature of the fiscal sovereignty of the state, but it set the stage for the modern history of money.

Money has traditionally been defined as currency, that is, as anything generally accepted as payment for goods and services and for the settlement of debts. A particular commodity, gold (along with other precious metals) functioned as the primary world currency from the beginning of the European colonial expansion until the 1970s. This meant that the supply and hence the value of money was dependent upon the chance discovery of precious metal mines and new techniques for refining these metals, because they affected the commodity value of the currency substance.[25] But the British invention of the modern central bank made the creation and fluctuation of monetary debt values realized in the capitalist accounting practices of private business enterprises an increasingly recognizable causal factor affecting the value of money. It also made the ability of states during crises, primarily wars, to issue paper fiat money, that is money whose acceptance is coerced by the state as legal tender and whose value is secured only by the general credit of the state, a third obvious determining factor. The creation and fluctuation of monetary value in capitalist societies thus appears to be triangulated between the changing market values of commodities and commodity currencies, the private monetary debt values created by trade credit and bank loans, and the standing public debt and issues of credit money of sovereign nation-states. That the value of money has become increasingly determined by the monetary values created in intermediated credit-debt relations, both private and public, rather than in the direct commercial exchange of commodities, is hardly news to economic historians. But economic models of the origin of monetary value do not take into account fatal accidents and other torts as an origin of novel debt liabilities and hence of new monetary values. To do so would be to acknowledge that death, the destruction of life, the very antithesis of an economically productive event, sometimes creates money.

23. This little-noted aspect of the famous "ship money affair" is mentioned in J. E. Neale, *Queen Elizabeth I: A Biography* (Garden City, New Jersey: Doubleday, 1957), pp. 176, 183–184.

24. For an excellent discussion of this, see John Brewer, *The Sinews of Power: War, Money and the English State, 1688–1783* (Cambridge: Harvard University Press, 1990).

25. I am referring to theories of money then current; the idea that prices were in truth more influenced by population growth was not part of orthodox economic theory prior to the nineteenth century. For a brilliant survey of price movements and their determinants, see David Hackett Fischer, *The Great Wave: Price Revolutions and the Rhythm of History* (New York: Oxford University Press, 1996).

The abolition of deodand: the money value of human life and immortal bodies without sovereignty

During what is still usefully referred to as the Industrial Revolution, capitalist manufacturing enterprise extended its dynamic drive toward technological innovation beyond the production and supply of wars and colonial adventures. It is undeniable that many of the new objects it produced in the world of early-nineteenth-century civil society were notable for their danger. Gas lighting, heavy machinery, even plate-glass windows became a new source not only of economic prosperity, but also of accidental death. Among these objects, the one with the greatest lethal potential was steam-powered transportation. In 1769 the inventor Nicolas Cugnot drove the world's first steam-powered land vehicle into a wall. (He was thrown into a French prison for being a danger on the road.) In 1801 at the trial run of the first English locomotive, the engine overturned and caught fire, while a demonstration two years later had ended with a boiler explosion and four deaths. I have described the accidental death of William Huskisson on the occasion of the opening of the first public railroad in 1830.

That no deodand was declared in Huskisson's death was important at the time, since powerful forces opposed the fledgling railroad industry. In those days a corporation such as the Manchester and Liverpool Rail-Road had to receive a special charter from Parliament. The fight to win this had been hard, since established interests, notably the owners of the canals with whom the railroads would compete for the domestic carrying trade, were adamantly opposed. As a publication called *The Anti-Rail-Road Journal* argued a couple of years later, the Manchester and Liverpool, which had turned a profit in its first years only because it had received a special tax exemption, benefited a relatively small number of investors, in contrast to canals, which had a far more extensive base of investors. The establishment of railroads inevitably diminished the property value of the canals in which many of the rural middle and upper classes had invested their capital, and these latter were the principal consumers who had created a prosperous internal market in England. This forecast of dire consequences for the general economy had a certain resonance in the depressed economy of the early 1830s. The antirailroad interests warned that a new and socially destructive principle had been introduced into the politics of corporations:

It is now to be laid down as a principle on which Parliament intends to act, that encouragement is to be afforded to every scheme which shall profess to be beneficial to its proprietors contrary or to the injury occasioned to property already in existence.[26]

The 1830s and 1840s do, in fact, represent the moment of the legal revolution that created modern corporations. The ancient law of corporations had concerned a special privilege granted by the state in the form of a charter to engage in and usually monopolize some socially beneficial—whether profitable or charitable—activity. The emergence of a capitalist economy required instead that incorporation be a routine procedure, a private right in civil society rather than a special privilege granted by the sovereign state. It also required that corporations be legitimized in terms of market competition rather than monopoly privilege. This entailed a theoretical contradiction between the right of property owners to enjoy a settled expectation in the stable value of the objects in which they had vested interests and the right of business owners to engage in free enterprise through market competition in which property values are always in flux and in which there are supposed to be both winners and losers (in this case, the railroad owners were the winners and the owners of canals and turnpikes the losers). This contradiction between the principles of property ownership and market competition was a fundamental problem underlying the later transformation of legal theory by such thinkers as Oliver Wendell Holmes.[27]

In this new institutional context, a parallel contradiction emerged in the sphere of public law; the state had a duty to protect the property and contracts of private individuals, but it also had a duty to act for the good of society as a whole. This often involved the confiscation of private property under the state's power of eminent domain or the diminishment of property values through state regulation, which happened to make some social groups winners and others losers. Indeed these contradictions determine the argumentative structure of legitimized politics within capitalist democracies. The logic of legitimate economic and

---

26. R. Cort, *The Anti-Rail-Road Journal; or, Rail-Road Impositions Detected, contains an answer to the Edinburgh Review and Mechanic's Magazine* (London: W. Lake, 1835), p. 52.

27. The argument of this paragraph and the one that follows relies heavily on Robert Meister's still unpublished study of American constitutional law.

political action that emerged in Anglo-American legal culture during the nineteenth century represented society as divided into two spheres, the public and the private. The public sphere of the sovereign state was conceived as a realm of coercive force that was justified only if it protected private rights in general and encroached on them only for reasons of the good of the whole society and not in a manner that deliberately redistributed wealth or power from one social group to another. The private sphere was conceived as a realm of voluntary association between private parties who established explicit reciprocal obligations by freely agreeing to enter into contracts. One thing Marx realized in his studies of revolution and class struggle in France at the end of the 1840s was that the discourse of political conflict between different groups in a modern society involved representing one's own group as acting in the interests of the whole society and opposing groups as acting in the interest of only their own part of society. Similarly, in legal disputes, a state's donation of land to the railroad industry, or a court's refusal to hold a railroad corporation liable for the burned wheat fields of farmers that had been ignited by a spark thrown from the wheel of a passing locomotive, could be justified by arguing that railroads and other embodiments of industrial progress benefited society as whole, whereas land owners or farmers represented only their own partial interests, and the public good outweighed these. Many of these legal controversies arose from wrongful injuries and deaths caused in unintentional accidents.

Within this new institutional and ideological context, there are two developments directly related to the emergence of a new model of the debt liability arising from accidental death. One was the civilization of such debt, in the original sense of the word "civilization": the transfer of social controversies that became justiciable cases from the criminal law of the state to the civil law of private individuals. The other was the institutional production of a new kind of (legally) immortal person: the modern limited liability corporation.

The civilization of accidental death was the issue that led to the abolition of deodand in 1846 as being "unreasonable and inconvenient." The 1840s was known in England as the decade of the "Railway Mania." By the early 1840s a disjointed network of railway lines had spread over England. This led to a proportionate increase in railroad accidents and a growing number of deodand judgments against locomotives, a very expensive capital asset. These raised

economic problems for railroad corporations and theoretical problems for law courts. For instance, a fatal accident on the Eastern Counties Railway in 1840 had resulted in four deaths and a judgment of deodand on a locomotive valued at 500 pounds; but did this mean that the company owed the crown a total of 500 pounds or did it mean that it owed 500 pounds for each death? One way or another deodand judgments on locomotives tended to get appealed all the way up to the Queen's bench, where they were almost invariably overturned. But local juries whose towns and farms had been invaded by the new reality of mechanized transportation were continuing to use the power of deodand to do justice as they understood it. There was no other way to compensate an accidental fatal injury. In cases where a person was maimed or mutilated, he or she could sue for damages. But in the case of accidental death, the injured party having ceased to exist, no one had standing to file a civil lawsuit. It was in order to pass the "Fatal Accidents Act" of 1846, which would allow this, that Parliament found it necessary to abolish the law of deodand.

The debate in Parliament emphasized the irrationality of deodand as a remnant of primitive law that should have passed away long ago. Deodands, said Lord Denman, were "a remnant of a barbarous and absurd law."[28] Lord Campbell, the great law reformer of his day, stated that certain doctrines of the revered common law were "not applicable to the present state of society. One of these doctrines was, that the life of a man was so valuable that they could not put an estimate upon it in case of a death by accident."[29] That is, the irrationality of deodand was that, in holding the value of human life to be infinite and hence unmeasurable, "compensation was made, not according to the extent of the injury inflicted, but according to the value of the instrument of injury."[30] The only cautionary note raised in the debate came from a politician who mused that, although he "was no advocate for the absurdity of the law of deodand," it seemed to him that "a simple compensation to the Crown was a very ready means of getting at the compensation which was due to the injured party."[31]

----

28. *Hansard's Parliamentary Debates*, 3d ser., vol. 87 (1846), col. 974. (Sixth session of the fifteenth parliament of the United Kingdom, House of Lords, 7 May 1846).
29. Ibid., col. 968 (24 April 1846).
30. Ibid., col. 626 (11 August 1846).
31. S. Wortley in ibid., col. 625 (11 August 1846).

This was a reference to the Scottish law of deodand, under which the state remained the party conducting the lawsuit and collecting the money due, but the state would then deliver the money to the closest relative of the deceased rather than to a charitable institution. The abolition of deodand meant that it would not be the powerful state that sued railroads and other corporations for compensations, but rather the relatives of the fatally injured person.[32]

There were a number of forces other than the modern industrial corporation that were working for the abolition of deodand. One of these was modern medical science, in the person of the coroner of Middlesex County, Thomas Wakely, one of the great medical reformers of the time. As editor of the journal *Lancet* and as a member of Parliament, Wakely tirelessly pressed for the reform of legal institutions in the name of modern medical science.[33] Wakely pushed the abolition of deodand in the House of Commons as part of his effort to restructure the office of the public coroner into something closer to that of a modern medical examiner. We should recall that this was an age still shocked by the scandalous activities of Burke and Hare, who robbed graves in order to provide corpses for doctors and medical researchers.[34] The transformation of the institution of the coroner into that of medical examiner was of some cultural importance, since it shifted the authority and the conceptual framework that provided the reasons explaining why a particular death occurred. Juries of ordinary citizens were basing their judgments of liability for death upon their response to the viewing of a dead body and their understanding of witnesses' narratives of what happened. Reformers like Wakely were revaluing the reasons for death within a scientific framework of purely physical causality from which moral considerations were, quite properly, removed.

The other important new social authority on death at this time that had an interest in the abolition of deodand was the insurance industry. The abolition of deodand and the passage of the Fatal Accidents Act meant that compensation for death was now a matter for civil remedies. These companies had such a remedy, a profitable one, in the form of life insurance and personal injury policies. It was the insurance industry that articulated the modern ideology explaining the proper monetary compensation for human life from a capitalist perspective. The best statement I have found of this appears in a fascinating book called *The Money Value of Man* that was published by two statisticians in collaboration with the Metropolitan Life Insurance Company. The book begins with a historical review of primitive modes for placing a money value on human life. One of these is compensation based of the value of noxious objects, as in the law of deodand. The other is, of course, human slavery. But the modern—and correct—approach, we are assured, is to view "man as a wage-earner or salaried worker."[35] Using actuarial tables of average life expectancy and the likely career trajectory and wage income of a person in a given occupation, one can calculate the amount of lifetime wage earnings lost by an individual killed in an accident before his natural time. In a capitalist society, this is obviously the correct logic for compensating a life, and we may note the class specificity it involves; people with different levels of income have differently valued lives. (The democratic wild card to this is the jury award of punitive damages, a practice the insurance industry is still ferociously fighting today.)

While medical reform and the rise of for-profit social insurance companies were important in the abolition of deodand, by far the greatest social force arose from the owners who managed and invested in corporations. The mid-1840s was the moment when the heterogeneous assemblage of rail lines built in the 1830s were gathered under the control of a few large corporations and when nearly all the liquid capital of England began to flow into railroad investment.[36] The reason for this was not

32. The debates also offer one harbinger of the coming class differential in monetary compensations for accidental death when Lord Campbell starts joking with the Lord Chancellor: "There is one objection to these Bills which I have heard. It has been said, 'Suppose the Lord Chancellor were to meet with an untimely end by a railway accident, which we all pray may never occur, how would the Jury estimate the loss to his family? What would be considered as the value of the tenure of his office? (The LORD CHANCELLOR: Hear, hear!) What would be considered a fair compensation to be awarded to his family for their loss?'" Ibid., col. 173 (7 May 1846).

33. For the important social contributions of Wakely, see S. Squire Sprigge, *The Life and Times of Thomas Wakely* (1899; reprint, New York: Krieger, 1974).

34. The role of British medical science in revising the institutions and ideology dealing with death in the decades prior to the 1840s, culminating in the Anatomy Act of 1832, has been discussed by Ruth Richardson in *Death, Dissection and the Destitute* (London: Penguin, 1988).

35. Louis I. Dublin and Alfred J. Lotka, *The Money Value of Man*, rev. ed. (New York: The Ronald Press, 1946), p. 3.

36. C. N. Ward-Perkins, "The Commercial Crisis of 1847," in *Essays in Economic History*, vol. 3, ed. E. M. Carus-Wilson (New York:

only high profit rates but also financial security. While railroads were a notably dangerous enterprise for their customers, they offered unparalleled safety to their investors. This is because railroads, in contrast to older corporations, had been granted the privilege of limited liability.[37] That is, investors were liable for the debts of the business entity in which they had invested only up to the amount of money they had actually invested. (The danger of unlimited liability has once again been demonstrated in the recent phenomenon of "debt millionaires" who invested in Lloyd's of London during its recent period of excessive speculation and fraud.) In the 1840s and 1850s, the advantage of the limited liability corporation form became evident to most corporations and investors, and a series of parliamentary acts were passed that established general limited liability as an essential quality of the modern corporation.

From the anthropological perspective I am adopting here, this represents the cultural production of a new kind of transhuman person (a corporation *is* a person in the eyes of the law) not subject to human mortality. The material assets of a corporation are owned by this entity and continue to be should any, or all, of its human owners die. In this, modern corporations are true immortal spiritual beings, as much as any god or sovereign. However, it is precisely their private status, the absence of the divinely legitimated power and the quasi-religious public duties of sovereignty, that distinguishes them. That these immortal beings are constituted through their monetary relation to the income-producing things they own is obvious to anyone who knows how to read a double-entry balance sheet; productive assets are represented as monetary values on one side of the sheet, while the mortal ownership of these assets appears as an equal amount of monetary value on the other side. The latter are divided into what is called "owner's equity," the portion of capitalized monetary value that belongs to the corporation's owners,

and liabilities, the balance of capital value that is owed as debt to outside creditors. It is debt that knits together the economic relations of different corporate entities and that becomes recognized as itself an asset in the balance sheets of banks and other financial corporations (and in the form of accounts receivable in commercial and industrial enterprises). That is, monetary debt, as constructed within this historically specific cultural system of economic accounting, is the fundamental medium of capitalist social relations.

Capitalism can fully establish itself as the structuring system of a social reality only to the extent that monetary debt in this sense becomes a practical logic and "felt necessity" in everyday social interactions. It may be that the historical limits of capitalist relations appear in those traumatic events that fall outside the economic realm of commercial exchange and contractual agreement, but whose material impact on individual human lives, in cases of accidental injury, and on whole peoples, in the form of war, nevertheless valorizes new debt relations that the modern social order must somehow realize in the form of monetary value. If there is a logic to the accumulation of such monetary values, I believe it has yet to be adequately theorized.

St. Martin's, 1966), p. 264. R. Dudley Baxter states that the capital speculatively invested in railroads at this time was "more than half as large as the national debt" so that railroads became "virtually mortgaged to the debenture and preference capitalist." "Railway Extension and its Results," in *Essays in Economic History*, vol. 3, ed. E. M. Carus-Wilson (New York: St. Martin's, 1966), p. 37.

37. "Railways had no old traditions to hamper their freedom. . . . It was the railways that won the acceptance of general limited liability." H. A. Shannon, "The Coming of General Limited Liability," in *Essays in Economic History*, vol. 1, ed. E. M. Carus-Wilson (New York: St. Martin's, 1966), pp. 375–376.

The constitution of Bohemia

JOSEPH RYKWERT

When Marcel Duchamp first visited New York in 1915, he was enthusiastic about the city (Calvin Tomkins reports), but especially about Greenwich Village: "a real Bohemia. Delightful. Why, [the place] was full of people doing absolutely *nothing*."[1]

He was introduced to the Village as an already famous painter, if only for the one picture, *Nude descending the Staircase*, which had been displayed in the Armory Show two years earlier. The Village was an obvious port of call, being the center of New York Bohemia: a place peopled by those "who did absolutely nothing" as well as their "natural" neighbors, artists.

This association of artists and layabouts in Bohemia is taken for granted, its relative novelty forgotten, and its harshly symptomatic nature neglected. I hope to direct attention to it in this essay—since I believe that the apparently trivial matter of the artists' social position and their image does point up a number of other issues and problems that our society and its masters have to face.

The association had first been made only about a century and a half ago, and the notion of the "artist"—musician, poet, painter, perhaps sculptor (even if more weighed down by his tackle, therefore more "stable" than the others)—as marginal to society, as irresponsible by profession, was first coined then. It follows the self-definition of a new middle class and attendant political upheavals (specifically the French political upheavals) that gave these events clearly visible and institutional representation.

A useful focus are the days in July 1830 when the last of the crowned, old-style Bourbon kings, Charles X, was deposed in favor of his cousin Louis Philippe. There was to be no coronation. The new King ascended the throne in the Legislative Chamber and signed (in triplicate!) a contract with the nation; he was King of the French by God's grace—but also the will of the People. His children went to public schools, and (unlike his predecessor) he was not really interested in the display of power.[2] A prudent businessman, he had managed the rump of his inherited estates so well before his accession that he was (privately) one of the richest men in France. Disillusion was to set in soon, of course, when he would appear as the bloated, pear-shaped monster familiar from the caricatures, but in July 1830 he was, however briefly, the one person who rallied liberal hopes—as Delacroix represented them in *Liberty guiding the people*; Marianne in her Phrygian cap storms the barricades leading a worker, a top-hatted bourgeois, and a uniformed student to freedom.[3]

The King had set an example to his fellow citizens: "*Enrichissez Vous*!" The slogan was attributed to François Guizot, the historian-statesman who often acted as the king's minister, even prime minister, through his

The Crown orb, the sceptre (*main de justice*), and sword were carried into the Chamber by Marshals of France, but the King merely touched them.

The princes were sent to the Collège Henri IV. As Duc d'Orléans, the King once observed: "*Je me moque absolument de l'étiquette*" and even after his enthronement, Victor Hugo reports in an undated note written sometime in 1830: "*Victor Cousin me disait hier: 'le Roi est désolé qu'on ne puisse pas le tutoyer. . . .'*" *Littérature et Philosophie Melées*, ed. Anthony R. W. James (Paris: Klincksieck, 1976), vol. 2, p. 314. On the other hand, Paul de Musset tells (*Biographie d' Alfred de Musset* [Paris: Hebert, 1888], pp. 181ff.) of his brother incurring royal displeasure when the then Duc d'Orléans—a school friend—showed the King a sonnet Musset had written on his escape (in 1836) from one of the attempts on his life. The king apparently disapproved of being *tutoie'd* in it. Maybe his views had changed in the six years. But see T. E. B. Howarth, *Citizen-King, the Life of Louis Philippe* (London: Eyre and Spottiswoode, 1961), pp. 136f.

Since François Guizot was aware of the incipient dissension between "academic" and "romantic" painters, he tried to signal the new Crown's neutrality in such matters by declaring a government-sponsored competition for a painting of the event, which was won by Amable-Paul Coutan, even though Ary Scheffer, the King's favourite painter, was one of the competitors. There were two more such competitions for canvases of "historical" events, but they were not a critical success and were discontinued. In 1848 another analogous competition was held for the figure of the Republic. See Albert Boime, *The Academy and French Painting* (London: Phaidon, 1971), pp. 116ff.; Raymond Escholier, *Delacroix* (Paris: H. Floury, 1926–1929), vol. 1, pp. 277ff.

3. The King bought the picture from the salon of 1831, though it was not much exhibited until 1848. On the novelty of the barricade and the political implications of the painting, see T. J. Clark, *The Absolute Bourgeois* (London: Thames and Hudson, 1979), pp. 17ff. On the figure of Marianne and the implication of the picture for the July Monarchy, see Maurice Agulhon, *Marianne in Battle* (Cambridge: Cambridge University Press, 1981), pp. 38ff. But see also Escholier (see note 2), vol. 1, pp. 266ff.

1. Calvin Tomkins, "Duchamp and New York," *The New Yorker*, November 26, 1996, p. 92.

2. The ceremony is described by David H. Pinkney, *The French Revolution of 1830* (Princeton, New Jersey: Princeton University Press, 1972), pp. 192ff. Eyewitness accounts (Duc de Broglie, Mme d'Agoult alias Daniel Stern, Alfred de Vigny, etc.) are reported by Jean-Louis de Courson, *La Révolution Tricolore* (Paris: R. Julliard, 1965), pp. 402ff.

eighteen-year-long reign.[4] Under the quasi-egalitarian rule of Louis Philippe, the middle class was finally seen to dominate French society, and the July Monarchy was the first royal government that deliberately embraced the aspiration of this new hegemony. A new kind of bourgeoisie had grown up in Europe, not primarily in France.[5]

Throughout the European Middle Ages and well into the sixteenth century, the urban middle class had contributed the manufacturing skill of craftsmen to the wealth of cities. These craftsmen were bound in guilds that both regulated and insured these workers and therefore often dominated local government. Merchants and bankers were important members of this class, but however great their power, they were numerically a small minority compared to the producers. In such a social structure, the role of those producers we now call artists—the painter, sculptor, mason, joiner—was integral to the social fabric. For financial, employment, and training purposes, they were organized in exactly the same way as weavers and tailors and blacksmiths. However, through the seventeenth century, the centralizing of patronage and the increasing demands of royal and princely courts would lead to the separation of the "fine artists" through their training in academies, and this isolated them from other craftsmen and made them directly answerable to princely authority. Yet throughout this changeover the "lifestyle" of the artist continued as before—as is obvious from the way in which artists represented themselves; their workshops are a common enough subject in European art. It usually shows the studio as a collective; the grinding of colors, the preparing of canvases goes on in that same space within which the master is working on the easel—whether elaborating a sketch or working from the model or yet giving instruction to his pupils and assistants, since the studio was also the only school for artists. Moreover it is their art gallery, their shop. The artist is sometimes shown dealing with critics and clients come to inspect or to buy his work and is often finely, nobly dressed. Occasionally he is shown relaxing before his unfinished canvas while playing a mandolin, and there are almost always musical instruments in the studio, as well as books, collections of engravings, works by other painters, and casts of body parts or famous sculptures, which could serve as props or teaching aids. The painter's studio was a place from which the master could deal as a responsible equal to other burghers, even to gentry and royalty. This busy, highly respectable and sociable view of his role was maintained in the early representations of the academies.[6]

The erosion of the political and financial power of organized guild craft in the arts by royal and princely authority during the seventeenth and eighteenth centuries was played out against the background of a great shift in the urban middle class. The factors that caused this realignment had emerged in the Low Countries but emerged even more energetically in Britain during the eighteenth century, specifically in London and Glasgow when foreign trade passing through London more than doubled and the new imperial market took over from the European one. A parallel growth in French trade concerned itself more with continental Europe, a shift that echoed earlier developments in Italy and in the Hanseatic towns of the Baltic. Power was passing from the manufacturers and their agents to growing groups concerned with distribution, services, and finance—products were turning into goods. The self-definition of this new class has occupied many sociologists, economists, historians—Spencer, Marx and Engels, Weber, Sombart, Simmel, Pareto—for over a century.

This new class asserted its power in the Revolution of 1789, and one of its most important economic and social enactments was the final dissolution of all guild organization. The new order inevitably evoked envy and opposition, much of it very clear-sighted and literate. Some came from the party of the aristocrats and friends of the ancien régime: Chateaubriand, Montalembert, the de Maistre brothers in France, and Herder and the Schlegels in Germany all spoke for the old social forms, as did Burke and Cobbett (or Pugin and Ruskin among artists) in Britain. More trenchant and aggressive were both social utopians as well as the leaders of proletarian movements; the names of Saint-Simon and Proudhon, Robert Owen and Charles Fourier indicate the enormous variety of that reaction.

---

4. The remark was extracted by Guizot's political opponents from speeches he made in 1843 and 1846. It was nevertheless the sense of his policy; as a faithful Calvinist, he was convinced that "God helps those who help themselves." He was also a firm advocate of free trade. See Gabriel de Broglie, *Guizot* (Paris: Perrin, 1990), pp. 333ff.

5. Even if North America has never had any other dominant class.

6. See John Walsh, *Jan Steen: The Drawing Lesson* (Los Angeles: The J. Paul Getty Museum, 1996), pp. 27ff.; a brief introduction by Michael Levey, *The Painter Depicted* (London: Thames and Hudson, 1981); Siegmar Holsten, *Das Bild des Kuenstlers, Selbstdarstellungen* (Hamburg: H. Chrisitans, 1978).

Many artists and men of letters were irked by the persistence of academic preferences in this novel situation. This impatience is sometimes presented all too simply as the dispute between "classicism" (following the old rules of propriety and composition) and "romanticism" (a demand for stylistic and expressive freedom, of which more will be discussed later). Classicism was identified to some extent with surviving absolutist governments; however while individual nineteenth-century monarchs certainly wanted to maintain the old patterns of royal patronage, the new finance-driven middle class also needed to create different conditions in which works of art might be exhibited and sold. Since the production of such works was still organized around the old academic disciplines, a conflict was inevitable. Training and production were no longer in harmony with display and marketing, and artists and their followers gradually found themselves marginal to the concerns and the lifestyle of the new class. Yet their products, being the trappings of "culture,"

were an essential mark of the social standing that the new bourgeoisie wanted to take over from the old aristocracy and the urban patriciate.

In this confused situation, artists were introduced forcibly to the demands and pressures of the market. By the middle of the eighteenth century, guild organizations had already become too weak to offer either stability or protection to them. Although they might not have articulated their unease, artists and literary folk seemed to understand even more clearly that their relation to the structures of power was becoming precarious, and they therefore often assumed combative, defiant attitudes for which the term avant-garde was later coined. However, a whole vocabulary of inclusion and exclusion that suggested the existence of quite separate, embattled nations was first formulated among them, and it soon passed into common speech. There were two words of exclusion, tinged with contempt, that would come to be used during the last quarter of the eighteenth and the first quarter of the nineteenth century to describe the

Figure 1. Jacques-Louis David, *The Tennis Court Oath*. Preparatory drawing on the canvas. Musee National du Chateau de Versailes.

public: "Philistine" in German, "Boeotian" in French. Both words have come to mean much the same: the gross, incomprehending, money-controlled bourgeois.

The "Philistines" of Scripture, with whom the Judges and the first kings of Israel had to fight, had moved into German student jargon towards the end of the seventeenth century (probably at the University of Jena). There had, it would seem, been a town-and-gown riot (not an unusual thing in university towns) in 1693. An innocent student had been killed and at his funeral the preacher[7] took as his text Judges 16:9: "And she [Delilah] said unto him, the Philistines be upon thee, Samson." Students therefore came to call townsfolk— and by extension, anyone external to the university— Philistines. The innkeepers became *Bierphilister*, landlords became *Hausphilister*, stable boys became *Pferdphilister*, and so on.

By the last quarter of the eighteenth century, Eichendorff, Goethe, Schiller, and Wieland were using the word to signify, generally, the unappetizing and art-alienated individual.[8] Even the very word *Buerger* was shifting; from the old sense of citizen, member of a craft, it was metamorphosing into a member of the *buergerliche Gesellschaft*—a group riven by impersonal economic competition, which only contractual agreements restrained within the social framework (the sense that it assumed for Hegel and more powerfully for Marx). Heinrich Heine (who, in his enthusiasm for the July Revolution, was inspired to move to Paris permanently) inevitably found "Philistine" a useful term of abuse.[9] About 1820, the word passed into English in the German form, "philister."[10] Through Thomas Carlyle and later Matthew Arnold, it was adpoted into general

English usage. It could even be given lyric form; Robert Schumann's *Davidsbuendlertaenze*, which ends with a rousing "March of the David-League against the Philistines," identifies King David, who killed the Philistine hero-commander, Goliath, as the archetype of the artist.[11]

The alternative term, Boeotian, comes from the Greek, in which it meant the coarse, beefy, greedy. The dull-witted people of Boeotia were (in later Greek literature) contrasted with the much cleverer and more refined Athenians. But a new currency was given to the word early in the eighteenth century by Alain Lesage's *Histoire de Gil Blas*,[12] a best-selling, quasi-picaresque novel about the evils of money-grubbing, and it was picked up by the novelists and journalists of the early romantic movement—by Balzac, Saint-Beuve, and Gautier—to mean much the same as "Philister" had in German. Now the English writers damned the Philistines following the Germans, as the Italians later in the century excoriated the Boeotians, following the French. But even though Gautier again—and Baudelaire—both used the word, the Philistines did not have as much currency as the Boeotians in Romance languages.[13]

The term with which the artists and the *littérateurs* came to label their way of life and show that they could keep a crass bourgeoisie at bay has a more complicated history. "Bohemian" definitely starts its existence as a polyvalent term of abuse[14] and never loses a disparaging undertone through the seventeenth century—so much so that when writing to the Dauphin in 1710 (in criticism of the depredations that the war of the Spanish

---

7. The pastor was the Generalintendant, Georg Goetze; see *Quarterly Review* (1899):438. The view that the incident is at the origin of the term was implied by Heinrich Grimm in his dictionary, s.v. "Philister."

8. The *Handbuch Deutschen Fremdwoerter*, s.v. "Philister," suggests that the sermon first took up a jargon term in 1687 to signify the town police in Jena.

9. But then Nietzsche uses the term *Bildungsphilister* for some of his opponents. *Kulturhilster* is coined with a similar intent—for those who abuse learning in the interest of pedantry and exploitation; while Adolf Hitler (*Mein Kampf*, p. 25) still explains *philister* as a virtual synonym of *petit-bourgeois*.

10. Though, of course, any group of enemies was commonly called "Philistines," and in canting language it signified the police. *A dictionary of the terms Ancient and Modern of the Canting Crew* (London, 1700), s.v. "Serjants, Bailiffs and their crew"; also, "Drunkards."

11. Op. 6, dated 1837; but the "March of the *Davidsbund*" also appears in op. 9, *Karnaval* (dated 1833–1835).

12. It was published in four parts: I and II in 1715, III in 1724, IV in 1735. He was by then a well-established playwright and translator (mainly from Spanish).

13. In Italian, for instance, while the ancient usage is familiar (to Vico), the modern usage is registered in Dossi, Gozzano, and D'Annunzio in the last quarter of the century. But although "Boeotian" does occur—in the old sense of thick-headed—even in Byron and Carlyle, it never assumes the full strength of exclusion that Carlyle already gave in 1828, when describing John Stuart Mill in a letter (7 March) as a "British-India Philister." However, Arnold, in his essay on Heine (in his *Essays in Criticism*, explicitly gives Carlyle's allusive usage general currency.

14. But Charles d'Orléans was already aware of that meaning at the beginning of the fifteenth century. In a *Rondeau* attributed in the manuscript to Pierre Chastelin, called Vaillant (Charles d'Orléans, *Poésises*, ed. Pierre Champion [Paris: Librairie H. Champion, 1923–1927], pp. 351f.), "*Pis suis que Boesme n'Yndien*," he says of himself as an unsucceful beggar for love.

Succession visited on the Kingdom), Fénelon complains that the Royal bailiffs are reduced to thieving and confiscation, living a *vie de Bohème* instead of administering. He uses the term in an offhand manner, taking its sense for granted,[15] though dictionaries now list this as the first written case of the usage. Furetière's *Dictionnaire* does not mention any connection between the Gypsy Bohemians and the inhabitants of the Czech lands, but derives the word from the old French *boème*, meaning "bewitched."[16] The eighteenth-century editions of the French Academy Dictionary list *bohémien* as meaning "Gypsies or Egyptians." It is not worth commenting on the literal meaning of Bohemian (the word for inhabitants of that part of the Empire called Bohemia) the Dictionary insists, but instead it concerns itself with those "vagabonds who wander round the country telling fortunes and thieveing expertly"; and it adds two metaphoric meanings: a "Bohemian" house is one that has no order or rule, while someone said to be living a "Bohemian" life is one *qui a ni feu ni lieu*. Much the same is the sense of the entry *Bohémiens* in the Great Encyclopedia of Diderot and d'Alembert. Yet in all of this there is not a word about painters or poets, since the figure of the respectable, bourgeois (in the old sense) citizen-artist had certainly not yet been affected by the change. Under princely patronage it might even be said to have shifted the position of the successful artist from that of the private citizen, the burgess, to that of a civil servant.

About the time of the July Revolution, the word changes definitively. Within two or three years a *boulevardier* of note, Félix Pyat, describes the rather miserable existence of aspiring artists living on the edge of society, dressing outlandishly, and speaking forms of canting language: "*Ils sont les bohémiens de nos jours*," he ends his account, as if the applying of such a term to people (some of whom he liked and admired) still required explanation.[17] Two or three years later, Lelio, the musician-hero of Georges Sand's *La Dernière Aldini*, justifies his equal enthusiasm for German and Italian music at the beginning of the novel with "*L'artiste . . . a pour patrie le monde entier, la Grande Bohème, comme nous disons.*" After he withdraws from two successive rich and noble marriages (to a mother, then to her daughter) so as to maintain his nomadic artist's life (in his case, that of a very successful opera singer), the novel ends with the toast: "Vive la Bohème." In both cases the sense is clear. It now has no particular reference to ethnic Gypsies.[18]

The ethnic nature of the terms Bohemian, Philistine, and Boeotian carried a charge of mutual distrust and aggression, which the modern half-joking (as Duchamp's) use of the words cannot convey.[19] The common French word for Gypsies was *Bohémien*, even if Molière already knew *Egyptien* as a synonym; *Gitanes* (after the Spanish *Gitano*) and *Tsiganes* were borrowed terms that were not accepted into general usage until the 1840s.[20] *Gitano*, like "Gypsy" is from *Aegyptos*, since Egypt is mentioned sometimes (though

---

15. François de Salignac de La Mothe Fenélon, *Oeuvres Complètes* (Geneva, 1971), vol. 7, p. 160: "*Les intendants font, malgré eux, presque autant de ravage que les maraudeurs. . . . On ne peut plus faire le service qu'en escroquant de tous côtés; c'est une vie de Bohèmes, et non pas de gens qui gouvernent. . . .*

Mme de Sévigné had already used the term to describe the bedraggled carriages of the Provençal M. & Mme de Valvoire (Letter 604, 29 August 1677: "*un équipage qui rassemblait à une compagnie de bohémiens,*" Marie de Rabutin-Chantal, Marquise de Sevigné, *Correspondance*, ed. Roger Duchene [Paris: Gallimard, 1972], vol. 2, p. 540). In English the word had appeared in the written texts even earlier. John Milton is reputed to have written about "Bohemians, the same with Gypsies, vagabonds that strowl about the country. . . ." quoted by Edward Phillips, *Letters of State . . . written by Mr. John Milton . . . to which is added an account of his Life* (London, 1694).

16. Antoine Furetière, *Dictionnaire Universel contenant . . . tous les Mots Francois. . . .* (The Hague and Rotterdam: Chez Arnoud et Renier Leers, 1690), s.v. "boème." With its quotation from Pasquier's Chronicle, it is the source of many later dictionary entries. Pasquier had reported the arrival of these "Christians from Lower Egypt" in 1472, but mentions an Ordonnance of the States at Orleans in 1560 demanding that they leave the Kingdom on pain of the galleys.

17. On Félix Pyat, see *A New History of French Literature*, ed. Denis Hollier and R. Howard Bloc (Cambridge: Harvard University Press, 1989), pp. 607, 689. The essay appeared in one of several anthologies popular at the time, *Nouveau Tableau de Paris au XIXme Siècle* (Paris, 1834). I owe this (and several other) references to Jerrold Seigel, *Bohemian Paris* (New York: Viking, 1985), pp. 16ff. Pyat appears as a sympathetic figure in Théodore de Banville's memoirs, in Augustin Cabanès, *Autour de la Vie de Bohème* (Paris: A. Michel, 1938), p. 11. He was benevolently caricatured (as the *orateur montagnard*) by Daumier when he became a deputy after the Revolution of 1848 (in *Charivari* 10.1.1849: delteil no. 1807).

18. (Paris: Felix Bonnaire, 1838). The hero-artist of the novel is a singer—who has free accesss to the aristocratic milieu, though he knows that marriage with him would have meant social disaster for either lady. His renunciation is partly due to an innate nobility and the artist's self-denial, but also the love of his true home, *la grande Bohème*.

19. See many of the extracts quoted by César Graña and Marigay Graña in *On Bohemia* (New Brunswick and London: Transaction Publishers, 1990).

20. There seems to be little doubt that Romany, the Gypsy language, is allied to northwestern forms of Hindi, with many

inexplicably) as their real home, though the word had little or no currency in France before Mérimé's *Carmen*. Popularized, it would seem by Liszt, the French *tsigane*, like the Slavonic *Cygan*, the Turkish *Çingeneler*, and the German *Zigeuner*, was derived from the Greek *athinganoi*, or the "untouched," or "touch-me-not," the name of an iconoclastic and perhaps judaizing heretical sect from Phrygia or even further east, whose devotees were known as fortune-tellers and magicians—heretics who seem to have been extirpated by the ninth century.[21] Yet the Byzantine Greeks already use a slightly different term, *atsinganoi* for a different group, "a Sarmatian people, descended from Simon Magus . . . famous for divining and spells," probably the ancestors of our Gypsies. Earlier legends, as well as the linguistic

evidence, all point to their having emigrated as a group, perhaps of musicians and entertainers, from or through northeast India and Persia sometime in the latter part of the first millennium.[22] At any rate they are first heard of in Byzantium in the reign of the Emperor Constantine Monomachus (1042–1055).[23] Various prohibitions and comminations are launched against them in the next centuries, while the term *Aegyptioi* seems already to be used interchangeably with *atsinganoi*.[24] However, a third term, the Rom, the Romani people (as they insistently call themselves) may have associated a word in their language to Romelia/Rumelia, the Turkish name for Thrace and Epirus, where many of them lived.[25]

The "Travellers" (as they also refer to themselves—in English, at any rate)[26] were often recognized as ethnically distinct and accorded self-government by a

---

admixtures from the languages of their several host countries. They appeared in the eastern Mediterranean at the break of the millenium.

A popular book by H. M. G. Grellmann, *Die Zigeuner: ein Historischer Versuch*, appeared in Dessau in 1783 and had another edition; it also appeared in French as *Histoire des Bohémiens* (Paris, 1810). A review of earlier scholarship is provided by A. F. Pott (a pupil of the great linguist Franz Bopp) in *Zigeuner in Europa und Asien*, 5 vols. (Halle: E. Heynemann, 1844–1845).

About the same time, George Borrow, who travelled (1835–1840) among the Spanish Gypsies for the British and Foreign Bible Society, published his *The Zincali; or an account of the Gypsies of Spain* (London, 1841); he would have much to say about the Gypsies in *The Bible in Spain* which had appeared in 1842/3, and his published fiction (*Lavengro, Romany Rye*) is also based on his Gypsy experiences.

21. J. Starr, "An Eastern Christian Sect: The Athinganoi," *Harvard Theological Review* 29 (1936):103ff. Since their teachings and practices (such as Sabbatarianism) are known largely through formulae of abjuration, a clear picture of them cannot be reconstructed. At any rate, they do seem rather different from the *atsinganoi* who appear somewhat later. Some lexicographers derive *Zingaro, Zinghero, Cygan*, and *Tsigane* from the Romany word *zengaris*, which I cannot find, however, in any of the Romany dictionaries to which I have had access.

A much earlier attempt to identify the Gypsies with a religious as well as an ethnic entity was made by a French student working in Rumania, J. A. Vaillant, "Origine, Langage et Croyances des Ro-Muni, Zind-Romes et Zind-Cali," in *Revue de l'Orient* (Paris: Societe Orientale, 1846), vol. 4, pp. 127ff., suggests that like the Bulgarians the Gypsies were Manicheans—a Godless people, *Athoi-genoi* to the orthodox—and derives a systematic account of their beliefs from their language. In his later publications (on which see Josette Blanquat, "Une Mythologie des Gitans Inspiratrice des Poètes?" in *Recherches sur le Monde Hispanique au Dix-Neuvième Siecle* (Lille and Paris: Universite de Lille, 1973, pp. 211ff.), Vaillant elaborated the system into a curious amalgam of Vico and Swedenborg; this was in part taken over by the popularizer-Magus who called himself Papus (Gérarad Encausse) and by another esoteric popularizer (and vociferous admirer of Wagner) Eduard Schuré and had a powerful unfluence on Parisian artists towards the end of the nineteenth century.

22. The recent studies are summed up by Angus Fraser, *The Gypsies* (Oxford: Blackwell, 1992), pp. 33ff.

23. They are associated with a number of heretical sectaries whom the Byzantine Emperors moved from Asia Minor to Rumelia—around Adrianople—in the ninth century. Hence perhaps the term "Romany."

Such an association of heretics with magicians may have worked the association of Bohemians as Gypsies with the Bohemian Brothers in France—much as the Bogomils (god-lovers) are assimilated to Bulgarians and corrupted to *bougre* and "bugger" in English.

24. A "Johannes Cinganus," the (presumably) Gypsy authority (or commander) at Nauplion is—apparently unlawfully—deprived of his post by the Venetian governor and restored by the Council of Forty. He had been appointed as *Drungarius* (a Byzantine military title) *Acinganorum* by Ottavio Bono, who was *Potestas et Capitaneus Neapolis Romanie* from 1398 until 1403–1404; he was deprived by his successor Matteo Barbaro and restored by the Forty in 1444. But see François de Vaux Forestier, *Mille Ans d'Histoire des Tsiganes* (Paris: Fayard, 1970), pp. 14ff. The best summary of the evidence is given by Fraser (see note 22); Fraser suggests (p. 47) that the Greek word *Aiguptissa* referred specifically to women fortune-tellers and had no ethnic reference.

Du Cange in his Glossarium only knows them as "'Aegyptiaci,' *Vagi homines qui Italis 'zingari,' Hispanicis 'gitani,' Gallis 'Bohemi,' 'Aegyptii,' 'Saraceni' appellantur*."

25. George C. Soulis, "The Gypsies in the Byzantine Empire and the Balkans in the Late Middle Ages," *Dumbarton Oaks Papers* 15 (1961):141ff. The term went on being used for what remained of Turkish possessions in Europe by the Treaty of Berlin in 1878, which were incorporated into Bulgaria in 1885. The association with Romania, the country, cannot predate its creation (out of Wallachia, Moldavia, and a part of Bessarabia) by the Treaty of Paris in 1856. A summary account of the different words the Gypsies use for themselves, *Manouch, Sinti*, and their divisions according to trade and origin is found in Fraser (see note 22), pp. 8f. But then, as he suggests, the *rom* words may simply mean "people."

26. On the sense of "travellers" in other languages, see Fraser (see note 22), pp. 7, 295ff.

number of European rulers as they moved north and west—notably early in the fifteenth century by the Emperor Sigismund (as King of Bohemia).[27] Although several other and later privileges are recorded—as far away as Scotland over the next century—the "Travellers" were most populous in the eastern reaches of what became the Habsburg Empire: Czech lands, Slovakia, Hungary, Transylvania, the North of Serbia, Croatia, and Bulgaria. It may well be that *Bohémiens*, the name they acquired in the fifteenth and sixteenth centuries, derives from the groups that entered France immediately from Bohemia. As they spread further into Europe under their various names, they acquired the reputation to which Fénélon referred: their caravans were bedraggled, their civic reputation was for shiftiness and irresponsibility, and worse. They were sometimes confused with the *Stradioti*, marauding bands of mostly dispossessed Slavonic (Albanian, Bohemian, Moravian, Polish, Ruthenian) peasants who acted as occasional mercenaries.[28]

Artists found them curious. In the earlier engravings—one by the "Master of the Housebook" of 1480 or thereabouts, another by Lucas van Leyden a decade or two later, and in the woodcut (in the second, illustrated edition) of Sebastian Muenster's *Cosmographia Universalis*[29]—they are distinguished by their horizontally striped cloaks and the men's peaked hats and the women's turban-covered basketwork hats. They appear sporadically in sixteenth-century painting; Titian's *Madonna degli Zingari* is simply a nickname for the dark-haired and dark-eyed model,[30] yet the portrait of a blue-eyed girl by the Cremonese Boccaccio Boccacini (in the Uffizi, Florence) is known as *La Zingarella*,[31] the same nickname was applied to a Madonna (with her tresses wound and covered with a handkerchief) and Child (presumably at rest on the Flight to Egypt, hence the informal posture and dress) by Correggio (which brought a reproof from Cardinal Francesco Borromini for showing the Madonna as a Gypsy) now in the Capodimonte Museum in Naples.[32] More ethnographically "correct" are the foreground fortune-tellers in Peter Breughel's *St. John Preaching* in the Museum of Fine Arts in Budapest (dated 1566 by the artist), shown telling fortunes in the foreground and identified by their "national" costume.[33] Jacques Callot produced a suite of four engravings showing a Gypsy caravan in 1621, and legend has it that he traveled with Gypsies when he went to Italy on his youthful journey there.[34] However the most popular "art" image of Gypsies was "coined" at the end of the sixteenth century by Michaelangelo da Caravaggio, whose palmist Gypsy girl points to the line of heart or the "Girdle of Venus" on the fine young man's hand as she slips a ring

---

The early form of Gipsy (plural Gypsies) was *gypean*, from *Ægyptius*; early in the sixteenth century John Skelton calls Maria Egyptiaca, "Mary Gipsey." The language of these "Egyptians" is first recorded by Andrew Boorde's *Fyrst Boke of the Introduction of Knowledge* (London: W. Copland, 1548). On the other early studies of the language of Gypsies, see Fraser (see note 22), pp. 186ff., though it is clear that many earlier students had some difficulty in distinguishing Romany from "Canting" language.

27. The much quoted imperial privilege to *Ladislaus Wayuda Ciganorum* is dated 1423 (quoted from the *Diarium Sexennale Andrei Presbyteri* in Felix Ofelius (von Oefele), *Rerum Boicarum Scriptores* [Augsburg 1763], vol. 2, p. 15). About the same time, a distressed "Count of Little Egypt" is given a grant of money by the citizens of Tours. By 1505 James IV of Scotland paid "Eigyptian" entertainers and wrote a letter of recommendation to "Antonius Gagino *ex Parva Egipto Comes* (Count of Little Egypt)," and they appear in England soon after.

The various dates of Gypsy appearance have been collected by S. S. Shashi, *Roma: the Gypsy World* (Delhi: Sundeep Prakashan, 1990), pp. 18ff. On the arival of the Gypsies in Spain, see Maria-Helena Sanchez Ortega, *La Inquisición y los Gitanos* (Madrid: Taurus, 1988), pp. 13ff. In France, see François de Vaux de Foletier, *Les Tsiganes dans l'Ancienne France* (Paris: Connaissance du Monde, 1961); and *Les Bohémiens en France au 19e Siècle* (Paris: Lattes, 1981). Francesco Predari's *Origine e Vicende dei Zingari* (Milano: Tip. di P. Lampate, 1841), although adding little to the scholarship, is almost unique in being illustrated.

28. John Hale, *The Civilization of Europe in the Renaissance* (London: Harper Collins, 1993), p. 165. The term seems also to have been a regional one—applied to the South Albanians whom the Venetians moved up the Croatian coast and spelled *stradiotti*.

---

29. The first edition also published in Basel in 1534 was unillustrated.

30. Harold E. Wethey, *Titian* (London, 1969), vol. 1, p. 98, no. 47; there is a replica in the Museo Civico in Rovigo. This nickname seems unknown to G. B. Cavalcaselle and J.-A. Crowe, *Tiziano, la Sua Vita e i suoi Tempi* (Florence: Successori Le Monnier, 1877), vol. 1, pp. 44ff.

31. This picture has also been attributed to Garofalo; on their relation, see Roberto Longhi, *Officina Ferrarese* (Florence: Sansoni, 1956), pp. 70ff.

32. Alberto Bevilacqua and A. C. Quintavalle, *L'Opera Completa del Correggio* (Milan: Rizzoli, 1970), p. 93; Cardinal Borromeo's reproof was in his *Musaeum* quoted by Arlene J. Diamond, *Cardinal Francesco Borromeo* (Los Angeles, 1974, microfilm), p. 235.

33. Gustav Glück, *Breugels Gemälde* (Vienna, 1951), p. 80, no. 35.

34. Jules Lieure, *Jacques Callot* (1924–1929; reprint, New York: Collectors Editions, 1969), pls. 374–378; Baudelaire's poem *Bohémiens en Voyage* (XIII in *Les Fleurs du Mal*) seems based on these engravings rather than any personal experience of Gypsy caravans and the poem certainly echoes one of the distichs on the engraving; though he also has a rhapsodic homage to them in his "Vocations" (*Oeuvres Complètes* [Paris: Gallimard,1975], vol. 1, p. 334). They also figure in his projected but not written libretto on "La Fin de Don Juan" (1975), vol. 1, p. 627.

off his finger.[35] The picture was admired, engraved, copied, and vulgarized throughout the seventeenth century, as was another theme he painted about the same time, that of the card-sharpers, a popular subject emulated (among others) by Georges de la Tour, though all of them have been overshadowed by the recently discovered and much discussed canvas of the smart young man having his purse cut by some Gypsies while others are telling his fortune. The old crone on the left of the young man, in her brocaded "Egyptian" blanket fastened at the shoulder over a chemise, like that of Caravaggio's Gypsy girl, becomes part of the lowlife repertory of *Caravaggisti*.[36] However, among the very same painters, another image of the Gypsy also appears—that of the young and apparently innocent fortune teller deceived by her own art and being fleeced by an adroit thief while engaged in telling another's fortune; the most famous is by Jean de Boulogne (who was known as Le Valentin), a French pupil of the *Caravaggista* Bernardo Manfredini. This representation is somewhat closer to the more sympathetic image of the Gypsies in literature, in which they mostly feature as stock characters.[37] Anyway, by the later sixteenth and seventeenth centuries, they provoke less literary wonder and more repressive action.[38] Cervantes may be the first to innovate by abandoning the stereotype; one of his *Novelas Ejemplares* (first published in 1613) called "la Gitanilla," seems to open with the usual recital of Gypsy vice:

> It seems that gypsies, both men and women, are only born into the world to be thieves: they are born of thief parents, they bear thieves, they train to be thieves and end up as fluent and thorough thieves in all seasons. . . .

Yet his heroine, Preciosa, who turns out not to be a Gypsy by blood after all (so that the novel can end with a good marriage), is not only beautiful and a great dancer, but also:

> . . . the most comely and prudent—not just of the gypsies—but of all the comely and prudent persons whose fame is known. . . .

This *discreción* has fascinated many writers, and although the literature of Gypsydom is thin enough,[39] *la Gitanilla* had repeated theatrical and even operatic reanimations into the nineteenth century.[40] It remains one of the earliest, and for a long time certainly the best-known and most-emulated of Gypsy stories.

---

35. *La Diseuse de Bonne Venture*, usually dated about 1595 now much restored, is in the Louvre, no. 1122.

36. The painting (now in the Metropolitan Museum, New York) was only discovered in 1946 and first shown publicly in 1960. There are two very close versions of a picture of a card-sharper by him, one with the ace of spades, the other with the ace of clubs, both in private collections and very similar in style to the "Fortune Teller."

37. In German there is Hans Sachs's farce, *Die Fuenf Elenden Wanderer*; in Italian, a Roman comedy by Gigio Artemio Giancarli, *La Zingana*; in Portuguese, Gil Vincente's *Farsa das Ciganas*.

38. Hans Sachs is the heroic (and very prolific) cobbler-poet of Nueremberg who cuts such a fine figure in Wagner's *Meistersingers*; Vicente was the court dramatist of John III of Portugal, and his play was performed before the King in 1516 at Evora. Incidentally, it is curious that the Portuguese base their word for Gypsy on *Tsigan*, while the Spanish *Gitano* was a corruption of *Egyptiano*.

39. Miguel de Cervantes, *Obras* (Madrid, 1993), vol. 3, pp. 21 ff. for the text. The two passages quoted are:

> *Parece que los gitanos y gitanas solamente nacieron en el mundo para ser ladrones: nacen de padres ladrones, crianse con ladrones, estudian para ladrones, y, finalmente salen con ser ladrones corrientes y molientes a todo ruedo . . .* and
> *la mas hermosa y discreta, no entre los gitanos' sino entre cuantas hermosas y discretas pudiera pregonar la fama. . . .*

Ben Jonson's "Metamorphosed Gipsies" (of 1621) are in fact masked courtiers who tell fortunes, and speak in canting talk, not Romany. Gypsies appear in Thomas Middleton's and William Rowley's "The Spanish Gipsie" (1623) already based on Cervantes *Gitanilla*; a number of minor late-eighteenth-century plays involving Gypsies are listed by Frank Wadleigh Chandler, *The Literature of Roguery* (Boston: Houghton Mifflin, 1907), vol. 1, pp. 268ff.

Gitanilla was therefore a child of gentlefolk stolen by Gypsies, much as half-a-century later, Molière's Zerbinetta, in "*Les Fourberies de Scapin*" (1671), would call them *Egyptiens*.

40. Antonio de Solis based *La Gintanilla de Madrid*, which appeared in 1671, on it; in French, *La Belle Egyptienne* was a title used for two versions, by Alexandre Hardy (1615) and Sallebray (1642). Middleton and Rowley's version was already mentioned. A number of Dutch versions were done in the seventeenth century; in German *Die Ziegeuner*, by Heinrich Ferdinand Moeller (1777); in 1821 the opera *Preciosa*, by Karl Maria von Weber sets to music a German version by Pius Alexander Wolff, and even later and in English is the almost equally famous *Bohemian Girl*, by Alfred Bunn and William Balfe, which was first shown in 1843; there were several others.

There were also many pseudo-Gypsies in seventeenth- and eighteenth-century literature, like Ben Jonson's *Gipsies Metamorphosed*, who are disguised courtiers using canting language, which with other underworld slang, is made to pass for Romany, though the troop of Gypsies with whom Ragotin gets blind drunk in Paul Scarron's *Roman Comique* are the real thing. Somewhat later, Sir Walter Scott seems to have known some Gypsies personally and taken a real interest in Romany. Hayraddin Maugrabin, who makes a curious appearance in *Quentin Durward*, which was published in 1823, describes himself as a "Zingaro, a Bohemian, an Egyptian, or whatever the Europeans . . . choose to call our people. . . ." He professes no

La Gitanilla's most famous descendant was a Gypsy proper, the beautiful Esmeralda, heroine of Victor Hugo's *Nôtre Dame de Paris*. The *Bohémienne* Esmeralda becomes *une Egyptienne* at the end of Hugo's book. Esmeralda is fatally attractive, yet an innocent victim of oppressive power.[41] A few years later, in 1845, yet another literary Gypsy, a victim also—but no innocent—begins her career. Carmen, "la Carmencita," is first a short story by Prosper Mérimée but is then taken up by Henri Meilhac and Ludovic Halévy,[42] to be transformed into the opera by Georges Bizet—first performed in 1875; after its first-night fiasco (which killed the composer), it quickly became a great international success, and it is now one of the two or three most frequently performed operas.

> *L'amour est un oiseau de Bohème*
> *Il n'a jamais connu de loi*

runs like a refrain through it.[43]

Real Gypsy-artists, musicians, and virtuosi from Hungary and Romania—where they were often court musicians of princes and great nobles—had by then also become well known in France and Germany. In 1839–1848, Franz Liszt, who had patronized bands of Gypsy musicians, revisited his native Hungary and found that the Gypsy bands produced a music that he considered part of a "fantastic *epopeia*: half Ossianic (for there pulses in these songs the feeling of a vanished race of heroes) and half gypsy."[44] *Des Bohémiens et de leur Musique en Hongrie*, when it was finally published in 1859, received much adverse criticism in Hungary, mainly for failing to identify the specific, un-Gypsy character of ethnic Hungarian music, and this caused Liszt a certain amount of trouble with his countrymen.[45]

Between Hugo's Esmeralda and Mérimée's Carmen, the identity of the Bohemian assumed its more or less modern meaning. Two minor writers, Adolphe Dennery and Eugène Grangé had a comedy—really a series of sketches—*Les Bohémiens de Paris* performed in 1848; Balzac, whose *Fantaisies de Claudine* of 1839 defines Bohemia as a land of the young "men of Genius in their own line, as yet almost unknown but with the ability to become known one day. . . ." changed the title of that novel into *Un Prince de la Bohème* on revising it in

---

religion, has no property, and obeys no laws. And he adds an ethnological note to the book, which shows that he was reading the philologists and historians who begin to take a serious interest in the language and the customs of the Gypsies (*Quentin Durward* [1823; reprint, Edinburgh , 1867], pp. 356ff., 395ff.). Scott had already said a little about the Scots Gypsies in *Guy Mannering*, but his interest appears in several letters; see *The Letters of Sir Walter Scott*, ed. H. J. C. Grierson (London: Constable and Co., 1933), vol. 5, pp. 282

41. It may be worth reminding the reader that Hugo pleaded the disturbances of the July Revolution as the excuse for delivering the manuscript of the novel late to the publisher.

42. Most famous in their time as the librettists for Offenbach. Prosper Mérimée also translated, as *Les Bohémiens*, Pushkin's "Tsygany." Interestingly enough, in the novel, the relationship between Carmen and José begins by their having a common language—Basque, not Romany. The Diderot and D'Alembert *Encyclopédie* makes the association already (s.v. "Bohémiens"): "*Les Biscayens & autres habitants de la meme contrée ont succédé aux premiers* bohémiens *et on leur a conservé le nom. Ils se mèlent aussi à voler le peuple ignorant. . . .*"

It was about this time that Mérimée translated into French Pushkin's *Tsiggany*, a brief rhapsodic drama, which Pushkin had written about 1825 in exile, in Kishinev in Bessarabia, and which plays on the nobly freedom-loving, untamelled character of the gipsy.

43. Though when they first meet, Carmen and Don Jose Lizzarrabengua (*vous connaissez assez l'Espagne, monsieur, pour que mon nom vous dise aussitôt que je suis Basque. . . .*) speak not in Romany but in Basque. Bizet's music takes up a very mellifluous version of the *Cante Hondo/Jondo*, the Andalusian "deep" song, which only came out of anonymity late in the eighteenth century (when Gypsy oppression by the Spanish crown was attenuated) and was not established as a recognized entertainment *genre* (now called Flamenco) until the 1840s, about the time when Mérimée wrote his short story; he certainly knew (and used) Borrrow's *Zincali*.

44. He based his *Hungarian Rhapsodies* on this music. That Liszt's "Gypsy" music included all sorts of extraneous elements—even Gypsy transpositions of modern "salon" music—has long been known. But, in fact, the major work on Hungarian folk music was done by Bartok and Kodaly in the twentieth century.

45. He presented a copy of the book as soon as it was published to Baudelaire in 1859, in exchange for one of *Les Paradis Artificiels*. But his attribution of some popular Hungarian tunes by living composers, as well as traditional Hungarian melodies, to the Gypsies was sharply criticised in Hungary. For the second edition of 1881 some parts (particularly those relating to Jews) were sharpened by Princess Sayn-Wittgenstein—Liszt did not see the manuscript or proofs; her daughter, Princess Marie Hohenlohe, revised them for the "popular" edition (Leipzig, 1911, vol. 3). See Alan Walker, *Franz Liszt* (Ithaca and London: Cornell University Press, 1987), vol. 2, pp. 334ff. About 1840 Liszt had half-adopted a Gypsy boy-prodigy violinist, Josi Sàrai, who had been given to him as a present (he had presumably been bought as a slave, as Gypsies often were) by Count Sàndor Teleki; he proved untameable and unteachable. Liszt wondered about his fate in *Des Bohémiens* though Josi, who had been returned to his tribe, was playing in a Gypsy band at Debreczen, had married a Gypsy girl, and called his son Ferencz, appointing Liszt his godfather *in absentia*. In the ensuing correspondence, Liszt expressed a strange and nostalgic admiration for the Gypsy life. Alan Walker (this note), vol. 2, pp. 339f. Of course, the researches of Kodaly and Bartok were undertaken to give back to the Magyars what Liszt had appropriated for the Gypsies.

1845.[46] However what gave the word its real currency was a great, best-selling operatic success, which has continued to the end of the twentieth century and shows no signs of abating, Henri Murger's *Scènes de la Vie de Bohème*, originally a series of *feuilletons* dramatized by the already very ill Murger himself in 1849 with another *boulevardier*, Théodore Barrière. This version was adopted towards the end of the century by Giacomo Puccini, whose *La Bohème* is even more popular than *Carmen*. Ruggero Leoncavallo (whose opera is now forgotten—completely overshadowed by Puccini's) also used a libretto drawn from the Murger-Barrière dramatization.

Murger's hero-artists had nothing at all to do with ethnic Gypsies. They were young provincials-come-to-Paris: Rodolphe, the poet; Marcel, the painter; Schaunard, a musician; Colline, the "philosopher."[47] Nor did the amiable but sickly Murger himself (one of whose characters, the poet-journalist Rodolphe, was autobiographical) ever reach literary fortune in his lifetime in spite of moderate fame; his great public success was that dramatized version of *Bohème*. Murger's tale manifested and confirmed the new status of the artist as one who will defy all social norms in his devotion to a particular lifestyle. It is therefore of no importance or even relevance if the artists shown in the *Scènes* are talented painters or composers, as there is nothing tragic about the scene in which Marcel turns his epic Biblical painting of the *Crossing of the Red Sea*, rejected by the *Salon*, into a signboard for an inn called "The Port of Marseilles."

Their lifestyle rather than their literary or artistic interests bound these young men into a mutually supportive group. Such informal groups, of which there were many in Paris, had no wish to better their lot through social reform but confirmed their status as social outcasts. They were talented perhaps, though not

necessarily so—but also irresponsible, immoral, louche, and as the century moves on, also drugged—of which more later. Although their function has sometimes been compared to that of the eighteenth-century *salons* (those semi-institutionalized gatherings in private houses usually presided over by women in which so much of the political and intellectual life of France was transacted from the days of Louis XIII onwards), they seem to have had a diametrically opposite purpose. The *salons*, even when they were gathering places of political opposition, even of conspiracy, were always intended to smooth the working of society; the Bohemian groups and chapels on the other hand were formed to disrupt the smooth surface of social activity—sometimes violently.

The bedraggled Bohemian became a constant figure of vaudeville and of the popular stage during the July Monarchy, and he was often represented in caricature and in many *Salon* paintings. This Bohemian artist is now quite a different figure from the honorable and laborious painter of the *Ancien Régime* and even the Empire theaters.[48]

Of course, it is virtually impossible to pinpoint the moment when the artist slipped into the Bohemian role—when the landlocked Bohemia of geography became Shakespeare's seaside realm or a shabby Land of Cockaigne. However, the text that is usually quoted as being the first to extol the figure of the antisocial artist—irresponsible, without fixed abode or any respect for social mores or even common honesty, though redeemed by his "genius," the very archetype of the Bohemian artist (even if it is far too early for him to be identified by that "Bohemian" label)—is Denis Diderot's *Neveu de Rameau*, which presents a conversation between the sensible, enquiring author and the cynical nephew of the great musician, whose quirky mindset depends on his not being sure that he is (rather suspecting that he is not) a genius, like his famous uncle, the great composer.[49] Diderot's little book was

---

46. Honoré de Balzac, *La Comédie Humaine.* Vol. 12, *Scènes de la Vie Parisienne* (Paris, 1846), pp. 97ff.

47. They were the kind of young men for whom the term *rapin* had also recently been coined to describe the down-at-heel, unsuccessful, feckless, and youthful. Their female opposites, the *grisettes* (Mimi, Musette) were their usual companions. Their situation was explained sometimes as that of being "on their way" to a prosperous career—exhibition in the *Salon*, membership of academies, even the Legion of Honour—but if you look at the lithographs of Gavarni and Daumier, many of them did not reach such elevated status.

Murger himself was Parisian born—although his father, who spelled his surname Mürger, was German.

48. Even though as late as 1841 Daumier was showing the *Bohémiens de Paris* as scavangers, toadies, and dog-barbers in *Charivari*, November 1841–February 1842 (d. 823–834).

49. The troublesome nephew was indeed a musician and a historical figure; see evidence collected by André Magnan, *Rameau le Neveu, Textes et Documents* (St. Etienne: Publications de l'Universite de Saint-Etienne, 1993). But see Yoichi Sumi, *Le Neveu de Rameau* (Tokyo: France Tosho, 1975), pp. 23ff. Diderot's text, after the Goethian adventure, was republished twice in 1821, again in 1847; a critical edition was done by Baudelaire's friend, Charles Asselineau in 1862.

probably written about 1760–1762 but was not issued at the time either in manuscript or in print. An incomplete copy was passed by an impoverished German officer in Russian service to a Riga publisher, through whom it reached Schiller. He gave it to Goethe, who translated and published it in German in 1805; the first French publication in 1823 was a retranslation of Goethe's version.[50]

Among Diderot's Parisian contemporaries, there were many poor artists eking out a living; even if Rameau's nephew was a proto-Bohemian, this had little bearing on the behavior of painters and sculptors at the time. Several more or less "academic" schools were training yet more postulants, while other artists complained about such a subproletariat. Diderot knew the situation well and in his *Salon* article of 1765—these articles form the bulk of his art-criticism—reported his friend Chardin's lament on this very subject.[51] Yet although Chardin was right about the numbers involved, many of these artists did earn a living as competent draughtsmen who made themselves available to the manufacturers of decorative objects—for weaving and printing patterns and for wallpapers and tapestries. Their work could not be rivaled elsewhere. Although many considered such skills to be unworthy of their high calling, they were the envy of other exporting nations (particularly of the British), and indeed Jean-Jacques Bachelier founded a school of specialist ornamental drawing (later it became

the *Ecole des Arts Décoratifs*) in 1762. By 1771 it had 1,500 pupils, many of whom were finding employment.

Poor painters and engravers were nevertheless becoming the subject of literary curiosity. In the latter part of the eighteenth century—and into the nineteenth—Parisian artists appeared often in fiction and in plays. They are presented as poor, decent, honest, responsible citizens. About the turn of the century the tone changes;[52] their characteristics are now most commonly recognized as "difficult"—because of independence and intransigence. They are presented as eccentric or given to low company, or as drunkards (though only exceptionally). One such figure is a semimythic painter-engraver who appears in some of the stories and is variously called Alexis or Jean Grimou. He also has the distinction of being about the first artist to be called *romantique*—though that label had not yet achieved the standing it would hold among nineteenth-century Bohemians. Yet his misdemeanors are not blamed on his profession; he is labeled a drunken Dutchman rather than a drunken artist.[53] Even *romantique* artists are usually shown to be honest, if poor, constant lovers, often responsible and settled family men—perhaps too credulous or too intransigent for their own good because of their very honesty. Another artist who turns up in several plays is Simon Mathurin Lantara, a minor landscape painter of some accomplishment, who was (somewhat arbitrarily) canonized as the "type" of comedy artist popular with the *littérateurs* of the late eighteenth and early nineteenth centuries. He is originally described as a responsible, if unfortunate, citizen, but in the first decades of the nineteenth century, he declines—posthumously—from the honest melancholic to the drunken sot. Even in his case, however, there is no question of "Bohemia." The

---

50. P. N. Furbank, *Denis Diderot* (New York: A. A. Knopf, 1992), pp. 242ff., 470ff. The autograph manuscript was found by Georges Monval on a Quai Voltaire bookstall in 1891.

Hegel quoted the Goethe translation in *The Phenomenology of the Spirit* as an instance of the disrupted spirit; the "restoration of the Spirit to itself" may only be achieved by a dialectical recognition of the reality of the ignoble and the discordant through which spirit may be restored to itself. Furbank (this note), pp. 254 ff; see G. F. W. Hegel, *Phenomenology of the Spirit*, trans. A. V. Miller and J. N. Findlay (Oxford: Clarendon Press, 1972), pp. 317f., 522.

All this may well be a historical accident, though to me it seems wholly right that the eccentric and irresponsible artist, the dubious, Gypsylike genius, did not find his public until well into the nineteenth century.

51. Diderot's *Salons*—critical accounts of the yearly official exhibition of painting and sculpture—were written for Baron Grimm's *Correspondance*, a handwritten "newspaper" that was circulated (to the Empress Catherine, King Stanislaus Augustus (Poniatowski) of Poland, and some German princely courts and was confidential (if only to maintain the subscribers' privilege), though various more or less expurgated editions appeared after Grimm's death in 1807. Chardin was a friend of Diderot's and often figures in the *Salons*. For the text of the complaint, see D. Diderot, *Oeuvres Complètes* (Paris: Le Club Français de Livre, 1970), vol. 4, pp. 16f.

52. For this and much that follows, see George Levitine, *The Dawn of Bohemianism* (State Park, Pennsylvania: Pennsylvania State University Press, 1978), pp. 21ff.; Marilyn Ruth Brown, *Gypsies and Other Bohemians* (Ann Arbor, Michigan: UMI Research Press, 1985), pp. 7ff.

53. The label *romantique* was applied to Grimou as well as to Antoine Watteau and Jean-Baptiste Santeree by Pierre-Charles Levesque in Claude-Henri Watelet, *Dictionnaire des Arts de Peinture, Sculpture et Gravure*, 5 vols. (Paris: L. F. Prault, 1792), vol. 5, p. 359.

It seems that there was both a Swiss Jean Grimoux (1674–?), and a near-contemporary French Alexis Grimou, Grimoud, or Grimoult (1678–1733)—who was no relation. Alexis's jolly self-portrait with a wine glass contributed to his reputation as a drunk and his Dutch trips to see Rembrandt's major paintings may have something to do with his assumed Dutchness. In fact he was nicknamed the "French Rembrandt."

Figure 2. Georges de la Tour. *The Fortune Teller.* 101.9 x 123.5 cm. The Metropolitan Museum of Art, Rogers Fund, 1960.

word does not occur in connection with artists as a social category until the 1830s.

The redefinition of the artist's social role (to which the "Bohemian" label was attached) not only follows, but is—at least in part—a consequence of the change in the way in which the painter reached his public, the way in which his wares were displayed and exhibited. Jacques-Louis David, the prince of French painting in his time, had an acute sense of the situation. Implicated as he was in the doings of the Convention and the Terror and imprisoned after the fall of Robespierre, he conceived a great peacemaking canvas, taking as his theme the reconciliation affected by the Sabine women between their new Roman husbands and their wronged, discarded Sabine menfolk. Once completed, the *Sabine Women* was exhibited to paid visitors for five years (1799–1804) in a room he had been lent in the Louvre. In this, David was also following the example of some British and American artists. In the event, he earned a

far larger sum from these ticket takings than he had ever received during years of royal and imperial patronage. This procedure became an important way for artists— from Géricault to Courbet—to measure themselves against market forces.[54]

The painting of the *Sabine Women* (so important as a marketing venture) reflected another inclination of David's, since the theme required him (or so he thought) to be even more "primitive" than his previous acclaimed masterpieces had allowed him to be. He is said to have let fall to one of his assistants a self-critical

54. Champfleury (Jules Husson), in a published letter to Georges Sand (reprinted in his *Realism*), begins by identifying the 1855 "exhibition of forty paintings of his work" (which followed the refusal of the *Atelier* by the Salon of that year), then calls it an "Exhibition in the English style . . . an incredibly audacious act; it is the subversion of all institutions associated with the jury; it is a direct appeal to the public. . . ." quoted by Linda Nochlin, *Realism and Tradition in Art* (Englewood Cliffs, New Jersey: Prentice-Hall, 1966), p. 37.

comment about his earlier overreliance on anatomy and on "classical" sculpture and his desire to concentrate on the outline of members as well as profiles in the manner of "Etruscan" vases and archaic relief sculpture. That casual remark was taken up as a text for the small group of "primitives" in his studio, enthusiastic critics of art and of the society that sanctioned it; there was even a break-off and more radical group among them who called themselves *Méditateurs* (if David's son and biographer is to be believed).

David himself worried that the group would go too far and got rid of the lot, so that he had to finish the vast painting with only one assistant "in silence and solitude." The defectors were now led by the brilliant and charismatic Maurice Quay,[55] who was to die in his early twenties, but the ideas that he formulated and championed were taken up by those of his friends and followers who also called themselves "primitives" (and were sometimes also known as *barbus* because of their habit of growing their beards—very unusual at the time). They interpreted David's self-critical remark as a call to purity, not only of art, but of intention. Quay himself was very good-looking and rather pious (a notable exception in irreligious, postrevolutionary Paris). The group also adopted a particular, pseudo-antique flowing form of dress (which they considered Phrygian, antique) in emulation of ancient heroes. It led to awkward scenes with the police. Interviewing Quay, who had been recommended by David as a drawing teacher for some Bonaparte children, Napoleon is reported to have asked: "why do you dress in a way which separates you from everybody?" To which the painter answered, "To separate myself from everybody."

The *barbus* had raised police suspicion by setting up common lodgings and studios in an abandoned convent at the foot of the hill of Chaillot, a district (unfortunately for them) then frequented by the politically disaffected of the time. They clearly considered ideas of a new direction in the arts to require a different, even a communal, way of life, and this would suggest more general social reform, of which that of dress was only a foretaste.

None of Quay's paintings seem to have survived, so he is now known through the memoirs of a fellow pupil of David's, Etienne Delécluze[56] and of Charles Nodier, then a very young and very rebellious writer, who had befriended the Chaillot fraternity; in 1803 he fictionalized the experience in a "Gothic" tale, *Le Peintre de Salzbourg*, which he followed with the brief and aphoristic *Méditations du Cloître* in which the suicidal exaltation (the painter of the title does—ambiguously—drown himself, but it may have been an accident) owes much to Goethe's *Werther*. But Goethian melancholia (French interest in German ideas and German literature was then at its height) is grafted onto the quasi-monastic sentiment of the Quay circle. "*Je le déclare avec amertume, avec effroi: le pistolet de Werther et la hache des bourreaux nous ont déjà décimé: cette génération se lève et vous demande des Cloîtres*" is the strange conclusion of his *Méditations*. The cloisters would provide the young with a refuge from political catastrophe and oppressive government, as well as from the incomprehension of coarse and moneyed patronage.[57]

In Germany such ideas had been burgeoning even earlier, though there they had a much less universalist, more nationalist cast to them. Perhaps the best-known—and rather light-hearted—documentation was a novel called *Ardinghello und die Glückseeligen Inseln* written fifteen years earlier by Wilhelm Heinse, an enthusiastic amateur of painting and a moving spirit in the German literature of his time. The hero is a pirate-painter "superman" (a fictitious pupil of Vasari) who, with some Greek friends, establishes a republic of justice, "virtue," and very free love on the island of Paros.[58] Heinse's Italianate and libertarian tone belies the important nationalist and quasi-religious tendency in both German and French art. Medieval architecture was being

55. On the *Sabine Women*, see Antoine Schnapper, *David* (New York: Alpine Fine Arts Collection, 1980), pp. 182ff. Quay is briefly mentioned (pp. 189 ff.). Delécluze spells him Quaï, but it is now clear that the more obvious spelling is the correct one; see Levitine (see note 52), pp. 46ff.

56. E. J. Delécluze, *Louis David, son Ecole et son Temps* (1855; reprint, Paris: Macula, 1983). Also Michel Salomon, *Charles Nodier et le Groupe Romantique* (Paris: Perrin et cie, 1908), pp. 41ff. Salomon also calls them "philadelphians."

57. Charles Nodier, *Oeuvres Choisies*, ed. Albert Cazes (Paris, 1923), pp. 52ff. It was published in 1803, immediately after his *Napoléonienne*, his anonymous attack on the First Consul, which caused a great deal of trouble. See the discussion in Malcolm Easton, *Artists and Writers in Paris* (New York: St. Martin's Press, 1964), pp. 12ff.

58. *Saemtliche Werke*, ed. Karl Schueddekopf (Leipzig: Insel-Verlag, 1924), vol. 4; in the preface he claims to have written the book before 1785; it is one of the many works of fiction of the time that claim to be a translation of an old manuscript found by chance. On Heinse, see Ladislao Mittner, *Storia della Letteratura Tedesca dal*

discovered as a forgotten heritage in France and Germany. A wholly Germanic identity of style in architecture was paralleled by an equally powerful movement in the other "fine" arts, whose gospel was a brief but eagerly read publication by the poet-painter Wilhelm Heinrich Wackenroder (another quickly burnt-out figure—he died in 1798, aged 25), the "Meditations of an art-loving Monk." This rather strange document, a rhapsodic mix of eulogies of artists, particularly of Dürer ("Master Albrecht . . . on account of whom I am glad I am a German"), Raphael, Francesco Francia, Leonardo, Piero di Cosimo—in the form of letters, essays, and poems, even hymns—presents an allegedly autobiographical picture of the total devotion of an artist to his art, a devotion that favors his (wholly fictitious) retirement to a cloister.[59]

Wackenroder's close collaborator and posthumous editor, Ludwig Tieck, was much longer-lived (he died in 1853). He is now remembered mostly as the cotranslator of Shakespeare with August von Schlegel. A brilliant and prolific man of letters, he also performed the posthumous editor's office for two much greater young writers: Heinrich von Kleist and Novalis. He attempted to fictionalize some of Wackenroder's ideas in *Sternbald's Wanderungen* of 1798, in which the hero, a pupil of Dürer's, makes a romantic pilgrimage round the ateliers of the Netherlandish painters of the time. In spite of its novel form, it did not attain the popularity of Wackenroder's book, which, published anonymously, was generally attributed to Goethe.[60]

Ludwig Tieck's brother, Christian Frederick, had been—for three years—a pupil in David's *atelier*. Before he left for Paris he had modeled a head of his dying friend, Wackenroder. Had Christian Tieck introduced David's disciples to Wackenroder's notion of the artist as a kind of monk and the artist's work as a form of priesthood, or were they simply developing such ideas in parallel? It is almost impossible to answer this question; at any rate, the group of David's pupils who had retired to Chaillot in 1800 broke up soon after the

death of Quay.[61] However, a much more influential German "sect" of artists was formed within a year or two—months almost. It all began when young Johann Friedrich Overbeck (himself born in 1789) was entered in the Vienna academy, directed by another pupil of Jacques-Louis David.

Overbeck rebelled at the academic discipline and (also a little) at Viennese frivolity. He came of a long line of Lübeck pastors and bankers, and his ideas had been informed by Wackenroder and Tieck and echoed some of the notions that had been formed and propagated by the *Barbus*. He now made common cause with a brilliant but consumptive artist, Franz Pforr. With four other fellow students they founded a "brotherhood" or "order" of St. Luke, dedicated to the revival of a true Christian art and modeled on Italian art before Raphael, as well as on the kind of German art incarnated in Dürer.

The "pre-Raphaelite" art of Italy had a strong pull; Overbeck and Pforr left the Vienna Academy for Rome in 1810 to establish an artists' commune, which would shelter in the Irish Franciscans' half-abandoned house, San Isidoro on the Pincian Hill.[62] There they were joined (shortly before Pforr's early death) by Peter Cornelius and a little later by Julius Schnorr von Karolsfeld, Friedrich Wilhelm Schadow (son of the Berlin sculptor), and Philip Veit (stepson of Friedrich von Schlegel).[63] Their withdrawal may have been a deliberate—or perhaps only half-conscious—replication of the *Barbus*'s rebellion, though their dogmatic insistence on the revival of true fresco technique was

---

Pietismo al Romanticismo (1700–1820) (Torino: G. Einaudi, 1964), pp. 439 ff (¶ 209). He was an associate of Friedrich Jacobi and an emulator of Christoph Wieland.

59. The brief *Herzensergiessungen* were published in 1796, but the writing collected by Tieck were published two years after his death, in 1799. But see P. Koldewey, *Wackenroder und sein Einfluss auf Tieck* (Leipzig: Dieterich, 1904).

60. Ludwig Tieck, *Franz Sternbalds Wanderungen: eine Altdeutsche Geschichte* (Munich, 1964).

61. Although several of them—notably the Brothers Francque as painters and Charles Nodier as a writer and polemist—had a great influence on later French intellectual life.

62. Aedan Daly, *Sant' Isidoro* (Rome: Marietti, 1971), pp. 27ff. The Academy had, in any case, ceased functioning for a while when Napoleon's troops occupied Vienna in 1809.

On their Roman associates, see Lionello Venturi, *Il Gusto dei Primitivi* (Turin, 1972), pp. 125ff.

63. Philip Veit and his older brother, Johannes, were the sons of the Jewish banker Stefan Veit and Dorothea, the daughter of the philosopher Moses Mendelsohn. After their divorce, Dorothea married Friedrich von Schlegel; they moved to Vienna, where the brothers joined them. The brothers both converted to Catholicism about this time and went to Rome, where Johannes settled (he died there in 1854), while Philip returned to Germany before 1840, was an influential teacher in Frankfurt, and moved to Mainz to fresco the cathedral and direct the Museum.

their own.[64] The notion of artists working in "communities" or "communes" was quite a novel idea—even when (as artists often did later) they invoked medieval guild practice. In fact the withdrawal to the still-Papal Rome was (for German artists) almost an equivalent to the withdrawal into Bohemia of the French (Rome, after all had no *bürgerliche Gesellschaft* to speak of). The "Brothers" never became Bohemian in the French sense, of course, even if the order of St. Luke soon acquired the sobriquet, "the Nazarenes," in Rome, a reference to their long hair as well as to the (medieval rather than antique) cloaks that they sported.

Yet the brotherhood did not last and had no immediate successors, either in Rome or in Germany. Overbeck became a Catholic in 1813, and stayed on in Rome until his death in 1869 as the keeper of the shrine. Many other Nazarenes returned to Germany and ended their working life as highly influential art school and museum directors: Tieck, as I said in Berlin, Schnorr von Karolsfeld in Dresden, Peter Cornelius in Duesseldorf and Munich. As a group, they had been socially much better connected than the *Barbus*. Crown Prince Ludwig of Bavaria (soon to succeed as King Ludwig I) saw a lot of them in Rome in 1824; he even sported their eccentric costume and later became Cornelius's main patron.[65] The quasi-religious atmosphere surrounding the *Barbus* and the Nazarenes was very different from that of the general Bohemia of which I spoke earlier, since they operated an almost sectarian procedure of inclusion and exclusion.

In an analogy to the Nazarenes, this period also saw the creation of quasi-religious societies—or even quite explicit ones—of the kind now called "utopian." France had never lacked utopian writers, since even Rabelais could be counted as one, who proposed a kind of ideal environment in his Abbey of Thelème. But the nature of utopian proposals altered about the time of the July Monarchy, and the disciples of the Comte Henri de Saint-Simon (who died in 1825) especially pioneered the direct application of the master's ideas in (not very successful) communes after his death. Like the Nazarenes—but quite unlike the various Parisian Bohemian groups—such communes secluded themselves so as to become the leaven which would transform all society.[66]

Yet a cause did present itself to unite a group of younger artists and their camp followers in a common antibourgeois action (which was a kind of "coming-out" for Bohemia) a few months before the July upheaval in Paris. February 25, 1830, was the first night of Victor Hugo's *Hernani*, so that the event came to be known as the "Battle of Hernani." During the performance, a "romantic" claque organized by a young architect (who came to be much better known as a poet and journalist), Petrus Borel, came to fisticuffs with the "academic" party—and won.[67] The skirmish affirmed the existence of Bohemia as a force and a presence—but also gave romanticism a physiognomy. In so far as romanticism was a definable movement rather than a sentiment—a bundle of associations—it was seen as concerned with the specificity of history as against the generality of myth—and with negative rules: a defiance of the unities of place and time, the breaking of the hierarchy of *genres*, and the direct setting out of emotion at the expense of any formal constraints.[68]

64. They had relied in Palazzo Zuccari on the technical help of an aged Roman plasterer who had worked for Raphael Mengs.

65. The painting of the Prince and his entourage drinking in the Spanish-Portuguese inn in Rome with Thorwaldsen and some of the Nazarenes by Franz Louis Catel is in the Bayerische Staatsgalerie in Munich. In the Residenz Schnorr von Karolsfeld painted his Niebelungen cycle for the King, while Cornelius's commissions are too numerous to specify here.

66. A convenient anthology of the relevant text is Frank E. Manuel and Fritzie P. Manuel, *French Utopias* (New York and London: Free Press, 1966).

67. The Classic account was given by Théophile Gautier in his "Première Représentation d'Hernani" reprinted in *Souvenirs Romantiques* (Paris: Garnier, 1929), pp. 80 ff; but see also Enid Starkie, *Petrus Borel* (London: Faber and Faber, 1954). pp. 30ff. Borel organized the event with the help of another young architect:

De bonne foi, Jules Vabre,
Compagnon miraculeux

Vabre, "the new Vitruvius," was to write an *Essai sur l'incommodité des commodes*; an advertisement for its forthcoming publication appears in Borel's *Rhapsodies* of 1832, but it seems not to have been completed. Vabre does not otherwise appear in the annals of French architecture, but see Louis Hautecoeur, *Histoire de l'Architecture Classique en France* (Paris: A. Picard, 1955), vol. 6, pp. 281f.; Jules Claretie, *Petrus Borel* (Paris: R. Princebourde, 1865), pp. 32ff. That little book is judged "fantastic and untrue" by Starkie (see note 67), but she knows nothing of Vabre.

68. Any definition is notoriously difficult; the Schlegels already found it so. It is often read as the succession and the development of a *Sturm und Drang* tendency, a label that takes its name from Goethe's *Wanderer im Sturm* (*Werke* [Zurich, 1960], vol. 1, pp. 331ff.) though it is often seen as originating in the anti-Enlightenment stance of Johann Georg Hamman; Hegel indicates this—and Benedetto Croce wanted to see the eighteenth-century philosopher (and critic of Cartesian

But the extreme consequence of this attitude was to see society as the destroyer of the artist, of genius. This was focused in the hero status accorded to Thomas Chatterton, a young English poet, famous as much for having attempted to pass a collection of imitation fifteenth-century pastiches as the work of one Thomas Rowley and failing to obtain patronage for his own genuine productions, as for committing suicide by taking arsenic. He was eighteen when this happened in August 1770.[69] Soon after his death, this was seen as a tragic sacrifice of the victim-genius to the indifference of bourgeois society. Certainly Coleridge, Keats, and Shelley saw him thus; as did Wordsworth: "the marvellous Boy, The sleepless Soul that Perished in his pride. . . ."[70]

But he becomes an emblematic figure for the French after 1830—especially in Alfred de Vigny's *Stellio* of 1832 and even more explicitly in a prose drama, *Chatterton*, which was performed to great applause at the Théâtre Français in February 1835, to an enthusiastic audience—presumably very similar to the one that had battled about Hernani five years earlier. The moral Vigny states explicitly in the preface in which he describes his work on the play ("Dernière Nuit de Travail du 29 au 30 Juin 1834"). His poet needs the leisure to hear the sounds that rise slowly in his soul and that the noise of the daily grind will drown: "such is the poet! . . . seek and find him ways to secure him a living—since on his own he will only find death!"

The poet can survive as a soldier, as a number-grinder, even as a man of letters, though in each case the voice of poesy in him will inevitably be drowned. If he cannot brook such compromise, suicide is his only alternative:

Celui (est la partie) que prit Chatterton: se tuer tout entier; il reste peu à faire. . . .

and having considered the matter further, Vigny concludes:

Quand un homme meurt de cette manière, est-il donc suicide? C'est la société qui le jette dans le brasier. . . .[71]

The hostility of society to the claims, the pretensions, of the artist can therefore be thrown back at it. That is why the inclination of artists to bind themselves into more or less exclusive groups according to schools and tendencies—or just personal sympathies—became part of a curdling of bourgeois society at its edges by its various enemies, of which the *barbus* withdrawal to Chaillot was a foretaste. The Nazarenes had taken up that protest by advocating a quasi-monastic community life. This last had no direct emulation in Bohemia, though artists were forming more or less extempore groups around a common cause. Hugo's circle was already known as the *Cénacle*. Charles Nodier, who provided the personal link with Quay's group, became their official host at the literary Sunday parties held at the Bibliothèque de l'Arsenal (whose director he had become). The leaders of the original *Hernani* claque (led by Gautier and Borel), called themselves (in order to be associated, yet clearly separated) *Le Petit Cénacle*, and later were transformed into a kind of spontaneous commune, *Les Jeunes France*[72]; Nodier and the *Cénacle* proper found *Le petit Cénacle* too rowdy and asked them to stay away.

At the battle of *Hernani*, Gautier, who had been trained as a painter but was moving to the position of a man of letters, was distinguished by his wild hair and his conspicuous scarlet velvet waistcoat.[73] Those Bohemians of the 1830s were not sloppy and careless about their clothes, yet they were often deliberately eccentric; it

rationalism) Giambattista Vico as a proto-Romantic figure. *Sturm und Drang* is also associated with certain proto-romantic music, that of Wolfgang Friedemann Bach and the late work of Haydn.

A bibliography of the question can be found in Austin Warren and René Wellek, *Theory of Literature* (London, 1954), pp. 381ff. Hegel was to give the term new coinage, of which more will be said later. In any case, it did not move from literature into the visual arts until Hegel's generation. In a way, the most powerful statement of what Romanticism meant at about the time of *Hernani* is set out by Hugo in the preface of a slightly earlier play, *Cromwell*, first published in 1828. Victor Hugo, *Théatre* (Paris: Hachette, 1858), vol. 3, pp. 14ff.

69. E. H. W. Meyerstein, *A Life of Thomas Chatterton* (London: Ingpen and Grant, 1930), for the details: on the suicide, pp. 414; on the posthumous fame, pp. 501ff.

70. William Wodsworth, "Resolution and Independence," in *Poetical Works* (London: Oxford University Press, 1969).

71. Alfred de Vigny, *Chatterton*, ed. A. H. Diverres (London, 1967), pp. 53f.

72. Théophile Gautier used the label for a collection of satirical stories about artists and men of letters published in Paris in 1894.

73. The red waistcoat Gautier wore on that occasion became his badge—as he himself complains in "La légende du Gilet Rouge":

si l'on prononce le nom de Théophile Gautier devant un philistin, n'eût-il jamais lu de nous deux vers et une seul ligne, il nous connaît par le gilet rouge que nous portions à la première représentation d'Hernani. . . .

in *Souvenir Romantique* (Paris, 1929), pp. 73ff. He remarks on himself at the time (p. 75) ". . . le rapin dominait encore chez nous le poète," using *rapin* in the precise sense of "apprentice painter."

was yet another way of defying the bourgeois. In their way they were fops—almost dandies.

Whatever the origin of the word "dandy," its meaning was fixed in England about 1815, and the reign of terror that "Beau" Brummel exercised over the London fashionable world (and even over the court) about this time already shows it fully developed. They were unlike the *merveilleux* or the *incroyables* of the *Directoire* and even early Empire, who exaggerated English fashion foppishly and wore their hair in extravagant fashion (including *à la Victime*—with long forelocks and the back cut short, to accommodate the Guillotine blade).[74] But the English dandy was never showy and the dandy's clothes never eccentric—only superlative. In Paris, a group of young Anglomanes, led by Lord Henry Seymour, had bound themselves into a kind of association of dandies soon after, during the 1820s. Seymour, in spite of his name, was only half-English (his mother was certainly the Marchioness of Hertford). This obsessively athletic, arrogant, and rather cruel young man made common (if the word can be applied to them) cause with another half-English, high-spending millionaire Charles la Battut and the Marquis de Saint Crique (famous for his practical jokes) to found a club for breeding pedigree horses (it became the Jockey Club in 1835).[75] They had nothing but contempt for the impoverished and literary Bohemians of their day—and vaunted their lack of any cultural baggage, even if their own homes had to have furniture, porcelaine, and even pictures, which had to be superlative, exactly like their clothes. Their cultivation of Anglomania was itself an antibourgeois stance, since it implied that one had been brought up in England—because one's parents were *émigrés*. Parisian dandies gave the word the somewhat

sinister and cruel undertone it acquired in French. And they promoted another scandalous activity— overindulgence in drugs. Indeed their only literate associate was a well-heeled, high-drinking man of letters—the poet and journalist, Roger de Beauvoir, who occupied the most ornate rooms in the Hotel de Lauzun on the Ile St. Louis (in which Baudelaire had more modest quarters). He befriended Gautier and his circle and introduced them to the pleasures of hashish, thus bringing drugs to the notice of Bohemia.[76]

Both hashish and opium had been recognized as therapeutic, but also narcotic, drugs all over the ancient world. Yet they had hitherto also been considered fairly beneficent substances; they were, for instance, consumed in large quantities as mild stimulants and as analgesics in Britain during the eighteenth century. The generation of Coleridge and de Quincey, however, began to treat opium as a stimulant to the imagination and as narcotic habit-making substance, more powerful in its effect than the wine or the coffee and tobacco to which some writers of the time (notably Balzac) frequently resorted. There is no record of drug addiction associated with the arts before the second quarter of the nineteenth century, thought it has grown steadily ever since.[77] Dandyism and Bohemia now came to be coupled with drug addiction during the 1830s.

Of course, the two types—the disciplined dandy and the dissolute Bohemian—would seem diametrically opposed, even hostile, to each other. Yet they become rather arbitrarily associated during the late 1830s as two aspects of the same antibourgeois stance. There were some who alternated between the two roles more or less unwittingly, notably Baudelaire, who was constantly short of money and whose drinking and *nostalgie de la boue* confined him to the Bohemia he despised, while he admired (and identified with) the dandy:

---

74. On these fashions, see Edmond de Goncourt and Jules de Goncourt, *Histoire de la Société Française pendant le Directoire* (Paris: G. Charpentier, 1880), pp. 404; Duchesse d'Abrantès (Mme Junot) *Histoire des Salons de Paris* (Brussels, 1838), vol. 3, pp. 96ff.

75. On the word and the notion, see J. Barbey d'Aurevilly, *Du Dandysme et de G. Brummel* (Paris: A. Lemerre, n.d.), pp. 13ff. The essay had originally (1841) been dedicated to the architect César Daly whose Fourierist activities as editor and essayist hardly seem to square with Brummel-like nonchalance. But then, as Barbey explains, you have to be English to be a dandy, which is why, he thought, the Comte d'Orsay, sometimes labelled as one, was for too sanguine to be saddled with that label.

A description of the Jockey Club appears a few year later by Charles de Boigne, *Le Diable à Paris* (Paris, 1846), pp. 237ff. On this whole episode, see also Starkie (see note 67), pp. 72ff.

76. Théophile Gautier in *Revue de Deux Mondes*, February 1846, quoted by Starkie (see note 67), p. 81. De Beauvoir was later (as a result of an unfortunate marriage and attendant lawsuits) to turn to Bohemia and indeed befriended Murger. But there is no doubt that in the 1830s he would be very much considered a dandy; the overlap is clear in Balzac's *Un Prince de la Bohème*, which I mentioned earlier, in which a character based, in part, on de Beauvoir has many more characteristics of the Dandy. Barbey d'Aurevilly, as the theoretician of dandyism, denied in his later life that he had ever been a Bohemian, though he is being "economical with the truth" in doing so.

77. Alethea Hayter, *Opium and the Romantic Imagination* (London: Faber, 1968), pp. 19ff.

(who) has to aspire to be constantly sublime. He must live and sleep in front of a mirror.[78]

This dandy of his, to whom he consecrates a longer study in *The Artist of Modern Life*, has nothing of the Bohemian of popular literature; rich and nonchalant, he is carefully—even meticulously—dressed and groomed. His very refinement sets him outside the bourgeois social norm.

Somewhere between the dandies and the Bohemians the attitude that came to be labeled *avant-garde* is formulated by the mid-century. It is not clear when this term, borrowed from some military manual, was applied to questions of art and literature. Perhaps this first happened in Saint-Simonian circles, since it carries an implication of a campaign against existing society, not merely a withdrawal from it. At any rate, the first recorded use of it in such a context is by a Saint-Simonian journalist, Gabriel-Désiré Laverdant, who, in an "inspirational" pamphlet on the artist's role during the July Monarchy maintains that the poet should not only be concerned with:

> . . . hymns to happiness, the mournful or despairing ode (but must . . .) lay bare all the brutalities, all the filth which are at the base of our society with a harsh and searching brush. . . .[79]

Fifteen years later, journalists must have found the term very useful, since Baudelaire treats "the avant-garde" as a generally current and highly offensive notion, certainly as far as the arts were concerned. Having listed the "military metaphors" to which—he considers—the French are fatally prone, he adds *Poètes de Combat* and *Les littérateurs d'avant-garde* to the list and continues, witheringly:

> this usage of military metaphors does not mark combative spirits, but ones made to be disciplined, that is to say for

conformity, spirits born to be servants, Belgian spirits who can only think in crowds (*en société*).[80]

While he damns the avant-garde, Baudelaire himself, alternating between the unruly and the disdainful, is constantly fired by hostility to the bourgeois society and its greedy comforts. For all his contempt, the energy and the aggression marks a stance that certainly deserves its military nickname.

In the same way that the Romany nation was never organized into a political force, so social Bohemia was too diversified and anarchic and too passive ever to be considered a transforming social power; yet once the social boundaries of that Bohemia had been drawn, the word seemed cleared of its ethnic associations. Nevertheless many Bohemians were on the edge of social reform and rebellion, and the creation of a "secular arm," a defensive-offensive force, an army that was to fight its battles, was almost inevitable. It grew within Bohemia, yet was not quite of it, and took on some of the testiness and obduracy of the dandies.

The Gypsy association continued to persist in connection with artistic groupings. Gypsies—particularly Provencal and Spanish Gypsies—also became a very popular subject for conventional artists during the 1840s and (in the wake of Esmeralda) appeared in fiction and on the stage, as well as in painting and sculpture (as it did in England, for instance, about the turn of the twentieth century—in both *pompier* Laura Knight and "advanced" Augustus John and Jacob Epstein). This exhibiting of the feckless artist to the responsible bourgeois seemed a necessary part of nineteenth-century attitudes. And it was read back into history, to show that artists had always corresponded to the personality type associated with Bohemian behavior.[81]

Thus Bohemia provided an image of an alien, unsettled, marginal existence, which the successful painters purveyed and the bourgeois patron demanded, perhaps even needed, to contemplate—a reassuring image of a disruptive and even threatening collective tamed by the painter's skill and isolated, contained within the ever-thickening gold frame, much as (later and at a socially somewhat inferior level) "cardinal pictures" (those meticulously painted images of high ecclesiastics flirting—not too indecorously—with

---

78. Charles Baudelaire, *Mon Coeur mis à Nu* (a title that he translated from Poe, "My heart laid bare"), in *Oeuvres Complètes*, ed. Claude Pichois (Paris: Gallimard, 1975), vol. 1, p. 678; vol. 5, p. 643).

See also Cesar Graña, *Bohemian vs. Bourgois* (New York: Basic Books, 1964); Geraldine Pelles, *Art, Artists and Society* (Englewood Cliffs, New Jersey: Prentice-Hall, 1963); Helmut Kreuzer, *Die Bohème* (Stuttgart: J. B. Metzler, 1968); Renato Poggioli, *The Theory of the Avant-Garde* (Cambridge: Belknap Press, 1968); Peter Gay, *The Bourgeois Experience* (New York: Oxford University Press, 1984), vol. 1, pp. 27, 42f.

79. Laverdant, who later contributed articles on such matters as crèches and their furniture to César Daly's *Revue des Travaux Publics*, published this pamphlet in 1845 in Paris. See Poggioli (see note 78), p. 9; Linda Nochlin, *Realism* (Harmondsworth: Penguin, 1990), p. 214.

80. Baudelaire (see note 78), pp. 690f.

81. The fruitlessness of such an endeavour was demonstrated by Rudolf Wittkower and Margot Wittkower, *Born under Saturn* (London: Weidenfeld and Nicolson, 1963), esp. pp. 292ff.

elegantly overdressed young women, or indulging in private gourmandising—reprobate images of *ancien régime* profligacy) confirmed the opulent prudence of their possessors.

Such pictures still command the modest sale-room prices that witness their limited but continued appeal, but twentieth-century society has in the main accepted and sanctioned the instabilities and informalities formerly associated with its Bohemian margins. Bohemia has become the convention therefore. On the other hand, the development of performance art and minimalism has forced the type of the artist into dandified patterns of behavior. In their wake, the increasingly monied and powerful world of academies, museums, galleries, sale rooms, and other agents of official patronage have taken some form of dandyism to be the appropriate stance for any proponent of artistic innovation and/or social protest without which any notion of the avant-garde would lose all its force and, it would seem, no vital art can be made.

The dandification of the avant-garde was already explicit in Marcel Duchamp's very patronizing reference to Bohemia with which I opened this paper. But like so many victories, their conquest of society is—as victories often are—Pyrrhic since, in conquering its institutions, the avant-garde has renounced any contact with everyday transactions of society.

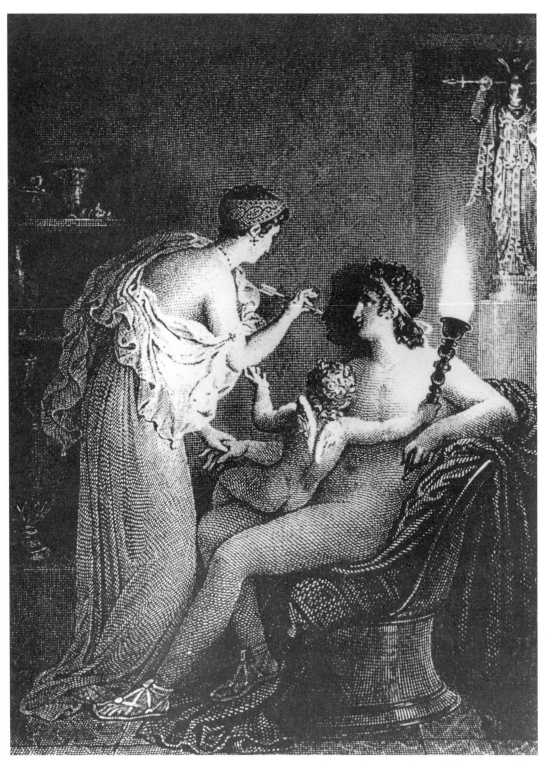

Figure 1. A.-L. Girodet Trioson, "The Origins of Painting." From *Oeuvres Posthumes* (Paris: J. Renouard, 1829).

Johann Caspar Lavater's *Essays on Physiognomy* and the hermeneutics of shadow

VICTOR I. STOICHITA
translated by Anne-Marie Glasheen

To the spirit of the Enlightenment, myths were nothing but fairy tales. Diderot, claiming to shed light on the dawn of painting, was no exception:

> The imagination is well practised in seeking the origin of Painting; and it is based on this, that poets have written the most charming of fairy-tales. If we are to believe them, then it was a shepherdess who, wanting to have the portrait of her lover, first drew a line with her crook around the shadow that the young man's face cast on the wall.[1]

This quotation from the *Encyclopédie*, casually amalgamates sources in a venture destined to blur the issue rather than clarify it. It seems to highlight an uncertainty that was already apparent in Pliny the Elder: *picturae initiis incerta*! This is one of the reasons why the allusion to be found in the first chapter of Rousseau's *Essai sur l'origin des langues* (1781) conceals a particular importance. As regards the "historical" debate surrounding the invention of art, the author opts for a more theoretical approach:

> It is said that love was the inventor of drawing. He might also unfortunately have invented speech; Dissatisfied with it, love spurns it, for there are more active ways of expressing oneself. She who so lovingly traced the shadow of her Lover had such things to impart! What sounds did she use to achieve these movements with her stick?[2]

This was the first time the Plinian fable had been explicitly regarded as a myth of love. Moreover, it was also the first time that the outlined shadow was considered to be—not a primitive mode of pictorial expression—but a primitive language through which love expresses itself.[3]

This is how, within the dream of origins that haunted the eighteenth century, the fable of Butades became one of the major themes of painting.[4] Something of Rousseau's spirit still survived at the beginning of the nineteenth century, in the way that Plinian iconography was addressed. In the engraving that illustrates Anne-Louis Girodet-Trioson's *Oeuvres posthumes* (fig. 1), it is the god of love himself who illuminates the scene with a torch and who guides the hand of the Corinthian girl while she traces her lover's profile with an arrow probably from Cupid's quiver. The scene is like an unbroken circuit; beneath the vigilant gaze of the statue of Minerva, goddess of wisdom, the two lovers' hands and those of Eros form a continuous chain that leads from the torchlight to the black portrait that stands out on the wall. This complicated body language is also a transformed, exalted "language of love." Seated between the two lovers, the small Eros covers the young man's unseemly nakedness, but—because of his position and through his symbols (wings, torch)—there is an echo of flight and passion. Censure and sublimation, the real themes of the engraving, end up on the path mapped out by Rousseau; Girodet is probably aware that in love, "there are more active ways of expressing oneself" than through the actual art of drawing, but he elects to portray the love scene as a "transfer of power" (or as he calls it in a poem appended to the engraving—a "heavenly transport") steering its erotic energy (which to Girodet was basically masculine) towards the (feminine) creation of a surrogate image:

This is a chapter of *Short History of the Shadow*, by Victor I. Stoichita, translated from French by Anne-Marie Glassheen, in press at Reaktion Books, London.

1. Diderot, *Encyclopédie* (Neuchatel: Chez Briasson, 1765), t. 12, p. 267.

2. J.-J. Rousseau, *Essai sur l'origine des langues* (Paris: Hatier, 1994), p. 35.

3. On this subject, see J. Derrida's commentary, *De la grammatologie* (Paris: Minuit, 1967), pp. 327–344.

4. R. Rosenblum, "The Origins of Painting. A Problem in The Iconography of Romantic Classicism," *Art Bulletin* 39 (1957):279–290; G. Levitine, "Addenda to Robert Rosenblum's 'The Origins of Painting': A Problem in the Iconography of Romantic Classicism," *Art Bulletin* 40 (1958):329–331; H. Wille, "Die Erfindung der Zeichenkunst," in *Beiträge zur Kunstgeschichte. Eine Festgabe für H. R. Rosemann zum 9. Oktober 1960*, ed. E. Guldan (Munich: Deutscher Kunstverlag, 1960), pp. 279–300; H. Wille, "Die Debutades-Erzählung in der Kunst der Goethezeit," *Jahrbuch der Sammlung Kippenberg*, n. f., 2 (1970):328–351; E. Darragon, "Sur Dibutade et l'origine du dessin," *Coloquio Artes*, 2d ser., 52, no. 1 (1982):42–49; J.-Cl. Lebensztejn, *L'Art de la tache. Introduction à la* Nouvelle Methode *d'Alexander Cozens* (Paris: Éditions du Limon, 1990), pp. 277–300; H. Damisch, *Traité du Trait/Tractatus tractus* (Paris: Réunion des Musées Nationaux), pp. 61–76.

And still to this sketch she brought her vows
In silent adoration, and the faithful image
Accepted the troth she plighted the model.[5]

At the time when Girodet was producing his poem and engraving, it was already accepted that the drawing of the outlined shadow was a primitive language of love. We find an excellent example of this in the first conference paper given to the Royal Academy of London (1801) by the Swiss Johann Heinrich Füssli:

> Greek painting took its first faltering steps, it was rocked in the cradle by the Graces and taught to speak by Love. If ever a legend deserved to be believed it was the love story of the young Corinthian girl who with her secret lamp drew the outline of her lover's shadow just before his departure, thus provoking our sympathy to trust in it, and leading us to make a few observations on the first complex effort at painting, as well as on this linear method which seems to have remained the founding act long after the agent for whom it was primarily conceived had been forgotten. . . . The earliest experiments in this art were the *skiagrams*, simple outlines of shadows—similar to those which have been circulated amongst the common people by amateurs and other parasites of physiognomy under the name of silhouettes.[6]

Füssli's observations connect early pictorial language to the fashion, during the second half of the eighteenth century, for cut-outs, which originated from a pun pertaining to Louis XV's Minister of Finance Etienne de Silhouette. It spread through the whole of Europe and was cherished by the upper classes as one of their most popular parlor games. Füssli's allusion is not without its ambiguities. Although he acknowledges that it is a legacy from Pliny's fable, he also seems to view the technique with obvious disdain, even though, a few years earlier, he had contributed to its popularity by helping to illustrate the English version of *Essays on Physiognomy* written by his compatriot Johann Caspar Lavater (published in London in 1792).

Lavater's book describes a new device for the creation of silhouettes (fig. 2). The illustration relating to this "machine" is much clearer in the English version than in the first German edition (published in Leipzig/Winterthur in 1776). If we compare the engraving in the *Essays on Physiognomy* with any

contemporary representation of the Butades fable (fig. 1), we see that the Plinian scenario of origins has been transformed into an actual posing session that aims to reproduce the profile through mechanical means. The allegorical décor has disappeared and the sexual roles reversed. The model—a woman—is seated on a special chair, which incorporates a screen mounted on an easel. On the other side of the screen stands the person who is capturing the contour of the model's profile projected by the candle burning nearby. For the method to succeed, the model must remain absolutely still and very close to the screen. As we can see, the process was devised in order to capture, as faithfully as possible, the profile's negative image, which is why it has often been regarded as one of the direct predecessors of photography.

We can only understand the functioning, or more particularly the function, of the "machine for drawing silhouettes" when we place it within the framework of Lavater's discourse on physiognomy, which we must now examine. I shall begin by quoting Lavater's definition of the shadow-image:

> Shades are the weakest, most vapid, but, at the same time, when the light is at the proper distance, and falls properly on the countenance to take the profile accurately, the truest representation that can be given of man. The weakest, for it is not positive, it is only something negative, only the boundary line of half the countenance. The truest, because it is the immediate expression of nature, such as not the ablest painter is capable of drawing, by hand, after nature.
>   What can be less the image of a living man that a shade? Yet how full of speech! Little gold, but the purest.[7]

To Lavater, the outlined profile of the shadow is the minimal image of man, his *Urbild*. And thanks to this quality it can also become the favored object of a hermeneutic of human nature. Through the ancient tradition of physiognomic studies, Lavater believed that a person's face bore the marks of his soul. He deviated from that tradition because he considered the outlined profile to be important:

> I have collected more physiognomical knowledge from shades alone than from every other kind of portrait, have

---

5. A.-L. Girodet-Trioson, *Oeuvres posthumes* (Paris: J. Renouard, 1829), t. 1, p. 48.

6. J. Knowles, ed., *The Life and Writings of Henry Fuseli* (London: Colburn and Bentley, 1831), vol. 2, pp. 26–27.

7. J. C. Lavater, *Physiognomische Fragmente zur Befärderung der Menschenkenntnis und Menschenliebe. Eine Auswahl* (Stuttgart: Reclam, 1984). Unless otherwise stated, all quotations from Lavater are taken from *Essays on Physiognomy*, trans. Thomas Holcroft (London: Ward Lock, 1840). Where the translator was unable to find the English version, she did them herself, basing them on the French version.

Figure 2. Thomas Holloway et al., "A Machine for Drawing Silhouettes." From Johann Caspar Lavater, *Essays on Physiognomy* (London, 1792).

improved physiognomical sensation more by the sight of them, than by the contemplation of ever mutable nature.

Shades collect the distracted attention, confine it to an outline, and thus render the observation more simple, easy, and precise. The observation, consequently the comparison.

Physiognomy has no greater, more incontrovertible certainty of the truth of its object than that imparted by shade.[8]

---

8. Lavater, *Essays on Physiognomy* (see note 7), pp. 188–189.

Through this assertion, the author of *Essays on Physiognomy* makes an important conceptual leap. In fact, according to him, it is not—as was accepted by tradition—the human face that is the reflection of the soul, but the shadow of this face. This is a fundamental difference since it exploits—probably subconsciously—another ancient tradition: the one which recognized in man's shadow his soul and in his soul, a shadow (fig. 4). The implications of this deviation are manifold. To analyze the shadow is tantamount to a *sui generis* psychoanalysis. To Lavater, the outlined profile is a hieroglyph that has to be deciphered. This work is regarded as a veritable hermeneutic, which has all the hallmarks of a translation from one language into the other:

> The true physiognomist unites to the clearest and profoundest understanding the most lively, strong, comprehensive imagination, and a fine and rapid wit. Imagination is necessary to impress the traits with exactness, so that they may be renewed at pleasure; and to range the pictures in the mind as perfectly as if they still were visible, and with all possible order.
>
> Wit is indispensable to the physiognomist, that he may easily perceive the resemblances that exist between objects. Thus, for example, he sees a head or forehead possessed of certain characteristic marks. These marks present themselves to his imagination, and wit discovers to what they are similar. Hence greater precision, certainty, and expression, are imparted to his images. He must have the capacity of uniting the approximation of each trait, that he remarks; and, by the aid of wit, to define the degrees of this approximation. . . . Wit alone creates the physiognomical language; a language, at present, so unspeakably poor. . . . All that language can express, the physiognomist must be able to express. He must be the creator of a new language, which must be equally precise and alluring, natural and intelligible.[9]

We may therefore be justified in referring to the formation of a Lavaterian "shadow-analysis," which was to become the focus of attack from enlightened circles heralded by George Lichtenberg:

> Nobody would laugh more than I, at the arrogance of that physiognomist who should pretend to read in the countenance the most secret thoughts and motions of the soul. . . .[10]

Despite all the criticism aimed at Lavater's method, it was widely practiced around 1800 and situated somewhere between entertainment and scientific experimentation. As a method, it regarded the shadow as a personal emanation more capable than the individual concerned of supplying us with authentic information on the person's inner self. Physiognomy does not interpret a person's "expression" (the model must remain absolutely still, immobile), but his "traits." Unlike expression (*der Ausdruck*), which reflects the soul's temporary state, traits (*die Züge*) relate to its deep structure.[11] It is for this reason that the captured shadow is more precious to the physiognomist than the actual living face in front of him. What the person conceals, the shadow reveals. This is one of the reasons why it was so popular as a parlor game; all those who took part, did so with a mixture of apprehension and anticipation—apprehension because they were worried they would reveal some terrible disorder of the soul, anticipation because they hoped they would reveal for all to see, inestimable, hidden qualities.

We would be mistaken if we believed that reading the four volumes of the *Essays on Physiognomy* would give us the key to deciphering the human profile. Lavater was in effect constantly revising the essays. They are a collection of repeated attempts to codify a language although the author never succeeded in establishing its grammar. And despite Lavater's efforts to interpret the line that runs from the brow to the chin (fig. 3) these remained experimental and intuitive. That is why our own investigations involve the origin and structure of Lavater's hermeneutic rather than its practical conclusions, since these belong in the realms of fantasy. Our task is not to judge whether the process is sound or absurd but to reflect on the fundamental fact that Lavater's hermeneutic aim was to understand man as a moral being, through his shadow. The symbolic significance of the method can only be understood if we bear in mind that the study of physiognomy, to Lavater, was the result of a religious vocation, which led him to train to be a Protestant pastor. Goethe, who was initially involved in the development of this physiognomic interpretation, admitted quite openly when speaking with Eckermann: "Lavater's method entails morals, religion.[12]

9. Ibid., p. 65.

10. G. C. Lichtenberg, *Werke in einem Band* (Stuttgart: Walter Hädecke Verlag, 1935), from *Remarks on an Essay upon Physiognomy*, in Holcroft's edition of *Essays on Physiognomy*, p. 267.

11. Lavater, *Physiognomische Fragmente* (see note 7), p. 60 (translator's version).

12. J. P. Eckermann, *Gespräche mit Goethe in den letzten Jahren seines Lebens* (Munich: C. H. Beck), 1984), pp. 273–274 (17 February 1829).

This is why Lavater maintained that the practice of physiognomic deciphering was an act of love, committed to searching out the divine in a human being. The full title of the work is more like a warning against possible slander: *Physiognomical fragments for the advancement of man's knowledge and his love for his fellow men (Physiognomische Fragmente zur Beförderung der Menschenkenntnis und Menschenliebe).*

The aim of Lavater's "shadow-analysis" is that it should be a new "cure for the soul" (*Seelensorge*). It starts off with a notion of man who takes his divine origins into account. Man was made in God's image and likeness. But sin drove him to lose his divine likeness. His relationship with the divinity was overshadowed by flesh.[13] Taking this kind of reasoning into account, we might wonder whether Lavater's claim that it was his search for the divine in man that led him to practice physiognomy was made in good faith. Or to be more precise, it raises the following question: are we really likely to encounter God in a *man's shadow*? We have every reason to believe the contrary; what Lavater was actually looking for was not the positive, divine side of man, but the negative, sinful side. This is a serious contention and needs to be justified.

Let us therefore examine once more the significance that the outlined profile assumed with Lavater. It only had a synechdocal value (*pars pro toto*) and was based on the notion that the human shadow is a meaningful image:

> I am of the opinion that a man seen in silhouette from all angles—from head to foot, from the front, from the back, in profile, in half-profile, three quarters, would allow fundamentally new discoveries to be made on the omnisignificant nature of the human body.[14]

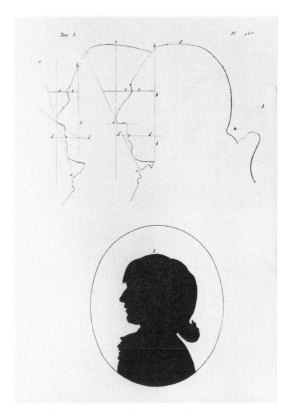

Figure 3. "Physiognomic Study." From Johann Caspar Lavater, *Physiognomische Fragmente* (Leipzig/Winterthur: Bey Weidmanns Erbe und Reiche, 1776).

What is quite implicit here is the notion that in the projection of the shadow, man is above all "himself." The importance bestowed on the profile resides in the fact that it is considered to be a direct externalization of the soul: his actual composition. The nose in particular with its more or less pronounced protuberance, is one of the most remarkable creations of internal forces; it is—Lavater believed—"the buttress, or abutment of the brain" (*Widerlage des Gehirns*).[15] The parallel, outline profile/ human soul, is in Lavater's opinion, so perfect that the expressions are interchangeable and often indiscriminately used. The outlined profile *is* the external soul, and physiognomy is an exercise capable of moving from the profile up to the psychic energies it is composed of:

---

13. For information regarding this problem, see E. Benz, "Swedenborg und Lavater. Ueber die religiäsen Grundlagen der Physiognomik," *Zeitschrift für Kirchengeschichte*, 3d f., 57 (1938):153–216; B. M. Stafford, *Body Criticism. Imagining the Unseen in Enlightenment Art and Medicine* (Cambridge: The MIT Press, 1991), pp. 84–103; E. Shookman, ed., *The Faces of Physiognomy: Interdisciplinary Approaches to Johann Caspar Lavater* (Drawer/Columbia: Camden House, 1993); K. Pestalozzi and H. Weigelt, *Das Antlitz Gottes im Antlitz des Menschen. Zugänge zu Johann Kaspar Lavater* (Göttingen: Vandenhoeck & Ruprecht, 1994).

14. J. C. Lavater, *Physiognomische Fragmente zur Befärderung der Menschenkenntnis und Menschenliebe*, vol. 2 (Leipzig/Winterthur: Bey Weidmanns Erbe und Reich, 1776) p. 132 (translator's version).

15. J. C. Lavater, *Essays on Physiognomy (Physiognomische Fragmente zur Beförderung der Menschenkenntnis und Menschenliebe*, vol. 4, (Leipzig/Winterthur: Bey Weidmanns Erbe und Reich, 1778), p. 390.

Physiognomy, in the narrow sense of the word, is an interpretation of the forces, or the science which studies the signs of the forces. . . .[16]

But the most important question remains unanswered. If Lavater's physiognomy is based exclusively on the interpretation of the *line of the profile*, then why do the illustrations show the whole of the man's head in the shape of a large dark stain rather than as a linear outline? The dilemma had cropped up earlier when, assisted by his friend Zimmermann, Lavater was finalizing the technicalities for the first edition of his *Essays.* Initially he was undecided, but he finally opted to have shadows rather than empty contours. It was Zimmermann who decided that "images of shadows should be dark" (*Schwarz sollen Schattenbilder sein*). Lavater appeared at first to be somewhat reticent, or to be more exact, cautious: "the silhouettes must be precise; we must distance ourselves from the black arts" (*Die Silhouetten sollen genau sein, können nicht Schwarzkunst sein*). He came up with the compromise solution of the grey shadow, only to abandon it at the last minute.[17] The first volume of the 1775 edition of *Essays on Physiognomy* was illustrated in the main with black outlined shadows, as were the three following volumes. But his initial reservations and final choice together demonstrate that the shadow-image, far from being devoid of symbolic implications, was so imbued with them that Lavater himself was worried that they were being over emphasized.

This point marked the birth of the fame Lavater's illustrations were about to gain; the context of the rhetoric of color that distinguished the final quarter of the eighteenth century allows us to understand Lavater's indecision. When in 1778, Alexander Cozens wanted to portray "simple beauty" (fig. 5), he chose a purely linear profile of a face, which resulted in the white background becoming integrated into the drawing's symbolism. He was aware however that his image was the product of a purely "statistical," intellectual process.[18] Cozens would probably never have dared to depict his *simple beauty* as a black shadow because black at the time was strictly

Figure 4. "The Man's Soul." From Commenius, *Orbis Sensualium Pictus* (Nürnberg, 1629).

codified as a key color within the framework of another aesthetic category: the sublime. Edmund Burke claimed that "darkness is one of the sources of the sublime," which, we should not forget, is a source of "aesthetic displeasure," combining admiration and fear, even terror. In one of the most important chapters of his treatise, devoted to the "power of black," Burke compares the perceptive power of black to the shock of a fall.[19]

The "danger of the precipice," which Burke discovered in the attractiveness of black, is in no way alien to Lavater who was quick to perceive the quasi-

---

16. J. C. Lavater, *Physiognomische Fragmente* (see note 7), p. 275 (translator's version).

17. See the texts in C. Steinbrucker, *Lavaters Physiognomische Fragmente im Verhältnis zur bildenden Kunst* (Berlin: W. Borngraber, 1915), p. 168.

18. A. Cozens, *Principles of Beauty, Relative to the Human Head* (London: James Dixwell, 1778), pp. 1–3, 7–10.

19. E. Burke, *A Philosophical Enquiry into the Origins of our Ideas of the Sublime and Beautiful,* sections XIV–XVII (1757; reprint, Oxford: Oxford University Press, 1906), vol. 1, pp. 55–219. See also M. Armstrong, "The Effects of Blackness: Gender, Race, and the Sublime in Aesthetics Theories of Burke and Kant," *Journal of Aesthetics and Art Criticism* 54 (1996):213–236.

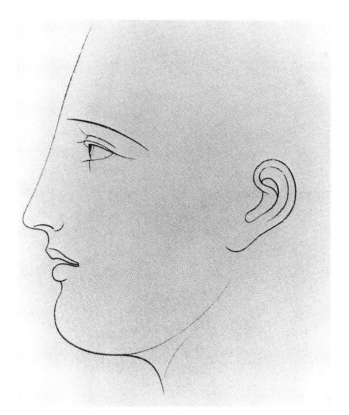

Figure 5. Alexander Cozens, "Simple Beauty." From *Principles of Beauty Relaative to the Human Head* (London: James Dixwell, 1778).

magical undertones that the manipulation of shadows contained:

> I teach no black art; no nostrum, the secret of which I might have concealed. . . .[20]

This statement is probably circumstantial. We know that Lavater elaborated a complete set of secret rules (*Geheimregeln*) so that the whole of the shadow could be read, however it was "not destined for the impure hands of the Public."[21] We also know that there were strange events in his personal life and immediate environment—these were not without their neuroses, suicides, and exorcisms. But since this is the stuff of

biographies,[22] we need only establish that, according to all probability, the short-lived success enjoyed by Lavater's physiognomy was largely due to the fact that it was another form of divination. While some of his contemporaries went in for palmistry, read the lines of the brow or coffee grounds,[23] Lavater read the shadow.

Paradoxically the process is a follow-up to investigations into myths undertaken in the spirit of Enlightenment. The momentous event that took place while Lavater was developing his method of examining the contours of shadows in order to understand the human soul and which indirectly explains it, was what could be referred to as "the death of the Devil."[24] The year 1776 was important in the history of demonology, for there appeared in Berlin, an anonymous work entitled *On the non-existence of the Devil (Ueber die Non-Existenz des Teufels)*. It was soon discovered that the author was Pastor Christian Wilhelm Kindleben,[25] who stated with unprecedented clarity that it was his opinion that the Devil only existed in the minds of theologians and in the hearts of evil men: "Do not seek the Devil outside, do not seek him in the Bible, he is in your heart" (*den Teufel nicht ausserhalb, suche ihn nicht in der Bibel; er ist in deinem Herzen*).[26] A significant step had been taken; the Devil makes way for Evil and becomes a psycho-philosophical principle that dwells in the heart of man.[27]

Lavater's shadow is therefore quite literally a shadow engendered by the Enlightenment. It is not a substitute for the Devil, but a physical manifestation of him.

In the light of these assertions, let us return to Lavater's "machine for drawing silhouettes" (fig. 2). It is

20. Lavater, *Essays on Physiognomy* (see note 7), p. 47.

21. Lavater, *Physiognomische Fragmente* (see note 7), pp. 377–394 (translator's version).

22. G. Gessner, *Johann Kaspar Lavaters Lebensbeschreibung von seinem Tochtermann G. G.*, 3 vols. (Winterthur: Steiner, 1802–1810); R. C. Zimmermann, *Das Weltbild des jungen Goethe*, 2 vols. (Munich: Fink, 1969–1979), vol. 2, pp. 213–234.

23. For example, C. A. Peuschel, *Abhandlung der Physiognomie, Metoskopie und Chiromantie* (1769).

24. See H. D. Kittsteiner, "Die Abschaffung des Teufels im 18. Jahrhundert. Ein kulturhistorisches Ereignis und seine Folgen," in *Die andere Kraft. Zur Renaissance des Bösen*, ed. A. Schuller and W. von Rahden (Berlin: Akademie Verlag, 1993), pp. 55–92.

25. Anonymous (C. W. Kindleben), *Ueber die Non-Existenz des Teufels. Als Antwort auf die demüthige Bitte um Belehrung an die grossen Männer, welche an keinen Teufel glauben* (Berlin: Bey Gottlieb August Lange, 1776), pp. 4, 17ff.

26. C. W. Kindleben, *Der Teufelein des achtzehnten Jahrhunderts letzter Akt. . . .* (Leipzig, 1779), p. 50.

27. Kittsteiner (see note 24), p. 73.

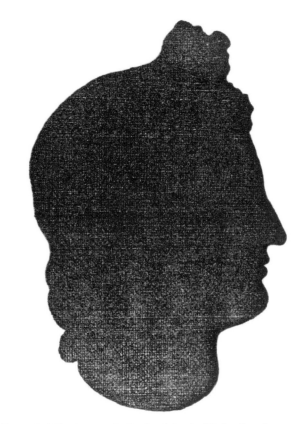

Figure 6. "Physiognomic Study of Apol of Belvedere." From Johann Caspar Lavater, *Physiognomische Fragmente* (Leipzig/Winterthur: Bey Weidmanns Erbe und Reiche, 1776).

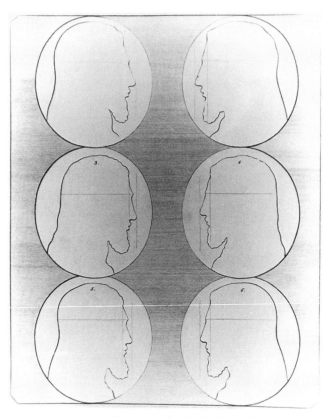

Figure 7. Thomas Holloway et al. after J. H. Fuseli, "Silhouettes of Christ." From Johann Caspar Lavater, *Essays on Physiognomy* (London, 1792).

possible that the lady in the chair, might not have sat down had she known that the man behind the screen was engaged in a practice verging on the unlawful. He was attempting to capture an image of her soul, as a first step in a hermeneutic process. It is interesting to note how Lavater's "machine" incorporates ideas inspired by the Plinian fable with an instrument traditionally used in Christianity (but abolished by Protestants) for the "therapy of the soul": the confessional.

The scene could *grosso modo* be regarded as a translation into visual terms of a confession. The verbalization of the inner life (common during confession) is replaced by the internal being projected to the external with the help of the shadow. Through the projection screen, the physiognomist watches the proffered image in much the same way that the priest listens to the anonymous voice that comes to him, filtered and without body, from the other side of the grill. Just like the confessor, the physiognomist has access to the secrets of the soul and just like him, he is more likely to discover the fallen man than the one created "in God's image." Lavater had this kind of process in mind when he described the physiognomist as a "Christian seer":

> He (the good physiognomist) must possess the character of those Apostles and early Christians who possessed the gift of recognizing spirits and reading the thoughts of the soul.[28]

Lavater, however, did not read the souls of men; rather he read their shadows. To him, the shadow was the imaginary area where the soul revealed itself to be full of sin. That is why the physiognomical hermeneutic

28. J. C. Lavater, *Von der Physiognomik* (Leipzig: Bey Weidmanns Erben und Reich, 1772), p. 79.

can be regarded as an exercise through which the shadow-soul is questioned and interpreted. To a certain extent it can also be seen as an act of love, but on one condition only: that we take into account a basic pessimism as regards human nature. This was not a feature of Lavater's philosophy alone, the pessimism was inherent to the Enlightenment. Diderot had something to say on this subject:

In the whole world there is not a single perfectly formed, perfectly healthy man to be found. The human species is just a mass of more or less deformed and sick individuals.[29]

We should not be too surprised, therefore, that Lavater went so far as to subject an image—which at the time was considered to be perfect—to a physiognomical analysis: Apollo of Belvedere (fig. 6). He does so with full knowledge of the facts since he quotes the enthusiastic appraisal of the statue made by Johann Winkelmann in his *History of Ancient Art* (1764):

Observe in spirit the kingdom of ethereal beauties and endeavour to guess the creator of this celestial nature and to fill your spirit with beauties which transcend nature. For nothing here is mortal and nothing has human means. No vein warms nor nerve animates this body. No, it was a celestial body which, flowing like a gentle stream, filled the whole contour of this figure.[30]

Lavater half listens to Winkelmann's appeal; it is a double illustration. The first contour, filled with the white of the page, is reminiscent of Cozens's illustration of "simple beauty" (fig. 5). The second reduces Apollo's head to an outlined shadow—not a very orthodox way to treat an immortal god. The beginning of the analysis is fairly positive, the conclusion borders on catastrophe:

Twice have I drawn this head of Apollo based on the shadow then reduced it and I think I have been able to bring to it something which confirms Winkelmann's feeling. One never tires of contemplating these contours. Really, we

can say nothing about them, we tremble and anything we say is intolerable. Nevertheless, from the confused mass we can highlight:

The sublimity of the forehead, how the forehead relates to the face as a whole; the curve of the brow in relation to the lower part of the face; the way the chin curves into the neck.

I believe that if the contour of the nose were a perfectly straight line, this profile would give the impression of even greater **noble power**, even greater **divine power**. The nose being completely concave to the contour of the profile is always indicative of a certain weakness.[31]

The effect of this final observation of Lavater's can be compared to the collapse of the entire structure that supports the moral values founded on the kind of aesthetic values Winkelmann had tried to construct around his fetish image. Everything hinges on Apollo's nose, whose weak character is *unveiled* by the shadow.

Let us examine Lavater's approach more closely. It is based on reductions that fit one inside the other. The statue is reduced to the head, the head to its shadow, the shadow of the head to the line of the nose. The problematic line demystifies a body (that of Apollo's) considered to be a model of perfection. The polemic is directly targeted against Winkelmann's text and the use he made of the notion of contour. In effect, to the art historian, the contour (*die Umschreibung*) was a *significant line*, since it was imbued (*ergossen*) with a divine spirit (*himmlischer Geist*). But if the divine spirit was, to Winkelmann, manifested through the contour of the body (*die Umschreibung der Figur*), to Lavater, who unscrupulously eliminated the body from the value system, another contour—that of the nose—cancels out the very existence of a divine power (*göttliche Stärke*) that could have been one of the founding principles of this "god" (of light), now reduced to a "shadow."

The process is symbolic and we must continue to examine it. Apollo is, indeed, the god of light. Lavater's reduction places shadow in direct antithesis to light thus directly targeting the Pantheon of the Ancients. It was not for another year that the key to the problem raised by the "shadow-analysis" of Apollo of Belvedere was finally found. It was in the second volume of his *Essays* (in 1776) that Lavater unveiled his prototype of

29. D. Diderot, *Eléments de physiologie*, ed. J. Mayer (1778; reprint,Paris: Librairie M. Didier, 1964), p. 266. Regarding this issue, see B. M. Stafford, "From 'Brilliant Ideas' to 'Fitful Thoughts': Conjecturing the Unseen in Late Eighteenth-Century Art," *Zeitschrift für Kunstgeschichte* 48 (1985):329–363, esp. 345.

30. On this question, see W. Sauerländer, "Überlegungen zu dem Thema Lavater und die Kunstgeschichte," *Idea* 7 (1988):15–30.

31. J. C. Lavater, *Physiognomische Fragmente zur Beförderung der Menschenkenntnis und Menschenliebe*, vol. 1 (Leipzig/Winterthur: Bey Weidmanns Erbe und Reich, 1775), p. 134 (Lavater's emphasis; translator's version).

physiognomical perfection (fig. 7). A glance at these illustrations, where he displays (in an overtly stereotypical manner) six profiles of Christ, instantly reveals the line of the nose whose absence in the Belvedere Apollo was so deplored by Lavater. The same glance will reveal that what differentiates the six silhouettes of Christ from the other plates in the book, is that they are all—could this have been otherwise?— what we could paradoxically term "profiles of shadows without shadows."

"Our own imperfect knowledge"

Petrus Camper and the search for an "ideal form"

NICHOLAS GRINDLE

Petrus Camper's treatise *On the Connexion between the Science of Anatomy and the Arts of Drawing, Painting, Statuary &c.* (1794) proposed that racial difference could be calibrated by means of a "facial line."[1] The line, drawn from the forehead to the upper lip, measured the angle of the jaw's protrusion (see figs. 1–2). Camper's theory inspired a host of works in a similar vein and has today become synonymous with the *Connexion*.[2]

Current interpretations of Camper's "facial line" focus upon the perceived treatment of Africans and Europeans as polarities in relation to the idealized forms of ancient Greek statuary.[3] It is debatable, however, as to whether the regulation of comparative anatomy was Camper's primary concern in the *Connexion*. Petrus Camper was a multifaceted scholar and practitioner, whose studies ranged from optometry, anatomy, and anatomical illustration to the practice of obstetrics. Given such wide interests, it seems unreasonable to assume that as innovative a work as the *Connexion* would not draw upon Camper's previous areas of scientific exploration. The *Connexion* is presented here in a brief outline that

seeks to integrate and clarify its content and objectives with an analysis of Camper's wider epistemological interests, as well as the more general intellectual climate of the later eighteenth century.

"Essential differences": form and color

Eighteenth-century Europeans regarded cognition as a formative principle of understanding, borrowing from John Locke's *Essay Concerning Human Understanding* (1690). The belief that sight informed ideas and actions can be viewed as a culturally diffused philosophy that had ideological implications in many areas of public life. The ramifications of this debate are to be seen most notably in the literature of the period, such as Swift's *Gulliver's Travels* and Voltaire's *Micromegas*. Yet the scientific community of eighteenth-century Europe strove to explore this debate further than the level of the "vulgar Lockeanism" that characterized public life. Its concern was with the scientific properties of optical cognition and the formation of knowledge regarding the physical world. Locke had proposed that the agreement or disagreement of any two ideas, or perceptions, may form the basis of understanding. The clarity of the agreement of two or more ideas became the degree of certitude of the knowledge itself. Methods of cognition that responded to mensuration thus assumed great currency in forming the basis of reliable knowledge. This is emphasized in Locke's *Essay* in the valorization of the mensurate qualities of objects, such as bulk, figure, and number, as "primary qualities" essential in the formation of rational understanding. Qualities such as color, which could not be abstracted from the objects themselves, could not be considered as constitutive of anything but an individual's perception and idea of an object. Mathematics had, paradoxically, become the substance of reality. What could be abstracted from the object would constitute its "primary qualities," while what could not be separated from the object itself was merely a subjective "secondary idea" of it.

It is upon these grounds that Camper identified the need for a thesis on the differences observable in racial

---

1. Petrus Camper (1722–1789), *The works of the late Professor Camper, on the Connexion between the Science of Anatomy, and the Arts of Drawing, Painting, Statuary &c.,* trans. T. Cogan, M.D. (London: C. Dilly, 1794), hereafter referred to as the *Connexion*. References to quotations from the *Connexion* will be given in parentheses in the text. Cogan's translation is accurate and should be considered faithful to the Dutch original of 1791 unless indicated. I am very grateful to Professor David Bindman for comments given on a draft of this paper.

2. See especially Charles White, *An Account of the Regular Gradation in Man* (London: C. Dilly, 1799); Johann Gottfried Schadow, *Polyclet, oder von den Massen des Menschen . . . als Fortsetzung des hierüber von P. Camper ausgegangenen* (Berlin: E. Wasmuth, 1834). Hugh Honour, *The Image of the Black in Western Art* (Cambridge: Harvard University Press, 1989), vol. 4, bk. 2, gives an excellent account of the impact of the facial line within the study of comparative anatomy. The *Connexion* itself ran through four editions in French, (1791 [twice], 1792, and 1803) and was reprinted once in English (1821). (Source: The National Union Catalog [pre-1956 imprints], Library of Congress Catalogs).

3. Examples of "current interpretations" of Camper's work are David Bindman, "Am I not a Man and a Brother?" *RES: Anthropology and Aesthetics* 26 (1994):80–82; id., *The Image of the Black in Western Art* (Cambridge: Harvard University Press, forthcoming), vol. 3, bk. 3; Honour (see note 2), pp. 13–14.

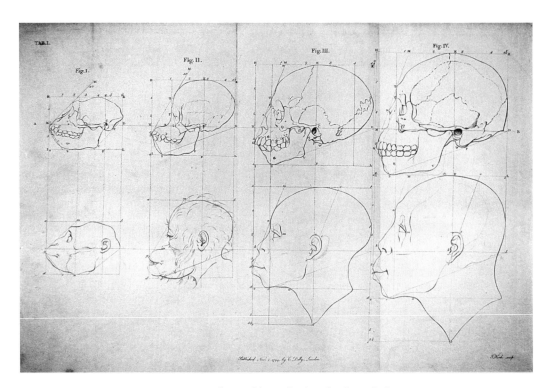

Figure 1. Petrus Camper, "Proportions observable in the heads of a tailed ape, an orang-outang, a young Negro, and a Calmuck, in left profile." From *The Connexion between the Science of Anatomy and the Arts of Drawing, Painting, Statuary, &c.*, trans. T. Cogan, M.D. (London: C. Dilly, 1794), pl. 1. Copper engraving: T. Kirk, 1794. 275 x 460 mm. Photograph: Francesca Berry. Courtesy of Professor David Bindman.

types—a thesis that realized a commensurate and methodological difference between form and color as categories of cognition and understanding. Camper's own interests in the scientific properties of optical cognition, which he had in common with many of his contemporaries, were extensive.[4] In the previous century, Locke had revised Newton's definition of color as light with "nothing but a certain power to stir up a sensation" to propose that color was not an innate objective property.[5] Following on from Locke, Camper's doctoral thesis, *Dissertatio de Optica Visu* (1746), showed color to be a variable quality of perception. It followed that a determination of the standards of

physical form would meet the criteria of an empirical and formalized understanding that the physical sciences demanded, while color as an indeterminate quality could not provide it. It was this that led Camper, in the *Connexion*, to reiterate that the idea of color was subject to the idioms of cognition that differed one man's perception from another; "objects have no color in themselves; the idea of color is excited in us according to the manner in which the ways of light are refracted" (p. 17).

The qualities of color could not therefore be shown to be subject to any particular rule as a mensurate property. As such, racial difference could not be reliably calibrated according to differences in skin color. Moreover, prior to the *Connexion*, Camper's lecture "On the Skin of Negroes" (1764) demonstrated that one individual's skin could change color over a period of time because the color originated from a tissue of middle membrane that was liable to be damaged or

4. For a further discussion of the early-eighteenth-century interest in visual cognition, see Michael Baxandall's essay on Chardin in *Patterns of Intention* (New Haven: Yale University Press, 1985).

5. Isaac Newton, *Opticks*, 4th ed. (reprint, London: G. Bell, 1931), bk. 1, pt. 2, pp. 124–125.

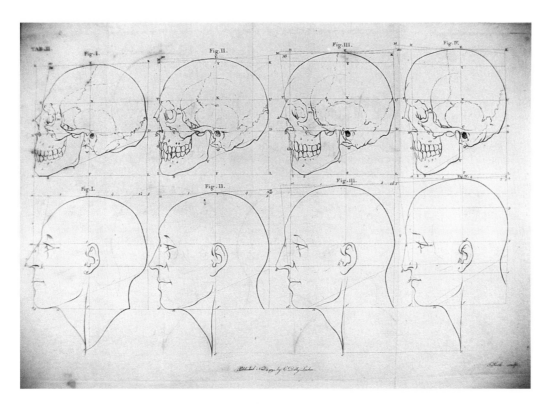

Figure 2. Petrus Camper, "Proportions observable in the heads of a European, a European-classical hybrid, a Roman bust, and a Greek statue, in left profile." From *Connexion*, pl. 2. Copper engraving: T. Kirk, 1794. 275 x 460 mm. Photograph: Francesca Berry. Courtesy of Professor David Bindman.

changed with climatic variation.[6] Reaffirming these findings in the *Connexion*, Camper's ideas of what constituted racial difference in both physiological and cognitive terms led him to conclude decisively that "Black, tawny and white men are simply varieties; [their variations in color], do not constitute *essential differences*" (p. 28).[7]

Within the study of comparative racial difference, the emphasis on form and mensuration was relatively new. Its significance may be seen when compared to the indeterminate and a priori theories of the renowned physiognomists Lavater and Swedenborg, on the one hand, and those natural scientists concerned with delineating a strictly hierarchical chain of being, such as Linnaeus and Buffon, on the other. Camper himself stressed the value of his work. He stated that up until that point, philosophers and scientists alike had attributed the difference in racial form to some "original artifice," namely, a postnatal cause dependent upon a

6. Petrus Camper, "On the Skin of Negroes," lecture at Groningen, 14 November 1764, cited in Sir William Jardine, *Memoir of Camper*, The Naturalist's Library, vol. 11 (Edinburgh: W. Lizars, 1843), pp. 1–67. A full transcript of the lecture with notes was published in Dutch as *Redevoering over de oorsprong en de kleur de Zwarten, voorgeleezen . . . door Professor Camper* (Lecture on the origin and color of the Blacks, as given . . . by Professor Camper) in the periodical *De Rhapsodist*, Tweede Deel, no. 3 (Amsterdam: Pieter Meijer, 1772), pp. 373–395. No English translation appears to exist.

7. Emphasis added. A firm monogeneisist, Camper's treatise on the skin of Negroes thirty years prior to the *Connexion* had already affirmed pan-human parity; "by anatomical observations on our

bodies, and particularly on our skin, there is no room for believing the race of Negroes does not extend from Adam as our own." He concludes in a spirit of Christian humanism, "nor will you hesitate with me to extend to the Negro a brother's hand" (Jardine's translation. Camper, On the Skin of Negroes, in Jardine [see note 6], p. 34; see De Rhapsodist [see note 6], pp. 392, 394).

"primitive" cultural tradition.[8] The mensurate properties of form led him to refute these degrading notions, however:

> I did not venture to oppose . . . such respectable authorities [that is, Buffon] until . . . the fetus of a female negro [sic] came into my possession. In this fetus, which was of about six months, all the features were so strongly marked, that every person could immediately distinguish the negro child, although the color of the skin was not changed into black (p. 22).

It is indicative of the increasingly empirical content of eighteenth-century approaches to physiognomic and other related studies that Camper's earlier work on optical cognition came to have currency within an area that had hitherto been the preserve of disciplines more speculative in nature.

The representation of form

Despite its valorization of the mensurate properties of objects, the debate on the qualities of form in the *Connexion* was not unanimous in its conclusions. Camper's thesis gave rise to a subtle distinction regarding the depiction of form as a passage to understanding. Following on from the issues raised in *De Optica Visu*, the *Connexion* was premised on the hypothesis that a distinction could be made between the representation of an idea of substance, on the one hand, and the representation of substance itself, on the other. Our own idea of objects might lead us to represent forms as in a painting. Camper argued that representation of actual substance must divest itself of the idioms of perception and follow a schematic procedure of production.

Again (and it is doubtful whether this can be stressed enough), it must be seen that the basis for Camper's proposals lay with Locke's *Essay*. Locke had said that schematic cognition may facilitate a perfect objective representation; "Numbers and Figures [that is, objects] can be set down, by visible and lasting marks, wherein the Ideas under consideration are perfectly determined."[9] Camper believed that his own work on optometry provided the knowledge and means necessary to schematically depict a "perfectly determined" form. He saw that such a uniform approach could profitably be used within the field of anatomical drawing, in which he had had an interest for many years.

It was to this end that Camper had engaged in a fierce dispute with his former tutor, Bernhard Siegfried Albinus. Albinus used a one-point perspective method in depicting anatomical models.[10] In negating the perspective method for an architectonic approach informed by his own study of optics, Camper was inspired by Locke's proposal to counter the erroneous methods of his tutor:

> In order to perceive the true form and relative situations of the parts, I did not view them from one fixed point, but my eye was always directed, in a right line, to the central point of the object, in the manner practiced by masons and architects; avoiding the rules of perspective, by which particular parts are always distorted and misplaced (pp. 33–34).

Camper's critique of the perspective method, and the solution he offers, are both extensions of the problematics of visual cognition identified in *De Optica Visu*: "Fallacies of vision are conclusions . . . which do not correspond with the objects themselves . . . suchlike errors are innumerable, for when we are not able to measure differences, our judgment must be absolutely false."[11] Perspectival views were liable to raise false ideas, he argued, in contrast to his own schematically uniform points of vision.

Camper's distinction between true and "false" judgment, indicates the extent to which the infallibility of scientific principle served as the basis upon which he assumed the intellectual and moral currency of his theories. The position of the *Connexion* in this analysis is best summed up in Book Two, where Camper treats of

8. *Connexion*, p. 22. "Herodotus, Hippocrates, Suidas, Aristotle, Pliny, P. Mela, and many other writers of antiquity, have uniformly maintained that the variety of forms observable in other nations, do not altogether arise from the climate and other natural causes, but also from some original artifice . . . and it seems to be confirmed by the remarks of numberless modern travelers." Camper contrasts the artifices of "other nations" to those of "polished nations," inferring a primitive state of the "other": "Manners and customs indubitably operate with great force on the form and posture of the body. A polished education renders the whole figure elegant. Of this we have daily instances in polished nations" (p. 29).

9. John Locke, *Essay Concerning Human Understanding* (London, 1690), bk. 4, chap. 2.

10. For a more detailed discussion of this debate, see K. B. Roberts and J. D. W. Tomlinson, *The Fabric of the Body—European Traditions in Anatomical Illustration* (London: Clarendon Press, 1992), p. 341.

11. Petrus Camper, *Dissertatio de Optica Visu* (Leiden, 1746), chap. 3.

the relative forms of animals in the same way as he does the human form in Book One.

> But you will enquire, Why then do we consider the pieces of the celebrated masters so beautiful? The explanation is not difficult. Our own *imperfect* knowledge of the exact form of animals, renders us contented with whatever is agreeably executed on the whole. We are enchanted by a graceful attitude, by a masterly stroke of the pencil, or by the finishing of the whole; *and this conceals our own ignorance*, as well as the imperfections of the artist (Bk. 2, p. 158).[12]

Camper draws a clear distinction between what is simply pleasing and what is perfect, and therefore truly beautiful. He aligns the painter's ability to excel, and the observer's capacity to appreciate, with his own critiques and hypotheses. This is indicative of his stark view of the artist's place within an epistemology that mediates between Lockean metaphysics, optical science, and the perennial problems of artistic representation.

The empirical grounding of Camper's argument is rather more evident in the original Dutch text of the *Connexion*, than the English translation.[13] In the latter, any acknowledgment of the *Connexion*'s scientific genesis is compromised when accounting for Camper's adoption of an "ideal" antique form as the meter by which racial difference is calibrated (see fig 3). An apparent use of an a priori standard of perfection is strongly at odds with the rigid empiricism that forms the basis of Camper's claims to scientific authority in the *Connexion*.

Yet what is given in the English translation as a philosophical ideal is, in fact, a "*kundige man inbeeldig.*" This translates as "the knowledge (*kunde*) of an idealized image (*inbeeld*) of man (*man*)."[14] Of significance is Camper's use of the verb *kunde*, which denotes empirical knowledge of man's image more than a passive and sophistic form of philosophizing. In this analysis, the human form becomes formalized by means

of optical mensuration as a property definable through the abstractions of proportion and equation. Camper was engaged in practices that gave substance to Locke's proposal that bulk and figure were the primary determinate and measurable qualities of a cognate world of objects. It is with this point in mind that Camper's valorization of the sculpture of Greek antiquity must be explored and the *Connexion* reassessed.

The mensuration of beauty

In "On Beauty," the Third Part of the *Connexion*, Camper takes his theses on optical cognition as the basis for determining beautiful forms. A standard of beauty is proposed that is predicated on a systematic mode of perception, formulating a thorough understanding and appreciation of unblemished form. Within an artistic context, this standard was taken by Camper to be embodied in the forms of antique statuary. As the basis of the aesthetic principles of the *Connexion*, Camper's praise of the antique form belies an assumption that Greek sculpture showed an understanding of the infallibility and truth of scientific principle.

> The proportions given by the ancients to their figures are not beautiful in our eyes, merely from a weak prepossession in favor of all they have handed down to us, *but because they have corrected the defects which arise from the laws of vision* (p. 82).[15]

Camper is concerned with delineating a notion of operative beauty that locates the beautiful within a set of commensurate, as opposed to canonical, relations.[16] If we can recall the debate discussed above, between depiction of perception versus depiction of substance, the ethical import given to the category "beautiful" might become clearer. Consider the following sentence from the introduction of the treatise, in which Camper conflates the capacity of form to be beautiful with the manner in which the form is perceived:

> In a separate chapter, on the constituent beauty of forms [that is, Part 3, chap. 1], I shall hereafter show how much depends upon avoiding a defective manner of viewing the object which is occasioned by the refraction of the rays of light (p. 6).

---

12. Emphasis added. The page numbers between the two books run consecutively from one to the other.

13. Petrus Camper, *Verhandeling over het natuurlijk verschil der wezenstrekken in menschen van onderscheiden landaart en ouderdom; over het schoon in antijke en gesneedene steenen* (Utrecht: B. Wild & J. Altheer, 1791).

14. *Kunde* is a verb denoting empirical knowledge. *Man*, for human, has the same connotations in Dutch as in English. *Inbeeldig* has its root in the noun *beeld*, meaning "image," and properly denotes "imagination," but retains a sense of empirical perfection, which the English use of "imagination" does not.

---

15. Emphasis added.

16. It should be noted, with relation to this, that throughout the treatise Camper uses only abstract measurements.

The "refraction of the rays of light" is a reference to the distortions of the perspective method. This passage follows directly from Camper's pronouncement that for artists, a knowledge of optics is requisite in the cognition of "true form" and the depiction of beauty (p. 6).

The role of the principles of optical cognition in the *Connexion* may become more evident if one considers the following: that in locating the beauty of the proportions of ancient statuary within criteria of scientific values, Camper took most of his aesthetic precepts from the Roman critic and rhetorician Longinus. He, of all the philosophers, had afforded Camper "the most satisfaction" in treating the constituents of beautiful form in a systematic manner (p. 78).

Camper's notion of a systematically determined, scientific beauty reflects Longinus's assertion that the execution of beauty in form serves to regulate the employment of the forms of inventive beauty. In this sense, operative beauty has a degree of jurisdiction over poetic and inventive beauty. Inherent in this empirical approach must be seen to exist a specific mode of observation and cognition. Such empiricism valorizes a purity of form as an idea and ingredient of beauty and places on the artist the burden of manifesting beauty. It relates closely to Longinus's metonymic position regarding the importance of vocabulary and diction in poetry; "the choice of proper and striking words . . . is the leading ambition of all orators and writers."[17]

Longinus extended his discussion regarding modes of beauty from poetry to sculpture. He argued that in sculpture as well as poetry, the choice of correct form ensures the presence "upon the fairest statues, of the perfection of grandeur, beauty, mellowness, dignity, force, power, and any other qualities there may be" (XXX, p. 119). Yet for Camper, there could be no choice of a vocabulary of form. As we have seen, the existence of laws of perception located within distinct scientific formulae provided the means by which "proper" forms may be identified, their propriety ensured by the infallible status of such modes of cognition. Longinus's aesthetic was here adapted to the values of scientific mensuration.

Yet form per se did not constitute beauty for Longinus. The regulative aspects of the sources of beauty were carried forward from its inventive and poetic content to its execution. "Among the chief causes of the [beautiful] . . . in the structure of the human body [in statuary] . . . is the collocation of members" (XL, p. 145). Individual elements may provide grandeur, dignity, power, and so on, but it is the unity of these forms in execution that ensures the presence of the universal quality of the magnificent or beautiful that may characterize a whole body: "a single member . . . possesses in itself nothing remarkable, but all united together make a full and perfect organism" (XLI, p. 146). Camper's own observations strongly reflected the dynamic of Longinus's aesthetic. "The idea of beauty," Camper wrote, "is excited by a certain conformity or proportion of component parts with each other" (p. 81).

For Camper, Longinus's notion of operative beauty was inherently organic in character. In the *Connexion*, the drive for the unity of forms was enacted through the relationships between forms that offered a higher order of purity in the abstraction of primary qualities. It is therefore arguable that if asked in precisely what manner a component part of a body should link with another, Camper would have replied that it should be through the formal value that all forms shared as properties of a normative mode of cognition. The harmonizing potential of such modalities of vision echo Longinus's observation that inventive and operative beauty "are for the most part developed through one another" (XXX, p. 119).[18]

It is upon this thesis that Camper argues for the excellence of the proportions of ancient statuary. The first chapter of "On Beauty" is concerned with the differences between the proportions of statuary and figures that the observer may have become accustomed to seeing and thinking beautiful. In Camper's analysis, each part of the body had a strictly formal value with regard to its compatibility with the other parts. It is for this reason, he states, that the ancients sometimes gave their statues proportions that appear to be "inconsonant

17. Longinus, *On the Sublime* XXX, ed. W. Rys Roberts (Cambridge: Cambridge University Press, 1899), p. 119. Future references to Longinus will be given in the text. The use of "sublime" for the Greek "hupsous" is questionable, and to avoid confusion with the Burkean sense of the word, I have substituted "beauty" or "magnificence" for "sublime."

18. In Chapter 6 of the first part of the *Connexion*, Camper gives examples of the manner in which the skull serves as the organism for constituting the shape of the rest of the figure. The organic nature of his anatomical theory proved attractive for artists. Henry Fuseli noted, "from a head so determined . . . the thinking artist could not fail to conclude the rest of the body." J. Knowles, ed., *The Life and Writings of Henry Fuseli* (London: Henry Colburn and Richard Bentley, 1831), vol. 2, lecture X, p. 380.

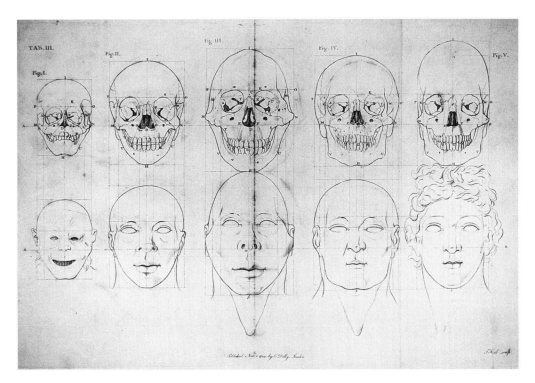

Figure 3. Petrus Camper, "Physiological examination of the differences in the features, when viewed in front." From *Connexion*, pl. 3. Copper engraving: T. Kirk, 1794. 275 x4 60 mm. Photograph: Francesca Berry. Courtesy of Professor David Bindman.

with all our ideas of beauty," but that ensured a dignified collocation of the members (p. 84).[19]

In demonstrating that the ancients were aware that the sources of beauty lay with cognitive precepts, Camper recalled that the Roman historian Pliny the Elder had made similar observations on the matter, with respect to the sculptor Lysippus:

> In order to avoid [a defective manner of viewing], it is . . . necessary to attend to the excellent rule of Lysippus, i.e. to make the head somewhat less, the body more slender and delicate than they really are, and they will be represented to a greater advantage than by the most scrupulous exactitude (pp. 6–7).[20]

Camper had earlier proposed that Albert Dürer, by looking at the object with both his eyes, had

misrepresented form, as binocular vision resulted in a slight broadening of the object (p. 6). The point of his argument was that the exactitude of Dürer was no guarantee against distortion in the representation of form, whereas a knowledge of optometry, was. Having shown that the relations of forms to one another may change in accordance with a given modality of perception, Camper could therefore posit that beauty, in this sense, "does not depend on certain immutable proportions" (p. 4).

With the aid of authority rooted in the maxims of Longinus's forms of rhetoric, Camper here achieves a two-fold objective. The first is that upon which he had criticized the aestheticians of modern times. They had, he states, only treated the sources of the manifestation of beauty in "a cursory manner, or by way of allusion" (p. 79). The great achievement of the *Connexion* in this respect is that it succeeds in making manifest forms of beauty and purging form of distortion and impurity. This is effected through a construction of related criteria that modes of perception may have to meet in order to

---

19. *Inconsonant* appears in the text itself as *consonant* and is indicated in the 1794 edition as a printing error.

20. Camper here refers the reader to Book 34 of Pliny's *Natural History*. See Pliny, *Natural History*, Loeb Classical Library (Cambridge: Harvard University Press, 1952), bk. 34, pp. 175–177.

correctly perceive and abstract the primary qualities of physical form. It is in this regard that Camper is able to argue for his treatise as rendering a "considerable service . . . to the science of painting" (p. 11). This leads to the second objective achieved in the *Connexion*. Camper saw the rendering of beauty as an activity reducible to scientific principles, and drawing and painting in this respect are given the status of "mechanic" arts (p. 79). His rigid methodology of perception came to form the basis of an affirmed truth that in turn granted his formulation of beauty an overtly moral dimension. The artist, presented with the infallible truths of scientific principle, was thus handed the burden of assuming these principles as the basis of their praxis.

A perfection of form

It is in this context that Camper praises the forms of antique statuary that the historian Johann Joachim Winckelmann (1717–1768) had argued as being almost perfect. The *Connexion* conflates Winckelmann's argument to Camper's own notion of the mensurate properties of form: "What this penetrating observer terms *ideal*, is in fact founded upon the rules of optics" (p. 4).

Such a specific identification of Winckelmann's use of scientific means to achieve philosophical ends deserves deeper consideration. Superficially, the parallels between Winckelmann's *History of the Art of Antiquity* (1764) and the *Connexion* are numerous. Not least, in both works, the debate within scientific circles between the merits of form and color in the formulation of understanding clearly valorized the formalism of the statuary of classical antiquity. Camper himself states that he had enjoyed the "excellent observations" of Winckelmann (p. 6). This is hardly surprising, as Winckelmann's *History* was hugely popular and influential in cultivating the taste for neoclassical forms. Yet, what makes Camper's interest in Winckelmann intriguing is the difficulty the latter had in defining his own notion of an aesthetic ideal and formulating it as an empirical phenomenon.[21] In Winckelmann's platonic conception of beauty, the absolute perfection required

in the formation of the ideal was compromised by the physical forms of nature from which it was to be constructed. The highest artistic style could be seen as a mode of beauty that borrowed and improved upon natural form, yet that could only refer the viewer to the higher and more perfect forms of an imaginary ideal. The purest form observable was not theoretically the purest conceivable, as the former borrowed from empirical forms whilst the latter envisaged an unobtainable ideality of form.

Camper's approach to natural form was intrinsically opposed to the a priori determinism of Winckelmann's image of the ideal, as defining the criteria by which objects are judged beautiful. Critically, for Camper, beauty was a construct of the rules of proportion. Any notion of a higher ideal, unobtainable in its purity, would be at odds with the empiricism that provided the epistemological foundation of the *Connexion*. To this end, beauty itself had to be a manifest and *perfectible* form. Hence, one may better understand the pertinence of Camper's attempt to place Winckelmann's aesthetic within the legitimizing paradigms of optical science. It is important to remember that Camper constantly sought to resolve the contradictory dialogue between idealism and empiricism that his commendation of Greek statuary suggests.[22] The *Connexion* attempts to formalize the philosophies related to classical forms and antique statuary within the borders of its own scientific project.

To this end, Camper proposed that the forms of Greek antiquity identified as a means to imagining an ideal by Winckelmann were in fact perfect because they *systematically* purged themselves of cognate impurity. As has been argued above, Camper's aesthetic precepts were informed almost exclusively by his hypotheses on optical acuity. Hence, when he wrote, "I was still unable to explain in what manner it was that the Greeks should have acquired . . . that single and defined expression which they gave to their figures" (pp. 7–8) he was trying to identify a manner and method of delineating beauty that could be considered, to a large degree, scientifically commensurate. It was the empirical foundation of the *Connexion*, the theory of the facial line, that Camper proposed as the means according to which the Greeks could have systematically elevated their forms to a

---

21. For a more detailed discussion of Winckelmann's aesthetic, on which this paper has drawn, see Alex Potts, *Flesh and the Ideal: Winckelmann and the Origins of Art History* (New Haven: Yale University Press, 1994).

22. Such conflict is not so evident in Camper's original Dutch text, where *schoon*, or "beautiful," has connotations of both beauty and purity; "On Beauty" is titled *Over het schoone* (On the beautiful/pure).

perfection of beauty. The facial line has given Camper much of his notoriety, and its popularity in the early nineteenth century inspired many similar works. Its primary use was perceived by Camper as a means by which artists could, with a degree of mensurate precision, valorize form over color in abstracting the salient features of race.

> When in addition to the skull of a negro [sic], I had procured one of a Calmuck. . . . I observed that a line, drawn along the forehead and upper lip, indicated [the] difference in national physiognomy. . . . Hence arose the first stage of my edifice (p. 9).

Camper had founded the validity of his theory on the fact that the angles that mark the countenance were calibrated in accordance with his architectonic method of viewing the subject. Yet scientific authority alone could not commend the facial line to an artistic milieu that was driven by the classicizing tendencies of public forms of academic art, which invariably placed a premium on the philosophical ideals of antiquity. In proposing that the Greeks were aware of the facial line as a means to calibrate a degree of optical acuity, Camper was harmonizing scientific and aesthetic authority.

> The second stage [of my edifice] was formed by a critical investigation of the line which the ancient masters preferred, in their best productions (pp. 9–10).

In this way, he hoped to impart a degree of artistic currency to both his newly discovered principle, as well as the theories on the properties of vision that lay behind it. The *Connexion* commends itself to artists on the premise that the perfect forms of the Greek ideal were realized by ancient artists only by means of a highly profitable interaction between science and art. As such, Camper's claim that ancient artists "seem to have paid great attention to the facial line" (p. 39) would invariably lead to the conclusion that they were concerned with similar issues and problems of a scientific nature. Camper is explicit in stating that his

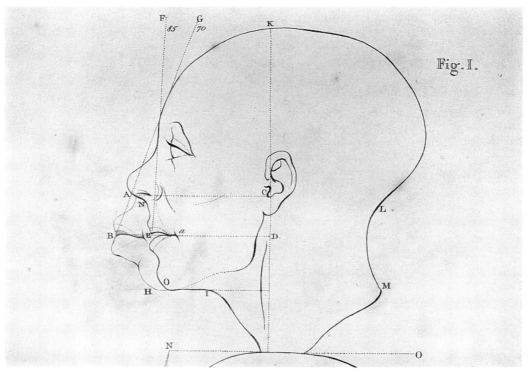

Figure 4. Petrus Camper, "A new method of delineating the head; the arrangement of the jaws of a European and a Negro according to the facial line." From *Connexion*, detail of pl. 6. Copper engraving: T. Kirk, 1794. 90 x 90 mm. Photograph: Francesca Berry. Courtesy of Professor David Bindman.

own thesis was invaluable as a rediscovery and substantiation of these praxes:

> I was able to distinguish immediately the [forms of the] Grecian artists. I flattered myself that [the principles of my knowledge] would prove acceptable . . . to those who admire the masterly performances of ancient artists (pp. 10–11).

This is not to say that Camper was simply applying a pseudo-scientific gloss to Winckelmann's valorization of Greek forms. The genesis of the facial line lies firmly in Camper's earlier work on optical acuity. Yet it is precisely this abstraction that enables Camper to conflate the scientific and aesthetic paradigms of the *Connexion*, bringing the two together as a united and operative concern.

It was undoubtedly the mensurate calibration of the facial line, as the foundation for an aesthetic principle, that provided the basis for the popularity of the *Connexion*. The ramifications of Camper's delineation of measured prognathism are already well known. Yet the importance of the facial line as a tenant of the *Connexion* itself has perhaps been over emphasized. I suggest that this has been at the expense of a consideration of the moral precepts and historical precedents upon which Camper hoped to commend his work to a wider readership.

Arguably, the authority of the *Connexion*, within the paradigms of eighteenth-century epistemology, is rooted in the moral currency that stemmed from the perceived infallibility of Camper's scientific principles. The *Connexion* may be seen, by extension, as having as its genesis a refinement of the psychological framework given in the second book of Locke's *Essay*. Yet it is doubtful whether scientific authority alone was sufficient to commend Camper's thesis to a wider artistic community. The *Connexion* acknowledges the more diffuse intellectual exigencies of the period in that it constantly evokes the suggestion that it was merely substantiating that which the artists of classical antiquity already knew and practiced. Such an appeal to the beauty of classical forms arguably compromised the scientific content of the *Connexion*. Even so, it must have given Camper great pleasure to apply his thesis to one of the eighteenth century's most prestigious areas of study, that of ancient Greek statuary. But it is the debt that is owed to Camper's earlier thesis on optical cognition, rather than any generalized cultural influences, that must be emphasized in an assessment of the aims and objectives of the *Connexion*. Camper's work must be seen as a facet of an epistemological milieu concerned with the commensurate formation of rational understanding.

Lectures and discussions

Redefinitions of abjection in contemporary performances of the female body

CHRISTINE ROSS

My paper deals with the recent profusion of the "question of the body" in the visual arts and the recurrent use of the category of the "abject" in its representation. My question, put in its simplest terms is the following: why this insistent resort to abjection? Is the use of revulsion and disgust a shock strategy elaborated in response to a cybernetic age where the body is threatened with disappearance into virtual reality? Is it merely a desire to "return to the body," a way to affirm the roots of the self in a time where traditional categories of identity (nation, religion, the family, etc.) are being radically challenged? In the specific case of the representation of the "female body," does the abject simply reaffirm the metaphysical definition of the woman *as* a dematerialized body? The hypothesis I want to develop here simultaneously asserts and refutes these conjectures, for what I believe is at play in the contemporary use of the abject is indeed a "return to the body," but one that produces an excessivity that problematizes the absence/presence duality and opens up new cybernetic definitions of subjectivity.

In *Powers of Horror: An Essay on Abjection* (1980), Julia Kristeva uses the notion of abjection to describe the revulsion and the horror experienced by the child as it attempts to separate itself from the pre-Oedipal mother in the passage from the Imaginary to the Symbolic Order.[1] Abjection, in its most archaic form, is an oral disgust, a refusal of the mother who is experienced as abject so that the child might expel itself from the mother-child dyad and become a subject. But for Kristeva, the experience of the abject doesn't stop there, for the abject never ceases to haunt the borders of identity; it constantly threatens to dissolve the unity of the subject. It is in fact an *integral* part of the identity process; as one attempts to ensure his or her subjectivity through the abjection of the other, one never quite

succeeds in differentiating the self from this abjected other. The abject belongs to the category of "corporeal rubbish," of the incorporated-that-must-be-evacuated, indicating the incapacity of Western modern cultures to accept not only the mother but also, as Elizabeth Grosz underlines, the materiality of the body, its limits and cycles, mortality, disease, corporal fluids, excrement, and menstrual blood.[2] Following this definition, Kristeva asserts that the bringing into play of the abject, especially in modern literature, as in the writings of Mallarmé, Céline, and Genet, is a critical practice that puts subjectivity into crisis; it is a work by which categories of identity are abruptly questioned, disrupted, and challenged.

In a discussion entitled "The Politics of the Signifier II: A Conversation on the *Informe* and the Abject," Rosalind Krauss states that Kristeva's project of abjection fails to effect what it should be producing and what Georges Bataille's *informe* succeeds in producing; that is, it fails to undermine *categorization*.[3] In other words, Kristeva's naming of the abject (as waste, excrement, menstrual blood, etc.) negates the potentially destabilizing effect of abjection; once it has been defined, the abject cannot be the means by which one undermines definitions. For Krauss, it is Bataille's *informe* and not Kristeva's *abject* that is subversive, it is the *informe*, as a project that puts into play the dissolution, decay and rotting of form that is the closest to abjection *as it should be*, a nonreifying and nonliteralizing process.

If indeed, the undermining of categorization is contradicted by Kristeva's definition of the abject and seems to be more in tune with Bataille's "undoing" on form, a closer examination of the abject permits one to see how it can (precisely when its act of categorization

1. Julia Kristeva, *Powers of Horror: An Essay on Abjection*, trans. Leon S. Roudiez (New York: Columbia University Press, 1982).

2. See Elizabeth Gross, "The Body of Signification," in *Abjection, Melancholia and Love: The Work of Julia Kristeva,* ed. John Fletcher and Andrew Benjamin (New York: Routledge, 1990), pp. 80–103.

3. Rosalind Krauss, "The Politics of the Signifier II: A Conversation on the *Informe* and the Abject," *October* 67 (1994):3–21.

is experienced by the viewer as an ambivalence) undermine some of the categories we perform to construct identity. This can only be understood if one acknowledges that categorizations are not only unavoidable, but that they can also be critical when they succeed in revealing how the identity of the viewer (and not only that of the represented body) is itself constructed through nominalist acts that never cease to abject the "other." So, in the 1990s, why should one still persist in favoring (as Krauss does) the work of Jackson Pollock and Cy Twombly to the detriment of John Miller and Kiki Smith, all of whose works were presented in one of the key exhibitions responsible for the labeling of "abject art," the Whitney's 1993 exhibition *Abject Art: Repulsion and Desire in American Art*?

What I want to argue, as I examine abject performances of the "female body" in the work of Mona Hatoum, Céline Baril, Kiki Smith and Jo Spence, is that this specific use of the abject can and should be understood as a strategy that seeks to disrupt the Kantian definition of aesthetics as pure pleasure, to produce a "body" that elicits other forms of unpredictable pleasures.[4] Aesthetics as pure pleasure corresponds to what the sociologist Pierre Bourdieu has called a "renunciation of pleasure, pleasure purified of pleasure"[5] by which the aesthete distances himself not only from the naked female body but more generally from the contingency of human corporeality, both of which threaten to disrupt the "disinterestedness" of Kantian aesthetic experience. Abject performances of the female body, of a body that is like "noise" to the picture (as in Cindy Sherman's *Madonnas* of 1990 and "bestial" performances of the mid-1980s), bring back the uncontrollable body inside the frame of art.

It is to this construct of the "uncontrollable body" through the use of categories of the abject that I want to refer here. Let us start by examining a video installation by Mona Hatoum entitled *Corps étranger* (a title that should be translated simultaneously as *Strange body* and *Foreign body*; see fig. 1). *Corps étranger* was originally produced for a 1994 exhibition at the Centre Georges Pompidou and was shown subsequently at the Venice Biennale and at the Tate Gallery in an exhibition titled *Rites of Passage* where Julia Kristeva explicitly designated the work as productive of the abject. A space partially closed upon itself, it consists of a circular area delimited by two semicircular partitions with two openings. On the floor, under a circular sheet of glass, one can see video close-up images of various internal and external features of Hatoum's body. Immediately upon entering the space, viewers are placed in a situation of exteriority vis-à-vis the images of a body that they must apprehend at a distance equivalent to their own body height, a distance measured from their feet (where the images play upon the screen) to their eyes and ears. But tactile contact with the images is also established through their feet; this is a crucial point to which I will come back later.

The most disturbing images of *Corps étranger* are surely those that show the visceral body, here defined by two types of optical instruments (the endoscope and coloscope) used to scan certain parts of the digestive system, colon, and intestines. This visual sequence is accompanied by an ultrasound recording of heartbeats echoing throughout different parts of the body, punctuated at regular intervals by the sound of Hatoum's breathing, which returns when the camera resurfaces. The body's deep cavities are illuminated and examined by the camera in its continual search for orifices. Deeper and deeper it moves, probing these visceral tunnels until, unable to advance any farther, it reemerges only to wander, compelled to go on solely for the sake of videotaping the interior of the artist's body.

One of the most striking ambivalences of this installation resides in the production, by the body, of effects that may be described as simultaneously incorporating and incorporated. In the space between the viewer and the images, a gradual oscillation develops between these two poles. In the first instance, the body is represented as incorporated (as much by the camera that penetrates it as by the viewer who follows its movement); in the second instance, the body becomes an incorporating power to the extent that, by following the intrusive action of the camera, viewers end up feeling themselves absorbed by what they are looking at so intently, as if they themselves were being pulled down into the profound darkness of the body's cavities. This ambivalence assumes its full meaning when one realizes that the body is the body of a woman. For it is the female sex in its cultural ambivalence—as both a body and a threatening sex—

4. On the feminist revision of aesthetics, see Amelia Jones, "Feminism, Incorporated: Reading 'postfeminism' in an Anti-Feminist Age," *Afterimage* 20, no. 5 (1992):10–15.

5. Pierre Bourdieu, *Distinction: A Social Critique of the Judgment of Taste*, trans. Richard Nice (Cambridge: Harvard University Press, 1984), p. 491.

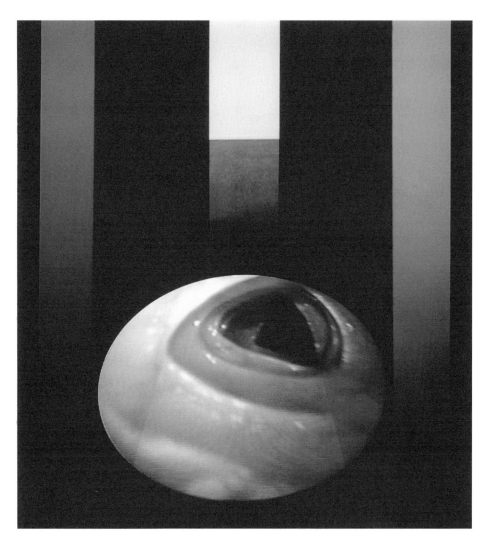

Figure 1. Mona Hatoum, *Corps étranger*, 1994. Video installation, 350 x 300 x 300 cm. Musée national d'art moderne, Centre Georges Pompidou, Paris.

that comes into play at this point. Thus the images we see here show a female body that reinscribes the link that Freud established between the death and life drives; in other words, *Corps étranger* reinscribes the fantasy of the *vagina dentata*, of the woman as vampire or animal equipped with a sexuality that is identified as devouring, enigmatic, dissembling, and castrating for men.[6] This fantasy is one that is also played out in the 1992

collages by Kathleen King that stage isolated, opened mouths, the teeth ready to bite anyone who dares to enter, protecting and locating the lips, fetus, or stitched up body parts in the inside. But instead of being kept outside by the threatening vaginal teeth, the viewer of *Corps étranger* is attracted towards the inside that he or she must resist so as not to be completely sucked into.

The installation also performs what recent phenomenology, particularly that exemplified in Drew Leder's *The Absent Body*, designates as the recessive visceral body, that is, the whole set of organs hidden under the skin, which functions as an absence,

6. On the *vagina dentata*, see Elizabeth Grosz, "Animal Sex: Libido as Desire and Death (Short Version)," in *Space, Time, and Perversion: The Politics of the Body* (New York: Routledge, 1995).

independent of the subject's awareness or control.[7] By exhibiting this phenomenologically "absent" body, the installation transforms the recessive into the ecstatic, producing an abjection effect insofar as it points to the fact that the use of endoscopy in medicine is prevalently associated with the diagnosis of illness, that is, with the existence of symptoms indicating that something, some "it," is acting in a dysfunctional manner. Endoscopy and coloscopy are hermeneutic practices that bring out what Drew Leder has dubbed an interiority in "dys-appearance," a visceral body that appears, that one becomes aware of, precisely because it is dysfunctional. Thus the foreign body is not so much the visceral body that tends to be absent from my consciousness as I move about in the world; it is also the dysfunctional body, a body both threatened and threatening, an "it" that reveals itself as something different from me, something stranger and harder to control. "Absent" and yet present in the manifestation of the *symptom*: a negative presence.

One can see here how Mona Hatoum brings together the visceral body, technology, and the female as incorporating threats, making each category a metaphor or metonymy of the other, projecting them over each other in order to consolidate an abjection effect. Being herself a foreigner living in London, a Palestinian in exile, she invests in the position of the stranger speaking about strangeness. Like in her videotape *Changing Parts* (1984), where Hatoum appears in a transparent box and smears the surface with blood so as to contaminate the protective screen that separates the viewer from the performer, *Corps étranger* is a work about the "other" as it starts to threaten "me" (the Westerner) because this "other" is out of place. The woman, the Palestinian, the visceral or dysfunctional body, that is, what *has to be ab-jected* by the Western subject to construct his or her identity, is now in the viewer's space, externalized, in proximity, indicating how the "difference" or the "distance" between the I and the other, the mind and the body, the healthy and the ill, is not so clear or predictable anymore. One is not in complete control of the situation. This is what disease is about; the body acts independently of your will, even from your consciousness.

It is interesting to note that the work of another important "abject" artist, Kiki Smith, also puts into play a similar sense of loss of control. Her bodies are usually represented not as a whole, but in parts; these parts often seem to have been torn off from the trunk as though following a catastrophe. Body fluids (such as semen and blood) are represented dripping out of a multitude of corporeal orifices, and organs are falling from the body, as though the skin is not functioning anymore as "container," like in the skinned *Virgin Mary* (fig. 2); the beings are constantly being defined by a corporeality that is in a state of ruin. About her work, Kiki Smith says:

> When people are dying, they are losing control of their bodies. That loss of function can seem humiliating and frightening. But, on the other hand, you can look at it as a kind of liberation of the body. It seems like a nice metaphor—a way of thinking about the social—that people lose control despite the many agendas of different ideologies in society, which are trying to control the body(ies) . . . medicine, religion, law, etc. Just think about control—who has the control of the body? Does the body have control over itself? Do you? . . . Does the mind have control over the body? Does the social?[8]

The loss of control or what should be called the contingency of the body and its failure to be what it is supposed to be in contemporary Western society (productive, healthy, and young), is also at play throughout the work of Jo Spence. And yet, this doesn't mean that the photographs of her *Cancer project* series are self-representations of a victim. On the contrary, they are part of a daily struggle to regain health, representing what she calls the "abject loneliness of the long struggle for health" so as to counteract the "narrative resolution of illnesses like cancer" that people usually expect.[9] Abject art, in the work of Spence, Hatoum, and Smith, is precisely this desire to break with resolution and categorization through the paradoxical use of categories of the abject. This strategy is subversive insofar as it manifests the failing of a subject to correspond to the predictable, disciplined, coherent body of contemporary discursive formations such as medicine, law, and psychology.

---

7. Drew Leder, *The Absent Body* (Chicago: University of Chicago Press, 1990).

8. Kiki Smith, in Robin Winters, "An Interview with Kiki Smith," in *Kiki Smith* (Amsterdam: Institute of Contemporary Art, 1990), p. 127.

9. Jo Spence, *Cultural Sniping: The Art of Transgression* (New York: Routledge, 1995), p. 122.

Figure 2. Kiki Smith, *Virgin Mary*, 1993. Bronze and silver, 167.6 x 68.5 x 48.2 cm. Collection of the artist.

As a result, what is being produced here is a more performative conception of the body. As Judith Butler states, the body is a materialization of a norm, it is the performance of an ideal construct, which one *has to comply with* to ensure his or her subjectivity so as not to be abjected, excluded, and marginalized into the spheres of nonsubjectivity.[10] But, as Butler also affirms, one *never quite succeeds in complying with* the norm he or she is supposed to reiterate. So abject performances of the female body are those where the failing to reproduce the norm is made manifest, where the spectre of abjection is being played out. Abject art is saying to the viewer: this failure is not necessarily unproductive, for it can have the effect of complexifying the body. When failing, mortality, catastrophe, noise, unpredictability, loss of control, nonorganicity, and contingency become *the* predominant components of the body, this means that a major redefinition of subjectivity is at play, one that seeks to displace the conception of the subject as presence to the detriment of the abjected female body, which represents lack and absence, to a conception of the subject as *both* presence and absence, pattern and randomness.

This means, as Katherine Hayles would argue, that what Lacan has called the floating signifiers of the modern sign are being troubled by the flickering signifiers of the computer age.[11] For Lacan, the meaning of things is never accessible but always constituted by the continuous sliding and displacement of the sign; subjectivity, like language, is founded on an absence, on the loss of the plenitude of the pre-Oedipal mother-child dyad forever broken as one becomes a subject. In this presence/absence dialectic, the abjected (the mother, body fluids, the female body, etc.) represents what has been lost and what *has to remain lost* to maintain one's subjectivity. In the case of abject art, this law of absence and lack has been somewhat subverted in order to produce a form of presence that is not founded on an absence, but *coexists* with absence. The body is not merely lacking. Its lack, failure or loss of control is productive as it brings into play unpredictable disorganizations and reorganizations that could lead to its deterioration but also to its increase in complexity. The flickering body as pattern *and* randomness is one

that cannot be completely programmed, one that can be defined as productive noise.

Randomness is a theoretical notion used in the study of complex systems to indicate the incapacity of the observer to predict the changes of the system under observation. It is defined as the agent that actualizes the unforeseeable potential of the system to adapt to "noise," that is, to what seems to be a distortion in the transmission of messages or a catastrophe within the environment.[12] When the system is able to adapt itself (to complexify itself or even to mutate), this means that it was able not to *resist* "noise," but to *use* it as an element of self-reorganization; for the observer, "noise" is an error, but when it has been integrated by the system, it loses this error quality. What is noise then, if it is not a form of abjection "produced by a complex dance between predictability and unpredictability, repetition and variation," (p. 78) a process by which the system under observation has perhaps ceased to properly signify for the observer, to the extent that it is now threatening the observer's identity boundaries, but that signals the unguaranteed possibility of a reorganization of the system which could lead to a higher level of complexity.

This specific way of thinking about social, aesthetic, and identity change is what is at play in the multimedia installation *The ant and the volcano* by Canadian artist Céline Baril (fig. 3). In this work, the abject is represented in the three giant ants installed on the floor. Carrying a video monitor in their abdomen that diffuses images of active volcanos, these ants are mutants of an era of telecommunication; they are science-fiction or horror-movie prehistoric dinosaurs of the future producing rumblings, magma, smoke, vapor, and sulphuric gas. But these monsters can only be understood once they are read in the context of the Chinese Diaspora that is depicted by the two other components of *The ant and the volcano*, a small video installation hanging from the ceiling composed of three monitors projecting images of Hong Kong and a feature film dealing with the 1997 retrocession of Hong Kong by the British Crown to China, a film that stages a young girl named Lihua, who will finally migrate to Iceland thirty years after her grandmother left communist China, but whose "new home" is disrupted by the eruption of a volcano.

10. Judith Butler, *Bodies that Matter: On the Discursive Limits of "Sex"* (New York: Routledge, 1993).

11. N. Katherine Hayles, "Virtual Bodies and Flickering Signifiers," *October* 66 (1993):71.

12. See Henri Atlan, *Entre le cristal et la fumée: essai sur l'organisation du vivant* (Paris: Editions du Seuil, 1979).

Figure 3. Céline Baril, *The ant and the volcano*, 1992. Multimedia installation, fiberglass, steel, and video, length of each ant: 300 cm. Collection of the artist.

Such a cultural contextualization provided by the film and the video installation has the effect of stereotyping "Chinese" as intrusive "ants." But if we are attentive to the film's narrative, it becomes clear that this categorization is one that occurs in the reception of the sign: the Chinese in diaspora is abject insofar as it is perceived as invading "our" territory and weakening "our" identity. For the Western observer, these three ants are like "noise" in his or her space. However, in the film, we are brought to listen to Lihua's story, which is one of a constant *unwriting* of the Chinese nation where individuals are continuously disorganizing and reorganizing their homes, territories, and identities following a series of geographical or political catastrophes. The year "1997" is *the* sign *par excellence* of uncertainty and unpredictability; it is, like the volcanic eruption, an anticipated catastrophe of the (yet uncertain) loss of democracy. Thus the monstrosity of the ants is a strategy elaborated in order to inscribe catastrophe in the construction of identity. As it indicates

the Westerner's fear of the other, it seeks to propose "noise" as constitutive (and not necessarily destructive) of more complex territories which do not have to be *preserved* to exist, but negotiated, unwritten-to-be-rewritten.[13] Territories are present, but as uncertainties.

Hence, the use of the abject in the representation of the body is one that recategorizes, that renames the other (that is, the "Palestinian," the "Chinese," the "female body" as *vagina dentata*, the visceral body) but only in as much as this renaming activates the desire or the need not to suspend categories as in the utopian "informe" but to re-orient them into a new logic of production where organization and disorganization, pattern and randomness coexist. This means that if, at first glance, the abjected bodies of Mona Hatoum, Kiki Smith, Jo Spence, Céline Baril, Cindy Sherman, and

---

13. On preservation versus negotiation, see Rey Chow, *Writing Diaspora: Tactics of Intervention in Contemporary Cultural Studies* (Indianapolis: Indiana University Press, 1993).

others produce the horror of loss, decay, and illness,
they are bodies that state that this loss is not necessarily
a death, a lack, or an absence from oneself but a pattern
indissociable from the randomness that has shaped it.
For the twenty-first century, what becomes important is
not the recovery of the lost body or the discovery of a
new body, but the quest for random "interrelationships
between them."[14] However, this shift to a
pattern/randomness dialectic can only be made possible
if the absence represented by the "abjected," that is, if
the lack of the feminine in the eyes of the masculine, is
overrun. This is precisely the process that is at play in
the abject performances of the body of the feminist
artistic practices I have just examined.

14. Ilya Kabakov, in Robert Storr, "An Interview with Ilya Kabakov,"
Art in America 83, no. 1 (1995):67.

Documents

A critique: Pevsner on modernity (1938)

MEYER SCHAPIRO
translated by David Craven

This book (*Pioneers of the Modern Movement*) is a careful, concise, and well-documented overview of the history of modern architecture and the industrial arts, up to the First World War. Pevsner traces the movement, which had its beginning with and was advanced by William Morris and his followers, who sought to reestablish the artisanal skills and aesthetics quality that had been lost during the decline of the Victorian Period. The movement included the following: an aesthetic opposition to the machine; the change of taste in the 1890s of the last century, from Pevsner's viewpoint, as much in architecture as in painting; the emergence of Art Nouveau; the extraordinary absorption of art into technology during the nineteenth century; the new *Grundbegriffe* (basic principles) of an art that applied new materials and was governed by the ideals of technology; and finally the confluence of three major sources—Morris, Art Nouveau, and the Industrial Arts—into a modern post-First World War style. While extremely sensible in his assessment of specific achievements, Pevsner is nonetheless contradictory and unclear in his general historical characterization and in his theoretical pronouncements. On the one hand, he to a certain extent explains the decline of art in the mid-Victorian Period by means of the devastating consequences of industrialism, yet, on the other hand, when he attributes art's revitalization in the nineteenth century to one of these developments, he does so by means of a reactive climate of spiritual opinion. This leads him as a result to group together otherwise basically different artists like Cézanne, Van Gogh, Munch, Rousseau, Valloton, and Seurat, as if they were all pursuing a common goal. The authenticity of their form, their intellectual integrity, their spiritual feelings, their abstractedness, and their intensity were supposed to have displaced the superficial sensuality and hedonism of Impressionism (Renoir!), which in turn supposedly reflected Victorian materialism. Similarly, Pevsner explains the movements of Symbolism and Art Nouveau of the same epoch in the nineteenth century, at one point, as coming from the dried-up sources of Realism and Impressionism and, at another point, as emanating from the ever strongly emergent projection of cheerfulness that brought fresh air and sunshine into the

David Craven would like to thank the late Meyer Schapiro and Lillian Milgram for reading over the translation in the spring of 1993, discussing it with him, and suggesting some minor revisions in keeping with the original intent of Schapiro's essay.

This is the first appearance in English of a review essay by Meyer Schapiro that was originally published in German in the *Zeitschrift für Sozialforschung* 7, no. 1/2 (1938):291–293. The *Zeitschrift für Sozialforschung* was the official publication from 1932–1941 of the Institute of Social Research (better known as the "Frankfurt School"). The Institute has been associated with the University of Frankfurt since 1923, except when it was affiliated with Columbia University from 1934–1944. Among the most notable essays to appear in this journal were those by Max Horkheimer (vol. 6, no. 2 [1937]) and by Herbert Marcuse (vol. 6, no. 3 [1937]), in which the term "critical theory" was coined and the theoretical concerns of the Frankfurt School were identified.

Among other journal articles that have since become well known are Walter Benjamin's essay on the work of art in the age of mechanical reproduction (vol. 5, no. 1 [1936]), Leo Lowenthal's critique of the novels of Knut Hamsen (vol. 6, no. 2 [1937]), T. W. Adorno's discussion of Thorstein Veblen's concept of art (vol. 9, no. 3

[1941]), and Friedrich Pollock's essay on state capitalism (vol. 9, no. 2 [1941]). Furthermore, over a third of each issue was taken up by a book review section that featured such critiques as those of Karl Korsch on Lenin and Sorel (1932, 1933), Georg Lukács on the Collected Works of Marx and Engels (1933), Ernst Bloch on John Dewey (1935, 1936), Henri Lefebvre on Paul Nizan (1937), Meyer Schapiro on Pevsner (1938), and Paul Mattick on New Deal Programs (1938).

In one of the best summaries to date of this journal's role, Jürgen Habermas has said of the *Zeitschrift für Sozialforschung* that, "It was the organizational core and the intellectual center of . . . a small group of scholars, who in the cramped space of emigration banded around the journal's standard." Furthermore, Habermas noted that "if ever there were a single datable and localizable Frankfurt School it was in New York, between 1933–1941." (See Jürgen Habermas, "The Inimitable *Zeitschrift für Sozialforschung*," *Telos* 45 [1980]:219–221.) Significantly, Meyer Schapiro executed a set of six portrait sketches in 1938 of various members of the Frankfurt School. Among those who can be identified are Max Horkheimer (editor of the *Zeitschrift*), Leo Lowenthal (reviews editor), Herbert Marcuse, Franz Neumann, and Erich Fromm.

stuffy Victorian world. But these movements are also still ultimately characterized by an "enervating atmosphere," a "muggy dream."

Van der Velde, a founder of the *Neuen Sachlichkeit* (New Objectivity), in Pevsner's account, appears than as an unhealthy aesthete, indifferent to unbearable disorder and to dirty conditions. Although Pevsner recognizes the tendency of William Morris's art to entail a medievalizing Romanticism, he neglects this reactionary side, as he did with Art Nouveau and symbolism, and he describes Morris's work instead as merely progressive because it provided a basis for the art of the twentieth century. Pevsner is forced to concede the substitution of Art Nouveau for Impressionism as involving a thoroughgoing transformation of the artistic impulse. Nonetheless, operating as he does with an erroneous construction that around 1890 there began an entirely new world (or a new *Geist*), he speaks emphatically of an irreconcilable opposition between the two styles. Since Pevsner does not distinguish between different phases and tendencies within Impressionism, he does not see the moment or aspect of continuity between it and the art that followed—Monet's Giverny Garden and decorative paintings, for example, have a very strong connection with Art Nouveau. The relationship between the formal and the technical aspects of architecture remains unsound within this argument, so that one begins to have the impression, on the one hand, that the form is the mere goal-directed solution of a technical problem and, on the other hand, that the form is the product of fantasy or the expression of a moralizing outlook.

The weak point in Pevsner's method, despite his scholarly care, can be located in his train of thought about the psychology of certain national folk characters and the nature of the present. No sooner has he used these ideas than he has a pronounced historical change to explain concerning the so-called *Volkseele* (national soul of a people); after 1900 the *Volkseele* of the English was transformed, bringing into being new forms, since the new forms were *necessarily* democratic and that would have been "to go against the core of the English character." Pevsner is, however, repeatedly contradictory in the characterizing of a people's folk character: in one passage, he gives the impression that the effusive, unbridled, energetic ornamentation of the architect August Endell embodies the "eternal unity of German art," yet, in another place, the same is true of the unornamented, stringent form of Gropius, whose

"uncompromising directness" represents the German national character.

This same tendency, to displace the analysis of an historical situation through a general psychological category, surfaces in the frequent references to the *Zeitgeist* and to the "essence" of the century as such. He advances from the representation of our time as a "practical" and "collective" century—somehow, the ordering structure of architecture reflects the *Geist* of rational planning in society—and forgets thereby the social conflicts and class divisions, all of which are subsumed under the collectively based sense of practicality. It is also entirely in the sense of an uncritical concept of mainstream society, with his erroneous judgment of society as "collective," that Pevsner rejects the subjectivity and individualism of the last three hundred years and sees in them instead the increasing acceptance of an idealistic and mystical outlook, to the development of which modern art is said to contribute. Cubism, though, is evaluated as the impersonal, decorative by-product of this collective architecture. "The artist," writes Pevsner, "who is a representative of our century must by detached, since he is entering a century quite cool with steel and glass, of which the precision allows less room for subjective expression than any epoch of the past."

A series of interviews (July 15, 1992–January 22, 1995)

MEYER SCHAPIRO and LILLIAN MILGRAM SCHAPIRO with DAVID CRAVEN

Introduction

From July 15, 1992, until October 1, 1995, I interviewed Meyer Schapiro and his wife Dr. Lillian Milgram about fifteen times. The longest of these interviews, those at their homes in Rawsonville, Vermont and on West 4th Street in New York City, lasted about six hours. The shortest of these interviews (by telephone) lasted only between twenty minutes and an hour. In July 1992, I first arranged to meet with the Schapiros for an interview and visit, after having been invited by Richard Wrigley to be the guest editor of a special issue of the *Oxford Art Journal* that would pay homage to Meyer Schapiro in 1994, the year of his 90th birthday.

As a consequence of the trust and friendship that developed between the Schapiros and myself through these interviews, they allowed me in May 1993 to consult the unpublished "Personal Papers of Meyer Schapiro" at his home in New York. This permission was granted in order to help me to clarify or amend various points about his views on art and politics in the art historical literature. The highlights transcribed here from this lengthy series of interviews disclose much that was not previously in print about Meyer Schapiro's lifelong commitment to social justice in tandem with vanguard art. I am much indebted to the late Meyer Schapiro and Lillian Milgram for sharing their rare time and numerous unpublished documents with me.

David Craven

Interviews with Meyer Schapiro and Lillian Milgram Schapiro (1992–1995)

David Craven: It has been suggested by some people that you were involved behind the scenes in the Erwin Panofsky/Barnett Newman debate that took place in the pages of *Art News* in 1961. Could you confirm or refute this claim?

Meyer Schapiro: Yes, I was in Israel in the Spring of 1961 when I read Panofsky's letter in *Art News*. I sent Barnie *one* letter, with the understanding that my counsel be kept confidential, in which I pointed out that Panofsky was wrong. I told him to check a large Latin Dictionary and he would see that *both "sublimis"* and *"sublimus"* are acceptable, as demonstrated by their appearance together in Cicero's citation of a passage from Accius. Both bits of advice appear in the first letter. Everything else in those two letters was contributed by Barnie himself.[1]

DC: What type of relationship did you have with the philosopher John Dewey?

MS: I was a student of John Dewey, whose classes I very much enjoyed. Dewey asked me to do a critical reading of *Art as Experience* in manuscript form.[2] The book is important, of course, but it is marked by a tendency to treat humanity and art as extensions of nature, as products of nature, without dealing with how humanity reshapes and remakes nature, hence also itself. This lack of emphasis on mediating nature, on humanity using craft and art to redefine itself, is a problem of the book.

DC: Did you ever meet the Marxist theoretician Karl Korsch when he was in the U.S.?

MS: I admire his work very much, but I only met him once or twice. His critique of the Stalinist misuse of Marx's thought is of fundamental importance.[3]

---

1. The letter by Panofsky initiating the debate appeared in the April 1961 issue of *Art News*. Newman's response, in the May 1961 issue of *Art News*, did include the above noted information supplied by Schapiro. The September 1961 issue concluded the exchange with yet another letter by Panofsky along with a fine response by Newman to it.

2. John Dewey, *Art as Experience* (1934; reprint, New York: G. P. Putnam's Sons, 1980). In the Preface, Dewey wrote: "Dr. Meyer Schapiro was good enough to read the twelfth and thirteenth chapters and to make suggestions which I freely adopted."

3. See Karl Korsch, "Leading Principles of Marxism: A Restatement," *Marxist Quarterly* 1, no. 3 (1937):356–378. As one of

---

In September 1996, Dr. Lillian Milgram kindly read my transcription of the interviews, in order to corroborate the accuracy of its content and to make some scholarly editorial suggestions.

Figure 1. Meyer Schapiro and Lillian Milgram, August 1991, Rawsonville, Vermont.
Photograph: Susan Raines.

DC: How often did you see Diego Rivera and Frida Kahlo when they were in New York City in the early 1930s?

MS: We met with Diego Rivera and Frida Kahlo several times. Diego was very entertaining and on one occasion he railed with great emphasis against color reproductions of artworks.

Lillian Milgram: Frida was quite taken with Meyer. She gave him gifts a few times, including a pre-Columbian figurine that we still have.

DC: On October 6, 1977, the French philosopher Jacques Derrida gave a presentation at Columbia University, in which he responded to your refutation of Martin Heidegger's interpretation of Van Gogh's 1886 oil painting of shoes that is now in the Van Gogh Museum in Amsterdam.[4] This presentation by Derrida would later appear in a longer version as "Restitutions" in his book *La Verite en Peinture* (1978).[5] Derrida's paper is surprising because of how the whole tenor of the piece becomes so shrilly *ad hominem.*

Yet on the one occasion when I had a chance to talk with Derrida up close, in April of 1983 when he was speaking at Cornell University, I found him to be quite approachable and unpretentious, even though I was taking issue with some things that he had said in his public talk about Western Marxism.[6] He welcomed this exchange and was much more put off by the sycophantic behavior of some other people in attendance. This is why I find Derrida's reaction to you so surprising and perhaps uncharacteristic. What happened at his presentation in 1977?

MS: He was challenged strongly by many people in the audience. I was abrupt with him, because he neither understood nor cared to understand the nature of my criticism. Furthermore, I discovered later that Heidegger changed his interpretation of the Van Gogh painting when he did an annotated commentary of his own essay and that he ended up admitting that he was uncertain about whose shoes they were. This material will appear in volume 4 of my selected writings. . . . One of Derrida's obvious shortcomings is that he entirely disregards artistic intention in his analysis.[7]

DC: How well did you know the remarkable school of political economists who edited the *Monthly Review*, which was started in 1949? I am thinking especially of Paul Sweezy and Leo Huberman, the latter of whom praised your editorial help in one of his most well-known books.[8]

MS: I knew Leo Huberman well in the 1930s, but we lost touch after that. I never met Sweezy, but I know and respect his writings.[9]

DC: Were you harassed by the U.S. Government during the McCarthy Period?

MS: The F.B.I. visited us in the 1950s to ask whether or not certain students of mine were "reds." They visited us again in the 1960s to ask me whether or not J. J. Sweeney was a "red," since he had once invited Leger to the US !!

---

the founding editors of this journal, Meyer Schapiro was among those responsible for the publication of this essay by Korsch. For a sustained discussion of the theoretical links between the two, see David Craven, "Meyer Schapiro, Karl Korsch, and the Emergence of Critical Theory," *Oxford Art Journal* 17, no. 1 (1994):42–54.

4. Meyer Schapiro, "The Still Life as a Personal Object—A Note on Heidegger and Van Gogh" (1968), in *Selected Papers of Meyer Schapiro.* Vol. 4, *Theory and Philosophy of Art* (New York: George Braziller, 1994), pp. 135–142.

5. Jacques Derrida, "Restitutions," in *La Verite en Peinture* (The Truth in Painting), trans. Geoff Bennington and Ian McLeod (1978; reprint, Chicago: University of Chicago Press, 1987), pp. 255–282.

6. Derrida only recently published an excellent defense of a certain reading of Marxism, specifically what he termed a critical "spirit of Marxism which I will never be ready to renounce." See Jacques Derrida, *Specters of Marx*, trans. Peggy Kamuf (New York: Routledge, 1994), pp. 88–92.

7. The text of Heidegger's handwritten revision of his position in his own personal copy of "Der Ursprung des Kunstwerkes," is published in Meyer Schapiro, "Further Notes on Heidegger and Van Gogh," in *Selected Papers of Meyer Schapiro.* Vol. 4, *Theory and Philosophy of Art* (New York: George Braziller, 1994), p. 150.

8. See Leo Huberman, *Man's Worldly Goods* (1936; reprint, New York: Monthly Review Press, 1952). In the Preface to this book, Huberman thanked "Dr. Meyer Schapiro, for his critical reading of the manuscript and stimulating suggestions."

9. Even before becoming a founding editor of *Monthly Review* in 1949 (he had taught economics at Harvard until 1946), Sweezy had made his name in 1942 in the field of economics with a celebrated book, *The Theory of Capitalist Development*. A revised edition appeared in 1970 through Monthly Review Press. As period remarks on the cover of the book declare, "Since its first publication in 1942, this book has become the classic analytical study of Marxist economics." For a very fine discussion of the contribution of the Monthly Review School of political economists to the emergence of Dependency Theory in the Americas, see Roger Burbach and Orlando Nunez Soto, *Fire in the Americas* (London: Verso Press, 1987), pp. 35–37.

LM: When they visited us in the 1950s, they had first asked all of our neighbors about Meyer's *communist affiliations*!!

DC: What do you think of Serge Guilbaut's book *How New York Stole the Idea of Modern Art from Paris*?[10]

MS: Not much. I never finished reading it. The title alone is rather silly. All art is "taken" from other art.

DC: What of your relationship with Clement Greenberg over the years? After all, his interpretation of Abstract Expressionism is quite at odds with yours.

MS: In the 1940s we were on friendly terms, but I grew increasingly disturbed by Greenberg's dogmatic formalism, by his refusal to grant artistic intention or social context, much less iconography, any place in analysis. . . . The problem is that Greenberg does not know how to *characterize* a painting. . . . In the early 1960s, I was asked to write a piece about Greenberg, which I did. But the essay was so negative that I decided to withhold publishing it.

From an interview at the summer home of the Schapiro's in Rawsonville, Vermont, July 15, 1992

DC: What of your political involvements on the left since the 1950s? This is a question that needs to be asked because there are those who erroneously claim that in the early 1940s you came to reject socialism and the writings of Marx.[11]

MS: What are the political credentials of those who say this? What type of activism have they engaged in? I am still a member of the steering committee of the Democratic Socialists of America and I am still on the editorial board of *Dissent*, a socialist magazine. I was a founding editor of the *Marxist Quarterly* and I continue to recommend that people read Marx as a way of discovering conceptual tools for grappling with an analysis of art and society. I am, like Irving Howe,

against all slogans and labeling. Our views of socialism often overlap.[12]

DC: Were you active in the anti-war movement in the 1960s and 1970s?

MS: Yes, I was always opposed to the war. In 1968 I spoke at Columbia's largest anti-war rally, along with a professor in physics.[13] I worked in the anti-war movement and the democratic socialist movement with Michael Harrington.

From a telephone interview, August 20, 1992

DC: Were you and T. W. Adorno friends when he was in New York City from 1938 to 1941 with other members of the Frankfurt School, all of whom were affiliated with Columbia University?

MS: Adorno and I were close then. I saw him constantly and he was very friendly with me. We usually discussed the political situation in Germany, which disturbed Adorno greatly. He lived on the Upper West Side near Columbia, so he would drop in on me often. While I was on the board of the Brooklyn Academy of Music, I arranged to have Adorno give a talk on Schonberg's music and also to have Walter Gropius speak on the Bauhaus. Both of these talks were held at the Brooklyn Academy of Music in 1939. . . . Of all the members of the Frankurt School, Leo Lowenthal was the one with whom I have had the longest relationship. We have been friends since the 1930s. [He died in 1993.] His primary field was European, specifically German literature, and he had a broad interest in theoretical problems. In the late 1930s, he was the book review editor for the *Zeitschrift fur Sozialforschung*. At a

---

10. Serge Guilbaut, *How New York Stole the Idea of Modern Art from Paris*, trans. Arthur Goldhammer (Chicago: University of Chicago Press, 1983).

11. This is of course what Guilbaut, among others, claims (see note 10), chap. 1.

12. For a moving tribute to Meyer Schapiro's lifelong commitment to democratic socialism, see Irving Howe, *A Margin of Hope* (New York: Harcourt Brace Jovanovich, 1982), pp. 237–238: "From the start [in 1954], Meyer Schapiro, the art historian served as an editor [for *Dissent*] . . . we were happy to have so eminent a mind ready to stand by us. . . . It mattered much that Meyer Schapiro attended some board meetings, speaking in his passionately lucid way about socialism as the fulfillment of Western tradition."

13. For a thoughtful and insightful look at Schapiro's relation to the anti-war movement, see Francis Frascina, "Meyer Schapiro's Choice: My Lai, Guernica, MOMA, and the Art Left, 1969–70," pts. 1–2, *Journal of Contemporary History* 30 (1995):481–511, 705–728.

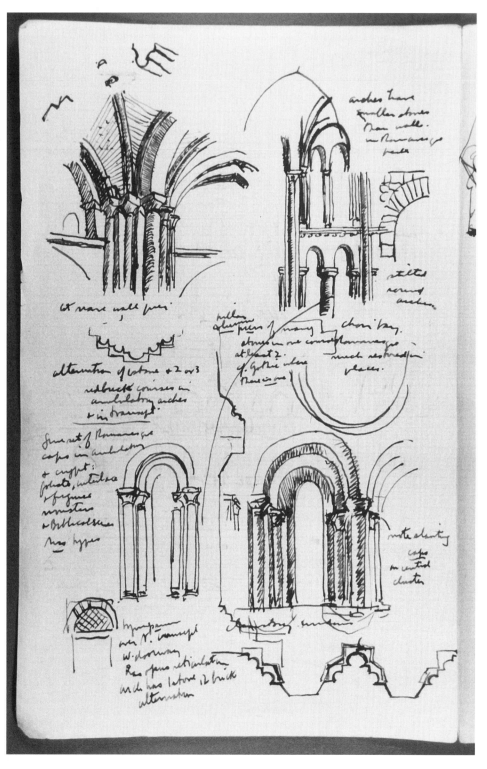

Figure 2. Meyer Schapiro, drawing of architectural components of Notre Dame de la Couture, Le Mans, late 1920s. Pen and ink. Photograph: Karen Berman.

memorial ceremony in 1967 at the Goethe House in New York City for Siegfried Kracauer, Lowenthal and I were the two main speakers.[14]

DC: What of your famous article on Santo Domingo de Silos?[15] Did it mark a fundamental shift in your approach to analyzing art? Was it influenced by Soviet thought, specifically by Mikhail Lifshitz's 1938 interpretation of Marxism and art?[16]

MS: I have never read the book by Lifshitz, nor am I interested in doing so. The conceptual framework for my 1939 Silos article was first used in my 1929 dissertation on Moissac. The third part of this dissertation, which has never been published, uses a Marxist concept of history.[17] Originally, after the first part of the dissertation appeared in the 1931 *Art Bulletin*, I planned to revise the second part on iconography and then to publish this plus the third part on the historical context for Moissac. For various reasons, I never found the time to complete the revision of this second part, so the last two parts have never appeared in print. . . . In 1927, I was a guest of the monks at Santo Domingo de Silos. Much of my article was conceived then and it was written long before it was published in 1939.[18]

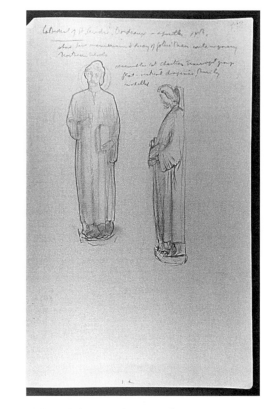

Figure 3. Meyer Schapiro, drawing of sculpted figures at the Cathedral of Saint Andre, Bordeaux, late 1920s. Pen and ink. Photograph: Karen Berman.

---

14. As Professor Martin Jay, a longtime friend of Lowenthal at Berkeley, informed me in a telephone interview of May 13, 1993, "Leo Lowenthal had immense admiration and respect for Meyer Schapiro. Lowenthal acknowledged having been given sound advice by Meyer Schapiro while Lowenthal was reviews editor for the *Zeitschrift fur Sozialforschung*." The Lowenthal-Schapiro correspondence is now in the Archives of the Institute for Social Research at Frankfurt University in Germany.

15. Meyer Schapiro, "From Mozarabic to Romanesque in Silos," in *Selected Papers of Meyer Schapiro*. Vol. 1, *Romanesque Art* (New York: George Braziller, 1977), pp. 28–101.

16. Karl Werckmeister speculates about such an influence in his well known essay on Schapiro's Silos article. See O. K. Werckmeister, "Review Essay on Meyer Schapiro's *Romanesque Art*," *Art Quarterly* 2, no. 2 (1979):214.

17. John Plummer, the Senior Research Fellow Emeritus at the Pierpoint Morgan Library in New York City and a student as well as associate of Schapiro's from 1945–1955, observed in an interview with me on May 20, 1993, that, "There is always a set of Marxian values submerged in Meyer's approach, however topical the article might seem. . . . He is a masterful dialectician. Kuspit's article on this aspect of his approach is excellent." See Donald B. Kuspit, "Dialectical Reasoning in Meyer Schapiro," *Social Research* 45, no. 1 (1978):93–129.

18. For an accessible reprint of section one of his dissertation, see Meyer Schapiro, *The Sculpture of Moissac* (New York: George Braziller, 1985).

DC: There is a certain reading of your 1936 essay "*The Social Bases of Art*" that has led to the belief that you had been opposed to modern art before a dramatic change of perspective in 1936–1937.[19] How would you respond to this claim?

MS: My essay on the social bases of art was never meant to be a blanket condemnation of modern art, but only a criticism of some aspects of it. I was never interested in any position that forced you to choose between social realism and modern art. In fact, members of the Communist Party and of the John Reed

---

19. Meyer Schapiro, "The Social Bases of Art" (1936), reprinted in *Artists Against War and Fascism: Papers of the First American Artists' Congress* (New Brunswick: Rutger's University Press, 1986), pp. 109–114.

Club, especially during the Burkewitz controversy of 1931, accused me of being against "art for the people," because I said that with one or two exceptions the social realists were bad artists from whom the people stood to gain little.[20]

From a telephone interview, February 19, 1993

DC: From how many languages have you produced translations for publication?

MS: From German and French, as well as from Latin and Italian. One of these articles was by an eighteenth-century German physicist named Lichtenberg, who wrote on Hogarth's work. . . . He stated in his essay on philosophy: "In all languages, the verb "*to be*" is irregular, hence metaphysics." I also translated and introduced an essay by Diderot.[21]

DC: What about twentieth-century French thinkers? Did you ever meet Jean-Paul Sartre?

MS: I read *Les Temps Modernes* when it first came out in 1945. And although I was unable to meet Sartre when he came to the U.S. in 1946, I subsequently met with him in the late 1940s.

DC: What about Merleau-Ponty?

MS: I spent more time in Paris talking with Merleau-Ponty, whose *Phenomenologie de la perception* (1945) I found to be impressive. Merleau-Ponty's thought was close to my own. His work on Cezanne and on the nature of perception shared a lot with my concerns.[22] No other philosopher seemed to know as much about the material process, the concrete techniques for making art or about the complexity of perception.

LM: We knew Jacques Lacan also, because he was Andre Masson's brother-in-law. We heard him lecture and read his books.

DC: Did you have any interchange with Bertolt Brecht when he was in the U.S. during the mid-1940s?

MS: I saw Brecht several times in this period. Once, we went with Brecht to dinner at the house of Max Wertheimer [of the Gestalt Psychology School]. Wertheimer, who was more conservative than Brecht, pressed him about the legitimacy of violent insurrection on behalf of bread. Brecht responded by saying, "In fact, if I had time, I would write a play called *A Piece of Bread.*" Through such a play, Brecht said he could go from looking at the struggle over bread to an examination of the production of bread to a consideration of the general structure of society. At this time Brecht was somewhat at odds with the members of the Frankfurt School over their criticism of Stalin and the Soviet Union.

DC: But of course you were even more critical of Stalin than were the members of the Frankfurt School?

MS: That is true.

From an interview at the home of the Schapiros on West 4th Street in New York City, April 3, 1993

DC: When did you first read Rosa Luxemburg's work?

MS: I first read her in the early 1930s and I admired her letters from prison a great deal. . . .[23] Paul Mattick, a friend of mine, was a Luxemburgian thinker of importance.

DC: On the cover of Arnold Hauser's *Social History of Art* (1951) are favorable comments by you and by Thomas Mann, the great German novelist.[24] Could you elaborate on this?

---

20. For a fine discussion of this article by Schapiro, see Andrew Hemingway, "Meyer Schapiro and Marxism in the 1930s," *Oxford Art Journal* 17, no. 1 (1994):20–22.

21. See Meyer Schapiro, "Diderot as Art Critic," *Diderot Studies* 5 (1964):5–11.

22. Maurice Merleau-Ponty, "Cezanne's Doubt" (1947), in *Sense and non-Sense*, trans. Hubert Dreyfus (Evanston: Northwestern University Press, 1964), pp. 9–25.

23. See Rosa Luxemburg, *Leninism or Marxism?* (1904), trans. Integer, in *The Russian Revolution and Leninism or Marxism?* (Ann Arbor: University of Michigan Press, 1961).

24. Arnold Hauser, *The Social History of Art*, 4 vols., trans. Stanley Godman (New York: Vintage Books, 1951). On the bookcover of each volume, Meyer Schapiro is quoted as follows: ". . . the most serious and comprehensive work of its kind that I know, a book based on great knowledge of both the arts and history. I have found in it many original, penetrating observations."

Figure 4. Meyer Schapiro, *Abstract Landscape*, 1950s. Oil on canvas board. Collection of Lillian Milgram.

MS: I wrote a prepublication discussion for the publisher of Hauser's book, whose wealth of knowledge and range I admired. Nonetheless, I had serious reservations about the study, since it was not sufficiently grounded in history. During the 1950s, while Hauser was teaching at Brandeis, he visited me in New York and we had a pleasant conversation about art.

DC: In your writings there is a conception of historical meaning as something that emerges from a dynamic interplay of subjectivity and objectivity, with neither one being the final determinant of truth value. One looks in vain for any traces of the type of epistemological realism that often marks the claims to complete objectivity or so-called "value-free" inquiry by orthodox Marxists and those Western scientists who are positivists. Could you say something about this?

MS: What is a fact? According to most languages it is a product of labor. Consider the word for fact in German, "*Tatsache*," which means "thing done"; in French, "*fait*," which means "made"; or even the Latin base for the English word "fact," which is the word "*factum*" and is related to *manufacture*, which means "made by hand." . . . What is the truth? The truth is what is *made*. There is an important letter in this regard by the scientist Galileo to the painter Cigoli, in which Galileo

spoke of the truth as a synthesis of the technique of the artisan plus the knowledge of the artist.[25]

From an interview at the home of the Schapiros on West 4th Street in New York City, May 20–22, 1993

DC: Did you have much interchange with Claude Levi-Strauss when he was in New York during the war?

MS: I knew Claude Levi-Strauss very well. We talked often during the mid-1940s. We also met with each other in Paris, as, for example, in 1952. He gave lectures at the New School of Social Research from 1942 to 1945. Once at least, he wrote a letter asking for my opinion on an anthropological point concerning an issue in folklore.[26]

At Columbia, Lillian and I studied anthropology with Franz Boas. Margaret Mead, who was Boas's assistant, subsequently marked Lillian's exams.

DC: Did you see Jackson Pollock and Lee Krasner much during the 1950s?

MS: Lillian and I saw Pollock, who was generally taciturn and drank heavily, on several occasions at the home of Jeanne Reynal, who was the daughter of the famous publisher, and her husband Tom Sills, who was an African-American painter. Lee Krasner was more approachable and sociable. On one occasion, at a Pollock Opening at the Betty Parsons Gallery, probably in 1950 or '51, I asked Pollock if he had made the right choice in using gold paint intertwined with other colors in one of his large all-overs and Pollock became *furious!*

25. On Galileo and Cigoli, see Erwin Panofsky, *Galileo as a Critic of the Arts* (The Hague: Mouton, 1954).

26. Some major early essays by Claude Levi-Strauss date from his stay in New York. See, for example Claude Levi-Strauss, "L'analyse structurale en linguistique et en anthropologie," *Word: Journal of the Linguistic Circle of New York* 1, no. 2 (1995). This essay appeared as Chapter 2 of his book *Structural Anthropology*, trans. Claire Jacobson and Brooke Schoepf (New York: Basic Books, 1962). There is also a fine essay by Levi-Strauss on New York City as he first came to know it in 1941, entitled "New York post—et prefiguratif," in *Le regard eloigne* (Paris: Plon, 1983), pp. 345–356.

For an incisive analysis of Levi-Strauss's view of New York City, see James Clifford, *The Predicament of Culture* (Cambridge: Harvard University Press, 1988), pp. 236–246.

Figure 5. Meyer Schapiro, sketch of Siena, late 1920s. Pen and ink. Photograph: Karen Berman.

He was very volatile if ever questioned about a choice he made while creating one of his works.

> From a telephone interview, November 11, 1993

DC: Did you ever discuss anarchism with Mark Rothko?

MS: I knew he was an anarchist, but we did not discuss his position at length. He was very inclined to support workers and to value workmanship.

> From an interview at the home on the Schapiros in New York City, June 5, 1994

DC: What is the source in your own analysis for the concept of "state capitalism"?

MS: It means a situation in which the state, like private capital, has a monopoly over the means of production, so as to disallow workplace democracy. It denotes an antidemocratic organization of the workplace and of society in general. Ultimately it is a critique of Leninism, as well as of capitalism. As for the source, it goes back to Luxemburg and Korsch.[27]

DC: What of Robert Motherwell's claim in his 1944 article "The Modern Painter's World" that "The modern states that we have seen so far have all been enemies of the artist"?[28]

MS: This view is too extreme and historically reductive. It is a position typical of much anarchist thought.[29]

---

27. See Karl Korsch, *Three Essays on Marxism,* introduction by Paul Breines (New York: Monthly Review Press, 1972).

28. Robert Motherwell, "The Modern Painter's World," *Dyn* 1, no. 6 (1944):9–14.

29. Elsewhere, Robert Motherwell wrote: "Society stands against anarchy; the artist stands for the human against society; society therefore treats him as an anarchist." See: Robert Motherwell, "Beyond

DC: You mean that Motherwell was insufficiently attentive to what was both progressive and reactionary about the state at any given historical moment?

MS: Yes. It is not merely a matter of the state's being the enemy or not. The secular state in the medieval period was not only an institution of repression. This was the case with the *communes*, which were sometimes at odds with other states or institutions, specifically those that were religious. The communes represented a state formation that was quite important for creating a space within which a type of artistic freedom could begin to emerge.[30]

From a telephone interview, January 22, 1995

the Aesthetic" (April 1946), in *The Collected Writings of Robert Motherwell*, ed. Stephanie Terenzio (New York: Oxford University Press, 1992), p. 38.

For a discussion of how Schapiro's values and his example influenced some of Motherwell's other views, see David Craven, "Aesthetics as Ethics in the Writings of Motherwell and Schapiro," *Archives of American Art Journal* (forthcoming).

30. For more on this, see Meyer Schapiro, "On the Aesthetic Attitude in Romanesque Art" (1947), in *Selected Papers of Meyer Schapiro*. Vol. 1, *Romanesque Art* (New York: George Braziller, 1977), pp. 1–3.

For two very fine and quite recent assessments of Schapiro's contribution to progressive art history, see Alan Wallach, "Meyer Schapiro, 1904–1996: Marxist Art Historian," *Against the Current* 62 (1996):52; Thomas Crow, "Village Voice: On Meyer Schapiro," *Artforum* 34, no. 10 (1996):9–10, 122. Crow justifiably concludes that Schapiro "almost single-handedly laid the foundation for the modes of advanced interpretation that we know today."

List of authors

JOAN R. BRANHAM is Assistant Professor of Art History at Providence College.

SARAH BRETT-SMITH is Associate Professor of Art History at Rutgers University.

DAVID CRAVEN is Professor of Art History and Latin American Studies at the University of New Mexico.

JULIET FLEMING is Assistant University Lecturer in the Faculty of English at the University of Cambridge.

NICHOLAS GRINDLE is a graduate student in the department of Art History and Theory at the University of Essex.

JEFFREY F. HAMBURGER is Irving E. Houck Professor in the Humanities in the Department of Art at Oberlin College.

JOSEPH LEO KOERNER is Professor of Fine Arts at Harvard University.

WILLIAM PIETZ is an independent scholar living in Los Angeles, California.

CHRISTINE ROSS is Professor of Art History at McGill University.

JOSEPH RYKWERT is Paul Philippe Cret Professor of Architecture at the University of Pennsylvania.

VICTOR STOICHITA is Professor of Art History at the University of Fribourg, Switzerland.

Res 32   Autumn 1997

Anthropology and aesthetics

Contents of upcoming issue

PEABODY MUSEUM

Peabody Museum publications are distributed by:

THE UNIVERSITY OF PENNSYLVANIA MUSEUM, PUBLICATIONS DEPARTMENT
33RD AND SPRUCE STREETS
PHILADELPHIA, PA 19104
(800) 306-1941, (215) 898-4124

Ceramics and Artifacts from Excavations in the Copan Residential Zone

Gordon R. Willey, Richard M. Leventhal, Arthur A. Demarest, and William L. Fash, Jr.

This is the first of two volumes that address the Harvard University excavations in an outlying residential zone of the Copan Main Ruin in western Honduras. The book offers detailed descriptions of the ceramics and all other artifacts that were recovered from a series of dwelling compounds during 1976–1977. The materials pertain largely to the Late Classic Period. Ceramics are presented according to the type-variety system.

1994 Peabody Museum Papers, vol. 80. 496 pp., 362 halftones, 495 drawings, 7 maps, 42 tables, biblios. Paper. ISBN 0-87365-206-1 $62.00

Corpus of Maya Hieroglyphic Inscriptions

Vol. 6, Part 2: Tonina, *Ian Graham and Peter Mathews*
Vol. 7, Part 1: Seibal, *Ian Graham*

The Corpus series is designed to make available in convenient form all of the extant inscriptions on stone and other media surviving from the ancient Maya civilization. Photographs and precise line drawings of each inscription are provided. Volume 6, Part 2 continues the detailed record of the monumental sculpture and hieroglyphic texts from Tonina, a major ruin located in the highlands of Chiapas, Mexico. Volume 7, Part 1 presents a complete compilation of the numerous inscriptions from Seibal, Guatemala, many of them notable for their late (Terminal Classic) dates.

1996 64 pp., 140 halftones, 103 drawings. Paper.
ISBN 0-87365-817-5 $50.00
1996 64 pp., 39 halftones, 31 drawings, 3 maps. Paper.
ISBN 0-87365-817-7 $50.00

Encounters with the Americas

Rosemary A. Joyce and Susan A. M. Shumaker
Photographs by Hillel S. Burger

Illustrated with historic black-and-white photographs, and featuring color plates of archaeological and ethnographic objects, this catalogue serves as an introduction to one of the most significant Latin American anthropological collections in the world. It highlights Peabody Museum holdings from Classic Maya sites such as Piedras Negras and Copan, and ethnographic costumes of Highland Maya and Amazonian peoples. Many of the objects represented have not been previously published. The book uses extracts from first-person accounts of sixteenth-century contact with the Aztec and Maya civilizations and post-Columbian encounters of native peoples with explorers and anthropologists.

1995 96 pp., 32 color plates, 40 halftones, 3 drawings, 2 maps, biblio. Paper. ISBN 0-87365-815-9 $25.00

Privatization in the Ancient Near East and Classical World

Michael Hudson and Baruch Levine, eds.

This is the first volume of a two-part colloquium that seeks to describe the increasingly autonomous private control of land, handicraft workshops, and credit from the Bronze Age through classical antiquity. The participants sought to develop a common vocabulary to clarify and debate the phenomena being discussed. The following colloquium, "Urbanization and Land Use in the Ancient Near East," is scheduled for 1996–97.

1996 Peabody Museum Bulletin 5. 320 pp. Paper.
ISBN 0-87365-955-4 $25.00

PUBLICATIONS

An Early Neolithic Village in the Jordan Valley, Part I and Part II

Part I: The Archaeology of Netiv Hagdud
Ofer Bar-Yosef and Avi Gopher, eds.
Part II: The Fauna of Netiv Hagdud
Eitan Tchernov

These volumes represent detailed studies of the Pre-Pottery Neolithic A (PPNA) village site of Netiv Hagdud, located just 13 kilometers north of Jericho in the Jordan Valley. Systematic excavations and good preservation conditions have resulted in a detailed description of exposed deposits dated 10,300 to 9500 B.P. The broader significance of this study lies in its application to the investigation of the transition from the Natufian period to the early beginnings of the Neolithic Revolution, just one stage before the distribution of plant cultivation and animal domestication in the Levant. Part I provides a description and analysis of the environment as well as specialized reports on the excavated houses, lithic assemblages, bone tools, obsidian sourcing, marine shells, and burials. Part II describes the collection of reptile, bird, and mammal remains.

1997 American School of Prehistoric Research
Bulletin 43. Part I. 288 pp., 74 halftones, 62 drawings, maps, and tables. Paper. ISBN 0-87365-547-8 $45.00
1994 American School of Prehistoric Research
Bulletin 44. Part II. 116 pp., 50 drawings and maps, 55 tables. Paper. ISBN 0-87365-548-6 $20.00

Hall of the North American Indian

Hillel S. Burger and Ian W. Brown
Barbara Isaac, ed.

After five years of preparation, the Peabody Museum reopened its Hall of the North American Indian in 1990. Since the late nineteenth century the Hall has presented to the public the most significant objects from the Museum's vast Native American collections. Their extraordinary nature, as well as the gallery's scope, is captured in this catalogue. Ian Brown describes how the exhibition considers change in Native American lifeways from prehistoric times to the contemporary scene. Hillel Burger's stunning color photographs complement the anthropological presentation of the exhibit and emphasize the aesthetic values of the pieces.

1990 136 pp., 94 color plates, 20 halftones, biblios.
Paper. ISBN 0-87365-811-6 $25.00

Shell Gorgets: Styles of the Late Prehistoric and Protohistoric Southeast

Jeffrey P. Brain and Philip Phillips

During the late prehistoric and protohistoric periods, shell gorgets engraved with sophisticated figural and geometric designs were made in many regions of the southeastern United States. They are an important component of the so-called "Southern Cult" phenomenon. In this heavily illustrated work, a corpus of 1,000 gorgets is classified into 50 detailed styles. Their archaeological contexts at more than 50 sites in the Southeast and Midwest are compared to align regional chronologies. The stylistic analysis is broadened to encompass other artifact categories. Their distribution is the basis for reinterpretations of the timing and nature of the Southern Cult.

1996 542 pp., approx. 2,600 illustrations, 57 maps and figures, bibliography, index. Paper.
ISBN 0-87365-812-4 $79.95

Origins of the Bronze Age Oasis Civilization in Central Asia

Fredrik T. Hiebert

This monograph concerns the development of the unique Oxus Civilization in the desert oases of Central Asia and is based on the first international collaborative excavation in former Soviet Turkmenistan (1988–1989) at Gonur depe, conducted by the Peabody Museum, the Ministry of Culture of Turkmenistan, and the Institute of Archaeology (Moscow). The Murghab River delta (ancient Margiana) had an extensive settlement during the late Bronze Age (2200–1750 B.C.), forming a man-made oasis in the desert. Gonur depe, the largest and most complex site in Margiana, provide a key to comprehending the large corpus of data from the extensive Soviet excavations over the last twenty years.

1994 American School of Prehistoric Research
Bulletin 42. 240 pp., 50 halftones, 100 line drawings and maps, biblio., index. Paper.
ISBN 0-87365-545-1 $40.00

Res

Anthropology and aesthetics

Res is a journal of anthropology and comparative aesthetics dedicated to the study of the object, in particular cult and belief objects and objects of art. The journal brings together, in an anthropological perspective, contributions by philosophers, art historians, archaeologists, critics, linguists, architects, artists, and others. Its field of inquiry is open to all cultures, regions, and historical periods.

Res also seeks to make available textual and iconographic documents of importance for the history and theory of the arts.

Res appears twice a year, in the spring and in the autumn. Subscriptions are filled only on a calendar-year basis:

$27 per year for individuals
$53 per year for institutions

Orders, which must be accompanied by payment, should be sent to a bookseller or subscription agent or directly to the University of Pennsylvania Museum Publications, 33rd and Spruce Streets, Philadelphia, PA 19104-6324. Claims for missing issues should be made immediately after receipt of the subsequent issue of the journal.

If ordering back issues (vols. 1–28), please contact Cambridge University Press, Journals Department, 110 Midland Avenue, Port Chester, NY 10573-4930 (for the United States, Canada, and Mexico) or Cambridge University Press, The Edinburgh Building, Shaftesbury Road, Cambridge, CB2 2RU, Great Britain (for all other countries). Volume 29/30 can be ordered from University of Pennsylvania Museum Publications, 33rd and Spruce Streets, Philadelphia, PA 19104-6324.

The publication of *Res* is made possible by a generous donation from the Fanny and Leo Koerner Charitable Trust.

We also gratefully acknowledge long-term support from the Pinewood Foundation.

Editorial correspondence should be sent to Francesco Pellizzi, *Res*, Editorial Office, 12 East 74th Street, New York, NY 10021.

Permission reprint requests for volumes 1–18 and 29/30 should be directed to the Peabody Museum of Archaeology and Ethnology, Publications Department, 11 Divinity Avenue, Cambridge, MA 02138; volumes 19/20–28 only to the Getty Research Institute for the History of Art and the Humanities, Publications, 401 Wilshire Blvd., Suite 700, Santa Monica, CA 90401-1455.